Personality and Social Behaviour

Personality and Social Behaviour

ADRIAN FURNHAM
Professor of Psychology,
University College London, London, UK

and

PATRICK HEAVEN
Associate Professor of Psychology,
iversity of Wollongong, Wollongong, New South Wales,
Australia

A member of the Hodder Headline Group
LONDON • NEW YORK • NEW DELHI

First published in Great Britain in 1999
This impression reprinted in 2002 by
Arnold, a member of the Hodder Headline Group,
338 Euston Road, London NW1 3BH
http://www.arnoldpublishers.com

Co-published in the United States of America by
Oxford University Press Inc.,
198 Madison Avenue, New York, NY 10016

British Library Cataloguing in Publication Data
A catalogue record for this book is available from the British Library

Library of Congress Cataloging-in-Publication Data
Furnham, Adrian.
    Personality and social behaviour/Adrian Furnham and Patrick Heaven.
    Includes bibliographical references and index.
    ISBN 0-340-67724-4 (hardcover). — ISBN 0-340-67725-2 (pbk.)
    1. Personality—Social aspects. 2. Individuality—Social aspects.
I. Heaven, Patrick C. L. (Patrick Charles Lionel) II. Title.
BF698 9.S63F87   1988
155.2—dc21   98-37860

ISBN 0 340 67724 4 (hb)
ISBN 0 340 67725 2 (pb)

3 4 5 6 7 8 9 10

Production Editor: Wendy Rooke
Production Controller: Rose James
Cover Design: Terry Griffiths

Typeset on 10/12pt Sabon by Photoprint, Torquay
Printed in India by Replika Press Pvt. Ltd., 100% EOU, Delhi - 110 040

> What do you think about this book? Or any other Arnold title?
> Please send your comments to feedback.arnold@hodder.co.uk

For Alison (A.F)
and
Leonora (P.H)

When money is on the table, when lives are at stake, normal people understand the importance of personality. Because money or life is rarely on the line in academia, academicians can pretend that personality does not exist and that they are not held accountable for their goofy ideas.

(Robert Hogan, *Reinventing Personality*, 1998)

Even now, the study of personality belongs to the adventurous, and not wholly respectable, frontier regions of psychology, which it is not altogether wise to explore without a safe academic reputation in some entirely reputable field, like colour vision, or the ability of rats to learn their way through a maze.

(Norcult, *The Psychology of Personality*, 1950)

Anyone disciplined in the old sciences, and with some knowledge of the history of scientific theory, cannot but deplore, with some disgust, what has long been, and still continues to be, served up to the student as 'personality theory'.

(R.B. Cattell, the leading psychometrician/psychologist of his day, 1979)

I would like to suggest that the root of many of the difficulties and disappointments found in psychological research, as well as the causes of the well-known difficulties in duplicating results from one study to another, lies in the neglect of individual differences.

(H.J. Eysenck, the most widely cited psychologist of recent years (1916–1997))

Personality psychology has a curious position in modern thought; although the public sees it as the most crucial and interesting part of psychology, academic psychologists seem to take the opposite view.

(Hogan, 1990)

Contents

Foreword

The vast majority of personality textbooks are structured around different theories – behavioural, psychoanalytic and trait. This book is different. Individual chapters are not dedicated to theorists, particular methodologies or specific philosophical approaches, but to areas of social behaviour such as health, education and work that are profoundly influenced by personality traits. The central questions addressed in each chapter are *which*, *to what extent* and *by what process* personality variables affect social behaviour in particular spheres of life. This is a radically different approach to the subject, and the authors have scanned a huge area of psychology to present a comprehensive, critical and accessible account of the role of personality and individuals in everyday life. *Personality and Social Behaviour* is a unique and essential supplement to traditional texts. It is particularly suitable for students and researchers from other areas of psychology and the behavioural sciences, as well as for those students who are seeking topic rather than theory based descriptions of the field of personality psychology.

Preface

The idea for this book came about in a restaurant in Ghent. At a meeting of the European Association of Personality Psychology, a group of individuals (with very distinct personalities) went off to eat at the end of a long day of giving and receiving papers. Conversation ranged from the usual academic gossip to the reflective. Most of the people present were very distinguished leaders in their fields – dare one say, even famous psychologists who had written various well-known and cited books and papers in the area of personality and individual differences. Despite their eminence, many complained that their field was not taken seriously by their colleagues, who were poorly informed about developments in the field. This was particularly galling because everyone felt that over the past decade (the late 1980s to the early 1990s) there had been enormous strides in the area. Behaviour genetics, evolutionary biology and multivariate statistics had had a powerful impact on personality theory and research. There is now a true consensus and a new excitement in the air. Personality research, we all felt, was making real and significant scientific progress.

Why then were there so few lecturers and researchers in the area in every department? Why was there still relatively little research money available for the study of personality? Why was it that the best students, powerfully attracted to working in the area, often decided (or more likely were persuaded) to turn their attentions elsewhere? Many partial explanations were proffered by the august company. However, all agreed that the mass of (mainly American based) textbooks in the field did not do it justice. This is true for a variety of reasons. First, they appear not to have changed much over a period of 20 to 30 years. Some famous texts are in their sixth or seventh editions, yet their structure and content remain unchanged. Revolutions have occurred, yet the world of the textbook writer is the same as it ever was. Secondly, traditional textbooks present theory after theory, but very little in the way of integration or criticism. Perhaps only the last of 10 to 20 book chapters would attempt this, but it was never serious, partly because it is so difficult. One wanted to know the answers to questions like the following. On what grounds should a theory be dropped or be deemed unworthy of a mention in the text? Why are obscure neo-Freudian theories from the 1920s still appearing in textbooks, while the exciting and powerful work of bio-logical psychologists is ignored? As recent US critics have noted, the time-honoured *theories of personality* approach is outdated and has little or nothing to do with current research by personality psychologists. Alas, textbook writers often do little research, while researchers tend not to write textbooks. Those who are exceptions always write different, untraditional and even 'quality' books that much better represent the field, but are not 'best-sellers' or adopted as textbooks. Thus there are books written from the constructionist, experimentalist, genetic, idiographic, lay, post-modernist and situationalist perspective. Although there are subtle, interesting and important differences between these various camps, there is a detectable left–right dimension, with the post-modernists, constructionalists and situationalists favouring an idiographic, lay perspective methodology over the traitist–experimentalists and geneticists (sociobiologists), whose star is now in the ascendant. This has been variously called the alpha–beta split, or the scientist–humanist dichotomy in personality theory. We believe that the traitist, the experimentalist, and those with an empirical sociobiological perspective on individual differences have most to offer, and that their recent research methodology is most profound and useful.

This set us to thinking about a radical new text. Maybe a textbook should be arranged like a conference, where papers in a similar area are grouped together. Thus all of the personality theorists who were interested in health would be in one symposium, while those interested in occupational behaviour would be in another. Although they might be influenced by very different theoretical models and use quite different methods, this arrangement always worked better because both the presenters and the audience would have more in common than if they were grouped by methodology or theory, irrespective of the content of the research. Furthermore, it could (and indeed can) be rather sad to see a lone researcher carrying the standard of a long defunct theory, method or questionnaire, who would have no peers to support him or her at a symposium.

So the idea was born to write a different textbook – one arranged by the particular areas or types of behaviour clearly related to individual differences. After proposing different chapter headings, we showed these to a few distinguished peers for comment. Had we left anything important out? Had we grouped the chapter topics appropriately? Did this better reflect the state of modern personality theory? Their comments were positive and helpful, as were reviews of the proposal. After a few changes, we set to work.

As co-authors, we are separated by some 10,000 miles. We first met some 15 years ago, and found we had a lot in common. We grew up in, but left, our country of birth for political reasons. We had always been interested in individual differences and their social behavioural correlates. We admired the leading researchers in the trait tradition and enjoyed psychometric work. The fax and, more particularly, e-mail, have meant that contact is not a problem, despite the distance involved. Furthermore, we are usually able to meet up at least once a year at one of those academic conferences that inspired the book in the first place.

There are, no doubt, errors of commission and omission in this book. It is increasingly difficult to be comprehensive in the journal-expanding world of psychological research. If you believe that we have left out important research, please let us know. We will be glad to include it in future editions. More importantly, if we have misrepresented a theory or finding, please put us right.

Writing a book is hard work. Both of us have heavy teaching commitments and an active research programme. Book-writing is, paradoxically, either not encouraged or even actively discouraged in the academic world, as academic evaluation exercises frequently do not include books. Yet it remains an interesting and challenging task, which ultimately certainly benefits one's own teaching and research, which fortunately is evaluated with increasing frequency.

Adrian Furnham
University College London

Patrick Heaven
University of Wollongong

January 1998

1

Introduction

1.1 THE SCOPE OF THE AREA

The etymology of the word 'personality' is the Latin word *persona*, which means mask. Synonyms might be façade, exterior, guise, identity or image. In this sense, the meaning of the word is the *public self*, which may or may not be different from the private self. However, as we shall see, psychologists have tended to use the word in a technical sense, to mean those internal stable factors that make people systematically and predictably different from one another.

Personality is that which makes individuals distinctively themselves. It is the stuff of biographers, playwrights and historians, but also of scientists and lay speculators. In a sense, we are all personality theorists. It is a difficult, multidisciplinary area of research. Personality is determined in part by genes, as well as by cultural factors, it operates at the conscious and unconscious level, and it both changes over time and remains stable. Both lay people and academic researchers ask many personality-related questions. The types of questions asked by lay people include the following. What is a personality clash? Do people with opposite personalities find each other attractive? Can someone have little or no personality? Academic questions are also of interest to the lay person, and might include the following. Does personality change much over time? What causes (shapes, determines) an individual's personality? What are the fundamental dimensions of personality? To what extent do personality differences (alone) determine such things as health? What causes a person to be an introvert or extravert (more likely an ambivert)? Can neurotics be cured effectively?

Personality psychology is often a child of its investigative method. The couch and the laboratory use different methods, and hence develop different concepts and theories of personality. Personality psychologists, unlike many of their biological and cognitive colleagues, are often 'whole-person' psychologists, not focusing exclusively on beliefs, emotions or cognitions. Many have tended to ask 'big' questions, such as the following. What is the relative importance of the past, the present and the future to the development of personality? What motivates human behaviour? How important is the concept of self? How consistent is human behaviour? (Hergenhalin, 1994). As Cook (1984) notes, there are many different and important reasons for studying personality – obviously to gain a scientific understanding, but also to assess people accurately and to try to change people. He also argues that some theories look at the development of personality and others examine the structure of personality, which attempts to get below the surface of observable trait-type behaviours by examining biological, phenomenal or motivational factors.

Carver and Scheier (1992) argue that, whereas some personality theorists (especially trait theorists) are interested in the *structure* of personality, others are more interested in its *functioning*. Both are important, but the result is often the development of separate theories and approaches. Personality theorists and researchers have influenced and have also been influenced by many other disciplines. Indeed, there is evidence that personality differences are related to different interests in psychology. Thus Zachar and Leong showed that pure (scientific) vs. applied (practitional) graduate students had quite different personalities.

> Pushing graduate students into strong practitioner-personality orientations to become scientists makes as much sense as trying to convert an introvert into an extravert. However, introverts may benefit from some training and social skills, just as practitioner-orientated graduate students can learn to think and evaluate their interventions scientifically without having to become a practising scientist.
>
> (Zachar and Leong, 1992, p.676)

Sociologists and anthropologists have influenced some personality theories by discussing what goes on 'outside, around and among' individuals, rather than what goes on inside them. Lately, however, it has been biologists and geneticists whose ideas and discoveries have most influenced personality research. Certainly this trend looks likely to continue. Behaviour genetics, cognitive neuropsychology and multivariate statistics probably represent the most influential contributions to the discipline at the moment (see Section 1.11).

Personality psychology aims to provide viable descriptions of and explanations for individual differences. It aims, by observation, hypothesis/theory development and experimental testing, to understand systematic human variability. Researchers hope to understand the basic *structure* of personality (the periodic table of individual differences), the *processes* whereby individual differences in observable behaviour occur, and the *development* of both over time. Those with a preference for a systems framework identify four overarching types, namely the identification/definition of personality, the components of personality, the organisation of those components, and the development of those components (Mayer, 1995).

Personality research is either exploratory or confirmatory. The former usually starts with *systematic observation* that generates hypotheses, which are tested by the latter (*empirical experiment*). However, all personality theories contain hunches, rather than hypotheses based on *intuitive knowledge, everyday observations*, or simple *rational deductions* from thinking about human behaviour. It is through observation, experiment and logic that theories are built, tested and refuted. Inevitably, some theorists rely more heavily on one of these models of theory-building than others. Ideally, personality theorists should aim for elegant, parsimonious, veridical theories of individual functioning.

However, description is not explanation – naming (labelling) is not explaining. Personality psychology is replete with overlapping and often rather vague concepts which, in providing complex or novel labels, look like explanations. Much effort has gone into description and taxonomisation, but far less into understanding dynamics and process (Meehl, 1992). It is only when one achieves an effective analysis of behaviour that one can provide an explanation in terms of a mechanism or process.

Personality psychology is at once both fascinating and infuriating. It is crammed with novel theories, unusual concepts and perspicacious insights, so that scanning the traditional textbook is like opening Pandora's box. However, few reviewers of the field have attempted a careful 'compare and contrast' approach to the theories, pointing out where they are *internally inconsistent* and *contradictory*, where there is *no evidence of proof* for specific hypotheses, or where all of the experimental evidence suggests that the hypothesis (or the entire theory) is *wrong*. Personality psychology reviewers seem to be either too humble or too incompetent to do the task. Worse, they do not keep up to date, and personality psychology becomes intellectually and socially isolated from other areas of psychology (Ehrenreich, 1997). Hence they are happy to lay out a 'flea market' of theories for the interested student, without any clear guide as to whether they should be taken seriously or not (see Section 1.6).

Most personality theorists have also eschewed grand theories that look too all-inclusive and non-scientific. An exception to this trend is sociobiology. The best books in the field offer a critical, comprehensive, comparative analysis that is unafraid to dismiss or ignore theories, however appealing, that have yielded precious little empirical support over the years. What is required is a method, and a series of criteria, that can be used to make a comparative analysis of all personality theories. Maddi has argued that personality psychology has had an 'unnecessarily prolonged infancy' because researchers have 'made little progress towards weeding out some theories as empirically unworkable' (Maddi, 1989, p.3).

Different personality theorists have stressed rather different factors as the determinants of personality. Recent research on identical twins, as well as adoption studies, have stressed the powerful role of *genetics* in determining personality. Others have preferred to stress *socio-cultural* determinants, such as child-rearing practices, political and religious institutions, formal and informal education, and economic opportunities. Some place greater emphasis on *personal learning* through patterns of reward and punishment in the family. There are those who follow the existential and humanistic social philosophers who stress *free will* and the belief that personality style is a matter of personal choice. There are still other theorists who believe that *unconscious mechanisms* set in place in early childhood are powerful factors in determining personality structure and process. For the past 20 years, the cognitive revolution in psychology has led a minority of personality theorists to stress the *cognitive processes* of perception and memory as being the fundamental factors that explain individual differences (Matthews and Deary, 1998).

As a result of these differences, personality theorists have answered the fundamental questions in their areas quite differently. Hence there appear to be rather different approaches in personality theory – the psychoanalytic, socio-cultural, trait, learning, sociobiological and existential-humanist approaches. Inevitably, therefore, it is a difficult area to cover or review. Hence textbooks arrange the subject according to different approaches or theories, assuming each is equally valid and important.

It is also possible to describe individual differences at quite different levels – ranging from fairly abstract to totally concrete. These may be labelled core vs. peripheral, abstract vs. concrete, inherent vs. learned, and pervasive vs. specific. Most theories include statements and descriptions at all levels. At the abstract/core/trait level, description is about structure and unique characteristics. In the words of trait theory, the levels are usually described as follows.

Superfactors These are the most abstract, unique, *independent, higher-order* factors. They are the periodic table of personality theory – the fundamental elements that make up personality. The past 20 years have seen a growing consensus about what these may be. We will discuss *The Big Five* in due course.

Primary factors This is one level down, where one takes a superfactor and divides it into *related* constituent parts. Thus the superficial extraversion may have two factors – sociability and impulsivity – which are primary factors, or six factors, such as warmth, gregariousness, assertiveness, activity, excitement-seeking and positive emotion.

Specific behaviour events These are behavioural manifestations of a primary trait. Thus the person who daily seeks out the company of friends and acquaintances for chats may be labelled sociable and extraverted.

ps¯
bio,
beh

Therefore personality theorists may work at different levels within different approaches or traditions, with different methods! Within the fields of personality research, different researchers seem happy working at rather different levels, which are partly dictated by their preferred methodological choices. Above, we specified the different levels within the trait approach. There are equally different levels of analysis when taking the psychoanalytic or neurological approach. One of the aims of science is parsimonious explanation – hence the attraction of working at the superfactor level. Over the years, an impressive amount of consistent and wide-ranging evidence has accumulated which has shown how superfactors relate to widely different but important behaviours. Thus the well-known dimension of introversion–extraversion (described by Hippocrates, Galen, Wundt, Jung, Eysenck and Costa, among others) has been shown to be directly related to mental health, learning and education, risk-taking and accident proneness, criminality and social behaviour, social and political attitudes, sexual attitudes and behaviour, social influence and affiliation, social attraction and personal perception and psychotherapy (Wilson, 1977). Traditional textbooks are often arranged according to traits, like extraversion and neuroticism, which look at correlates of each. This book is arranged in the opposite way – the rows have been replaced by columns. Thus each chapter covers a particular type of area/issue, such as leisure and health, and we shall consider the (main) personality correlates of each.

However, in the words of Costa and McCrae (1992), we do believe that trait psychology has come of age – it is a mature science with established and replicable methods and findings. As a consequence, most of the chapters of this book will examine trait correlates of behaviour.

1.2 A (VERY) SHORT HISTORY OF PERSONALITY

Personality psychologists have been particularly sensitive to fashions in philosophical thinking. They are commonly involved in frequent and profound discussions about methodology and theory. As Caprara and van Heck (1992) have noted, three movements provided the premises of modern personality psychology, namely psychiatric concern about taxonomising mental illness, the development of mental testing, and an interest in instincts and the development of personality.

The earliest books on personality theory as such were written in the 1930s (Lewin, 1935; Allport, 1937; Murray, 1938). There are now probably at least 100 personality textbooks in print (in English alone). Personality psychology was a European concern until the 1940s, since which time it has been dominated by American researchers. It has seen periods of excitement and growth (the 1950s and 1980s) and of decline (the 1960s and 1970s). It goes through periods of crisis and rejuvenation, and it has survived a 'near-death' experience and seen a modest academic renaissance. It has been characterised by a myriad of micro-theories, specialist methodologies and measures which go in and out of fashion, although the psychometric tradition appears to have endured.

Ignoring the philosophical considerations of the ancient Greeks and medieval scholars, it is possible to detect various themes in the way in which the scientific study of personality has developed since the middle of the last century. The first discernible of these were *phrenology* and anatomical psychology, which attempted to look for clear anatomical markers of personality. This type of approach is far from dead, both in the bogus scientific world (e.g. palm-reading) and also in the sociobiological literature, linking such factors as head size (volume or circumference) with intelligence. However, it is neuroanatomy, rather than physiology, that has seen a powerful resurgence of research interest. Indeed, it is on the anatomical structure and functioning of the brain (along with genetic work) that many current theorists have pinned their hopes for a modern scientific breakthrough in the understanding of normal, and especially abnormal, personality functioning.

The beginning of the twentieth century saw a great deal of interest in intelligence and possible *genetic* determinants of the latter. These structural and biodeterminist views spread to the world of personality testing. Over the past few years, powerful new technologies looking at genetic fingerprinting and DNA mapping have made this area one of the most exciting and important for understanding individual differences. It is now widely agreed that personality traits are largely inherited, with perhaps 50 to 60 per cent of variance being accounted for by genetic factors (Plomin and Nesselrode, 1990).

However, from the end of World War One until well into the 1960s, ideas from *classical* and *operant conditioning* seemed to imply that personality and individual differences were 'learned'. The behaviourists suggested that by observation, imitation, identification and the rules of reward and punishment, people learned, unlearned and changed their personalities. Despite a relatively long and sustained research interest in this tradition, it seems to have fallen out of favour lately. This is not to deny the importance of early learning or experience, but to deny that it is primarily conditioning that determines personality. Radical behaviourists or situationalists even denied the reality of personality, preferring to believe that social situations (their rules and equivalents), not inherent traits, were the primary determinants of nearly all behaviour, particularly 'social behaviour'.

Ideas from *psychoanalysis* were (and indeed still are) constantly being introduced into English-speaking personality theory during the period from 1920 to 1960. This was perhaps the most fecund time for psychoanalysis. There seems to have been a recent renewal of interest in some Freudian ideas. Condemned by many scientists from the 1950s to the 1980s, psychoanalytic research retreated into its own small world, but now various Freudian concepts (reaction formation and repression) are slowly being revived, and there is a growing *rapprochement* between radically different fields of psychology (such as psychoanalysis and cognitive psychology).

Freud was a trained psychiatrist and used biological explanations (instinctive drives, stages, etc.), although many of his followers stressed the social determinants of personality, such as unconscious motives. The case-study method still predominates in Freudian personality theory. Because all psychoanalysts distinguish between what is superficially observable and what lies beneath, meaning and symbolism take on a central importance in this conception of personality functioning.

Freud also used nineteenth-century steam-engine energy metaphors. This energy (the medium of sexual and aggressive drives) needs to be redirected in problem cases. The Freudians separate the structure, development and dynamics of personality. The structure involves the primitive *id*, dominated by the pleasure principle and wish fulfilment. The *ego*, or self, is the objective part, dominated by the reality principle. The *superego* is the seat of conscience. Personality develops and is marked by stages of growth and crises such as weaning, which may determine whether one is an *oral* personality, and potty training, which may be related to *anal* traits. The Freudians see the id, ego and superego as being in constant conflict, and the necessity for people to develop ego defence mechanisms (such as denial, repression and projection) to cope with them. Some of the defences, such as displacement and sublimation, are considered to be healthy.

The *phenomenological/humanist/third force* ideas, stressing the importance of self-concept, were most influential in the 1960s and 1970s, but have currently ceased to have much influence. Even the self-theorists appear to have lost their following. This approach represents an uneasy coalition between existentialists, humanists and phenomenologists. They agree on the supremacy of the subjective experience of individuals, their attempts at learning, experience and realising their potential. Conscious experience – how people see, think about and experience their world – determines personality. For many humanistic psychologists, self-concept is personality.

This 'physical' or biological approach to personality has historically included two types of approach, with a third being comparatively recent. The first, which has a long history, focused on body build and structure. Some (the phrenologists) concentrated on the head, while others concentrated on the hands, but probably the most celebrated work is that of Sheldon (1940) on the three classic body types – endomorph, ectomorph and mesomorph. It was assumed that body shapes affected and reflected personality. However, the evidence for those theories has been weak. Some geneticists assumed that genes determine body build independently of personality, while others have pointed out that body build might have a powerful influence on the development of personality. Sociobiologists have argued their point by proposing the theory that thin bodies (ectomorphs) are less good at physical work and also inherit a preference for solitude and intense thinking.

Behaviour genetics is showing on an almost daily basis the extent to which personality variables are inherited. Few dispute the impressive accumulation of evidence that the heritability index for most traits is between 0.5 and 0.7. Twin and adoption studies, as well as DNA analysis, seem to point consistently to genetics being a major determinant of all dimensions of personality. Evolutionary biologists have also focused on potentially evolutionary cases of personality development.

There remain at the heart of psychology in general, and personality research in particular, two very different approaches, first pointed out by Cronbach (1957) over 40 years ago.

Experimental psychologists   These psychologists study the impact of experimental manipulations on specific responses in particular situations. They tend to focus on one or two specific but important determinants of behaviour. Personality and individual differences are ignored, rather than being systematically varied or controlled. It is considered to be error variance. They also tend to focus on behaviour that is influenced by (short-lived) laboratory manipulations and (transient) situational variables.

Personality psychologists   These psychologists search for consistencies in behaviour that allow them to infer traits, processes and the consequences of behaviour. They seek to discover the psychological dimensions along which people differ, and how traits cluster with individuals. Often they ignore the impact of experimental manipulations and the processes underlying them for an understanding of the outcome or content of those processes.

Psychologists who are not specialists in personality and individual differences are often seriously out of date with regard to the thinking and research in the field. This is particularly true of those psychologists – educational, occupational and health – who doubtless do not have the time to follow other areas, and seem to be 20 or 30 years out of date. Some still believe that the concept of stable traits died with the attack of the situationists (Mischel, 1968), or that everyone is now an interactionist (Argyle *et al.*, 1981). Experimentalists who see individual differences as error variance or noise in the system have long dismissed the point of measuring personality, and hence take little interest in the area (Furnham, 1988). Specialist psychologists each have their own agenda, which leads them to take a particular view with regard to personality. Hence cross-cultural psychologists rejoice in demonstrating consistent and coherent cultural differences in social behaviour, while personality psychologists have done exactly the opposite, namely by demonstrating the invariance of personality structure across widely different population groups. Indeed a very recent issue of the *Journal of Cross-Cultural Psychology* (1997) celebrated the fact that the 'Big Five' personality factors were stable across very different cultures.

There is no doubt that, over the past 50 years, personality psychology has attracted many good researchers, students and writers. The *Annual Review of Psychology* had its first chapter dedicated to personality in 1950, and seems to have had an update about every 5 years. Furthermore, successful textbooks such as Hall and Lindzey (1957) have sold nearly three-quarters of a million copies. There has, of course, been tension between clinically and experimentally orientated researchers, and the cognitive revolution profoundly affected personality theory. Personality theorists have teamed up with both clinical and social psychologists. Thus we have had journals like the *Journal of Abnormal and Social Psychology* and the *British Journal of Social and Clinical Psychology*, and still have the *Journal of Social and Clinical Psychology*. The close relationship between personality and social psychologists can be currently seen in such journals as the *Journal of Personality and Social Psychology* and the *Journal of Social Behaviour and Personality*.

More recently, personality theorists have been interested in themes like the relationship between affect, cognition, motivation and behaviour, personality and behaviour genetics, and personality and health. As Pervin (1996a, b) notes, certain topics wax and wane in the level of interest they generate, while others remain constant. Thus interest in authoritarianism (rigidity, conservatism), so popular in the 1950s and 1960s, seems to be of little interest to personality psychologists nowadays. However, topics such as the way in which personality variables affect physical health and productivity at work are of great interest at the moment. It is not always clear why interest in certain topics is so sensitive to fashion, but few disappear altogether.

Eysenck noted that 'what we have is not the evolution of a paradigm, but a Dutch auction in ideas, alien to the spirit of science, and conducive to arbitrary choice in terms of existing prejudices on the part of the student' (Eysenck, 1983, p.369). Many others have described the field as splintered, non-paradigmatic, pre-scientific, directionless, fragmented and faddish. Yet Eysenck and many more recent reviewers have begun to detect clear evidence of both a theoretical and a methodological paradigm around the trait construction of personality (Matthews and Deary, 1998). It is on this conception that we shall concentrate most in this book.

1.3 DEFINITIONS OF PERSONALITY

There is no shortage of definitions of personality. Most do not mention physical factors (e.g. height, weight) or mental abilities. Some definitions stress the impression a person creates on others and their environment, while others look at habits and stable responses to the environment. However, most definitions focus on intervening variables, attempting to describe the nature, function and organisation of the variables below the surface.

Definitions of personality for psychologists have various themes. For some, the essence of the definition is how people respond or react to the people or situations they have encountered. For others, it is the biophysical, inherited, organic component that is crucial. Still others stress the organisational or patterning feature of personality that brings consistency and stability to behaviour. Clinicians stress the adjustment to the environment in definitions of personality. Finally, there are those who see personality as the expression of uniqueness in individuals.

Consider the following three definitions:

> Personality is a dynamic organisation, inside the person, of psychophysical systems that create the person's characteristic patterns of behaviour, thoughts and feelings.
>
> (Allport, 1961)

> Personality is that which permits a prediction of what a person will do in any given situation.
>
> (Cattell, 1965)

> Personality is a stable set of tendencies and characteristics that determine those commonalities and differences in people's psychological behaviour (thoughts, feelings, actions) that have continued in time and that may not be easily understood as the sole result of the social and biological pressures of the moment.
>
> (Maddi, 1989)

Definitions of personality are as varied as writers of textbooks. This is not of great concern, as definitions are not very important in the development, or even demarcation, of a discipline. However, all definitions seem to have quite specific themes:

- individual differences – people are unique, but can be described and categorised parsimoniously along various fundamental dimensions or into specific categories;
- personality dimensions are behavioural dispositions in the sense that they correlate with determination and drive, to affect social behaviour;
- personality dimensions are relatively stable over time and manifest consistently and coherently over varying social situations;
- the personality of a person can, and must, be decomposed into its specific and fundamental parts, elements and building blocks, but also combined into an organised whole system in order to understand its functions.

1.4 TWO DIFFERENT APPROACHES TO EVALUATING THE LITERATURE

Textbooks on personality theory in psychology fall essentially into two types. The first type is probably the most common, partly because it is the easiest to write, but also because it presents personality theories historically. This approach has been described as *benevolently eclectic* because the textbooks usually group theories into categories such as Freudian approaches, trait approaches, cognitive theories, etc., and then present the theories descriptively. The theory and its peculiar and particular concepts are usually described uncritically. Although the experimental literature and studies testing the theory may be reviewed, it is rarely the case that the author offers major criticisms of the theory, arguing that no further work needs to be done in the area. By virtue of the fact that theory appears in the book, it is assumed to be worthy of study. This type of approach is termed benevolent because it tends to accept all theories as being equally worthy of study. The student is therefore presented with a long and venerable list of thinkers in the area of personality – Freud, Jung, Adler, Horney, Allport, Murray, Eysenck, Gray, etc. They are presented as different but equal, in terms of their insights and veridicality, so the student reader ends up with a lot of theories about personality, some of which are contradictory, and many of which have been shown to be fundamentally wrong or, at best, to have no evidence to support them – that is, they may be unproven or unprovable. It is, in a sense, like wading through a venerable gallery of thinkers in this area.

Personality theories are simply summary statements or interrelated axioms that describe some class of event. They should explain what is known, and be able to predict possibilities not yet examined. They are – or should be – in a state of flux as they are modified and refined to take into account recent findings. If the theory is presented in the same way year after year, this usually means that no one is working on it, rather than that it is completely correct. It is certainly interesting that some personality theorists have come up with fascinating insights, counter-intuitive ideas and, on occasion, explanations for the processes by which people do the things they do. Another reason why many of these thinkers are interesting is that they have come from a clinical, case-study tradition.

Yet the problem for both the student and the researcher is how to integrate these lists of theories. Learning the sub-dialects of each theory is not difficult, but it seems to leave many readers incapable of doing a 'compare and contrast' exercise. In fact, this approach is more akin to philosophy or theology, where different thinkers' ideas are juxtaposed. Curiously, this approach occurs nowhere else in psychology, and has recently attracted criticism. Pervin (1996b) has only recently acknowledged problems in the textbooks in the area. In the preface to his latest text, he writes:

> To my knowledge, personality is the only area of psychology in which the leading texts do not present the field as it currently exists . . . the typical, time-honoured approach to teaching undergraduates – namely a Theories of Personality course – is misleading and uninformative. The material presented in such a course is outdated and of limited scientific relevance and has little to do with research actually done by personality psychologists.
>
> (Pervin, 1996b, pp.v–vi)

He believes that: 'Personality as a science rests largely on observations concerning human functioning that can be replicated by other observers and on efforts to formulate principles and laws that can be tested through further observation' (Pervin, 1996b, p.2).

A second approach, in contrast to benevolent eclecticism, is *partisan zealotry*. Indeed, most personality theories start out this way. Those who prefer this approach simply disregard or criticise all other theories, and present their theory as *the* theory in psychology. Thus they are openly partisan, often demanding unreasoning allegiance from disciples, and zealous in their ardent eagerness to further the faith in the theory. There is, of course, a tendency when taking this approach to minimise the problem of findings that do not confirm or disconfirm the theory. Another danger is getting too caught up in a private theoretical or conceptual language that has to be mastered before the theory is understood.

Those books that propound a single, coherent, considered and thoroughly researched theory are rare. They are often more likely to be speculation or presentation of a partially tested theory. Kelly's (1955) theory of personal constructs is an excellent model of this genre. A less well-known example is Schultz's (1967) theory.

Once again, these books are interesting to read, but they often give one a very biased picture of the field of personality. It is rare for a partisan zealot to encourage theoretical and empirical criticism of the theory – even if it makes it better. Hence the world of personality theory is littered with feuds between orthodox and revisionist believers, the psychoanalytic feuds with the crypto-orthodox neo-Freudians being a fine example. One can equally find passionate debates in other fields, such as the trait psychologist over the fundamental traits of personality.

Ehrenreich (1997) content-analysed 15 current personality textbooks. He found surprising omissions, such as recent developments in psychoanalysis, as well as major breakthroughs in biological and cognitive psychology.

> Topics such as intelligence, attitudes, values and creativity were omitted entirely. . . . Discussions of the impact on personality processes and behaviour of the mere presence of others; of participation in long-term groups; of membership in families; and of ethnic, racial, gender, cultural and historical identity were almost entirely absent . . . the failure of the authors of these contemporary textbooks to discuss them suggests a peculiarly narrow and isolated perspective on human personality.
>
> (Ehrenreich, 1997, pp.38–9).

1.5 COMPARING AND CONTRASTING THEORIES

Most textbook writers, particularly those in the benevolent eclecticism model, and reviewers of the field feel the need to undertake a taxonomisation or *categorisation* of the different theories. This, at least, helps the reader to understand some of the major underlying axiomatic differences between different research traditions.

The goal of personality psychology is to understand (i.e. describe *and* explain) individuality. Nearly all personality theorists admit that people are biosocial organisms, but they differ in the extent to which they stress the nature of one aspect or the other (i.e. biology or socialisation), and the nature of the interaction. The way in which they define personality varies greatly with the kind of behaviour thought to be relevant (i.e. obedience and conformity vs. deviance, selfishness vs. altruism, neuroticism vs. stability) to the study of human beings and the constructs used to describe and conceptualise that behaviour. It is because different theorists have been rather interested in highly varied kinds of individual differences in specific behaviour and different concepts (metaphors) used to describe and explain them that the field of personality is currently so messy.

Some personality theorists are attracted to the inner-man, deep-seated homunculus levels of psychic processes that simply change the level and type of concepts used. Others only feel comfortable with biological, physiological descriptions/explanations which are often left at the level of unverified hypothetical constructs, or are not treated as responses themselves.

Nearly all textbook writers have attempted some sort of grouping of theorems. It is not an easy task, and they have chosen to do it in rather different ways. For instance, Hall *et al.* (1985) selected nine dimensions of difference. These were as follows:

1. whether human behaviour is controlled by rational, conscious, aware processes, or by unconscious, irrational or a-rational processes of which we are unaware;
2. whether it is the learning process (how behaviour is modified) or its acquisitiveness, or outcomes (structure) that is most important;
3. whether behaviour is primarily determined by hereditary/genetic or environmental factors;
4. whether the key to understanding a person's current behaviour is in the past (infancy, childhood) or the present (and immediate past);
5. whether people are better understood in terms of an organic whole or analytically, in terms of smaller, discrete units of behaviour;
6. whether behaviour is seen as largely the product of the (inner) person, or of the external situation or environment;
7. whether human behaviour is purposive, teleological and goal-driven, or mechanistic and explicable entirely in terms of antecedent events;
8. whether behaviour is determined by a few primary (innate) motives or by many acquired motives;
9. whether one understands the normal by studying the abnormal, or whether normality is qualitatively and quantitatively different.

However, they also very wisely suggested that theories may be divided in terms of their fruitfulness as generators of research.

Cook (1984) has suggested one way to categorise personality theories based on two dimensions – above or below the surface, and three lines, namely the biological, phenomenal and motivational lines. Above the surface is the trait or factor level of description. Below the surface are three lines, namely the *biological* line, which looks at temperament, the *phenomenal* line, which looks at self, and the *motivational* line, which looks at motives.

Schultz (1993) laments the number of theories on personality, but felt able to group them in eight domains as follows: psychoanalytic; neo-psychoanalytic; trait; lifespan; humanistic; cognitive; behavioural; and limited-domain. This is a fairly typical list. Formal explicit theories are contrasted with personal implicit theories, although it is acknowledged that, like novelists, theorists rely on their own lives as a primary source of empirical material.

Ewen (1993) attempts to classify many of the classic personality theorists along the following set of dimensions, which he thinks are particularly relevant:

- *the basic nature of human beings* – the extent to which human nature is inherently malignant or benign. Freud tended to be on the malignant end, with his emphasis on innate incestuous and destructive drives, while Rogers tended to typify the optimistic viewpoint;
- *drive reduction* – the extent to which all motivation can be explained in terms of drive reduction. Freud and Cattell believed that the basis of all motivation was drive reduced. Maslow and Allport believed that pleasurable tension-maintaining and increasing concepts need to be included;
- *the dynamics of human nature* – the extent to which all behaviours are determined by prior causes (causality), or in terms of purpose and goals that people make for themselves (teleological). Freud and Skinner, rather uncomfortable bedmates, are located at the causality end, with Allport and Kelly at the teleological end;
- *the importance of unconscious motives* – the extent to which true self-knowledge is difficult to attain. For all of the Freudians, the importance of the unconscious can be overrated, while for the behaviourists, such as Skinner and Bandura, it is less important;
- the extent to which *structural concepts* and *intra-psychic conflicts* are important. Interestingly, both Freud and Cattell thought that they were both important, while Adler and Bandura thought both were unimportant;
- the importance of *anxiety* and *defence*. Here, some Freudians (Freud, Horney and Sullivan) are at the extreme (high) end, while others (Adler) are at the opposite end;
- the *development* of personality – the importance of events in infancy and early childhood. Freud rated this as very high, and Allport, the trait theorist, rated it as very low.

The list in Table 1.1 illustrates the very different theoretical concepts used by the established personality theorists. It helps to explain the particular focus on and concepts used by individual theorists. Ewen (1993) also offers an interesting table, looking at the applied interests of the famous personality theorists. Whilst not everyone would agree with his list, nor accept the theorists he includes and excludes, it provides some insight into why some chapters in this book are longer than others. Certainly it demonstrates the many spheres in which personality is thought to play an important role.

Hjelle and Ziegler (1981) also attempted a twofold 'compare and contrast' task in their review of 10 major personality theories. First, they looked at nine basic assumptions that the theorists appear to make about human nature (Table 1.2).

More importantly, they chose six major scientific criteria (or barometers), as follows:

1. verifiability – theories are explicitly defined, logically interrelated, and amenable to empirical validation/investigation;
2. heuristic value – the degree to which the theory stimulates thinking, theorising and, most importantly, future research;
3. internal consistency – the extent to which the theory is integrated and does not contradict itself;
4. parsimony – the idea that the preferred theoretical account is that requiring the least (but most powerful explanatory) example;
5. comprehensiveness – the range and diversity of phenomena encompassed by the theory;
6. functional significance – simply the extent to which the theory helps people, as well as scientists, to understand everyday human behaviour.

This may be expressed as in Table 1.3.

Finally, from the perspective of the early 1980s, the authors believe that there are several areas worth developing which are, in fact, the new frontiers in personality research. Some, with hindsight, have proved to be less important than others, whilst others have been omitted, such as the study of *cognitive processes* as it relates to personality. This is doubtless a reaction to the cognitive revolution in psychology from social and clinical psychology to physiological psychology. Some personality theorists (e.g. Kelly, Wilkins) were always cognitive in approach, but newer models like that of Seligman (1992) emphasise that personality shapes and is shaped by how people reason about and explain their world. Attention, memory and information-processing are increasingly seen to be important correlates of personality traits, especially neuroticism.

The study of the *physiological* and *neurological determinants* and bases of personality Even more than advances in biochemistry, psychopharmacology and neurophysiology, it is behaviour genetics that seems to offer most to our understanding of personality. Indeed, it may well be that unknown genetic

Table 1.1 The application of different theories to areas of social behaviour

Theorist	Dream interpretation	Psychopathology	Psychotherapy	Work	Religion	Education	Literature	Laboratory research
Freud	+	+	+	–	✓	–	✓	–
Jung	+	+	+	–	+	✓	+	–
Adler	✓	+	+	+	✓	+	–	–
Horney	✓	+	+	✓	–	–	–	–
Fromm	+	+	+	–	✓	–	+	–
Sullivan	✓	+	+	–	✓	–	–	–
Erikson	✓	+	+	–	✓	–	✓	–
Allport	–	–	–	–	✓	–	–	+
Murray	–	+	–	–	–	–	–	+
Kelly	✓	+	+	–	–	✓	–	+
Rogers	–	+	+	–	–	+	✓	+

Applications

Maslow	−	+	+	+	✓	✓	−	+
May	+	+	+	−	✓	−	✓	−
Cattell	−	+	−	+	−	+	−	+
Skinner	−	✓	✓	✓	✓	+	✓	+
Dollard and Miller	−	+	+	−	−	−	−	+
Bandura	−	+	+	−	−	−	−	+

Applied interests of various personality theorists and behaviourists: + = substantial interest; ✓ = some interest; − = little or no interest.
Source: Ewen, R. (1993) *An introduction to theories of personality.* Hillsdale, NJ: Lawrence Erlbaum Associates, 532.

Table 1.2 A 'compare and contrast' exercise

	Strong	Moderate	Slight	Mid-range	Slight	Moderate	Strong	
Freedom	● ○ □		❀	△ ★		◇	★ ❀ ■	Determinism
Rationality	○ ❀ ■ △ ★	● △					✳	Irrationality
Holism	○ ● □ ◇	❀ ★ ■				△	◆	Elementalism
Constitutionalism	○ □ ◇	✳ □ ■	○	❀ ● ■			◆ △ ◇	Environmentalism
Changeability	◆ △ ◇			❀	■	★ ■	● ✳	Unchangeability
Subjectivity	○ ● ★ □	■	❀ ✳	△		◇	◆	Objectivity
Proactivity	○ ● ❀ □	✳ ■ ◇		△			◆	Reactivity
Homeostasis	✳ ■					◇	● ❀ □	Heterostasis
Knowability	✳ ◆ △	❀ ◇		■			● ○ □ ✳	Unknowability

✳, Freud; ◇, Erikson; △, Bandura; ★, Kelly; ●, Adler; ■, Murray; ◆, Skinner; ❀, Allport; ○, Maslow; □, Rogers.
Source: Hjelle, L. and Ziegler, D. (1981) *Personality theories*. New York: McGraw Hill, 443. Reproduced with permission from Larry Hjelle.

factors may prove to be the key to some of the most important issues in personality theory.

The study of *personality development* in middle and old age   Despite the interest in lifespan developmental psychology, and gerontology in particular, work in this field does not appear to have contributed significantly to the understanding of personality and individual differences.

Table 1.3   The positions of personality theorists on the six major criteria for evaluating theories of personality (a designation of 'high' indicates that the theory in question generally meets the criterion in question)

	Low		Moderate		High	
Verifiability	Freud Adler Erikson Allport	Maslow	Murray Kelly		Skinner Bandura Rogers	
Heuristic value	Erikson Allport Kelly Maslow		Adler Murray		Freud Skinner Bandura Rogers	
Internal consistency			Freud Allport		Adler Erikson Murray Skinner	Bandura Kelly Maslow Rogers
Parsimony	Murray		Freud		Adler Erikson Skinner Bandura	Allport Kelly Maslow Rogers
Comprehensiveness			Erikson Murray Skinner Bandura	Allport Kelly Maslow Rogers	Freud Adler	
Functional significance	Murray Allport Kelly		Adler Erikson Bandura		Freud Skinner Maslow Rogers	

Source: Hjelle, L. and Ziegler, D. (1981) *Personality theories*. New York: McGraw Hill, 447. Reproduced with permission from Larry Hjelle.

The study of *self-regulating processes* and plans The interest in self-efficacy and attribution style in the early 1980s led personality theorists to believe that self-control concepts may grow to explain important personality differences. Although this remains an interesting area of research, it has not been integrated well into personality theory.

The study of especially productive, talented, *creative people* This has not taken off particularly well. Two factors have led to this approach being somewhat neglected. The first concerns the definition of these 'superior' creative people, which is highly problematic, and the second concerns the limitations of the case-study method. However, recent work by Eysenck (1995) seems to herald a rejuvenation in this area.

The study of *person–situation interaction* Although this issue was being debated in the 1980s, it is now largely resolved. However, much work remains to be done on developing a useful taxonomy of situation.

The study of problems relevant to the *practical world of human affairs* The extent to which the study of modern issues such as AIDS, unemployment, drug addiction, suicide, etc., has or will ever influence personality theory is debatable. However, what it may do is point to the relevance of individual differences to those who are not sufficiently aware of their importance.

1.6 PERSONALITY RESEARCH AND THEORY-BUILDING

Maddi (1989) has tried to explain, quite straightforwardly, what researchers in the field of personality (personologists) do. Personologists are described as experts in the study and understanding of the consistent patterns of thoughts, feelings and actions that people demonstrate. They tend to study groups of people (or interesting individuals), noting *commonalities* among a representative group of persons. Yet in doing so, they also attempt to identify and classify differences between people. Some researchers seem more interested in demonstrating uniqueness, and others commonalities, but all of them are by definition interested in systematic individual differences. It is their ultimate quest to discover the fundamental, unique traits or 'styles of being'.

At the centre of personality theory is an interest in individuality – the occurrence of individual differences where biological or social pressures are the same, or indeed the converse, where almost identical behaviour is apparent where biological and social conditions are quite different. It is how individual differences develop and change *over time* that is of particular concern and interest to the personality psychologist. Determining that characteristics are stable over time is of especial interest.

As Maddi (1989) notes, the personologists tend to restrict their attention to behaviours that are of psychological importance (such as thoughts, feelings and attitudes), and tend not to be very interested in animal studies. This is not to neglect or reject biological or animal research, but rather to believe that it only answers specific questions.

Pervin (1996b) has argued that there are three distinct research traditions within the domain of scientific personality research. The *clinical* approach involves the systematic, in-depth study of individuals. Psychiatrists such as Freud, doctors such as Murray, and clinicians such as Rogers and Kelly favoured this approach. The obvious strength of the method is the wealth and richness of observations made – some intuitive, others not. Yet the limitation must remain the reliability of those observations, and the testability of the hypotheses, which is frequently not the real concern of the practising therapist. Furthermore, many are fascinated by abnormal rather than normal personality processes.

The *correlational* approach involves looking at the statistical relationship between various objectively defined measures on which individuals have been found to differ. Galton, Eysenck and Cattell are some of the most famous names in this area, which is often called psychometrics. The approach is clearly scientific in the sense that it calls for careful measurement of behaviour, even though it is often based on self-report questionnaires and sophisticated statistical techniques which can explore the complex pattern underlying behaviour. It has been pointed out that multivariate statistics (like factor analysis) make a good servant but a poor master. On the other hand, if the measures are superficial, biased or trivial, no amount of statistical sophistication can compensate for this.

The *experimental* approach involves the systematic manipulation of variables in an attempt to establish causal relationships. It attempts to discover and describe general laws of psychological functioning. Wundt and Skinner are the founding fathers of this approach, which has all the advantages and disadvantages of the experimental approach, although neither of them were personality theorists. Problems of ecological validity, experimenter and expectancy effects, and evaluational apprehension dog all experimental work. On the other hand, it is by far the best method for investigating causal relationships and testing specific hypotheses.

Personality theories differ on various dimensions (see Section 1.5). Some are popular in both psychiatry (even literature) and psychology, like neo-Freudian theories, while others have a small, dedicated following, but have never enjoyed wide popularity. Some were postulated a century ago – others less than a decade ago. Of the many theories, some arise from observations made in the clinic or on the couch, while others are derived and tested in the university laboratory. Some theories stress emotional phenomena, while others emphasise cognitive biases. While some theories attempt to be inclusive and comprehensive, others seem content to describe and explain a small but important area of human individuality.

One can look at each theory in terms of different characteristics such as hypotheses, research and applications (Eysenck, 1991). Theories can be evaluated on numerous criteria. Any good theory of personality must include a clear statement of the data which it is attempting to explain. It requires the use of clear, defined and useful terms that are sensitive and sufficiently differentiating to provide an accurate description. Many theories need operational definitions which explain how to measure a characteristic in ways that differ from the data which it is meant to explain. In this way, one can see the difference between description and explanation. Equally, one could examine the quality, quantity and coherence of experimental research that has been conducted on any one theory. The testing of theories is of the utmost relevance to the development of personality as a science.

Maddi (1989) has listed six criteria of formal adequacy of a good theory. A good theory should be:

1. *important* – it deals with issues that really matter, as opposed to trivial, limited, inconsequential ideas. Theories built almost exclusively on psychotherapeutic observation or animal learning studies in the laboratory often run the risk of being trivial;
2. *operational* – the theory allows the meaning of a concept to be determined by the measurement operations associated with it. It ensures a level of predictions. However, if theorists use measurement operations to define a concept, rather than first defining it, the concept is nothing more than an arbitrary symbol;
3. *parsimonious* – the theory should be as simple as possible, but not more so. It should strive to be stated in the fewest but clearest statements possible. Being unparsimonious is common, and even regarded by some as clever;
4. characterised by *clarity* – good theories avoid figurative, metaphorical or analogical language which creates ambiguity and inconsistency. The clearer the language in a theory, the easier it is to apply it to observations of people in order to understand them better;
5. *empirically valued* – theories should be able to derive hypotheses which have been empirically tested and validated by disinterested researchers using very reliable experimental methods. To test any predicted hypothesis, it must be determined whether relevantly collected data, obtained under strict scientific standards, confirm or disconfirm the theory;
6. *stimulating* – a theory should be capable of provoking others to thought and investigation. Important as this goal is, it cannot be an important criterion until the above factors have been confirmed.

Matthews and Deary (1998) believe that, for personality theories, one can distinguish between *horizontal* and *vertical* validation: *Horizontal* validation refers to finding the same underlying factor structure in different groups of people. It also involves finding convergent (similarities) and discriminant validity when the traits are compared with other psychological concepts and measures. With regard to *vertical* validity, *upward* validation involves finding real-life (e.g. health, work, socially related) correlates of trait differences, while *downward* validation looks at physiological and pharmacological underpinning of traits.

In this book, we shall be concerned with both types of validity. However, in the above terminology it is the upward vertical validity that is of most concern here. It may also be called 'applied personality theory' because, although some of this research may be conducted in the laboratory or the consulting room, it is most often done in the clinic, the classroom, the office or the sports club.

1.7 DIFFERENT APPROACHES

There have been different approaches to personality in general. Perhaps the most important of these are the trait approach (see Section 1.6) and, to a far lesser extent, the situational approach. Without doubt it is the trait approach that has dominated recent developments in personality theory (Matthews and Deary, 1998), and this book is, in part, a celebration of that approach. However, there have been various other approaches, and three of the more recent ones are summarised below.

1.7.1 The implicit or constructionist approach to personality

Does personality reside *inside* the person observed, or *inside* the observer? Do we all have implicit theories which we project/attach to others that are more a function of us than of them? In this sense, is personality constructed rather than real? Given the results of experiments which have shown that if one factor-analyses the ratings of imaginary people, one seems to get the same kind of factors/results, compared with the ratings of real known people, it has been suggested that factor analysis of ratings tells us more about the language of personality description than actual people. Hence some believe that people themselves may not be the best judges (the questionnaire respondents) of their own personality (Hofstede, 1994).

Those who support the long tradition of implicit personality theory research (D'Andrade, 1974; Schweder, 1987) argue that people develop a set of assumptions about the structure of personality which they apply constantly when they make judgements about others. They (the raters/observers) assume a behavioural association between certain concepts – nurturant and feminine, clever and witty – which may be behaviourally unrelated.

Social constructionists reject the idea that traits are primary causes of behaviour, or that they are in some sense fundamental. Rather, they see personality as being constructed (and therefore easily de-, re- or unconstructed) by people in everyday intercourse. Personality traits are seen to be constructed by the product of social interaction (Hampson, 1988). Hampson has distinguished between what people display to others about themselves (explicit personality), how they are construed by others (implicit personality), and how they construe themselves (self-perspective). Social constructivists reject the objective existence of personality, which they see as a social artefact. They believe that people attach meaning and significance to behaviour, and thus infer personality characteristics.

Everyone is in the business of constructing their own and others' personalities – hence concern with identity, reputation and image. Underlying this approach is the idea of change. Hampson notes:

> The construction of personality is a social process, involving the active participation of the actor, observer and self-observer. Removing social support (as in long periods of solitary confinement), or radically changing it (as in moving to a foreign country) is likely to result in the adjustment problems associated with the deconstruction of personality (ie breakdown). However, on the positive side, the constructivist view allows for more possibility of personality change than do many of the traditional personality theories. Instead of being at the mercy of genetics or condition, we can play an active role in the construction of our own personalities.
>
> (Hampson, 1988, p.200).

Put simply, the constructivist view is that personality is no longer regarded as residing exclusively or primarily within the individual. It is seen as the product of an ongoing process, with meaning and concepts being attached by observers and self-observers to social behaviour. Personality occurs between and among – not within – people. In this sense, one has different personalities for different people. Personality is therefore really a persona – a mask – that is, in part a result of active impression management. For some Eastern European researchers such as Strelau (1985), the word 'personality' has a social constructionist, or at least socially defined, ring about it, while 'temperament' refers to biologically determined traits. However, Western psychologists still use the word 'personality' in a technical sense to mean both approaches, although traitists definitely take a temperament perspective.

The idea that personality is a mask that can be relatively easily removed is attractive to many. It fits the current *Zeitgeist*. However, many people point to the clinical literature on attempts to change, and seem less convinced. The increasing evidence for the stability of behaviour over time, as well as the evidence of genetic, biological and pharmacological correlates of stable, internal traits renders the power of the constructivist position ever weaker.

1.7.2 The lay perspective

Lay people – that is, those who are not educated in personality theory (including many psychologists) – are nearly all trait theorists. In other words, they appear to believe that people possess traits which mean they are consistent and stable. Trait words claim that people's behaviour originates from 'within'. It appears to be a parsimonious, culturally shared way of describing the prominent features of individuals. For the lay person, personality is something that is the property of a person. It is psychological in nature,

Table 1.4 Possible dimensions along which prototypically 'scientific' vs. 'common-sense' lay theories differ

	'Scientific' theories	'Lay' theories
1. Explicit and formal	Frequently explicit	Rarely explicit
2. Coherent and consistent	Frequently consistent	Rarely consistent
3. Verification vs. falsification	Falsification, deductivism	Verification, inductivism
4. Cause and consequence	Rarely confuses cause and effect	Often confuses cause and effect
5. Content vs. process	Often process-orientated	Often content-orientated
6. Internal vs. external	Cognisant of both factors	Underestimates external factors
7. General vs. specific	Mostly specific, some general	Mostly general, some specific
8. Strong vs. weak	Strong	Weak

it is general in its manifestations, it is what characterises people as being different, it endures over time, and it can be functional and healthy, or dysfunctional and abnormal. Indeed, various personality tests have their roots in folk concepts of personality (McCrae *et al.*, 1993).

Lay people assign themselves to others' traits. They certainly have enough to choose from – 17,953 trait terms in English, according to Allport and Odbert (1936). The interest in lay (previously known as implicit) theories, lies in how people acquire them, their contents and how they operate. There is also considerable interest in how they differ from explicit scientific theories of personality.

Furnham (1988) attempted to describe how lay theories differed from scientific theories (Table 1.4).

He also attempted to spell out some of the more interesting and important questions that one would ask of any lay (or scientific) theory of personality:

1. What is the aetiology or development of the individual differences observed? For instance, what part does heredity versus environment play in the origin of stable individual differences?
2. What is the relationship between different aspects, features, or dimensions of personality? For instance, if one comes up with a taxonomy or typology, one would want to know how one type (extraverts, endomorphs, Aquarians) are related to, or correlated with, other types (introverts, mesomorphs, Librans).

3. How do these individual differences or personality factors function? That is, what is the process, mechanism or biology that determines how individual differences occur? Related to this is the question of the function of holding any particular theory by any one individual.

4. Are individual differences and personality features stable across time and consistent over situations? This question, widely debated in academic circles, is of course crucial to the definition of personality.

5. What are the consequences of being one type/having a trait? That is, what are the characteristics of people with different personalities – what are their strengths and weaknesses?

6. How can one change one's personality or another person's personality? For instance, can one change one's personality, and if so, how?

7. How does one particular theory of personality relate to another? That is, what is the overlap between various concepts? For instance, it has been suggested that Eysenck's concept of extraversion, Zuckerman's of sensation-seeking, Mehrabian's of stimulus-screening, Strelau's of temperament, and Rosenman's of A-type are all closely linked. To what extent are lay theories essentially the same, but using different terms?

8. How useful are the language, analogies and models of the theory? Nearly all theories use analogies to explain or describe phenomena, and some of these are more or less useful.

(Furnham, 1988, pp.183–4)

The lay perspective is not really an alternative approach. Rather, researchers have been interested in the congruence between lay and scientific accounts of personality, as well as in cultural differences in descriptions of personality.

1.7.3 The act frequency approach

Situationists from various backgrounds have always rejected the idea that traits are the source or origin of behaviour that somehow exists at a deeper level inside the person. Some, like Buss and Craik (1984), have regarded traits as *labels* that sum up a collection of behavioural acts. Thus it is simply a *summary statement*, not an explanatory concept or hidden essence. Saying that someone is anxious or outgoing or creative simply means that person performs acts thus labelled more often than do other people. Traits are summaries of general trends in behaviour, and they refer to acts which vary in prototypicality. Hence, personality descriptions are simply statements about the frequency with which a particular person acts in a particular situation, and say nothing about why they act in this way. Thus this approach works at a different level (see Section 1.1).

The act frequency approach is related to the band-width controversy. Is it more useful and desirable to measure personality in terms of a large number of *narrower*, more specific, homogenous traits, or more *broadly defined*, higher personality traits. The principle of parsimony would suggest the latter, since it has long been suggested that broad, global personality constructs seem to predict broad behavioural criteria with moderate validity, while narrow, specific constructs predict more detailed behavioural criteria with maximum validity (Cronbach and Gleser, 1965).

1.8 THE DOMINANT APPROACH: TRAITS

Lay people, like most modern personality theorists, are trait theorists. Trait theory, like psychology in general, has a long history but a short past. The ancient Greeks, and before them the Chinese, both had clear trait theories of personality. Most people are familiar with Galen's theory (AD 200) of humours or bodily fluids leading to four temperaments – choleric, melancholic, phlegmatic and sanguine. Clear dimensions of extraversion–introversion and neuroticism–stability can be traced through many philosophical speculators until the very turn of this century (Eysenck, 1983).

There is no doubt that over the past decade, and probably since the mid-1980s, there has been a tremendous reawakening and reinvigorating of personality trait research (Deary and Matthews, 1993; Matthews and Deary, 1998). McCrae and Costa (1995) posed the fundamental question: are traits mere descriptions of behaviour, or do they offer a legitimate and useful explanation for individual differences? They argue that they do, but that they cannot be complete explanations. Thus explanations in terms of roles, abilities, expectancies, habits and situational demands are also legitimate. However, traits do contribute causally to the development of habits, attitudes, skills, etc. McCrae and Costa believe that:

1. Personality traits are not descriptive summaries of behaviour, but rather dispositions that are inferred from and can predict and account for patterns of thoughts, feelings and actions.
2. Scientific evidence for the existence of traits is provided (in part) by studies that show patterns of covariation across time, twin pairs, and cultures – covariation that cannot be readily explained by such alternatives as transient influences, learned responses and cultural norms.
3. Patterns of covariation provide non-circular explanations, because observation of some behaviours allows the prediction of other, non-observed behaviours.
4. Psychological constructs give conceptual coherence to the covarying patterns of thoughts, feelings, and actions; good constructs have surplus meaning that points beyond the known correlates of a trait.
5. Trait explanations are not themselves mechanistic; the mechanisms through which they operate may or may not be specified in a psychological theory.

6. When trait standing in an individual is assessed using a validated method, knowledge of the trait's manifestations can legitimately, albeit fallibly, be invoked to explain that individual's behaviour.
7. Personality traits are hypothetical psychological constructs, but they are presumed to have a biological basis.
8. Over time, traits interact with the environment to produce culturally conditioned and meaning-laden characteristic adaptations (such as attitudes, motives, and relationships).
9. Specific behaviours occur when these characteristic adaptations interact with the immediate situation; traits are thus best construed as indirect or distal causes of behaviour.

(McCrae and Costa, 1995, p.248)

Others believe that traits are necessary but not sufficient to explain social behaviour. Diener (1996), like others, believes that we need more than traits to explain individual differences in behaviour. He dismisses the idea that traits are mere labels without true explanatory power. He notes:

Trait correlations do not explain underlying processes, other variables are inevitably important at least in some instances, and traits do not explain intra-individual variation. . . . We need to understand how traits influence behaviour and how they interact with the environment. We need to understand how traits arise and how they are stored in the nervous system.

(Diener, 1996, p.397)

There are almost 20,000 trait words in English. Some are used by psychologists in a 'technical' sense, and others are almost ignored by trait researchers. Lay people describe and explain behaviour that they see (in others) by the use of trait words, e.g. 'He is an extravert', 'She is impulsive', 'They are neurotic'. However, because these words are used to describe and explain, this does not mean that they are always scientifically useful. Even some psychologists never escape the tautological loop of, for example, saying that an extravert is impulsive and sociable, and that sociable and impulsive people are extraverts, but never offering an explanation for the origins of traits and the mechanisms and processes whereby they influence behaviour. Most scientists and lay people believe in the *causal primacy of traits*. Although it is agreed that this works at many levels, and can be indirect, it is assumed that traits shape and structure (and hence predict) behaviour. Furthermore, most agree that traits are fundamental (biologically based, and stable over time), not simply a superficial mask that is negotiable in different social encounters.

Trait psychologists aim to develop a comprehensive but parsimonious and powerful theory of personality. Early attempts at scientific research in Europe (by Galton and Spearman in the UK and Her and Heymans in the Netherlands) were greatly fascinated by the development of statistics. For nearly 100 years the psychometric approach has been characterised by the construction and refinement of questionnaires through multivariate statistics. The fundamental aim is to develop reliable and valid measures that accurately measure the fundamental traits. Some theories attempt to combine measures of ability, motivation, personality and mood, but most stick to traits alone.

Perhaps the most celebrated of all traits is extraversion. This construct can be found in the writings of Hippocrates and Galen, Wundt and Jung, and Eysenck and Cattell. It can be measured by self-report (questionnaire) and by ratings by others, as well as by indirect or objective measures such as salivation after receiving 'lemon drops' in the mouth, colour preference or speed of reaction.

Moods, by definition, vary – traits do not. Thus one could distinguish between trait and state anxiety (Spielberger *et al.*, 1970). Hence even very low trait-anxiety people can exhibit – quite normally – high state-anxiety. They often look similar and can be measured in the same way, but they are psychometrically different. Therefore trait anxiety should correlate with neuroticism (another trait), whilst state anxiety does not. Equally, state anxiety should correlate with other concurrently assessed negative mood measures, whilst trait anxiety does not. Usually, trait factors are better predictors of behaviour than state factors, but in extreme situations, various state factors can have very powerful effects on behaviour.

State factors, like trait factors, can be measured by questionnaire, and it is possible to try to determine the fundamental dimensions of mood. Thus many have talked of positive or energetic arousal and negative or tense arousal (Thayer, 1989). Experimentalists find that mood is fairly easy to manipulate through films, music or drugs, to test their effects on behaviour. Yet moods are a mix of biological, cognitive and social influences.

It is also important to distinguish between traits and types. *Types* (e.g. gender) are regarded as categories of membership that are distinct and discontinuous. People are either the one or the other. In *trait* theories, people differ in amounts on a continuum. Trait theorists see the difference between individuals quantitatively rather than qualitatively. Typologies are out of fashion because assignment has often proved to be too arbitrary and unreliable. After all, even gender is not absolutely perfect. Trait theories often talk in typological terms, but think of traits as continuously (often normally) distributed. One way to contrast the two is shown in Table 1.5.

The world of psychiatric diagnosis still seems to use types in the sense that people are either labelled/diagnosed X (depression, anxiety, schizophrenia) or not. Typological theory suggests a discontinuity between similar behaviours, while trait theory does not. Trait theorists believe that on all variables there is a continuum, and that cut-off into types is therefore arbitrary, or at least follows a set convention. There remain few modern personality psychologists who actively follow the type strategy (Meehl, 1992). Between the 1940s and 1970s, many trait measures were devised to measure single trait concepts as well as multiple traits. They differed enormously in approach, the amount of

Table 1.5 The differences between traits and types

Trait theory	Type theory
Concerned with universals possessed in different amounts	Concerned with preferences which are perhaps inborn or learnt
Involves measuring	Involves sorting
Extreme scores are important for discrimination	Midpoint is crucial for discrimination
Normally distributed	Skewed distribution
Scores mean *amount* of trait possessed	Scores indicate confidence that sorting is correct

effort put into questionnaire development, and the sophistication and resulting evidence of their reliability and validity.

Two major events have occurred over the past 30 years to shake and reinvigorate trait research. The first was the advent of *situationalism*.

Trait theorists believe that people are relatively consistent across situations, and stable over time. The situationalists (Mischel, 1968) argued that the evidence for the cross-situational consistency of behaviour is very poor, *and* that traits were demonstrably poor predictors of actual behaviour. Thus the radical situationalists believed that all (social) behaviour was primarily a function of the situation people were in, rather than of their (innate) personality traits. To a large extent, the situationalist critique was full of red herrings and straw men. No trait theorist or situationalist ever really believed that either factor alone accounted for all of the variance (Argyle *et al.*, 1981). All of them were, and are, to some extent situationalistic. To a large extent, the debate was methodological and researchers have subsequently shown that if people were measured appropriately over different situations, their behaviour was surprisingly consistent (Kenrick and Funder, 1989). In this sense, a trait may be seen as the probability of a particular type of behaviour in a specific situation. Over time, the theoretical and methodological criticisms made by situationalists were refuted. However, the debate did demonstrate a number of points.

- It is best to take multiple behaviour ratings (by self or others) in order to obtain a reliable measure of a trait (or indeed of a behaviour that one is trying to rate).
- Raters of others have to be fairly familiar with them (i.e. have a good data bank of experience).
- Using multiple observers or raters improves reliability.

- Dimension/behaviours that are publicly observable yield more reliable ratings.
- Some situations/behaviours are more relevant to the measurement and study of traits than others.

Certainly traits are more important and powerful predictors of behaviour when the context is familiar and informal (as opposed to novel and public), when there are many options as to how to behave (rather than few), when the setting endures over a reasonable period of time (rather than being very brief), and when the acceptable possible behaviours are numerous rather than few.

The issue of stability over time is more difficult to demonstrate because of the necessity for longitudinal research, but it is interestingly counter-intuitive. Studies conducted over 10 to 30 years report correlations of 0.65 to 0.80. Furthermore, using different tests and different methods over long periods of time, it is possible to demonstrate an impressive level of stability (Conley, 1985). The results of these studies are surprisingly unequivocal. There is overwhelming evidence for the stability of personality traits (particularly extraversion, neuroticism and conscientiousness) over time (Costa and McCrae, 1992). For many individuals, this is self-evidently true of others, if not of themselves. Many people like to believe that they have changed, almost always for the better (being wiser, more mature and more insightful), but that others have not – but in this they are mistaken!

In fact, there is also impressive evidence that the structure and correlates of traits are consistent across cultures (Eysenck and Eysenck, 1985). Thus traits seem to be remarkably resilient. Only major trauma seems to change personality, which implies that the situationists and interactionists may be over-stressing the role of social and contextual variables in changing or shaping behaviour.

Deary and Matthews (1993) argue that the trait approach is not only 'alive and well', but flourishing. They highlight various 'bright spots' in current trait theory:

1. growing agreement concerning the number, character and stability of personality dimensions;
2. a greater understanding of the heritability of personality traits, and hence a greater appreciation of the role of the environment;
3. a growing sophistication of research which aims to elucidate the bio-logical and social bases of trait differences;
4. an appreciation of the extent to which personality differences predict outcomes, or act as moderators, in cognitive and health settings.

They assert, as many others have done before them, two fundamental points:

1. *the Primary Causality of Traits* – the idea that causality flows from traits to behaviour and that, although there is a feedback loop, it is less important;

2. *the Inner Locus of Traits* – the idea that traits describe the fundamental core qualities of a person that are latent rather than manifest.

The causes of personality traits have always been acknowledged to be both biological *and* social. The evidence for the former is primarily based on behaviour genetics. The fact that there were so many competing theories, typologies and measures of traits did not serve the trait position well. The pre-paradigmatic state of affairs meant that it was difficult to take the trait arguments seriously. However, there is growing consensus over the emergence of the 'Big Five' as fundamental higher-order orthogonal factors. The 1980s and 1990s have been dominated by the five-factor model (FFM) of traits. What this means is that many personality psychologists have accepted that there are five fundamental (higher-order) orthogonal (independent of one another) personality traits (these will be described later). The origin of the model lies in very different methods and areas. It is open to question how much agreement there really is for this position, when Eysenck (1991) claims three factors, Cattell (1960) 16 factors and Brand (1994) six, and furthermore the labelling of the factors within the Big Five tradition is not consistent.

Essentially, differences between the various theorists can in part be resolved by understanding a few salient issues. First, researchers have used rather different methods, such as studies of natural language in questionnaire construction, and this has naturally had an effect on the labelling of the factors. Secondly, different factor-analytical methods yielded two different results. The dispute between Cattell and Eysenck is really about whether to use an orthogonal or oblique rotation – the former trying to render factors independent of one another and the latter attempting to maximise variance. Thirdly, a number of researchers have concentrated on 'unpacking' some of the fundamental traits, rather than looking at the relationship between them – that is, they investigate them at rather different levels (see Section 1.1). Hence there appears to be more disagreement than there really is.

Various attempts to re-analyse others' data (Noller *et al.*, 1987; Deary, 1996) have shown how similar, rather than how different, are the resultant higher-order factors. Even single-trait personality theories seem to be able to be nicely 'slotted in' to the Big Five framework. Moreover, these factors can be 'recovered' from different types of data as well as self-reports such as the report ratings of others who know them well (Muten, 1991). Furthermore, data from different countries, using widely different languages for the ratings, have yielded similar results. Finally, it is also worth noting that all of these traits seem to be remarkably stable over time.

Whilst there remains almost total agreement about the existence of two fundamental unrelated factors (extraversion and neuroticism), the debate is about what the others are and should be labelled. The evidence for five factors appears to be growing from many sources – from longitudinal studies over time, from different groups of individuals, and from studies in different languages (Goldberg, 1993). However, it is equally true, and important to point out, that the five factors found by different researchers do not always equivocate, and that doubts still remain as to whether five is either too many or too few. Some researchers are eager to change their system to psychobiological processes, or mental illness, or natural language, and each of these influences naturally shapes what factors they believe to be important and how they label them. Thus whether intelligence, self-rated intellect or culture is part of personality remains a fundamental question, as does the variable labelled 'openness to experience'.

Digman (1990) traced the history of classificatory work (often factor analysis) of personality dimensions over a 40-year period. Despite the use of rather different methods, samples and terms, it appears to be possible to align radically different theories in order to show their overlap, as has been done by Carver and Scheier (1992) (Table 1.6).

Cattell and Eysenck, who both did their PhDs at University College London, have a lot in common, but also showed some important differences. Both sought, through factor analysis, to 'let reality reveal itself'. Cattell began with *lexical criteria*, by using 171 trait names for this factor analysis. Using different types of data (self-report, observational and objective), he made many discoveries and conducted many exploratory factor analyses on many data sets. He settled on 16 factors, which can be described in either technical or everyday language.

Eysenck argued that it was better to develop and test theories (a practice now called confirmatory factor analysis), rather than to discover factors. He set about measuring and testing the two Galen-inspired 'superfactors'.

Table 1.6 Labels used by various authors to refer to the so-called 'Big Five' factors in personality

1	2	3	4	5
Social adaptability	Conformity	Will to achieve	Emotional control	Enquiring intellect
Surgency	Agreeableness	Conscientiousness	Emotionality	Culture
Assertiveness	Likeability	Responsibility	Emotionality	Intelligence
Extraversion	Friendly compliance	Will to achieve	Neuroticism	Intellect
Extraversion	Agreeableness	Conscientiousness	Neuroticism	Openness to experience
Power	Love	Work	Affect	Intellect

Labels in the rows are (in order) from Fisk (1949), Norman (1963), Borgatta (1964), Digman (1990) and Costa and McCrae (1985). The final row provides a characterisation by Peabody and Goldberg (1989) of the life domain to which the trait pertains.
Source: Carver and Scheir (1992) *Perspectives on personality*. Boston, MA: Allyn & Bacon, 74.

McCrae and Costa (1995) believe that earlier criticisms that personality traits are either simple descriptions or cognitive fictions can now be refuted in part because of evidence of the heritability of most personality traits. However, it should not be assumed that the five-factor model is without critics (Block, 1995). McAdam (1992) has offered six criticisms:

1. the inability of the model to address core constructions of personality functions beyond the level of traits;
2. limitations with respect to the prediction of specific behaviour and the adequate description of people's lives;
3. failure to provide compelling causal explanations for human behaviour and experience;
4. disregard of the contextual and conditional nature of human experience;
5. failure to offer an attractive programme for looking at the organisation and integration of personality;
6. reliance on simple, contingent, implicitly comparative statements about personality.

Nevertheless, the fact that so many personality researchers are working within the five-factor model framework must be good for an erstwhile fragmented field. There is an impressive research library on the social behaviour correlates of the Big Five described in this book.

1.9 THE DEVELOPMENT OF TRAIT MEASURES AND CONCEPTS

Furnham (1990) has argued that the development of single-trait theories appears to go through most of the following stages. There are, of course, many problems associated with any stage-wise theory, such as how long each stage lasts, what determines movement from one stage to the next, whether one can skip a stage or not, whether one might return to an earlier stage, and whether all phenomena pass through all stages. Nevertheless, there does seem to be a logical series of steps that researchers follow before a trait is 'discovered'. Eight stages of development can be identified.

1. *Identification of the phenomenon.* This may occur as a result of laboratory experimentation or observation in a clinic, at work, or through critical reading. It may occur when a researcher operationalises that which is well known in literature into a psychological measure. However, what is more commonly the case is that a researcher observes a psychological phenomenon to which he or she gives a name. First, the researchers who originally made the observations need not necessarily be the same ones who develop the single-trait theory or the self-report measure. Secondly, the phenomenon is often 'new' only in the sense that it has not been recorded before in quite the same way. Thirdly, this stage

often occurs in the laboratory as a by-product of observational studies, or occasionally from the systematic behaviour of their patients. Rarely are the researchers intentionally engaged in developing a trait measure of theory.

2. *Replication of the effect.* The second stage is characterised by replications and considerably more experimental work on the nature of the effect observed. The aim of this phase is to test the robustness of the findings, often by subtle yet simple means – a case of data-gathering in an attempt to find support for observations made, while other series of studies attempt to test the various hypotheses that make up the nascent theory.

3. *The development of a self-report measure.* Despite the fact that the original researchers may not be personality, clinical or social psychologists, and may in fact have little faith in self-report measures, the next stage does involve the development of a self-report measure. The questionnaires used may be of highly variable psychometric quality, and the research that goes into establishing them can be somewhat inadequate. Reliability, validity and normative statistics may be fairly minimal to begin with, and it is unlikely that the first versions to be published are validated in a manner that is acceptable to psychometricians. Frequently, the self-report measure is developed some years after the concept/behaviour pattern has been described in the literature. In this case, what might happen is that, over the space of a few years, a number of similar (but not highly correlated) measures will be developed.

4. *Validation of the measure.* The fourth phase may continue for some time, and involves numerous experimental and correlational studies of various types, all aiming to validate the measure and its underlying concepts. Studies often include a programmatic series designed to test corollaries of the theory. What links the studies is the unidimensional trait measure used to assess the independent variable. A large number of these studies are essentially attempts to establish the concurrent, construct and predictive validity of the self-report scale by correlating it with other well-known measures or behaviours. Paradoxically, it is not a lack of validity that prevents research into a measure or concept, but more likely the extent to which the measure taps into the *Zeitgeist* of (North American) psychology.

5. *Factor-analytical work and multidimensionality.* Although researchers may identify what they believe to be a single – albeit complex – dimension or phenomenon, and hence develop a unidimensional scale, subsequent multivariate statistics (cluster analysis, factor analysis and multidimensional scaling) nearly always show the measure to be multidimensional with specific interpretable primary factors which may be orthogonal or oblique. Factor-analytical work usually poses problems for the original author, because the theory upon which the measure is founded usually assumes a unidimensional concept. Three responses are possible. One is to maintain that the concept, measure and trait are unified at a higher

order (i.e. superfactors) and that, although it may have various components, these are second-order (secondary) distinctions/factors which do not threaten the theory. A second approach is to revise the scale, either by attempting to eradicate items that load on irrelevant factors, or by building a truly multidimensional instrument. A third approach is to conduct a meta-analysis of factor-analytical studies, to decide on the factor structure, and to accept the original scale as multidimensional. This phase may last for many years, but may help to resolve equivocal findings when they can be attributed to the multidimensional structure of the trait measure.

6. *Multiple, multidimensional measures.* The malaise that follows repeated psychometric investigations of an established, single-trait measure often leads scholars to despair because, as has been noted, it is uncertain at which level analysis should proceed. However, a common response is for a team of psychometrically oriented researchers to develop a new, better scale or self-report device. These new 'improved' measures often have various specific features. First, they are nearly always multidimensional in the sense that they provide subscale scores which may or may not be combined into a single score, depending on the needs of the researchers. Secondly, many researchers develop sphere-specific scales to measure the trait, belief or behaviour system within a very restricted range of behaviours, as this has been shown to improve the predictive validity considerably. There are, of course, problems with this proliferation of measures because studies that use different measures are not strictly comparable. It is possible that a person may score high on one measure, but low on a related measure. Some authors have attempted to produce not so much a multidimensional measure as sphere-specific measures which set out to measure the same beliefs in different contexts.

7. *Doubts about the original concept.* It is not infrequently found that, after a decade or so of intensive psychometric work on a measure/concept, authors begin to have doubts about its conceptual and psychometric status. Researchers concerned with the measurement of assertion construct now believe that it is outmoded and should be relinquished. The complexity of measurement and the equivocal nature of the findings leads reviewers to conclude that the original concept/phenomenon/behaviour pattern, and all of the questionnaires that attempt to measure it, should be abandoned, either in favour of a new concept – usually a subscale of the former – or else totally in that the original behaviour pattern is too unstable to be considered a trait. This stage, not unlike the last two, is characterised by increased empirical work, but also by theoretical reconceptualisation. Naturally, the commitment of researchers to a particular concept or scale means that they are loath to relinquish it, but happy to make further attempts to refine it.

8. *Acceptance and 'text-bookisation'.* Having gone through the above seven stages and having survived the last one, the concept and its measures are

usually accepted into the canon of individual differences measures. A sure sign of this process is inclusion in the numerous textbooks on personality. By this stage there is probably a sizeable literature on the concept and the measure, as shown by citation counts. However, one should not assume that because a test (and concept) has won through the above baptismal and confirmatory process, it is therefore necessarily a psychometrically valid, theoretically important or diagnostically useful measure. Small bands of zealots wedded to the original ideas in the scale can propel a measure of dubious theoretical and psychometric validity into the textbooks and research consciousness. Equally, extremely good measures based on sound theory and careful psychometric work can get 'lost' and never make it to the laboratories of the world.

Like all stage-wise theories, the above sequence has its limitations and unanswered questions. Despite some unresolved questions, it may be useful to adapt the above stage-wise model to evaluate the progress of a trait measure, or indeed to predict further development. It should not be assumed that a robust, valid and universally accepted measure undergoes no further development or refinement because it appears in textbooks. For example, through exhaustive and extensive work on its factor structure, construct validity and theoretical parsimony, Eysenck and Eysenck (1985) have revised the Eysenck Personality Questionnaire – Revised (EPQ-R) in order to make the measure as psychometrically sound as possible.

The issue of broad vs. narrow traits has been somewhat misleadingly titled as the band-width–fidelity trade-off because it has been suggested that the broader the measurement (of the higher-order or super-factors) the more it precludes high-fidelity assessment (Ones and Viswesvaran, 1996).

1.10 THE IDIOGRAPHIC CRITICISM

The idiographic criticism of modern (trait or cognitive) psychology is both one of the most fundamental and one of the most long-lasting. According to one established adage, 'Science does not deal with individual cases' (*scientia non est individuorum*), and hence laws and theories have nothing to say about individuals (Western, 1996).

Yet, since the *Verstehen* movement in Germany, many personality psychologists have favoured the *idiographic* as opposed to the *nomothetic* approach. The former favour an intuitive, holistic approach, aimed at a comprehensive and empathic understanding of the quality of the unique make-up of single individuals. It has also been noted:

> No matter how intensively prolonged, objective and well controlled the study of a single case, one can never be sure to what extent the lawful regularities found can be generalised to other persons, or in what way the findings will turn out to be contingent on some fortuitously present

characteristic of the subject – until the investigation is repeated on an adequate sample of persons. As excellent a way as it is to make discoveries, the study of an individual cannot be used to establish laws.

(Holt, 1967, p.397)

Quick (1997) has attempted a clarification of the differences between the two approaches, as shown in Table 1.7.

The fight, or disagreement, between the idiographic and the nomothetic, is frequently between the tough- and tender-minded personality psychologists. Idiographic researchers tend to be tender-minded, believing that personality is 'more than' any simple description. They are often seriously opposed to what they see as the mechanistic qualification and reductionist analysis of essentially the whole person by the nomothetic school (Valentine, 1992). At the

Table 1.7 The idiographic–nomothetic dimension in scientific enquiry

	Research paradigm	
	Nomothetic	**Idiographic**
World definition	Determinate	Indeterminate
World hypothesis	Mechanism	Contextualism
Core processes	Analysis Integration Reductionism	Synthesis Dispersion Holism
Method	Experimentation	History
Metaphor	The machine	The historical event
Interactions	Cause–effect	Reciprocal–transactional
Knowledge attribute	Positivistic–pragmatic	Hermeneutic–spiritual
Treatment of facts	Exclusive	Inclusive
Key strengths	Breadth Precision Replicability Prediction	Depth Richness Uniqueness Comprehensiveness
Key limitations	Lack of richness	Lack of precision

Source: Quick, J. (1997) Idiographic research in organizational behaviour. In Cooper, L. and Jackson, S. (eds), Creating tomorrow's organizations. Chichester: Wiley, 478. Copyright John Wiley & Sons Limited. Reproduced with permission.

heart of the issue is the vexed question of whether a science of the individual is possible. Neuroscientists often report single-case unique studies of individuals who have suffered extreme trauma. However, as Valentine notes:

> ... the results of such studies are scientifically uninterpretable unless an adequate baseline for comparison is provided (either in the form of the patient's performance before the onset of the illness, usually unavailable, or scores from a normal population on standardised tests). In isolation, it is difficult to determine whether or not the results from a single case are due to chance and, without replication, whether or not they are generalisable. Such data are insufficient to establish general laws.
>
> (Valentine, 1992, p.190)

The idiographic researchers are fond of pointing out the *uniqueness of individuals*, that the qualitative properties of individuals cannot be subjected to *qualification*, and that it is the unique combination or structure of traits, abilities, needs, etc., that are important. The *nomothetic* researchers respond by pointing out that if there were no commonality between individuals, idiographic research would be pointless. They also vigorously dispute that all aspects of human behaviour – even values, moods and capricious dreams – cannot be accurately and reliably measured. Finally, they argue that, in fact, the empirical method is the best way to examine complex structures (e.g. DNA). If there is a systematic, underlying structure to people, the quantitative method is the best way to investigate it.

Thus the nomothetic scientists argue that truly idiographic methods cannot be scientific and, furthermore, that they are really only nomothetic measures applied to individual cases. In this sense, 'idiographic' is really only a value label that flags up a focus on the individual. Psychologists who favour the nomothetic approach, which has dominated trait psychology over the past 30 years, do not reject the idea that each human being is unique. However, they view uniqueness as reflecting a *unique combination* of levels on trait dimensions, with the dimensions themselves being the same for all. As Eysenck has put it: 'To the scientist, the unique individual is simply the point of intersection of a number of quantitative variables' (Eysenck, 1952, p.18).

Lamiell (1981) argued that personality theories are rather ineffective for describing the personality of any given individual. He proposed an *idiothetic* approach, which used idiographic methods for personality description and nomothetic principles for studying personality.

> The nomothetic approach (to personality) finds trait dimensions relevant to everyone and calculates where on the distribution a particular individual may be located. ... The idiographic approach stresses describing each individual in whatever terms are appropriate for him or her. The description should be derived from a variety of sources: self-view and views of significant others, as well as more objective descriptions of the person's behaviour.
>
> (Hampson, 1984, p.110)

Allport used the idiographic approach to propose that traits can be classified according to how prominent they are in a person's personality. Some people have qualities that are pervasive, virtually dominating their existence. Allport called such a trait a *cardinal disposition*, and he believed that such traits are rare. Few people are so fully dominated by a trait, even a pathological one, that it deserves that label.

For most people a few traits stand out, although less so than would a cardinal disposition. These salient traits are referred to as *central dispositions*, and most people have several of them. When asked to describe someone they know well in words or phrases, people seem to use between 3 and 10 characteristics per person, with an average of around 7. Most people have a fairly broad range of central dispositions, with relatively few dominated by a cardinal disposition. Traits that are less salient and more restricted in their applicability are termed *secondary dispositions*. A secondary disposition is a trait that may operate only in a limited setting, or it may reflect a tendency that has only a weak influence.

Whilst there remain some personality theorists dedicated to the idiographic, biographical method, most work within the nomothetic tradition. However, clinically orientated personality theorists often derive many interesting hypotheses within the idiographic methodology.

1.11 PSYCHOLOGY AND SOCIOLOGY

Textbooks in general and social psychology in particular often include large sections on obedience and conformity. Indeed, perhaps the most famous psychological 'experiment' of all time was Milgram's (1969) *Obedience to Authority* study, followed closely by Asch's (1952) often replicated study on *conformity*. Psychologists – and personality psychologists in particular – are interested in individuality, and puzzled and intrigued by conformity. As the individual is the unit of analysis, they find 'group behaviour' an issue worthy of research.

On the other hand, textbooks on sociology usually include chapters on deviance (delinquency). Sociologists are interested in large (and small) human groups such as families, gangs, factories (and even strata of society), and take for granted the following of norms and social roles. They are puzzled by those who break the rules, deviate from the group, and refuse to toe the line. Individuality is the puzzle, and hence there is little consideration of systematic individual differences.

Psychologists are happy with physiological, biological and genetic explanations for behaviour, while sociologists prefer economic and structural explanations. Thus when there are multiple theories for a phenomenon, the psychological and the sociological often focus on different features. For example, a sociological explanation for anorexia nervosa might be the number of very thin models in magazines and the electronic media, while a psychological explanation might be expressed in terms of attempts to deny sexuality, control over authority, or even physiological problems in the brain. Equally, sociologists observe that behavioural problems often are not evenly distributed across the population, and hence may be influenced by social factors. Thus the fact that working class women over 50 years of age are a very high smoking group suggests that these factors are important in the origin and maintenance of smoking. On the other hand, psychologists are equally impressed by the facts that extraverts smoke more than introverts, and that schizophrenics are particularly heavy smokers (especially when they are medicated), suggesting powerful individual difference factors that may, in part, determine smoking behaviour. Personality psychology might, as a result, be less sensitive to sociological variables that may influence behaviour.

1.12 CURRENT REFLECTIONS AND PREOCCUPATIONS

Approaching the millennium has made personality psychologists look both back to the past and forward to the future. Many believe that personality theories have no time perspective or sense of history (Caprara and van Heck, 1992), while some believe that the important questions remain the same – and unanswered – and that so-called innovations are new, incorrect reformulations of old problems.

The renaissance of personality theory in the 1990s has resulted in many researchers reflecting back to lessons of history, as well as to the future of personality (Pervin, 1996a; Sarason, Sarason and Pierce, 1996). There is now more than mere lip service being paid to the idea that we are simultaneously biological *and* social beings, shaped by evolutionary and current factors. They argue that there appear to be three paths to integrating personality theories more effectively, namely using better research designs that take account of all the complex and relevant factors involved in individual reaction, stressing internal processes more (i.e. how individuals appraise their world), and stressing how people change over time.

Carver (1996) detects, through very diverse research traditions, the rediscovery of an old concept – *approach-avoidance* – and the idea that there are two distinct biologically based structures that are independent of one another. Data and theories from neuropsychology, psychopathology, animal conditioning and psychopharmacology all point to an approach activation system (aiming at engagement facilitation) and an aversive, withdrawal, inhibition system. Thus different systems seem to be apparent at the level of affect attitude as well as at the level of self. Carver also detects the rediscovery and subsequent acceptance of various *psychoanalytical* concepts, which seem to be closely linked to evolutionary concepts. In Carver's words, we have new lenses and old ideas. A final theme is the re-emphasis on the *social nature* of personality, based on concepts such as attachment and group pressures.

Epstein (1996) argues that trait theory is not sufficient either to account for differences in behaviour in different situations, or to capture the complex uniqueness of individual identities. Like others, he feels that motivational constructs (goals and needs) are, or should be, of central importance in personality psychology. Yet the importance and relevance of biological, evolutionary and genetic principles cannot be underestimated.

McClelland (1996) detected various themes regarding the present and the future.

- Personality is still largely a study of the self-image – that is, data is still self-report data, collected via questionnaires.
- Personality psychologists study primarily conscious, cognitive variables, and very little research is dedicated to unconscious factors.
- Personality research is not a cumulative science – most researchers work alone on their own 'new' approaches, rather than building upon earlier, systematic theories.
- Personality psychology is based more on process than on content – for example, researchers are interested in strength, rather than content, of beliefs.

The mid-1990s have led to much reflection about both the future and the past in personality (McAdam, 1996; Pervin, 1996a). This is perhaps to be expected, as the field regroups with greater enthusiasm and a sense of direction.

Recent reviewers of personality theory and research are, overall, bullish. Pervin (1996), an acknowledged reviewer and textbook writer in the field noted the following.

1. Interest in the field has reached astonishing proportions.
2. There appear to be as many definitions of personality as there are authors.
3. Clarification of the concept of types would be an invaluable service to the field.
4. The tide has turned toward greater faith in the innate determination of traits.
5. There is increasing dissatisfaction with the more artificial pencil-and-paper or laboratory methods.
6. The principal source of disagreement is the issue of specificity versus generality, with common sense postulating the latter and experimental studies giving results that are interpreted in either direction, often according to the inclination of the author.
7. Although there is value in studying the same phenomenon in many subjects, there is particular value in seeing relations among the parts in the individual organism.

8. Although the formulation of adequate theories of personality lags behind research, this research is so flourishing that the outlook for a future systematic psychology of personalty is bright indeed.

(Pervin, 1996b, p.1)

Buss (1995) has succinctly reported some of the current debates, and disputed issues around the trait perspective. A central question concerns how *powerfully* behaviour is predicted by traits. This is often about the size of the relationship between a trait and its manifest behaviour. Recent studies which aggregate the impact of traits appear to show that they are as powerful predictors of behaviour as *situational constraints*. Since Mischel (1968), it has been argued that powerful situations (e.g. stimuli, manipulations) negate the effect of a trait. Yet some traits (like anxiety) may be important *only* when the manipulation is strong. In essence, it seems that where the *context* (i.e. situation) of behaviour is private, informal and familiar, when the *duration* is extensive, when the possible range of *responses* is wide, and when there is considerable *choice* between different types of behaviour, trait-like consistent behaviour is observable. Much of this (never-ending) debate concerns such issues as the *units and classes of behaviour* that one is trying to predict, the breadth of behaviour or situation under inspection, the amount of aggregation which has occurred in data collection, and the consistency of behaviour one expects.

Consider the final issue, namely the consistency of behaviour. We know, as Buss (1995) has pointed out, that behaviour is affected by methodological factors (ranking yields more consistency than rating), the traits themselves (inherited, stylistic and self-related traits are more consistent) and other genetic variables (the more observable the trait, the more extreme the rating, and the more consistent it is).

1.13 UNRESOLVED (AND UNRESOLVABLE) PROBLEMS IN PERSONALITY

There is a long list of issues or debates in modern personality theory which has never been fully resolved. They include the following.

Heredity vs. environment This difference is also referred to as nature vs. nurture, or even nature *via* nurture. What is more important: genetic and biological factors, or influences from the environment? The issue is whether personality differences develop primarily from genetic, environmental or interactive factors. Trait theories have been divided on this issue. Freudian theory depends heavily on heredity, whereas humanistic, learning, cognitive and self theories all emphasise either environment as a determinant of behaviour or interaction with the environment as a source of personality development and differences. It may well be impossible to separate these two factors whose interaction is so complex. Therefore this may be a 'red herring'.

Learning processes vs. innate laws of behaviour   Should emphasis be placed on modifiability, or on the view that personality development follows an internal timetable? Again, trait theories have been divided. Freudian theory has favoured the inner determinant view – a pessimistic one – while humanists postulate an optimistic view that people change as a result of their experiences. Learning, cognitive and self theories clearly support the idea that behaviour and personality change as a result of learned experiences. The question is not so much whether people learn and change – that is self-evident – but when, how and why they do, and why some learn faster than others.

Emphasis on past, present or future   Trait theories emphasise past causes – whether innate or learned, Freudian theory stresses past events in early childhood, learning theories focus on past reinforcements and present contingencies, humanistic theories emphasise present phenomenal reality or future goals, and cognitive and self theories emphasise past and present (and the future, if goal-setting is involved). Those personality psychologists who are interested in personal goals and scripts are among the few who emphasise the influence of the future on the present.

Consciousness vs. unconsciousness   Are personality processes conscious, preconscious, subconscious or unconscious? Indeed, is reference to how people think, feel and perceive essential to a personality description? Freudian theory emphasises unconscious processes, whereas humanistic, learning and cognitive theories emphasise conscious processes. Trait theories pay little attention to either consciousness or unconsciousness, and self theories are unclear on this score. The topic of consciousness – surely one of the most important and difficult in psychology – is attracting more attention. Increasingly, the idea that some important personality processes are unconscious is being accepted by personality theorists of all persuasions.

Internal disposition vs. external situation   Learning theories emphasise situational factors, trait theories play up dispositional factors, and the others allow for an interaction between person-based and situation-based variables. We certainly have a good idea about the internal, person-based factors, but we know much less about the situational, external factors.

Situational vs. 'personological' approaches to human behaviour   Do people vary because they respond differently to situations which they (by fate) find themselves in, or because they have different personalities which create, choose and change those situations?

The mind vs. body problem of personality   Should we consider personality differences to have a physiological basis, or are they socially or self-constructed? The former view implies difficulty in change, whereas the latter does not. This is one of the oldest debates in philosophy, and is of direct relevance to personality issues.

Folk vs. scientific psychology of personality Do non-experts have different, perhaps more sophisticated and variable descriptions of personality? Are all folk descriptions irrelevant because they are unclear, ambiguous and contradictory? Certainly the self-perspective of the lay person on personality theory was considered to be of the utmost relevance until recently.

Finally Cook (1984), like many reviewers, has tried to understand the reasons for 'slow progress' in personality psychology. They include the following.

The response class problem What is the unit of analysis personality is meant to predict? How big or small should that be? Thus, in the world of education, should one expect personality to predict overall examination success, individual examination scores, separate correct answers, stylistic features only (such as length (per word) of answer), preferred pen and writing style, or related issues such as 'how long' before the examination started the candidate arrived.

The situation taxonomy problem Personality theorists accept that situational factors inevitably influence and shape behaviour, but which features of situations? At what level should one describe these – stimulus, situation, setting or environment? We need a taxonomy of situations as well as of personality in order to predict behaviour accurately.

The sheer number of variables Behaviour is simultaneously determined by genetics, personality, mood, historico-cultural ability and situational variables. The exhaustive assessment of an individual or act inevitably requires the measurement of many variables both within and outside the expertise of psychologists.

Unknown critical events Long forgotten or even fantastical 'inner events' can influence the personality as a whole, as well as behaviour in particular situations. These events are difficult to identify and access.

Chance events and the random walk Chance events, such as meeting someone at a party, accepting a job offer, or reading a magazine in a particular waiting-room, can have long-term dramatic positive or negative effects on a life course which are impossible to predict.

Vicious circles and autocatalytic processes Chance events can spiral out of control. Seeing a film about an operation could make one phobic about operations, which could in turn lead to anxiety about hospitals and the people in them.

Idiographic uniqueness Every individual, like every animal (or indeed living thing) is unique in terms of their make-up and experiences. However, one can still look for general principles.

Nuisance variable These are factors that are difficult to control or take account of. They include culture and class. Are gender differences biological or environmental? To test this, we need to look at people who grew up in a feminine, matriarchal society, with all other factors kept constant, but this is impossible.

Ethical constraints Many famous studies, like the Milgram experiment on ethics, are now deemed unacceptable by ethics committees. Separating identical twins at birth and bringing them up in radically different homes is a very desirable piece of research, but quite ethically unacceptable behaviour.

Research pressures Work pressures to publish and get grants do mean that much psychological research is a cottage industry, and that it is too easy for researchers to 'do their own thing', cultivate their own garden, and cause hundreds of bizarre theories and tests to be developed, which may or may not be similar to each other.

Rules and norms There are laws, norms and rules and everyday etiquette which dictate how people 'behave in society', whether they want to or not. In this sense, social behaviour may be very constrained.

Feedback loops Parents influence their children, therapists influence their patients, and consultants influence their clients, and vice versa. These feedback loops can be complex, subtle and difficult to understand.

Fluctuating correlations Personality is partly defined by social behaviour, which is influenced by culture and sub-culture. Thus two identical studies in two different sub-cultures will not yield identical results.

Conceptual drift Many personality variables (e.g. intelligence, extraversion) are not precisely defined, and many drift over time, even within the writings of a particular individual.

Reliance on human judgements Many even dispassionate, disinterested and well-trained observers have biases and show inter-rater disagreement. These inevitable human errors make any form of assessment difficult.

Reliance on words Words are vague and have multiple meanings. What does 'her behaviour was satisfactory' really mean? Even questionnaires which provide numerical data are ratings of words, which are inevitably vague.

Hall *et al.* (1985) believe that personality theory needs to be simultaneously more imaginative and more evaluative. Scientific enterprises in personality theory need to be less risk-averse. They argue that theoretical formulation is truly a free enterprise activity. However, they see in the future fewer grander, inclusive theories and more mini-theories, which some day will have to be incorporated into a general theory of behaviour. Whose task that may be, and when it is likely to occur are, however, crucial questions. They list various areas that have influenced, are influencing and will, in their view, influence the future of personality theory:

- neuroscience, biology and evolutionary theory;
- social development and the evolution of 'higher-order' behaviours such as altruism, equality and role tokens;
- cognitive science, especially that which focuses on how people learn and use what they learn;
- behavioural medicine as it links individual differences and illness;
- causal modelling and structural equation modelling to understand the complex patterns found among personality data.

It would be premature to create a synthesis of existing personality theories. Existing theories are imprecise, they conflict in many ways, their findings are still conjectural, and the merging that has already taken place has not produced a single consensus. To impose an artificial synthesis at this stage would preclude giving existing theories every possible opportunity to contribute to the understanding of personality.

(Hall *et al.*, 1985, p.591)

Psychologists who are not specialists in personality and individual differences are often seriously out of date with regard to the thinking and research in the field. This is particularly true of those psychologists – educational, occupational and health – who doubtless do not have the time to follow other areas and seem to be 20 or 30 years out of date. Some still believe that the concept of stable traits died with the attack of the situationalists (Mischel, 1968), or that everyone is now an interactionist (Argyle *et al.*, 1981). Experimentalists who see individual differences as error variance or noise in the system have long dismissed the point of measuring personality, and hence take little interest in the area (Furnham, 1988). Specialist psychologists each have their own agenda, which leads them to take a particular view with regard to personality. Hence cross-cultural psychologists rejoice in demonstrating consistent and coherent cultural differences in social behaviour, while personality psychologists have done exactly the opposite, demonstrating the invariance of personality structure across widely different population groups.

1.14 CONCLUSION

In this chapter we have, perhaps rather brashly and adventurously, attempted an overview of the issues in personality psychology. It is a field that many reviewers have noted is in a state of renewal. As Hogan notes:

We have clear evidence that personality measures predict a range of significant outcomes – including academic performance, vocational choice, job performance, and income level. . . . And we can predict significant life outcomes over periods as long as 20 or 30 years.

(Hogan, 1998, p.4)

We have examined different empirical and theoretical approaches, yet in this book, we shall be less concerned with theory testing or methodological arguments than with the observable behaviours that are linked to personality traits. We shall examine eight broad areas ranging from crime to consumption, and from health to education, focusing on the systematic trait correlates of specific behaviours in that area of enquiry.

REFERENCES

Allport, G. (1937) *Personality: a psychological interpretation.* New York: Holt.

Allport, G. (1961) *Pattern and growth in personality.* New York: Holt, Rinehart & Winston.

Allport, G. and Odbert, H. (1936) Trait names: a psycho-lexical study. *Psychological Monographs* **47**, 211.

Argyle, M., Furnham, A. and Graham, J. (1981) *Social situations.* Cambridge: Cambridge University Press.

Asch, S. (1952) *Social psychology.* Englewood Cliffs, NJ: Prentice Hall.

Block, J. (1995) A contrarian view of the five-factor approach to personality description. *Psychological Bulletin* **117**, 187–215.

Brand, C. (1994) Open to experience – closed to intelligence. *European Journal of Personality* **8**, 299–310.

Buss, A. (1995) *Personality: temperament, social behaviour and the self.* Boston, MA: Allyn & Bacon.

Buss, A. and Craik, K. (1984) The act frequency approach to personality. *Psychological Review* **90**, 105–26.

Caprara, G-V. and van Heck, G. (1992) *Modern personality psychology.* London: Wheatsheaf.

Carver, C. (1996) Emergent integration in contemporary personality psychology. *Journal of Research in Personality* **30**, 319–34.

Carver, C. and Scheier, M. (1992) *Perspectives on personality.* Boston, MA: Allyn & Bacon.

Cattell, R. (1965) *The scientific analysis of personality.* Harmondsworth: Penguin.

Conley, J. (1985) The hierarchy of consistency. *Personality and Individual Differences* **5**, 11–20.

Cook, M. (1984) *Levels of personality.* London: Holt, Rinehart & Winston.

Costa, P. and McCrae, R. (1992) Trait psychology comes of age. In Sonderegge, T. (ed.), *Nebraska Symposium on Motivation.* Lincoln: University of Nebraska Press, 169–204.

Cronbach, L. (1957) The two disciplines of scientific psychology. *American Psychology* **12**, 671–84.

Cronbach, L. and Gleser, G. (1965) *Psychological tests and personnel decisions.* Urbane, IL: University of Illinois Press.

D'Andrade, R. (1974) Memory and the assessment of behaviour. In Blacock, H. (ed.), *Measurement in the social sciences.* Chicago: Aldine & Atherton, 74–95.

Deary, I. (1996) A (latent) big five personality model in 1915. *Journal of Personality and Social Psychology* **71**, 942–95.

Deary, I. and Matthews, G. (1993) Personality traits are alive and well. *The Psychologist* **6**, 299–311.

Diener, E. (1996) Traits can be powerful, but are not enough: lessons from subjective well-being. *Journal of Research in Personality* 30, 389–99.

Digman, J. (1990) Personality structure: emergence of the five-factor model. *Annual Review of Psychology* 41, 417–40.

Ehrenreich, J. (1997) Personality theory: a case of intellectual and social isolation. *Journal of Psychology* 131, 33–44.

Epstein, S. (1996) Recommendations for the future development of personality psychology. *Journal of Research in Personality* 30, 435–46.

Ewen, R. (1993) *An introduction to theories of personality.* Hillsdale, NJ: Lawrence Erlbaum Associates.

Eysenck, H. (1952) The effects of psychotherapy: an evaluation. *Journal of Consulting Psychology* 16, 319–25.

Eysenck, H. (1983) Is there a paradigm in personality research? *Journal of Research in Personality* 17, 369–97.

Eysenck, H. (1991) Dimensions of personality: 16, 5 or 3? Criteria for a taxonomic paradigm. *Personality and Individual Differences* 8, 773–90.

Eysenck, H. (1995) *Genius: the natural history of creativity.* Cambridge: Cambridge University Press.

Eysenck, H. and Eysenck, M. (1985) *Personality and individual differences.* New York: Plenum.

Furnham, A. (1988) *Lay theories.* Oxford: Pergamon.

Furnham, A. (1990) The development of single-trait personality theories. *Personality and Individual Differences* 11, 923–9.

Goldberg, L. (1993) The structure of phenotypic personality traits. *American Psychologist* 43, 23–34.

Hall, C. and Lindzey, G. (1957) *Theories of personality.* New York: Wiley.

Hall, C., Lindzey, G., Loehlin, J. and Manosevitz, M. (1985) *Introduction to theories of personality.* New York: Wiley.

Hampson, S. (1984) *The construction of personality.* London: Routledge.

Hampson, S. (1988) *The construction of personality.* London: Routledge.

Hergenhalin, B. (1994) *An introduction to theories of personality,* 4th edn. Englewood Cliffs, NJ: Prentice Hall.

Hjelle, L. and Ziegler, D. (1981) *Personality theories: basic assumptions, research and applications.* New York: McGraw Hill.

Hofstede, W. (1994) Who should own the definition of personality? *European Journal of Personality* 8, 149–62.

Hogan, R. (1998) Reinventing personality. *Journal of Social and Clinical Psychology* 17, 1–10.

Holt, R. (1967) Individuality and generalization in the psychology of personality. In Lazarus, R. and Opton, J. (eds), *Personality.* Harmondsworth: Penguin.

Kelly, G. (1955) *The psychology of personal constructs.* New York: Norton.

Kenrick, D. and Funder, D. (1989) Profiting from controversy: lessons from the person-situation debate. *American Psychologist* 48, 26–34.

Lamiell, J. (1981) Toward an idiothetic psychology of personality. *American Psychologist* 36, 276–87.

Lewin, K. (1935) *A dynamic theory of personality: select papers.* New York: McGraw Hill.

McAdam, D. (1992) The five-factor model of personality: a critical appraisal. *Journal of Personality* 60, 329–61.

McAdam, D. (1996) Alternative futures for the study of human individuality. *Journal of Research in Personality* 30, 374–88.

McClelland, D. (1996) Does the field of personality have a future? *Journal of Research in Personality* 30, 429–34.

McCrae, R. and Costa, P. (1995) Trait explanations in personality psychology. *European Journal of Personality* 9, 231–52.

McCrae, R., Costa, P. and Piedmont, R. (1993) Folk concepts, natural language and psychological constructs. *Journal of Personality* 61, 1–26.

Maddi, S. (1989) *Personality theories: a comparative analysis.* Chicago: Dorsey Press.

Matthews, G. and Deary, I. (1998) *Personality traits.* Cambridge: Cambridge University Press.

Mayer, J. (1995) A framework for the classification of personality components. *Journal of Personality* 63, 819–77.

Meehl, P. (1992) Factors and taxa traits and types, difference of degree and differences in kind. *Journal of Personality* 60, 117–74.

Milgram, S. (1969) *Obedience to authority.* London: Tavistock.

Mischel, W. (1968) *Personality and assessment.* New York: Wiley.

Murray, H. (1938) *Explorations in personality.* New York: Oxford University Press.

Muten, E. (1991) Self-reports, spouse ratings, and psychophysiological assessment in a behavioural medicine programme: an application of the five-factor model. *Journal of Personality Assessment* 57, 449–64.

Noller, P., Law, H. and Comrey, A. (1987) Cattell, Comrey and Eysenck personality factors compared: more evidence for five robust factors. *Journal of Personality and Social Psychology* 53, 775–82.

Ones, D. and Viswesvaran, C. (1996) Bandwidth-fidelity dilemma in personality measurement for personnel selection. *Journal of Organizational Behaviour* 17, 609–26.

Pervin, L. (1996a) Personality: a view of the future based on a look at the past. *Journal of Research in Personality* 30, 309–18.

Pervin, L. (1996b) *The science of personality.* New York: Wiley.

Plomin, R. and Nesselrode, J. (1990) Behaviour genetics and personality change. *Journal of Personality* 50, 191–219.

Quick, J. (1997) Idiographic research in organizational behaviour. In Cooper, L. and Jackson, S. (eds), *Creating tomorrow's organizations.* Chichester: Wiley, 475–91.

Sarason, I., Sarason, B. and Pierce, G. (1996) Views of the future. *Journal of Research in Personality* 30, 447–53.

Schultz, D. (1993) *Theories of personality.* Monterey, CA: Brooks/Cole.

Schultz, W. (1967) *Joy.* New York: Grove.

Seligman, M. (1992) *Learned optimism.* New York: Pocket Books.

Sheldon, W. (1940) *The varieties of human physique.* New York: Harper.

Schweder, R. (1987) How to look at Medusa without turning to stone. *Contributions to Indian Sociology* 21, 37–56.

Spielberger, C., Gorsuch, R. and Lushene, R. (1970) *The State Trait Anxiety Inventory manual.* Pala Alto, CA: Consultants Psychological Press.

Strelau, J. (1985) *Temperance, personality, activity.* London: Academic Press.

Thayer, R. (1989) *The biopsychology of mood and arousal.* Oxford: Oxford University Press.

Valentine, E. (1992) *Conceptual issues in psychology.* London: Routledge.

Western, D. (1996) A model and a method for uncovering the nomothetic from the idiographic. *Journal of Research in Personality* 30, 400–13.

Wilson, G. (1977) Introversion–extraversion. In Blass, T. (ed.), *The psychology of social behaviour.* New York: Lawrence Erlbaum Associates, 179–218.

Zachar, P. and Leong, F. (1992) A problem of personality: scientist and practitioner differences in psychology. *Journal of Personality* 60, 665–7.

2

Personality and Health

INTRODUCTION

It is widely held that personality disposition is linked to health status. Indeed, many academic definitions of health recognise this fact and view health not simply as an absence of illness, but also as involving body, mind (personality) and social factors (Taylor, 1991). Even among lay people, it seems to be generally recognised that 'emotional factors' may predict one's health status at any given time (Furnham, 1994). Thus it is clear that, in addition to the physical dimension of wellness–illness, it is recognised that physiological, emotional and social factors also play an important interactive role in determining one's health status. Thus an individual who *believes* that he or she is unlikely to contract HIV/AIDS is probably more likely to engage in risky sexual behaviours with multiple partners or to share needles with others. Equally, conscientious people may take their doctors' advice seriously and follow instructions rigorously, while neurotics may be hypochondriacal.

Although the development of the biopsychosocial model, as this more inclusive approach is called, has occurred only relatively recently in western behavioural sciences and medicine, it has enjoyed prominence in eastern, notably Chinese, culture for much longer. According to Bishop (1994), Chinese medicine has long recognised the role that emotional health plays in the aetiology of illness. For those practitioners, illness is just as likely to be due to a physical condition as 'emotional imbalance', and today there is still a close nexus between the mind and the body in Chinese medicine. Indeed, the rather spectacular rise in popularity of complementary medicine is in part attributable to the recognition of emotional and personality factors in the maintenance of health (Vincent *et al.*, 1995). Increasingly, this view has gained in prominence in contemporary psychology. We must adopt what has been referred to as a 'systems' or 'organistic' approach to understanding the causes of illness:

The type of 'either-or' thinking that has so long characterized single-discipline research (e.g. defining risk for cardiovascular disease in terms of whether one has evidence of coronary heart disease *or* not in one's family history, whether *or* not one smokes cigarettes, exercises *or* not, is obese *or* not, or is Type A *or* not) does not apply here.

(Gentry, 1984, pp.6–7)

This chapter reviews recent research which explores the links between personality functioning, health and illness. In particular, it addresses personality influences on cardiac disease and cancer, and also explores the role of explanatory (attribution) style on illness. In addition, it will assess the links between personality and subjective well-being. However, it is appropriate first to examine conceptual approaches regarding personality and illness.

2.2 THE ROLE OF PERSONALITY IN UNDERSTANDING ILLNESS

According to Ranchor and Sanderman (1991), the links between personality and health can be conceptualised in a number of different ways. One way is to draw a distinction between the *specificity* and *generality* approaches with respect to health outcomes (Cohen, 1979). According to the specificity approach, personality is a causal factor in disease. Research areas that are referred to here include, for example, the role of personality in the aetiology of cancers or cardiovascular disease. One of the earliest researchers who followed this line of research was Alexander (see Suls and Rittenhouse, 1987, p.157), who postulated the existence of seven psychosomatic diseases, each having its own underlying unconscious cause. These were peptic ulcer, essential hypertension, bronchial asthma, thyroid toxicosis, rheumatoid arthritis, ulcerative colitis and neurodermatitis (see also the early observations on the Type A behaviour pattern).

The generality approach, on the other hand, argues that personality factors mediate or buffer the effect of a causal factor on illness. As Ranchor and Sanderman (1991) suggest, such factors 'facilitate' or 'inhibit' the influence of causal factors. Examples included here are factors such as locus of control, hardiness and self-esteem, to mention just a few. Strickland (1989) reviewed the health locus of control literature and concluded that those who are internally controlled generally engage in more health-enhancing behaviours. Internals take more interest in messages about health, and take active steps to control their health status. Equally, conscientiousness is linked to better health through more careful following of specialist and general health advice.

Other psychological factors which can also be included are individual perceptions or explanations of events. For instance, just how we interpret or react to life events (e.g. the death of a spouse or loved one, interpersonal conflict in the workplace) has been shown to have important consequences for our health status. Thus it is likely that factors such as coping or attributional style or traits like neuroticism style may play an important part in how life events affect health outcome. An important consequence of some of this work was to remind physicians and non-physicians alike that psychological factors may indeed be related to illness, and that they need to be considered if one is striving for an inclusive view of the aetiology of illness (Carson, 1989). Much research effort has consequently been expended in uncovering which personality factors are important, and precisely how they relate to health status through specific processes.

Krantz and Hedges (1987) adopted a slightly different, although related approach. They distinguished between the aetiological trait approach, the stress moderators approach and the illness behaviour approach. As with the specificity approach, the aetiological trait approach sees a direct causal link between personality factors and illness or 'health-damaging physiological changes' (Krantz and Hedges, 1987, p.352). In their view, only a few traits have received sufficient empirical support to be classified here, including the Type A behaviour pattern and inhibited power motive.

By stress moderators, Krantz and Hedges (1987) are referring to one's coping styles. Healthy coping styles (e.g. by seeking social support) enhance one's ability to resist stress and consequently disease. According to these authors, specific abilities are linked to healthy coping styles, such as optimism and explanatory or attributional style. Thus those individuals with a negative attributional style are more likely to explain positive events as being due to external and uncontrollable causes, which is likely to be related to increased risks for illness (e.g. depression).

Smith and Williams (1992) have also noted three pathways by which personality factors might influence health outcome. First, it is possible that personality dispositions could have an effect on the duration or the intensity of stress responses, and this could be an important consideration in the development of later disease. Secondly, as has already been noted, personality might have direct causal effects on health outcome. Thirdly, it is possible that certain personality factors, such as a particular attributional style, could moderate the impact of a stressor.

Finally, it is possible to distinguish the illness behaviour approach. It is suggested that there are individual difference factors which determine just how one perceives one's health status and whether one is likely to seek out medical attention. However, these factors have traditionally enjoyed less research attention. In this chapter the tendency will be to focus more on the first two approaches, which may be seen as complementary rather than as alternatives.

2.3 PERSONALITY AND CORONARY HEART DISEASE

Although Friedman and Rosenman (1974) can be credited with popularising the links between personality factors and coronary heart disease, it was Osler (1910, cited in Eysenck, 1985), nearly 100 years ago, who first remarked that those likely to suffer angina were of a particular disposition and temperament. As he pointed out, they were characterised as 'the robust, the vigorous in mind and body, the keen and ambitious man, the indicator of whose engine was always at full speed ahead' (Eysenck, 1985, p.545).

The links between the so-called Type A behaviour pattern (TABP) and heart disease were first recorded empirically several years ago by Friedman and Rosenman (1974), who traced over 3000 men in the Western Collaborative Group Study for more than 8 years. They observed that those men who were at risk for heart disease could be classified as Type A individuals who always tried to achieve as much as possible within a short space of time. Invariably, Type A individuals were also characterised as being very competitive, impatient, hostile, restless and alert, as well as displaying a strong need for advancement. Early depictions of this syndrome were of an anxious and compulsive person with little time for relaxation (see also Table 2.1). Support for many of these general characteristics was obtained by others, notably by Haynes and Feinleib (1980) in the Framingham Heart Study. Some researchers (e.g. Dembroski and Costa, 1987) have questioned the passive acceptance of many generalisations regarding the profile of the Type A person, suggesting that the cultural background and age distribution of respondents, as well as genetic factors, should also be considered.

Early work on the Type A syndrome generated extensive research into its relationships with other psychological constructs. For instance, the links between extraversion and neuroticism and heart disease were confirmed by several authors (e.g. Eysenck and Fulker, 1983; Byrne et al., 1985; Llorente, 1986; Myrtek, 1995; but see Booth-Kewley and Friedman, 1987) using different measures of the TABP. For example, Byrne et al. (1985) used the Structured Interview, the Jenkins Activity Survey, the Vickers Scale, the Framingham Type A Scale and the Bortner Scale in their study. All of these measures except the Jenkins Activity Survey (total score) showed a significant

Table 2.1 Early depiction of the Type A personality

Strenuous worker	Poor sleep pattern
Compulsive tendencies	Aggressiveness
Depressive/neurotic tendencies	Angry
Impatience	Low on introspection
Anxious	Hard driving
Little time for relaxation	Conscientious

Adapted from Dunbar, 1943; Miles et al. 1954; Peete, 1955.

positive correlation with E and N, although findings regarding the role of N are more equivocal (see Costa and McCrae, 1987).

Some research studies have focused on the links between impulsiveness and Type A measures (e.g. Innes, 1980; Heaven, 1989), Heaven having noted important gender differences in their relationships among 17-year-olds. It was observed that Type A scores correlated with *total* impulsiveness among males, whilst among females Type A scores also correlated significantly with particular *submeasures* of impulsiveness. Other studies among young people have demonstrated that high-TABP adolescents report significantly higher self-ratings of stress and tension than do low-TABP individuals (Eagleston *et al.*, 1986).

Over the last few decades great strides have been made in our understanding of the psychological predictors of heart disease (Carson, 1989). Whereas it was earlier thought that cardiovascular disease is best predicted by the different components of the TABP, it is now generally held that negative affect, anger/hostility as well as antagonism and self-involvement are closely associated with susceptibility to heart disease (e.g. Siegel, 1982; Booth-Kewley and Friedman, 1987; Dembroski and Costa, 1987; Byrne *et al.*, 1989; Thoresen, 1991; Bishop, 1994), as are 'vigorous voice mannerisms' (Dembroski and Costa, 1987). A recent meta-analysis by Myrtek (1995) found renewed support for the relationship between hostility (anger-in and anger-out) and heart disease, whilst Scheier and Bridges (1995) noted the importance of the factors 'potential for hostility', 'anger directed outward', 'frequent experience of anger' and 'being irritated when standing in queues'. Moreover, it would seem that emotional suppression (or the tendency not to express anger) may also be related to heart disease in women, but not in men (Scheier and Bridges, 1995).

Dembroski and Costa (1987) have referred to the anger/hostility factor as *potential for hostility*, which, in their view, is a reasonably stable personality trait. They define this attribute as the tendency:

- to experience varying degrees and combinations of anger, irritability, resentment, and related negative effects in response to common, everyday events that are likely to arouse them in individuals who are prone to react in such ways, and/or
- to react with expressions of antagonism, disagreeableness, rudeness, surliness, criticalness, and unco-operativeness.

(Dembroski and Costa, 1987, p.224)

It is possible to gauge the presence of potential for hostility by any number of ways including use of the Structured Interview (Dembroski and Costa, 1987). Clear indicators can be manifested in several different ways, including content of response (e.g. anger, irritation and resentment), the intensity of the response (e.g. the level of irritation and annoyance), and style of interaction with the experimenter (e.g. how rude or argumentative the respondent is).

It is well documented that there are different types or aspects of hostility, and Smith and Williams (1992) have reviewed evidence to indicate that verbal aggression, rather than anger, irritability and resentment, is a better predictor of heart disease. It has also been shown that a marker for this trait exists in the well-known Big Five measure of personality, namely the NEO (Costa and McCrae, 1985). Empirical evidence now indicates that antagonism (a facet of agreeableness) is a better indicator of later heart disease than neurotic hostility (see also Smith and Williams, 1992).

Why does the Type A behaviour pattern predict coronary heart disease? One possible answer may pertain to the way in which Type A individuals respond to or interpret stressful and not so stressful events, whilst another possibility lies at the psychophysiological level (Bishop, 1994). It is well established, for instance, that Type A individuals report significantly higher stress and tension levels than do Type B individuals (Eagleston *et al.*, 1986), while work with adolescent samples has demonstrated that those young people who *perceive* the environment as being hostile or demanding show increases in systolic blood pressure (Matthews and Jennings, 1984; Thoresen, 1991). There is also evidence of changes in heart rate and catecholamine levels during stressful or demanding tasks (Bishop, 1994).

Are Type A individuals satisfied with themselves? Do Type A individuals enjoy being competitive and pushed for time? A study by Henley and Furnham (1989) attempted to answer these questions by asking respondents to indicate the extent to which 20 positive and 20 negative traits applied to them, and also how much the traits describe how they would ideally like to be. It was found that Type A (but not Type B) individuals tended to describe themselves in negative rather than positive terms (see Table 2.2). Thus they saw themselves as being demanding and dominating, matching their ideal ratings. The authors warn against equating these self-ratings with low self-esteem. It could very well be that Type A individuals regard these negative traits as highly desirable.

Table 2.2 Significant and ideal-self ratings of TABP individuals

Type of rating	Traits
Self-ratings	'Demanding, dominating, patient (negative rating), outspoken, calm (negative), mild (negative), forceful, enterprising, irritable, aggressive, restless, tense, enthusiastic, self-centred, conceited, energetic, relaxed (negative), argumentative, alert, dreamy (negative), excitable, gentle (negative), stubborn'
Ideal ratings	'Dominating, demanding, self-confident, meek, conceited'

Adapted from Henley, S. and Furnham, A. (1989) The Type A behaviour pattern and self-evaluation. *British Journal of Medical Psychology* **62**, 51–9.

In summary, the Type A behaviour pattern is a well-established individual difference factor that has been shown to be linked to health outcome, particularly coronary heart disease. There can be no doubt that the presence of Type A characteristics in an individual together with more traditional risk factors, such as hypertension, is a significant predisposing factor for heart disease. Perhaps the greatest challenge for psychologists is to modify Type A behaviour in individuals, not only for the sake of their own health, but also for that of their children. Indeed, there is growing evidence that children may learn Type A behaviours in the home. As Thoresen (1991) has argued, these parents very often encourage their children to try again and again in order to succeed, and are more critical of their children's achievements.

2.4 SMOKING AND HEART DISEASE

In some individuals coronary heart disease can result from a particular lifestyle, and smoking is an important lifestyle factor said to be associated not only with heart disease, but also with lung and throat cancer (US Surgeon General, 1990). This section will not review that evidence, but will instead examine the personality differences between smokers and non-smokers. Because smoking is under volitional control, its role in heart disease takes on an added interest for personality psychologists.

Smokers are characterised by higher extraversion scores such that, as one's level of extraversion rises, so too does one's use of cigarettes (Ashton and Stepney, 1982). In a Dutch sample (Kuiper and Feij, 1983), extraversion, impulsiveness and sensation-seeking were found to be associated with cigarette smoking. Research by Cherry and Kiernan (1976) found neuroticism and extraversion to correlate significantly with cigarette-smoking, with deep inhalers forming the most neurotic group. Male smokers had higher mean extraversion scores than females.

Patton et al. (1993) conducted an epidemiological study of alcohol use and smoking among 1257 adult Canadians. There were 348 current smokers, 486 subjects who never smoked, and 417 quitters in the sample. Current male smokers were found to be significantly more extraverted than the group who never smoked and the quitters. With regard to neuroticism, male smokers were significantly more tense and anxious and had significantly lower self-esteem scores than the other groups, and they also scored significantly higher on Eysenck's P scale. Quitters were higher on ego strength than smokers. Likewise, women smokers were significantly more extraverted than non-smokers and quitters, although there were no differences with regard to neuroticism. Female smokers scored significantly higher on the P dimension than the non-smoker and quitter groups.

This gender difference with regard to neuroticism and smoking is an interesting one. Several studies have noted that female smokers are no more or less neurotic or anxious than females who do not smoke or who have quitted.

However, there are significant differences among males. Male smokers have significantly higher neuroticism scores than do quitters or those who have never smoked. Thus males are less well prepared to cope with stress than are females. One coping strategy for males is to take up smoking, thereby reducing anxiety levels (Patton *et al.*, 1993).

It was concluded by Patton *et al.* that the fact that smokers score high on the psychoticism (tough-mindedness) dimension

> is consistent with the conceptualization of psychoticism as low empathy, high hostility and impulsivity, and a high degree of non-conformity. This latter point, a lack of interest in conforming, may relate to the idea that smokers are engaging in a behaviour that is becoming less and less socially acceptable.
>
> (Patton *et al.*, 1993, p.660)

Many studies on the psychological predictors of smoking can be criticised because of their assumption that only one or two factors predict smoking. Thus some researchers have examined the role of contextual factors such as peer pressure and conformity to group norms, whilst others have tended to focus on one or two personality variables. A large Australian study of over 7000 high-school students went some way towards examining the influence of individual and contextual factors on the propensity to smoke (Byrne *et al.*, 1993). For both sexes, factors such as friends who smoke and perceived peer pressure were stronger predictors of smoking than were neuroticism and low self-esteem (see Box 2.1). Curiously, extraversion and psychoticism were not included as independent variables.

Byrne *et al.* (1995) traced these students for 12 months. Those who were not smokers at the onset of the study (Time 1), but were smokers 12 months later (Time 2), were found to have significantly higher neuroticism scores than those who remained non-smokers. Those who smoked at Times 1 *and* 2 had even higher mean neuroticism scores. These effects were strongest for girls. Moreover, non-smokers at Time 1 who remained non-smokers at Time 2 scored significantly lower than later smokers on the following experiences of stress: stress of school attendance, stress of family conflict, stress of parental control, stress of school performance, stress of perceived educational irrelevance.

In conclusion, there is abundant evidence that personality factors are implicated in heart disease through the Type A behaviour pattern and through smoking. Important personality differences have been found to exist between smokers and non-smokers, and it is also apparent that these factors interact with one's experiences of stress in predicting smoking, at least among young people. Finally, there is much scope for further work on the role of the Big Five factors in Type A and smoking behaviour. For instance, given the links between Eysenckian psychoticism and smoking, it could be predicted that

BOX 2.1

Psychosocial predictors of smoking among 7000 teenagers
The psychosocial correlates of cigarette-smoking were examined among a sample of over 7000 high-school students aged 12 to 17 years and in grades 7, 8, 9, 10 and 11 (Byrne *et al.*, 1993). In total, 11.5% of 12-year-olds and 53.3% of 17-year-olds indicated that they were regular smokers. The following factors best discriminated regular smokers from non-smokers. The factors are arranged in order from the most to the least important.

Boys	Girls
1. Friends who smoke	Friends who smoke
2. Smoking–health link (low recognition)	Smoking–health link (low recognition)
3. Peer pressure	Peer pressure
4. Low self-rated school performance	Neuroticism (high)
5. Personal physical condition (low importance)	Exemplar pressure[a]
6. Smoking boys more popular	Mother smokes
7. Exemplar pressure[a]	Smoking girls popular
8. Low self-esteem	Low self-rated school performance
9. Age (high)	Conformity (low)
10. Neroticism (high)	Family modelling to smoke (yes)

[a]Includes reasons such as 'People teenagers want to be like smoke' and 'People teenagers look up to smoke'

'agreeableness' and 'conscientiousness' are likely to be negatively related to smoking.

2.5 PERSONALITY AND CANCER

Following the assertion by Galen in the second century that 'melancholy' women are likely to develop breast cancer, it now seems to be generally held that personality factors may indeed be implicated in the development of cancers (for reviews see Contrada *et al.*, 1990; Scheier and Bridges, 1995). Some writers have speculated that stress factors and the loss of emotional relationships may also be linked to cancers (e.g. Goodkin *et al.*, 1986), marital disruption (such as divorce or bereavement). Others refer specifically to a syndrome of psychosocial factors – the so-called 'Type C' personality disposition – which is said to be related to cancer. This personality type is characterised by the suppression of emotion, and by depression, hopelessness/helplessness, disrupted social support, the inability to express

Table 2.3   Traits linked to the development of cancers

Over-cooperation
Appeasing
Unassertive
Over-patient
Avoiding conflict
Suppressing emotions (e.g. anger and anxiety)
Coping with repression
Self-sacrificing
Rigidity
Hopelessness
Depression

Source of information: Eysenck, H. (1994) Cancer, personality and stress: prediction and prevention. *Advances in Behaviour Research and Therapy* **16**, 167–215.

negative emotion, and low levels of emotional expressiveness (Contrada *et al.*, 1990; Eysenck, 1994) (see also Table 2.3). According to Eysenck (1994), these factors can be reduced to two broad dimensions, namely suppression of emotions and inappropriate coping styles.

Perhaps the best-known prospective study on the aetiology of cancer was that conducted by Thomas *et al.* (1979). They interviewed over 1000 medical students, and then interviewed them again some years later when the students had reached middle age. No personality traits (such as depression, for example) were found to be linked to cancer, although it was possible to differentiate those individuals who had developed cancer from healthy individuals in terms of their reported closeness to their parents. Those who developed cancers were found to have had very poor relationships with their parents compared to those who did not have cancer.

More recently, Kavan *et al.* (1995) reported prospective data examining the personality factors associated with colon cancer. They obtained data for 61 male veterans who completed the Minnesota Multiphasic Personality Inventory (MMPI) between 1947 and 1975 and were diagnosed with colon cancer between 1977 and 1988. These respondents were matched with 61 male veterans who also completed the MMPI between 1947 and 1975, but who had not developed cancer at the time when the study was conducted.

The researchers found that the best discriminator between those who developed cancer and those who did not was aggressive hostility. The authors suggest two possible explanations for these results. In the first place, it is likely that hostile people manifest particular physiological responses in the face of stressors. For example, these researchers suggest that anger alters the functioning of one's immune system, resulting in higher levels of neuroendocrine responses and accompanying immunosuppression (Kavan *et al.*, 1995, p.1035). Thus it is likely that such individuals may be more vulnerable to 'oncogenic' viruses. Secondly, it is possible to explain these results in terms of the Health Behaviour Model. This suggests that hostile individuals are less likely to be susceptible to cues to practise adequate health care, and are more likely to engage in risky behaviours such as cigarette-smoking or alcohol consumption.

There appears to be more evidence (albeit qualified) for the aetiological importance of other factors. For instance, aspects of social support that are deemed to be important in the possible development of cancer are early loss or lack of parental closeness, a recent loss reported by newly diagnosed cancer patients, and inadequate social support affecting long-term outcome (Contrada *et al.*, 1990).

There is more suggestive evidence that emotional suppression is linked to the development of cancers. 'Non-expression of emotion' refers to those who simply accept their fate, are emotionally constricted and 'bland'. 'Low emotional expressiveness' refers to those who hide their anger and strive for 'emotional control' (Contrada *et al.*, 1990). Greer and Morris (1975) conducted a semi-prospective study which showed that those women who were diagnosed with breast cancer displayed significantly more emotional suppression than women with benign breast disease, especially among individuals under 50 years of age. Interviews with these women and their husbands revealed that emotional suppression had been characteristic of the cancerous women for most of their lives.

Further support for the importance of emotional suppression was obtained by Cooper and Faragher (1993), who administered a range of psychosocial indicators to women undergoing breast-screening. Those who were found to have developed a breast malignancy differed significantly from those who were free of cancer. After controlling for the age of the respondents, it was found that experiencing a major stressful event was a significant predictor of cancer, especially in those women who did not express anger, but who used denial as a form of coping with the situation. Thus it would seem from these results that stressful life events and our ways of coping with them (through the use of denial) may be linked to cancer development.

Following suggestions by Eysenck (1985), several authors have pursued investigations into the links between cancer and personality as measured by the Eysenck Personality Questionnaire (EPQ). Thus Wistow *et al.* (1990), for example, examined the links between physicians' health ratings of their patients and those patients' scores on the EPQ. The main findings from this study can be summarised as follows:

- *psychoticism* – positively linked to cardiovascular symptoms;
- *neuroticism* – positively linked to stress symptoms, and negatively related to cancer;
- *extraversion* – no significant relationship.

Similar results have been obtained by other researchers (for a review see Eysenck, 1985). For instance, it has been documented that, whereas the lung cancer mortality rates for individuals low on N are 296 per 100,000 individuals, for those high on N the mortality rates are only 56 per 100,000. Others (e.g. Coppen and Metcalfe, 1963; Hagnell, 1966; both cited in Eysenck, 1985) have found significant links between cancer and extraversion.

In conclusion, it is highly likely that personality traits play a causal role in the aetiology of some cancers (see also the work of Grossarth-Maticek and Eysenck, which will be addressed in Section 2.6). However, it is worth noting that not all authors are convinced about the role played by psychosocial factors in the development of cancers. As Contrada *et al.* assert, the links between personality and cancer are only suggestive. They argue that:

> A fuller understanding of the nature of the 'cancer-prone personality' and the mechanisms by which it exerts its effect can best be achieved by examining the psychosocial factors that comprise it in conjunction with physiological processes that may mediate its effect on cancer outcome.
>
> (Contrada *et al.*, 1990, p.659)

Support for the findings of Wistow *et al.* (1990), described earlier, is also evidenced by research which has examined the adjustment of patients after mastectomy (for a review see Meyerowitz, 1980). In one study, those who made a better adjustment after surgery were individuals who scored significantly *lower* on a neuroticism measure. They also tended to score higher on external locus of control and to have been married for a longer period. This suggests that good social support acts as a buffer against cancer. It has also been observed (Eysenck, 1985) that women who survived breast cancer for longer tended to have a 'fighting spirit', and were less depressed and more angry than those who died sooner.

Self-perceptions at the time when cancer is first diagnosed also play an important role in later (post-diagnosis) adjustment. For instance, Malcarne *et al.* (1995) found that individuals who engaged in characterological self-blame (that is, who endorsed 'It is my lot in life to develop cancer') were more likely to suffer psychological distress 4 months later. Moreover, psychological distress as measured at Time 1 was significantly linked to characterological self-blame at Time 2. Thus these patients appeared to be caught in a never-ending cycle of distress and self-blame, with harmful effects on their ability to cope with cancer.

A recent prospective study by Buddeberg *et al.* (1996) found little support for the suggestion that personality, and more specifically coping styles, are linked to survival rates. They traced 107 women with early breast cancer for up to 6 years after primary surgical treatment. Only about one-third showed some spread of cancer to the lymph nodes at the time of surgery. After 3 years, 66 women remained in the study, 14 women having died of cancer. Coping strategies as well as medical condition were monitored intermittently throughout the study.

It was found that the best predictors of death from cancer were not the patient's coping strategies, but the size of the tumour and the patient's nodal stage. Thus the authors cautioned as follows:

> Media interest in investigations reporting that psychosocial factors or events might influence either the cause of disease or the outcome of cancer has important clinical ramifications. Some patients may assume a burden of guilt in accepting the notion that their personality, lifestyle or coping behaviour have caused or influenced the course of their illness. Other patients may reject cancer treatment in favour of psychotherapy to cure the psychological roots that they believe are related to the cause of their disease.
>
> (Buddeberg *et al.*, 1996, p.262)

In contrast to adult samples, not much research into living with cancer has been conducted among teenagers. An exception is a study by Madan-Swain *et al.* (1994). They compared adolescents who had been free of cancer for 5 years with matched controls, and found that the cancer survivors experienced greater body discomfort and significantly less self-criticism than controls.

Finally, it is important to note that the role of personality in predicting cancer development has come under careful scrutiny in recent times. A review of post-1988 research suggests that few personality differences exist between cancer and non-cancer patients, with cancer patients being somewhat less anxious (Van't Spijker *et al.*, 1997). They suggest the following explanations for their results.

- Cancer treatment is much improved these days – hence the prognosis is better.
- People with cancer make a conscious effort to suppress negative thoughts about their condition.
- People with cancer make a conscious effort to deny their true feelings of anxiety or depression, rather than have to deal with those feelings.

2.6 THE DISEASE-PRONE PERSONALITY

Eysenck and colleagues (e.g. Eysenck, 1991; Grossarth-Maticek *et al.*, 1997) have postulated the existence of a disease-prone personality. Based on two large long-term prospective studies in Yugoslavia and later in Germany, they proposed the existence of particular personality types which predict the onset of cancer and heart disease. They proposed four (followed later by two more) types which differ in their relationships with illness as follows (adapted from Eysenck, 1991).

- *Type 1*. This is the cancer-prone type. Individuals show understimulation and want to be emotionally close to a highly valued person (or object);

they experience stress when they are distanced from him or her, and they show suppression of emotions.

- *Type 2*. These individuals are prone to heart disease. They are over-aroused. A highly valued emotional object is viewed as a source of stress and unhappiness. They are highly dependent on the object and cannot disengage from it.
- *Type 3*. These are ambivalent types who alternate between Types 1 and 2. They alternate between feelings of hopelessness and anger.
- *Type 4*. These individuals see links between their own autonomy and happiness.
- *Type 5*. This is a rational type with links to rheumatoid arthritis and cancer.
- *Type 6*. This is a criminal and psychopathic type.

Eysenck (1991) has stressed that what distinguishes the individual types is their reaction to interpersonal stress. Using a questionnaire measure of the first four types, Grossarth-Maticek and Eysenck (1990) conducted a longitudinal study of a large sample consisting of several thousand relatively elderly Yugoslav respondents. The eldest person in every second household in a town of 14,000 people was interviewed using questionnaire and observation strategies. The usual medical observations, such as height, weight, blood pressure and smoking behaviour, were made periodically. Some 10 years after the start of the project, a physician made further medical observations and/or recorded the information on the individual's death certificate. Among this sample, more than 45 per cent of deaths among the Type 1 individuals were due to cancer, whilst almost 30 per cent of deaths among the Type 2 respondents were due to heart disease. Types 3 and 4 were classified as healthy. Similar results were later obtained using a German sample.

These data suggest that cancer can be linked primarily with a personality disposition described as *suppressing emotion* and as being *helpless and depressed*. Heart disease, by contrast, was associated with an over-aroused and aggressive disposition. Importantly, these general principles have been replicated by other authors. For example, Quander-Blaznik (1991) administered measures of the first four types described above to 113 individuals who had been referred to a lung hospital. It was found that the best predictor of lung cancer was being classified as Type 1 – that is, as someone who suppresses emotion. Smoking and older age were also found to increase the success of prediction of lung cancer.

Further statistical analyses have recently been conducted on the Yugoslav data in an attempt to determine whether particular personality dispositions are related to specific cancers in women (Grossarth-Maticek *et al.*, 1997). Respondents completed a 15–item questionnaire 'specifically designed to differentiate between the different types of cancer' (Grossarth-Maticek *et al.*, 1997, p.952). Factor analysis of these items revealed four underlying factors, namely blocking of feelings, sudden losses in important current relationships, blocking of needs and feelings towards one's parents and, finally, a factor describing attraction to someone followed by frustration.

It was found that specific cancers can be predicted by scores on these psychosocial variables. For instance, women who later went on to develop breast cancer scored significantly higher on blocking of needs and feelings towards their parents and present partners. Those who developed cervical cancer scored higher on blocking of feelings and needs in relationships currently thought to be important. Cervical cancer patients scored highest on items dealing with frequent change of sexual partners, and 'sado-masochistic' tendencies (Grossarth-Maticek et al., 1997).

These findings have not gone unchallenged. Amelang (1996) recently questioned the methodology employed in the original Yugoslav and German studies, concluding that the typology used is no more accurate in predicting illness than are other established factors such as depression and neuroticism. It was also found in a Dutch study of over 2000 men that, contrary to predictions, 30 per cent of respondents were classified as *more* than one type, and almost 40 per cent obtained a score that placed them *below* the highest quartile of any of the six types (Ranchor et al., 1993).

Finally, procedural concerns have also been expressed about some aspects of Grossarth-Maticek's data collection strategies. For instance, Van der Ploeg and Vetter suggested that some interview data may have been used twice calling into question the 'trustworthiness' of these data (Van der Ploeg and Vetter, 1993, p.66).

2.7 EXPLANATORY STYLE AND ILLNESS

It has been argued that being helpful, optimistic and active is linked to good health, whilst hopelessness, passivity and pessimism are associated with disease (e.g. Peterson and Seligman, 1987; Scheier and Carver, 1987). Attributional theorists have identified an attributional style that individuals habitually use when explaining events. According to the reformulated learned helplessness model of depression, three dimensions (locus, stability and controllability) are important.

Someone with a negative (depressive) attributional style typically attributes failure to some permanent feature of him- or herself, whilst someone with a positive attributional style sees failure as a temporary set-back, usually caused by factors outside the individual's control. Moreover, one's response to why something has happened is likely to shape one's future expectations. Thus negative attributional style has been linked to loneliness, depression and low self-esteem (Feather, 1983) and poor health outcomes over the longer term (e.g. Scheier and Carver, 1987; Peterson et al., 1988). Negative expectancies, together with a sense of little control, increase the likelihood of symptom reporting, all of which are negatively related to optimism (Wenglert and Rosen, 1995).

Empirical support for these views has been obtained from carefully controlled laboratory experiments on animals, showing that feelings of helplessness are associated with premature death. For example, cancerous tumours have been found to grow more quickly in animals that experience inescapable shock. Moreover, inescapable shock has also been linked to changes in the functioning of the immune system of animals (see Peterson and Seligman, 1987).

In an unpublished study reported by Peterson and Seligman (1987), researchers asked college students to complete an attributional questionnaire, the Beck Depression Scale, and an illness scale. Students reported any illness experienced during the past month (Time 1), and again at Time 2 (1 month later) and Time 3 (about 1 year later). At Time 3, respondents were asked to report on their frequency of visits to a medical practitioner. The follow-up success rate at Time 3 was 86 per cent. Most of the illnesses reported at Times 2 and 3 included infectious illnesses such as colds, sore throats, venereal disease, etc. The researchers found that their composite stability/globality dimension was the best predictor of illness at Times 2 and 3, even after controlling for depression at Time 1. In other words, explanatory style is linked to subsequent illness even after controlling for possible confounding factors. In a similar vein, it has been observed that individuals with an optimistic view of their personal risk for illness tend to regard disease as something which is preventable (e.g. Peterson and De Avila, 1995).

More recently, a Swedish longitudinal study of over 2000 men found that those who were rated as moderately or extremely hopeless at Time 1 were, respectively, more than twice and three times at risk of all-cause mortality 6 years later than those who were rated low on hopelessness (Everson et al., 1996). Mortality included death due to cancer, cardiovascular disease and violence (e.g. accident or injury). These results suggest that beliefs about the future and the perceived inability to reach goals are linked to the aetiology of disease. Thus hopelessness is a 'maladaptive psychological response' (Everson et al., 1996, p.119), but one with vital implications for health and well-being.

Why does it appear that optimists experience better health than pessimists? One possible explanation is that optimists are more likely to engage in health-promoting behaviours. Scheier and Carver (1987) have summarised some of the behavioural differences. First, optimists use different coping strategies when faced with a stressful situation. They are much more likely to use problem-focused than emotion-focused coping mechanisms. In other words, they use more active methods of dealing with a situation than do pessimists. Secondly, optimists have different (and more effective) health habits. For instance, it has been documented that they exercise more (e.g. Kavussanu and

McAuley, 1995), and it is suggested that they are also more likely to follow 'a prescribed medical regimen' (Scheier and Carver, 1987, p.192).

Research evidence points to the fact that optimists respond with less intense cardiovascular reactivity to stressful situations, thereby reducing the risk of disease. Finally, it has also been reasonably well documented that empirical links exist between feelings of hopelessness and suicide (e.g. Kazdin *et al.*, 1983), whilst Scheier and Carver (1987) have noted links between pessimism and hopelessness. Thus it seems feasible to expect optimism to act as a buffer against suicide and suicidal ideation. As they explain, 'these findings are quite consistent with the notion that negative outcome expectancies lead to a disengagement tendency that can manifest itself in active and profound ways' (Scheier and Carver, 1987, p.193).

According to Kobasa (1982), a particular personality type – the so-called hardy personality – is resistant to experiencing stress, and the ability of hardiness to predict health status has been established (e.g. Kobasa *et al.*, 1982; Kobasa and Puccetti, 1983). Kobasa (1982, pp.6–7) sees the hardy individual as having an 'optimistic orientation', and hardiness as being comprised of commitment, control and challenge. Commitment is seen as 'the ability to believe in the truth, importance and interest value of who one is and what one is doing', whilst control is to 'believe and act as if one can influence the course of events'. This latter characteristic is of itself likely to result in good coping skills and an effective response repertoire. Challenge is viewed as 'the belief that change, rather than stability, is the normative mode of life'. Thus individuals come to expect (and perhaps look forward to) the unexpected and novel.

The similarities between this conception of hardiness, optimism and attributional style discussed above are striking. Indeed, as Hull *et al.* (1988, p.506) put it, hardiness may be an effective predictor because of the way in which we *perceive* events around us. Those who perceive a stressful event as being *less* stressful than does another person are more likely to cope with the situation. In other words, they suggest that attributional style may mediate the effects of hardiness. There is some evidence to support this suggestion. Hull *et al.* found that, when presented with a negative event, those who were highly committed made external, unstable and specific attributions, and regarded themselves as not personally responsible. When presented with positive events, high-commitment individuals made internal, stable and global attributions and viewed themselves as personally responsible.

Hardiness has failed to ignite research passions to the same extent as other constructs, such as Type A. This may be due to the fact that Funk and Houston (1987) argued that hardiness is more closely associated with depression than it is with physical illness. Perhaps the most telling blow, and contrary to the predictions of Kobasa (1982), was the finding that hardiness does not buffer against the effects of stress (Funk and Houston, 1987), and that the concept itself is not well operationalised (see also Carson, 1989).

2.8 PERSONALITY AND SUBJECTIVE WELL-BEING

Subjective well-being can be defined as a function of the amount of joy/ happiness or sadness/fear that one experiences. Joy and happiness refer to positive affect, whilst the latter are indicative of negative affect. A further component of subjective well-being is life satisfaction, which Emmons and Diener have defined as 'a cognitive, judgmental process – a global assessment of one's life as a whole' (Emmons and Diener, 1985, p.89).

Ryff and Keyes (1995) have recently proposed an alternative model of well-being, suggesting that it consists of distinct dimensions including autonomy, environmental mastery, personal growth, positive relationships with others, purpose in life, and self-acceptance. These components are only moderately related, suggesting some distinctiveness, and all of them have good convergent validity. For instance, all measures correlate in the expected direction with measures of happiness, life satisfaction and depression (see also Table 2.4).

It is important to study the personality correlates of subjective well-being, Emmons and Diener (1985) having noted the significant links between negative affect, worry and psychosomatic symptoms. Indeed, Feist *et al.* found that subjective well-being can be a cause as well as an effect of daily hassles and physical health (Feist *et al.*, 1995).

There are several different measures of subjective well-being currently in use (see Diener, 1984), ranging from single-item measures of questionable reliability and validity (e.g. 'how are things these days?') to multi-item multi-dimensional measures. Some inventories (such as the Oxford Happiness Inventory) measure happiness, whilst others measure mood, level of affect and level of lonely dissatisfaction.

Table 2.4 Components of subjective well-being

Components	Description
Self-acceptance	Feels positive about self
Positive relationships with others	Is trusting of others and concerned with their well-being
Autonomy	Can think and act independently
Environmental mastery	Has a sense of control; can choose situations that fit with their needs and values
Purpose in life	Has a sense of direction in life
Personal growth	Believe they have the ability to realise their potential

Adapted from Ryff, C. and Keyes, C. (1995) The structure of psychological well-being revisited. *Journal of Personality and Social Psychology* **69**, 719–27.

A number of personality factors have been shown to be related to subjective well-being, such as positive self-esteem, internal locus of control, and extraversion (Diener, 1984). Emmons and Diener (1985) asked volunteers in their study to keep a daily record of their mood levels. At the end of each day, respondents rated themselves on measures of positive and negative affect (e.g. happy, pleased and unhappy, worried, respectively). Respondents completed their mood reports for between 56 and 84 consecutive days. Not surprisingly, those who were designated over this period as experiencing positive affect were classified as extraverted. In particular, they scored high on warmth, social boldness and surgency. By contrast, negative affect was related to components of anxiety, namely tender-mindedness, guilt proneness and being tense.

Furnham and Brewin (1990) assessed the relationships between personality and scores on the Oxford Happiness Inventory (OHI). The OHI yielded three factors, namely satisfaction with personal achievements, enjoyment and fun in life, and vigour and good health. As predicted, these factors were significantly positively related to extraversion and significantly negatively related to neuroticism. Of some interest was the finding that scores on the achievement and enjoyment scales correlated significantly with scores on the Lie scale for men, but not with those for women – that is, men faked a good response on these two scales more than women.

Although research has found significant relationships between extraversion and subjective well-being, it is highly likely that other factors might qualify this relationship. Hotard *et al.* (1989) went some way towards addressing this question by examining the effects of social relationships on the personality–happiness relationship. They found that extraverts tended to be happy regardless of the number of social relationships they had, whilst introverts with several good social relationships also scored high on subjective well-being measures. Low levels of subjective well-being were more closely associated with individuals classified as neurotic introverts.

An important question is whether personality disposition actually predicts later subjective well-being. Costa and McCrae (1980) examined this question, and found that neuroticism at Time 1 showed a significant positive correlation with negative affect 10 years later (Time 2), whilst extraversion at Time 1 was found to correlate significantly with positive affect at Time 2.

Is it possible that the significant links observed between extraversion and subjective well-being may, in part, be artefactual or due to social desirability influences? In a study by Pavot *et al.* (1990), respondents were asked to complete the NEO inventory as well as a variety of different mood measures over a 2-week period. It was concluded that the link between extraversion and subjective well-being is indeed a substantial one, and that it is not situationally specific.

2.9 THE BIG FIVE AND HEALTH

It is only relatively recently that studies have begun to appear in the literature specifically addressing the question of the extent to which the Big Five are implicated in health status. This research has tended to confirm the important role of factors such as neuroticism and extraversion, and has also demonstrated the importance of the remaining factors. From our discussion thus far it is clear that researchers have used a number of different variables (e.g. sense of control, hardiness) to predict health. Marshall *et al.* (1994) were interested in the underlying structure of several such commonly used research tools, as well as the extent to which the factor scores are related to the Big Five.

Three higher-order factors emerged from their analysis, namely *optimistic control* (e.g. optimism, hope, internal control), *anger expression* and *inhibition* (e.g. anger inhibition, rumination). The authors found that none of the factors were uniquely identified with a particular personality domain, but rather that they were related to most of the Big Five dimensions, therefore showing considerable overlap as shown below.

- Optimistic control: positively correlated with E, O, C, A; negatively correlated with N.
- Anger expression: positively correlated with N; negatively correlated with O, C, A.
- Inhibition: positively correlated with N, O.

Similar trends have been observed by Booth-Kewley and Vickers (1994), although it should be noted that conscientiousness was the strongest predictor even after controlling for the other personality domains:

- Wellness behaviours: positively correlated with E, C.
- Accident control: positively correlated with E, A, C.
- Traffic risk-taking: negatively correlated with A, C.
- Substance risk-taking: positively correlated with O.

Taken together, these sets of results point to the fact that the Big Five domains are related in logical and predictable ways not only to lower-order measures (e.g. internal control), but also to health behaviours (e.g. risk-taking). Moreover, it would seem that conscientiousness appears to be particularly important, based not only on the findings noted above (Booth-Kewley and Vickers, 1994), but also on other work which has noted the ability of conscientousness to predict longevity (Friedman *et al.*, 1993).

2.10 CONCLUSION

This chapter has shown the important effects that personality functioning and emotional factors have on one's health and well-being. These studies lend valuable support to the view that psychosocial factors are implicated in health, and help to dispel the myth that illness is caused primarily by biological factors. Many of the studies reported here show very clearly how personality traits and feelings of optimism are able to predict health status over time.

It is quite evident from the numerous studies reviewed here that in recent decades psychologists have made important conceptual advances in the area of health and personality. Compare, for example, our earlier conceptions of the link between the Type A behaviour pattern and coronary heart disease with the view now widely held that verbal aggression, rather than anger or irritability, is predictive of heart disease. Recent work has also narrowed the range of possible psychological causes of some cancers, suggesting that different emotional states may be important causal factors for different cancers.

Several studies have documented the association between explanatory style and illness, and have shown that optimists tend to be healthier than pessimists. Peterson and De Avila (1995) have warned of the risks of 'unrealistic optimism', suggesting that these types may, in fact, disregard or ignore their health. They offer a possible solution to this problem by pointing out that optimists are more likely to take control of their lives and to believe that potential health problems are controllable.

Finally, research data are now beginning to emerge specifically addressing the links between the Big Five and health. Conscientiousness and agreeableness, together with the well-established factors extraversion and neuroticism, seem to be important and will no doubt be the focus of many studies in the future.

REFERENCES

Amelang, M. (1996) *Personality, stress and illness: facts and fiction in the prediction of cancer and coronary heart disease*. Paper presented to the 8th European Conference on Personality, 8–12 July, Ghent, Belgium.

Ashton, H. and Stepney, R. (1982) *Smoking: psychology and pharmacology*. London: Tavistock Publications.

Bishop, G. (1994) *Health psychology*. Boston, MA: Allyn & Bacon.

Booth-Kewley, S. and Friedman, H. (1987) Psychological predictors of heart disease: a quantitative review. *Psychological Bulletin* **101**, 343–62.

Booth-Kewley, S. and Vickers, R. (1994) Associations between major domains of personality and health behaviour. *Journal of Personality* **62**, 281–98.

Buddeberg, C., Sieber, M., Wolf, C., Landolt-Ritter, C., Richter, D. and Steiner, R. (1996) Are coping strategies related to disease outcome in early breast cancer? *Journal of Psychosomatic Research* **40**, 255–64.

Byrne, D.G., Rosenman, R., Schiller, E. and Chesney, M. (1985) Consistency and variation among instruments purporting to measure the Type A behaviour pattern. *Psychosomatic Medicine* **47**, 242–61.

Byrne, D.G., Reinhart, M. and Heaven, P. (1989) Type A behaviour and the authoritarian personality. *British Journal of Medical Psychology* **62**, 163–72.

Byrne, D.G., Byrne, A. and Reinhart, M. (1993) Psychosocial correlates of adolescent cigarette smoking: personality or environment? *Australian Journal of Psychology* **45**, 87–95.

Byrne, D.G., Byrne, A. and Reinhart, M. (1995) Personality, stress and the decision to commence cigarette smoking in adolescence. *Journal of Psychosomatic Research* **39**, 53–62.

Carson, R. (1989) Personality. *Annual Review of Psychology* **40**, 227–48.

Cherry, N. and Kiernan, K. (1976) Personality scores and smoking behaviour: a longitudinal study. *British Journal of Preventive and Social Medicine* **30**, 123–31.

Cohen, F. (1979) Personality, stress, and the development of illness. In Stone, G., Cohen, F., Adler, N. *et al.* (eds), *Health psychology: a handbook. Theories, applications and challenges of a psychological approach to the health care system.* San Francisco, CA: Jossey-Bass, 27–40.

Contrada, R., Leventhal, H. and O'Leary, A. (1990) Personality and health. In Pervin, L. (ed.), *Handbook of personality: theory and research.* New York: The Guilford Press, 638–69.

Cooper, C. and Faragher, B. (1993) Psychological stress and breast cancer: the interrelationship between stress events, coping strategies and personality. *Psychological Medicine* **23**, 653–62.

Costa, P. and McCrae, R. (1980) Influence of extraversion and neuroticism on subjective well-being: happy and unhappy people. *Journal of Personality and Social Psychology* **38**, 668–78.

Costa, P. and McCrae, R. (1985) *The NEO Personality Inventory.* Odessa, FL: Psychological Assessment Resources.

Costa, P. and McCrae, R. (1987) Neuroticism, somatic complaints, and disease: is the bark worse than the bite? *Journal of Personality* **55**, 299–316.

Dembroski, T. and Costa, P. (1987) Coronary prone behaviour: components of the Type A pattern and hostility. *Journal of Personality* **55**, 211–35.

Diener, E. (1984) Subjective well-being. *Psychological Bulletin* **95**, 542–75.

Dunbar, F. (1943) *Psychosomatic diagnosis.* New York: Hoeber.

Eagleston, J., Kirmil-Gray, K., Thoresen, C. *et al.* (1986) Physical health correlates of Type A behaviour in children and adolescents. *Journal of Behavioral Medicine* **47**, 341–62.

Emmons, R. and Diener, E. (1985) Personality correlates of subjective well-being. *Personality and Social Psychology Bulletin* **11**, 89–97.

Everson, S., Goldberg, D., Kaplan, G. *et al.* (1996) Hopelessness and risk of mortality and incidence of myocardial infarction and cancer. *Psychosomatic Medicine* **58**, 113–21.

Eysenck, H. (1985) Personality, cancer and cardiovascular disease: a causal analysis. *Personality and Individual Differences* **6**, 535–56.

Eysenck, H. (1991) *Smoking, personality, and stress.* New York: Springer-Verlag.

Eysenck, H. (1994) Cancer, personality and stress: prediction and prevention. *Advances in Behaviour Research and Therapy* **16**, 167–215.

Eysenck, H. and Fulker, D. (1983) The components of Type A behaviour and its genetic determinants. *Personality and Individual Differences* **4**, 499–505.

Feather, N. (1983) Some correlates of attributional style: depressive symptoms, self-esteem, and Protestant ethic values. *Personality and Social Psychology Bulletin* **9**, 125–35.

Feist, G., Bodner, T., Jacobs, J., Miles, M. and Tan, V. (1995) Integrating top-down and bottom-up structural models of subjective well-being: a longitudinal investigation. *Journal of Personality and Social Psychology* **68**, 138–50.

Friedman, H., Tucker, J., Tomlinson-Keasey, C. *et al.* (1993) Does childhood personality predict longevity? *Journal of Personality and Social Psychology* 65, 176–85.

Friedman, M. and Rosenman, R. (1974) *Type A behaviour and your heart*. London: Wildwood.

Funk, S. and Houston, K. (1987) A critical analysis of the hardiness scale's validity and utility. *Journal of Personality and Social Psychology* 53, 572–8.

Furnham, A. (1994) Explaining health and illness: lay perceptions on current and future health, the causes of illness, and the nature of recovery. *Social Science and Medicine* 39, 715–25.

Furnham, A. and Brewin, C. (1990) Personality and happiness. *Personality and Individual Differences* 11, 1093–6.

Gentry, W. (1984) Behavioral medicine: a new research paradigm. In Gentry, W. (ed.), *Handbook of behavioral medicine*. New York: The Guilford Press, 1–12.

Goodkin, K., Antoni, M. and Blaney, P. (1986) Stress and hopelessness in the promotion of cervical intra-epithelial neoplasia to invasive squamous cell carcinoma of the cervix. *Journal of Psychosomatic Research* 30, 67–76.

Greer, S. and Morris, T. (1975) Psychological attributes of women who develop breast cancer: a controlled study. *Journal of Psychosomatic Research* 19, 147–53.

Grossarth-Maticek, R. and Eysenck, H. (1990) Personality, stress and disease: description and validation of a new inventory. *Psychological Reports* 66, 355–73.

Grossarth-Maticek, R., Eysenck, H., Pfeifer, A., Schmidt, P. and Koppel, G. (1997) The specific action of different personality risk factors on cancer of the breast, cervix, corpus uteri and other types of cancer: a prospective investigation. *Personality and Individual Differences* 23, 949–60.

Haynes, S. and Feinleib, M. (1980) Women, work, and coronary heart disease: prospective findings from the Framingham Heart Study. *American Journal of Public Health* 70, 133–41.

Heaven, P. (1989) The Type A behaviour pattern and impulsiveness among adolescents. *Personality and Individual Differences* 10, 105–10.

Henley, S. and Furnham, A. (1989) The Type A behaviour pattern and self-evaluation. *British Journal of Medical Psychology* 62, 51–9.

Hotard, S., McFatter, R., McWhirter, R. and Stegall, M. (1989) Interactive effects of extraversion, neuroticism and social relationships on subjective well-being. *Journal of Personality and Social Psychology* 57, 321–31.

Hull, J., Van Treuren, R. and Propsom, P. (1988) Attributional style and the components of hardiness. *Personality and Social Psychology Bulletin* 14, 505–13.

Innes, J. (1980) Impulsivity and the coronary-prone behaviour pattern. *Psychological Reports* 47, 976–8.

Kavan, M., Engdahl, B. and Kay, S. (1995) Colon cancer: personality factors predictive of onset and stage of presentation. *Journal of Psychosomatic Research* 39, 1031–9.

Kavussanu, M. and McAuley, E. (1995) Exercise and optimism: are highly active individuals more optimistic? *Journal of Sport and Exercise Psychology* 17, 246–58.

Kazdin, A., French, N., Unis, A., Esveldt-Dawson, K. and Sherick, R. (1983) Hopelessness, depression, and suicidal intent among psychiatrically disturbed inpatient children. *Journal of Consulting and Clinical Psychology* 51, 504–10.

Kobasa, S. (1982) The hardy personality: toward a social psychology of stress and health. In Sanders, G. and Suls, J. (eds), *Social psychology of health and illness*. Hillsdale, NJ: Lawrence Erlbaum Associates, 3–32.

Kobasa, S. and Puccetti, M. (1983) Personality and social resources in stress resistance. *Journal of Personality and Social Psychology* 45, 839–50.

Kobasa, S., Maddi, S. and Kahn, S. (1982) Hardiness and health: a prospective study. *Journal of Personality and Social Psychology* 42, 168–77.

Krantz, D. and Hedges, S. (1987) Some cautions for research on personality and health. *Journal of Personality* 55, 351–7.

Kuiper, C. and Feij, J. (1983) Adolescents: personality and complaints, spending of leisure time, smoking and drinking. *Tijdschrift voor Psychologie* 11, 168–81.

Llorente, M. (1986) Neuroticism, extraversion and the Type A behaviour pattern. *Personality and Individual Differences* 7, 427–9.

Madan-Swain, A., Brown, R., Sexson, S., Baldwin, K., Pais, R. and Ragab, A. (1994) Adolescent cancer survivors: psychosocial and familial adaptation. *Psychosomatics* 35, 453–9.

Malcarne, V., Compas, B., Epping-Jordan, J. and Howell, D. (1995) Cognitive factors in adjustment to cancer: attributions of self-blame and perceptions of control. *Journal of Behavioral Medicine* 18, 401–17.

Marshall, G., Wortman, C., Vickers, R. *et al.* (1994) The five-factor model of personality as a framework for personality–health research. *Journal of Personality and Social Psychology* 67, 278–86.

Matthews, K. and Jennings, R. (1984) Cardiovascular responses of boys exhibiting the Type A behaviour pattern. *Psychosomatic Medicine* 46, 484–97.

Meyerowitz, B. (1980) Psychosocial correlates of breast cancer and its treatments. *Psychological Bulletin* 87, 108–31.

Miles, H., Waldvogel, S., Barrabee, E. and Cobb, S. (1954) Psychosomatic study of 46 young men with coronary artery disease. *Psychosomatic Medicine* 16, 455.

Myrtek, M. (1995) Type A behaviour pattern, personality factors, disease, and physiological reactivity: a meta-analytic update. *Personality and Individual Differences* 18, 491–502.

Patton, D., Barnes, G. and Murray, R. (1993) Personality characteristics of smokers and ex-smokers. *Personality and Individual Differences* 15, 653–64.

Pavot, W., Diener, E., Colvin, C. and Sandvik, E. (1990) Further validation of the Satisfaction With Life Scale. *Journal of Personality Assessment* 57, 149–61.

Peete, D. (1955) *Psychosomatic genesis of coronary artery disease*. Springfield, IL: Thomas.

Peterson, C. and Seligman, M. (1987) Explanatory style and illness. *Journal of Personality* 55, 237–65.

Peterson, C. and De Avila, M. (1995) Optimistic explanatory style and the perception of health problems. *Journal of Clinical Psychology* 51, 128–32.

Peterson, C., Seligman, M. and Vallaint, G. (1988) Pessimistic explanatory style is a risk for physical illness: a thirty-five-year longitudinal study. *Journal of Personality and Social Psychology* 55, 23–7.

Quander-Blaznik, J. (1991) Personality as a predictor of lung cancer: a replication. *Personality and Individual Differences* 12, 125–30.

Ranchor, A. and Sanderman, R. (1991) The role of personality and socio-economic status in the stress-illness relation: a longitudinal study. *European Journal of Personality* 5, 93–108.

Ranchor, A., Sanderman, R. and Bouma, J. (1993) The assignment of subjects to disease-prone personality types: a comment on Schmitz (1992). *Personality and Individual Differences* 14, 483–4.

Ryff, C. and Keyes, C. (1995) The structure of psychological well-being revisited. *Journal of Personality and Social Psychology* 69, 719–27.

Scheier, M. and Carver, C. (1987) Dispositional optimism and physical well-being: the influence of generalized outcome expectancies on health. *Journal of Personality* 55, 169–210.

Scheier, M. and Bridges, M. (1995) Person variables and health: personality predispositions and acute psychological states as shared determinants for disease. *Psychosomatic Medicine* 57, 255–68.

Siegel, J. (1982) Type A behaviour and self-reports of cardiovascular arousal in adolescents. *Journal of Human Stress* 8, 24–30.

Smith, T. and Williams, P. (1992) Personality and health: advantages and limitations of the five-factor model. *Journal of Personality* 60, 395–423.

Strickland, B. (1989) Internal–external control expectancies: from contingency to creativity. *American Psychologist* 44, 1–12.

Suls, J. and Rittenhouse, J. (1987) Personality and physical health: an introduction. *Journal of Personality* 55, 155–67.

Taylor, S. (1991) *Health psychology*, 2nd edn. New York: McGraw-Hill.

Thomas, C., Duszynski, K. and Shaffer, J. (1979) Family attitudes reported in youth as potential predictors of cancer. *Psychosomatic Medicine* 41, 287–302.

Thoresen, C. (1991) Type A and teenagers. In Lerner, R., Petersen, A. and Brooks-Gunn, J. (eds), *Encyclopedia of adolescence. Vol. 2.* New York: Garland Press, 1168–80.

US Surgeon General (1990) *The health benefits of smoking cessation.* Washington, DC: US Department of Health and Human Services.

Van der Ploeg, H. and Vetter, H. (1993) Two for the price of one: the empirical basis of the Grossarth-Maticek interviews. *Psychological Inquiry* 4, 65–9.

Van't Spijker, A., Trijsburg, R. and Duivenvoorden, H. (1997) Psychological sequelae of cancer diagnosis: a meta-analytical review of 58 studies after 1980. *Psychosomatic Medicine* 59, 280–93.

Vincent, C., Furnham, A. and Willsmore, M. (1995) The perceived efficacy of complementary and orthodox medicine in complementary and general practice patients. *Health Education Research* 10, 395–405.

Wenglert, L. and Rosen, A. (1995) Optimism, self-esteem, mood and subjective health. *Personality and Individual Differences* 18, 653–61.

Wistow, D., Wakefield, J. and Goldsmith, W. (1990) The relationship between personality, health symptoms and disease. *Personality and Individual Differences* 11, 717–23.

3

Personality, Learning and Performance

INTRODUCTION

There is abundant scientific evidence that personality traits are related to human performance and learning. Furthermore, every parent knows that school performance is partly predicated on the child's level of interest, motivation and conscientiousness. This chapter will address some fundamental questions regarding the role of personality in education and learning performance. It is becoming increasingly important to understand how one's psychological characteristics, and personality traits in particular, affect training as well as academic and job performance. To what extent do factors such as anxiety affect one's performance? Do extraverts excel at some academic activities, but not at others? How well do different personality types function when distracted? Do people differ in how they go about studying new material? Are other social and contextual factors (e.g. type of school, parental social class) more important in predicting academic excellence than personality? Are some personality types attracted to particular courses of study? Indeed, are some personality types better at some jobs than others?

Few doubt for a moment that different educational and social factors are important in predicting one's level of academic ability. It is well established that students from private schools tend to outperform those in state schools, suggesting that type of school and parental socio-economic background are implicated in children's academic performance. Evidence shows that students from private schools are more likely than their state counterparts to complete more schooling and to attend university (Byrne and Byrne, 1990; Jones, 1990). Likewise, the socio-economic status of parents is important in predicting who will stay on at school and who will proceed to university. It has been argued that parents with high socio-economic status have certain values and beliefs that increase the likelihood that their children will be academically successful (Argyle, 1994).

There is also a continuing debate about the merits or otherwise of single-sex vs. coeducational schools (Foon, 1988), it being suggested that girls in government coeducational schools are less likely to enrol in higher level mathematics or science courses. Some evidence suggests that girls from single-sex schools may prefer science-based subjects. Thus class ideology within the wider societal context is mirrored in many coeducational schools such that class and gender interact, lowering the academic aspirations of many girls in state coeducational schools (Jones, 1990).

Nevertheless, we argue that for too long the role of personality factors in helping to determine learning and performance has been overlooked. As Eysenck (1971) has remarked, when personality factors such as extraversion or neuroticism are added to other variables such as type of school, researchers are able to increase significantly the proportion of variance explained. Thus personality factors add an important dimension to our understanding of a range of different performance and educational issues, as will be shown below.

3.2 TASK PERFORMANCE

It is well documented that personality traits differ in their psychophysiological and behavioural manifestations (e.g. Eysenck, 1967; Eysenck and Eysenck, 1985; Eysenck and Gudjonsson, 1989; Gale and Eysenck, 1992). It is beyond the scope of this chapter to discuss all of these behavioural differences in any detail, but here we shall pay particular attention to the influence of personality on vigilance tasks and verbal learning and memory.

How good are you at detecting changes to sensory stimuli over time? Put another way, would you detect changes on a radar screen after, say, 30 minutes, 1 hour, or even longer? If you were watching a radar screen for signs of enemy activity, it would be essential that you were up to the task.

Several authors have documented the fact that success in vigilance tasks is normally enhanced by raising one's level of arousal. Given that introverts tend to be over-aroused compared to extraverts, it is not surprising to learn that introverts tend to perform better at vigilance tasks. This is a well-established finding. Recently, for example, Aladjalova and Arnold (1991) found that male introverts outperformed extraverts on a vigilance task after both normal sleep and one night of sleep deprivation. Moreover, the data showed that the differences in performance between these two personality types was greater toward the *end* of the task.

One explanation for the finding that extraverts do not do as well on vigilance tasks may be due to the fact that they show greater vigilance decrement (Eysenck and Eysenck, 1985) or a lowering of arousal, although Koelega (1992) notes that most decrement occurs in the very early stages of the task. Indeed, physiological indicators of arousal levels (e.g. heart rate and skin resistance) show decreases over the duration of a task (Eysenck and

Eysenck, 1985). Vigilance decrement is not automatic for extraverts. Eysenck (Eysenck and Eysenck, 1985) reports that explanations for this decrement could include the possibility that extraverts simply become more cautious over time. After beginning the novel task in a 'hypervigilant' state (Koelega, 1992), they soon settle down, with extraverts showing less decrement when attending to more interesting tasks. In any event, it does seem possible to reduce the decrement gap between introverts and extraverts by creating arousal-enhancing conditions, including the use of white noise, caffeine or electric shocks.

Research findings in this area have not been unequivocal, and some researchers have failed to detect the expected differences between extraverts and introverts. In a recent meta-analytical review of extraversion and vigilance performance, Koelega (1992) found support for Eysenck's (1967) arousal theory, but concluded that the effects were rather small. In particular, introverts were more successful at detecting signals, attaining hits, and adopting more severe response criteria.

Enthusiasm for Eysenck's (1967) arousal theory is not shared by all researchers, who emphasise different aspects. Some emphasise the effort expended by the individual, whilst others focus on reward and punishment systems (see Box 3.1).

Extraverts and introverts differ in many ways, including their verbal learning and memory skills, and it is widely believed that arousal levels are implicated. According to Eysenckian theory (Eysenck, 1967), the

BOX 3.1

Eysenck (1967) explains behavioural differences between introverts and extraverts in terms of his arousal theory. However, Koelega (1992, p.240) reminds us of other interpretations, some of which are emphasised below.

Gale and Edwards (1986):	In their view the role of arousal has been 'over-inflated'.
Humphreys and Revelle (1984):	They emphasise arousal *and* effort.
Brebner and Cooper (1985):	Introverts and extraverts analyse and respond to stimuli in different ways.
Gray (1981):	Introvert–extravert differences are explained in terms of reward and punishment systems operating within the brain.
Eysenck (1988):	He emphasises arousability and suggests that introverts/extraverts differ in *how* they respond to certain conditions.

extraversion–behaviour link is arousal mediated – that is, extraversion is linked to arousal which is linked to performance. As far as behavioural differences are concerned, extraverts do better under high levels of arousal, whereas introverts perform better under low arousal conditions. Extraverts are much better at learning more complex (and more arousing) tasks, while introverts are better at learning less complex and less arousing tasks (see also Matthews *et al.*, 1990). The evidence also shows that extraverts do better than introverts at short-term recall, whilst the pattern is reversed for long-term recall. Howarth and Eysenck (1968) showed very clearly that, with regard to short-term recall (after 1 minute), extraverts performed significantly better than introverts, although this pattern was reversed after 1 day.

However, not all studies support these trends, and Eysenck (1976) notes three interpretative problems with the research which supports the expected findings. First, it is not clear whether the results reflect the level of subject arousal at *input* or during *retention*. Secondly, it is possible that introverts rehearse the information while it is being stored. Thirdly, it is not clear what effect the retention interval has on the arousal levels of introverts and extraverts.

Introverts and extraverts differ in their ability to complete a task under distracting conditions. For instance, evidence shows that introverts tend to study in more isolated sections of the library than extraverts (e.g. Campbell and Hawley, 1982). Some research has shown that the performance of extraverts actually improves under distracting conditions compared to their performance in silence, whilst the performance of introverts deteriorates during distraction (Morgenstern *et al.*, 1974). In contrast, work by Furnham (Furnham *et al.*, 1994; Furnham and Bradley, 1997) has shown that distraction in the form of pop music or television noise has a negative impact on the reading comprehension and memory tasks of both introverts and extraverts, although the effect is greater for introverts.

Another personality factor related to learning and performance is anxiety. Following the now well-known formulations of Spielberger (1966), many theorists distinguish between state and trait anxiety. Whereas state anxiety is more transitory (e.g. 'I feel anxious today'), trait anxiety is a relatively stable individual difference factor. As state anxiety is affected primarily by external stressors such as an imminent important examination, it follows that performance is more a function of state than of trait anxiety (Eysenck and Eysenck, 1985).

Spence and Spence (1966) have postulated a theory regarding the effects of anxiety on performance. They proposed that strength of learning (as indexed by habit) multiplied by drive produced what they referred to as 'excitatory potential' (Eysenck, 1981). When the excitatory potential and drive exceed a certain threshold, the strongest habit will lead to performance. In short, these interactions are predicted to have different effects for different tasks. Anxiety increases performance on relatively simple tasks, but not on more complex tasks. The reason is that in the case of complex tasks, anxiety strengthens incorrect responses in relation to correct responses, although this may not happen under all conditions (see Eysenck, 1981). One problem with this view, according to Eysenck, is that 'it assumes that the effects of anxiety are centred exclusively on retrieval processes and that anxiety does not affect other aspects of information processing (e.g. attentional and encoding processes and the response threshold)' (Eysenck, 1981, p.175).

Eysenck proposed that anxiety has either a beneficial (i.e. motivational) effect or an inhibitory effect (see Eysenck and Eysenck, 1985). Whereas worry is clearly a cognitive component of anxiety, the emotional component is linked with affect. Moreover, it is the cognitive rather than the affective component of anxiety that is likely to have a negative impact on performance.

These ideas have been taken up by several writers. Recently, it has been suggested that anxiety often manifests itself as 'fear of failure' or 'test-taking anxiety', and both tend to be related to lower levels of achievement (De Raad and Schouwenburg, 1996). Those who are test anxious are very often characterised by their 'self-deprecatory thinking', rather than focusing on the task at hand (De Raad and Schouwenburg, 1996, p.320). Eysenck (1981) has likewise reviewed the role of cognitive factors in anxiety. According to some evidence, anxiety is composed of displeasure, high arousal and submissiveness, with the displeasure component based on cognitive appraisal. This is reminiscent of the view that anxiety can be subdivided into two components, namely worry and emotionality, defined as follows:

- *worry*: the cognitive aspect of anxiety; concerned about one's performance; contains negative task expectations and negative self-evaluations;
- *emotionality*: has a physiological basis; manifested as uneasiness, tension and nervousness.

(Eysenck, 1981, p.177)

Worry and emotionality are not necessarily linearly related. One study by Spiegler *et al.* (1968, cited in Eysenck, 1981) showed that worry scores among university students were elevated several days before and after an important examination. Emotionality scores, on the other hand, decreased from immediately before to just after the examination.

Markham and Darke (1991) have also examined the inhibitory and beneficial effects of anxiety on verbal reasoning and spatial reasoning tasks. As predicted, they found that high anxiety inhibited the verbal reasoning task when the processing demand was high, although this was not found to be the case for the spatial reasoning task. They therefore concluded that 'cognitive self-concern' seems to have different effects on the verbal and visual domains of the working memory system.

Finally, it has been argued that neurotic introverts are perhaps more likely than neurotic extraverts to be susceptible to the limiting effects of worry. As Eysenck explains:

> Since introverts generally condition better than extraverts, it might be expected that neurotic introverts would be more susceptible than neurotic extraverts to conditional anxiety in the form of worry or psychic anxiety. On the other hand, neurotic extraverts with their low level of arousal and high level of autonomic activation may be liable to the more somatic components of anxiety resembling emotionality.
>
> (Eysenck and Eysenck, 1985, p.293)

The available evidence suggests that performance is affected by personality traits. In particular, extraversion–introversion and levels of anxiety have been found to be important. The impact of factors such as these also depends on the type of task being completed, the presence of distracting factors, and the complexity of the task.

3.3 ACADEMIC PERFORMANCE

The possibility that personality functioning may affect academic performance has not only important theoretical implications, but also important practical ones. For example, such knowledge would allow for more effective vocational guidance, as well as resulting in more careful selection of candidates for particular courses of study.

The literature on personality and performance of whatever kind is a wide and scattered one representing work from quite diverse research traditions and paradigms. Some of it (e.g. the work on learning styles and cognitive styles) appears somewhat muddled. According to Braden (1995), this large body of work can be said to cover one of four main areas.

Need for achievement The first area represents work on need achievement which itself is included in some personality inventories, e.g. the Sixteen Personality Factor Questionnaire (16PF). Braden notes that, as not many predictions from this theory have been confirmed, it is not represented in more contemporaneous work.

Locus of control There is a very large literature which shows that internals make different attributions for success and failure than do externals. This work overlaps with that on attributional style.

Attributional style People with a pessimistic or negative attributional (explanatory) style explain their failure to achieve in terms of internal, stable and global attributions. These modalities are used by those with a positive attributional style to explain their successes.

Anxiety and performance Anxiety has an impact on one's ability to perform certain tasks, and this relationship is mediated by arousal. Thus there are performance differences between extraverts and introverts.

Interest in the possible links between personality (or 'non-intellectual' factors) and academic performance has persisted throughout this century. One of the earliest attempts was that of Webb (see De Raad and Schouwenburg, 1996) who, in addition to mental abilities, also suggested the existence of a second group of character traits, labelled motives or will, which were said to be associated with academic performance. Other traits, such as originality and perseverance, were later identified and regarded as being crucial in academic performance (De Raad and Schouwenburg, 1996).

As a result of his experimental work on the nature of individual differences, it was Eysenck (1967) who, many years after Webb, argued that introverts and extraverts differ in their level of academic achievement, which is also a function of the type of task completed. He found evidence to show that introverts are much more successful at rather tedious, relatively boring and lengthy tasks. Extraverts, on the other hand, seemed to perform better at shorter and more interesting activities. Likewise, we know that introverts are more successful than extraverts at vigilance tasks (Eysenck and Eysenck, 1985; see previous section), whilst it has been noted that introverts are better equipped to consolidate new material and hence improve their chances of academic success (Child, 1989).

Recent research has shown, quite predictably, that extraverts are much better suited to seminar-type activities than are other personality types. Rothstein et al. (1994) found that classroom performance was best predicted by extraversion as well as by agreeableness and openness to experience, although these factors did not predict performance with regard to written work. This measure of performance was best predicted by verbal and quantitative aptitudes.

Furnham and Medhurst (1995) found that extraverts (as measured by the EPQ) were more likely to participate in seminar activities, but were less successful at other tasks, such as essay-writing. Similar results were obtained with Cattell's 16PF. Extraverts participated more and were not averse to making oral presentations, but anxious individuals, by contrast, performed poorly on oral tasks. However, the overall best predictor of seminar outcome was an individual's score on Eysenck's P scale, with these individuals significantly *less* likely to show any of the following characteristics (Furnham and Medhurst, 1995, p.200):

- a good grasp of the subject matter;
- good work habits;
- motivation;
- good written expression;
- good oral expression;
- participation in seminars.

In further work, Furnham and Mitchell (1991) conducted a longitudinal study to examine the ability of personality factors to predict academic performance at the end of the first, second, third and fourth years of

Table 3.1 Predictors of academic performance over time

	First year		Second year		
	Anatomy	Psychology	Psychiatry	Medicine	Absenteeism
Predictors	Extraversion (-)		Sentience (-) Achievement Nurturance	Achievement	Lie Achievement (-) Nurturance Social anxiety (-)

Adapted from Furnham, A. and Mitchell, J. (1991) Personality, needs, social skills and academic achievement: a longitudinal study. *Personality and Individual Differences* **12**, 1067–73.

professional study. Performance was ascertained in first-year anatomy and psychology, and in second-year psychiatry and medicine. In addition, an overall absenteeism score for each student was computed. The personality measures used were the EPQ, a measure of nine different needs, the self-monitoring scale, a measure of social anxiety and distress, a measure of assertiveness, and a measure of locus of control. The main predictors of each dependent variable are shown in Table 3.1.

Table 3.1 shows that in fact few personality factors were significantly related to academic performance during the first 2 years. At the end of the third year, neurotics did less well in a course in communication and management skills, whilst none of the EPQ dimensions was able to predict the students' final overall results. Finally, and perhaps importantly, the highest correlation obtained was − 0.17, between sentience and performance in second-year psychiatry. This accounts for only a very small proportion of the variance in performance. On the basis of this study, therefore, one must conclude that personality factors play a modest role in predicting academic performance, and that other non-personality factors that were not measured here are probably more important in explaining academic outcome.

Entwistle (1972) found extraversion to be an important factor in explaining the academic attainment of primary-school children, while introversion seemed to be much more important among college and university students. Support for this transition comes from a study by Goh and Moore (1978), who found that introversion was the strongest predictor of grade-point average in university students, followed by study hours, and Raven's progressive matrices. Introversion was also the strongest predictor for students studying 'hard sciences', but not for 'social' sciences students. For the latter, the strongest predictor was a low score on Eysenckian psychoticism. None of these factors predicted academic performance among high-school students.

Possible explanations for these findings may be that highly extraverted or sociable children fall behind in their studies, or that capable students become more introverted as they get older (Eysenck and Eysenck, 1985). Entwistle

(1972) also showed that the academic performance–personality relationship is complicated by the effects of such factors as the student's intellectual level, the type of school he or she attends, and the subject being studied (see also Anthony, 1973). In a Bulgarian study, Paspalanov (1984) also found differential effects for extraversion depending on the field of study. Extraversion was shown to be related to achievement motivation for groups of high-school students and skilled industrial workers, as well as for gifted and high-school students, and eminent musicians and artists. However, the effect of extraversion was much stronger for the latter group.

Heaven (1990) examined the personality correlates of achievement motivation among two samples of Australian teenagers attending high school. Extraversion was found to be the most consistent correlate of achievement motivation for both sexes in both samples, followed by psychoticism and neuroticism (negative correlations).

The research results discussed here show quite clearly the extent to which extraversion–introversion predicts performance in academic settings. These data were found to be qualified by the age group of the respondents and the nature of the academic task being completed.

Although research using the Big Five factors has recently begun to appear in the literature, comparatively few studies have looked at the Big Five traits and learning. By and large, research using the extraversion and neuroticism scales supports earlier findings. In short, introversion appears to be significantly linked to high performance at university level, while extraversion is linked to success at school. Neuroticism is associated with poor academic performance (De Raad and Schouwenburg, 1996), whilst it has also been shown (De Fruyt and Mervielde, 1996) that high-N individuals tended to obtain their degree only after several attempts at the final examination.

Recent research using a Belgian version of the NEO inventory has uncovered personality differences in university students according to their major area of study (De Fruyt and Mervielde, 1996). Thus, for example, it was found that language and history students scored highest on the neuroticism scale, followed by psychology and education students, and then students of the natural sciences and engineering. Language and history majors as well as bioengineers scored lowest on extraversion, whilst psychology, social sciences and natural sciences students scored highest on openness to experience. Law and economics students tended to score lowest on this dimension. High conscientiousness scores were characteristic of students of law, economics and the natural sciences, while low conscientiousness was typical of bioengineering, language, history, psychology and education majors. Students of the natural sciences scored highest on agreeableness.

To date, there is little direct evidence linking agreeableness to academic performance. However, given the idea that a 'peaceful attitude' probably facilitates learning, De Raad and Schouwenburg (1996) suggest that there is a significant association between agreeableness and motivation to learn. In support of this view, they cite evidence which shows that aggressive and withdrawn children tend to have lower grades than non-aggressive and more outgoing children.

According to De Raad and Schouwenburg (1996, p.325), conscientiousness is the 'main psychological resource in learning and education'. Conscientious individuals possess the attributes necessary to succeed in academic and occupational pursuits. These include drive, carefulness, concentration, endurance, and being organised, systematic, efficient, practical and steady. It is perhaps not surprising that conscientious students tend to attain their degree after the first rather than subsequent examination periods in Belgium. Indeed, conscientiousness is significantly negatively correlated with the total number of re-examinations (De Fruyt and Mervielde, 1996).

The fifth element of the Big Five taxonomy has been referred to by some researchers as openness to experience, and by others as intellect (e.g. John, 1990). Invariably, most researchers seem to agree that this dimension refers to someone who is resourceful as well as original and having foresight. Thus a positive association between this personality dimension and learning and performance is quite conceivable and highly likely. The Belgian data indicate that those students who score high on openness to experience are more likely than not to attain their degree after the first examination period (De Fruyt and Mervielde, 1996).

De Fruyt and Mervielde (1996) also examined the relationships between students' educational outcome and the facet scales of the Belgian NEO. The facet scales of the dimension 'conscientiousness' appear to be most important in predicting academic success (see also Wolfe and Johnson, 1995). Thus it was found that grades obtained after the first examination period as well as final grades were significantly related to competence, order (males only), dutifulness, achievement striving, self-discipline and deliberation (males only). The number of re-examinations attempted tended to be negatively related to these lower-order personality traits. The other traits which appear to be only moderately important in explaining grades obtained are anxiety, depression, impulsiveness, vulnerability (N; negative correlations), activity (E; positive correlation), fantasy and aesthetics (O; negative correlation).

To summarise, the Eysenckian and Big Five personality taxonomies are useful for understanding and perhaps also predicting academic success and courses of study. Clear patterns have emerged from the existing literature which show differences in learning between extraverts and introverts, whilst there is growing evidence of the importance of conscientiousness in academic success for both males and females. As De Fruyt and Mervielde suggest:

> Hardly anybody questions the contribution of general mental abilities to academic achievement across a range of majors. . . . Conscientiousness can perhaps be conceived of as the non-cognitive counterpart of the cognitive g factor, explaining part of the variance in various educational outcome measures across academic curricula.
>
> (De Fruyt and Mervielde, 1996, p.420)

In addition to the work that has specifically assessed the Eysenckian and Big Five taxonomies, other researchers have examined the links between single traits, learning and performance. For example, several studies have demonstrated the importance of locus of control (e.g. Prociuk and Breen, 1974; Fry and Coe, 1980). However, this relationship is not as straightforward as it first appears. For instance, Fry and Coe found in the USA that the relationship is more complex among black than white undergraduates. They found that performance among black students varies and is a function of whether respondents 'are co-operating with blacks or competing against whites' (Fry and Coe, 1980, p.166). Black students who were classified as internals tended to perform best when competing against a white student or when collaborating with another black student.

Dorsey and Jackson (1995) were interested in why black undergraduates attended a predominantly white university and what factors predicted their academic success. Included in the research were both internal and external factors (e.g. self-concept, personal motivation, faculty relationships, etc.). A higher level of academic performance was found to be related to levels of motivation, high aspirations and positive self-concept. These students also tended to rely on a particular faculty member for support and mentoring, although they tended to experience a sense of alienation from the wider university community. It is not clear whether these personality predictors of academic success will be found among black students at predominantly black institutions, and this question needs to be addressed in follow-up work.

In a rare Indian study of over 500 teenagers, Jindal and Panda (1982) examined the relationships between level of anxiety, low self-esteem, locus of control and achievement motivation. They found a significant negative association between achievement motivation and anxiety for males only – that is, achievement-motivated males tended to be less anxious. No explanation for these sex differences was offered.

Scott and Scott (1989) conducted an impressive study of children's adjustment to high school among 1825 respondents from seven different countries, namely Australia, Canada, the USA, Japan, Hong Kong, Germany and Taiwan. One of the measures of school adjustment was academic performance as appraised by teachers' and students' judgements. After discounting various judgemental biases through cross-source analyses, the researchers found that students' views of parental nurturance and punitiveness were linked to academic performance through personality. Self-esteem mediated the effect of parental nurturance on good academic performance, whilst high levels of hostility mediated the effects of parental punitiveness on low academic performance.

Boekaerts (1996) has recently alluded to the importance of what she refers to as 'personality style', which is closely related to self-concept and refers to one's self-descriptions and self-prescriptions. It comes as no surprise, therefore, that learning and performance are particularly affected by one's achievement-related cognitions. Such cognitions are reflected in a certain attributional style, one's beliefs about self-efficacy, one's expectations about succeeding, the value one places on academic success, and so on.

Not all of the evidence supports the personality–academic performance link suggested above. Some researchers have argued (not unreasonably) that a host of other factors, such as socio-economic background or school type, may be better predictors of academic outcome. Indeed, Entwistle expressed this sentiment in the following terms:

> One should not make . . . wide generality in statements about the relationship between personality and academic attainment. Age, ability, sex, geographic area, classroom organisation, class size, teaching methods and teachers' personality may all affect these relationships to some extent.
>
> (Entwistle, 1972, p.147)

In a similar vein, Kline and Gale (1971) found little evidence of the personality–academic performance link. Of eight studies that they reviewed, seven showed a significant – albeit low – correlation with academic performance. In their own longitudinal research, the authors found very few significant relationships between extraversion and academic performance. Ferrari and Parker (1992) found no evidence that either self-efficacy or locus of control were related to semester credits completed or Grade Point Average (GPA) among a sample of 319 students.

Given that not all extraverts perform poorly, Gallagher (1996) postulated that those extraverts who do perform well have probably altered their sociable behaviour so as to create an environment more conducive to high achievement. As it is quite reasonable to regard such altered behaviour as a form of coping, Gallagher examined the relationships between coping style, personality and academic achievement among 364 introductory psychology students. They completed a coping measure, the EPQ, and also provided their scores on a mid-term and final assessment. The results indicated the existence of two underlying coping styles, namely irrational coping as well as a style characterised by seriousness, being alone and achieving.

As one might expect, Gallagher (1996) observed that irrational coping was not associated with high achievement, although neurotic and stable introverts tended to outperform extraverts. In further analyses he assessed the coping style of those extraverts who did do well. Compared to introverts who did well, high-performing extraverts tended *not* to engage in a form of coping referred to as 'avoiding social support'. In other words, they tended to be *more* sociable. As Gallagher concluded, it would seem that when extraverts are facing an academic stressor they express their emotional distress to others, and that:

> extraverts who are willing to do so, and who also take their work seriously, are the ones who are able to circumvent the general tendency of extraverts toward lower academic performance . . . high performing extraverts utilize social support in ways different from low performing extraverts. . . . High

> performing extraverts may engage in a kind of social interaction that is intended to ameliorate their troubling and, perhaps, distracting emotional experience. Lower performing extraverts' interactions, in contrast, may be of a character that aids them in avoidance, but not relief.
>
> (Gallagher, 1996, p.428)

3.4 LEARNING AND COGNITIVE STYLES

The influence of personality on academic performance is moderated by one's learning style (see, for example, Furnham, 1995; Grigorenko and Sternberg, 1995). Indeed, this makes perfect sense – one person may prefer a much more structured approach to learning, while another may be more suited to a less structured, highly informal experiential approach to learning. Importantly, these two quite different strategies may be very effective for the individuals concerned. As Grigorenko and Sternberg have noted, academic performance is not simply a function of one's level of intelligence *or* of one's personality, but also of something referred to as *style* – that is, an 'interaction of intelligence and personality' (Grigorenko and Sternberg, 1995, p.205).

A review of the literature will show that many researchers use the terms 'cognitive' and 'learning style' interchangeably and, as they appear to have developed slightly different literatures, they will therefore be discussed separately. One can also distinguish between various approaches to the study of styles (Furnham, 1995; Grigorenko and Sternberg, 1995), it being possible to distinguish the cognition-centred approach, the personality-centred approach, and the activity-centred approach. The latter approach is often referred to as 'learning style'.

3.4.1 Learning Styles

There is no universally agreed definition of learning style, and authors differ in what is for them the defining question that needs to be answered. Grigorenko and Sternberg (1995) have noted some of the more influential approaches to understanding the nature of learning styles, each of which focuses on a different perspective, as shown in Table 3.2. What is clear is the wide diversity of approaches, ranging from an emphasis on behaviour to sensory modalities, to information-processing.

Kolb (1976, 1984) devised the Learning Style Inventory as a measure of one's characteristics as a learner. It measures four different styles, namely, 'converging', 'diverging', 'assimilating' and 'accommodating'. The convergent individual is especially competent at problem-solving and has good practical skills. The divergent thinker has excellent imaginative capabilities and is thus well equipped to generate a range of different ideas. The assimilating type prefers to function at the abstract level, and likes to produce models and taxonomies of how things ought to work or how problems should be solved.

Table 3.2 Different conceptions of learning styles

Questions asked by different researchers
'What conditions will facilitate any learning?'
'Which behaviours indicate how I learn from and adapt to my environment?'
'How do those with specific problems learn?'
'Are particular sensory modalities linked to particular types of learning?'
'Do particular personality characteristics have behavioural implications for learning situations?'
'Do people differ in their learning abilities?'
'Is learning a function of different ways of processing information?'

Source of information: Grigorenko, E. and Sternberg, R. (1995) Thinking styles. In Saklofske, D. and Zeidner, M. (eds), *International handbook of personality and intelligence.* New York: Plenum, 205–29.

These individuals are thus very often well suited to work in planning and research-type occupations. Finally, the accommodator is characterised by action – he or she is an opportunist and risk-taker, and is always eager to 'do something' when the need arises.

Students with particular learning styles seem attracted to specific courses of study. Green *et al.* (1990) found that divergers were least sure of their career choice, although assimilators had very good quantitative skills. Convergers had an interest in scientific occupations, but accommodators tended to be indistinguishable in terms of career choice. Similarly, convergers without computer experience can improve their performance much more quickly than those with other learning styles when they combine 'hands-on' applications with abstract conceptualisation (Sein and Robey, 1991).

The four styles described above are really a function of how one collects and processes information (Furnham, 1995). It is possible to gather information through concrete experience or abstract conceptualisation, whilst information-processing occurs either through reflective observation or by active experimentation. According to Kolb (1976, 1984), the four different styles gather and process information as follows:

- *accommodators*: concrete experience + active experimentation;
- *divergers*: concrete experience + reflective observation;
- *assimilators*: reflective observation + abstract conceptualisation;
- *convergers*: active conceptualisation + active experimentation.

More recently, Honey and Mumford (1992) have proposed a taxonomy that bears a striking resemblance to that of Kolb. They proposed the following styles: 'activists', 'reflectors', 'theorists', and 'pragmatists'.

Activists These individuals are open-minded, and are enthusiastic about new experiences, but not about long-term planning and consolidation. They are sociable and enjoy being at the centre of whatever is happening. Activists also tend to be flexible in their thinking, although they do act somewhat impulsively.

Reflectors These individuals are more cautious and carefully consider the situation before acting. They appear slightly aloof and distant, yet are thorough and methodical, listening to all points of view. On the negative side, reflectors are somewhat slow at reaching a decision, and are not sufficiently assertive.

Theorists These are analytical individuals who like to propose models and theories; they therefore prefer things to be clear and logical. Not surprisingly, they follow a disciplined and methodological approach to knowledge acquisition, preferring the objective to the subjective. One of the weaknesses of this approach is that they have no stomach for uncertainty and ambiguity.

Pragmatists These individuals like to solve problems and are practically minded. They will experiment with new ideas or strategies to solve a problem which is invariably viewed as challenging. They much prefer structured to open-ended discussion. A disadvantage of this approach is their emphasis on the practical rather than the theoretical, and these individuals will often decide on a solution to a problem as a matter of sheer convenience.

Is it possible to differentiate between men and women in terms of their learning styles? This was the question asked by Philbin *et al.* (1995). A sample consisting of 72 respondents of differing ages, ethnicity and gender completed Kolb's Learning Style Inventory and a measure of educational dialectics. This questionnaire contains 12 statements such as 'How do you prefer to behave in an educational setting? Listen/participate verbally' and 'What method of analysis do you value most? Subjective/objective'.

Most of the men in the sample (48 per cent) were classified as assimilators and therefore liked to produce models and taxonomies. Only 8 per cent of the men were in the diverger category, indicating a reliance on imaginative capacity. On the other hand, women were more evenly distributed across the different learning styles, with the lowest number (20 per cent) in the assimilator category. Accommodators represented 22.2 per cent of the sample, divergers represented 28.9 per cent and convergers represented 28.9 per cent of the sample.

Studies by Furnham (1992) and Jackson and Lawty-Jones (1996) were designed to examine the interrelationships between learning styles and personality as assessed by the EPQ. The main results are shown in Table 3.3 and are consistent with our knowledge of the different personality types. Extraverts were found to perform well as activists and pragmatists, but not as reflectors. The findings with respect to neuroticism are equivocal, while those high on the P scale tend to be activist in their approach, but not theoretical.

Table 3.3 Personality correlates of learning styles in two studies

Extraversion	Psychoticism	Neuroticism	Lie
Activitist[a]	Activitist[a]	Theorist[b]	Activitist(-)[a]
Reflector(-)[a]	Theorist(-)[a]		Reflector(-)[a]
Pragmatist[a]	Reflector[b]		Theorist[b]

[a] Results obtained in both studies.

[b] Results obtained by Jackson and Lawty-Jones (1996) only.

Sources: Furnham, A. (1992) Personality and learning style: a study of three instruments. *Personality and Individual Differences* **13**, 429–38 *and* Jackson, C. and Lawty-Jones, M. (1996) Explaining the overlap between personality and learning style. *Personality and Individual Differences* **20**, 293–300.

Research by Drummond and Stoddard (1992) assessed the extent to which scores on the Gregorc learning style inventory and the Myers-Briggs personality scale are correlated. Several significant correlations were obtained, but only two are really of interest from our point of view. The authors found that extraverts tended to score lower on the abstract sequential scale – that is, they tended not to be sequential, studious, logical and analytical whereas the opposite was the case for introverts.

3.4.2 Cognitive Styles

Cognitive style has been defined as an individual's 'preferred way of making decisions, solving problems, and construing change' (Tullett and Davies, 1997) or as 'a preference for perceptual organization that includes an individual's self-concept, worldview, typical instrumental responses, and values. . . . (It) determines the mode and accuracy of perception, thinking style . . . and focus of attention' (Furnham, 1995). In other words, cognitive styles have an effect on how we think about the environment or world in which we live (Riding *et al.*, 1995).

According to Messick (1984), cognitive style can be seen to consist of the following: broad vs. narrow categorising, cognitive complexity vs. simplicity, field dependence and independence, levelling vs. sharpening, scanning vs. focusing, converging vs. diverging, automatisation vs. restructuring, and reflection vs. impulsivity. Riding and Wigley (1997) have surveyed the many different approaches to conceptualising cognitive style and concluded that they can be subsumed under two broad and independent categories as follows.

- *Wholistic–Analytic*: does the person process information in parts or in wholes?
- *Verbal–Imagery*: does the person represent information during thinking in a verbal way or with mental pictures?

Imagers have been found to prefer pictorial representations over verbal ones, whereas the reverse is true for verbalisers. Imagers are better at recalling descriptive text, which is not the case with imagers. Not surprisingly, therefore, the exact way in which material is presented will affect subsequent recall or performance. Riding and Douglas (1993) found that the performance of imagers was enhanced if material was presented as text plus pictures, rather than as text only. Contrary to belief, however, verbalisers did equally well under the text only *and* text plus picture conditions. It was thought that the *nature* of the verbal explanation given to the students may have contributed to this result.

Among adults, neuroticism was not found to be significantly related to either cognitive style, but rather it was related to their admixtures. Thus those who could switch from one style to another were found to be most susceptible to neuroticism. 'Wholistics' can see the whole picture, and analytics have everything under control. Thus they tend not to be susceptible to stress.

Cognitive style has been found to be related to personality descriptors in children as young as 12 years. Riding *et al.* (1995) asked children to complete the cognitive styles measure and then nominate classmates on particular personality characteristics. Imagers were seen by others as being more responsible than verbalisers. Verbalisers were perceived as more active (lively and outgoing) than imagers. There was no difference between verbalisers and imagers on the trait 'modest' (shy and quiet). Thus to some extent these styles fit logically with our knowledge of the major personality domains.

Although it is reasonable to suggest that intelligence is implicated in cognitive styles, personality factors are important for explaining *how* we arrive at a particular solution to a problem (see also Kossowska and Necka, 1994), and differences have been noted *within* broad categories. Thus analytical subjects do not differ significantly from 'global' subjects in mean processing time on a task, but they do differ in how they allocate time. Kossowska and Necka (1994) found that analytical subjects spent more time on the preparatory stages of a task (a 'step-by-step' approach), whilst global subjects spent more time on the executive stages of a task. Neurotic subjects were found to be faster than emotionally stable ones on a similar task, and opted for the analytical rather than the global strategy (but see Riding and Wigley, 1997, discussed above).

According to Crozier (1997), the cognitive style that has given rise to considerable research is Wik's conception of field-independence/field-dependence. Individuals classified as field-independent tend to be active learners, and they like to impose structure on material, to use mnemonic strategies for effective storage and retrieval of information, and prefer to learn general principles whilst acquiring them quite easily (Furnham, 1995). Field-dependent learners are characterised by their use of salient features for generating predictions, they tend to be passive learners, they use the existing organisation of material, and so forth.

Table 3.4   Personality differences between field-independent and field-dependent subjects

---

Field-independents tend to:
- separate their feelings and cognitions;
- be independent of other people;
- be demanding and manipulative;
- perform well in science and mathematics;
- aspire to be architects or engineers.

Field-dependents tend to:
- be warm, affectionate and tactful;
- maintain effective interpersonal relationships;
- aspire to nursing, social worker or personnel manager occupations.

Source of information: Crozier, W.R. (1997) *Individual learners: personality differences in education.* London: Routledge.

With regard to their personality correlates, Crozier (1997, p.10) has speculated on the differences between field-independent and field-dependent subjects (see Table 3.4). In summary, whereas field-independents are found to be manipulative, field-dependents are warm and affectionate.

What are the differences between ability and cognitive style? Furnham has noted the following.

> Whereas ability deals with how much and what, style refers more to how. Style refers to the way in which material is processed; ability refers to accuracy or the speed of the response. We may have a lot of or very little ability in a particular area, whereas style is bipolar. While we have abilities in a particular domain, our styles cut across domains.
>
> (Furnham, 1995, p.399)

3.4.3   Explanatory Style

Explanatory or attributional style is a characteristic way of responding to or dealing with events, and as such could be construed as a cognitive style. The study of attributions is important to psychologists, since attributions link the stimuli that we encounter to individual behaviour (Ross and Fletcher, 1985). Attributions therefore have implications for behaviour.

Individuals with a negative attributional style tend to explain negative events (such as examination failure) in terms of stable, internal and global causes. Thus an individual with a negative attributional style might argue that he or she failed an examination because of a lack of intelligence. There is very little the person can do about this, and they would very often believe that they were likely to fail again some time in the future. If we believe that we are unintelligent and doomed to failure, we are less likely to study for an examination and more likely to be unsuccessful.

Peterson and Barrett (1987) found support for these ideas among a small sample of 87 first-year university students. Even after controlling for possible confounding factors, such as depression, gender of respondent, and scholastic aptitude test, those who made internal, stable and global attributions for negative events tended to have significantly lower grade-point average scores. Subjects with higher grades tended to make internal, stable and global attributions for positive events. Thus those who succeed explain their success in terms of their ability. There appear to be some exceptions to these general principles (e.g. Chapman and Lawes, 1984). Low-achieving individuals have been found to attribute success to external causes, whilst some sex differences have also been noted, with females more likely than males to make external attributions for success and failure.

Of importance from our perspective is the suggestion that attributional style is linked to personality. Rim (1991) found that emotionally unstable women as well as extraverted women were more likely to make internal attributions for adverse events than emotionally stable or introverted women, although this was not the case for men. Lie (or dissimulation) scores were related to a composite index of negative attributional style as well as negative attributional style for affiliative conditions among UK salesmen, but not among male volunteers (Corr and Gray, 1995).

This finding in itself is quite curious, as a positive attributional style has been found to be related to sales productivity in the UK. In addition, it should be noted that the observed correlations were modest (the highest value was 0.251), suggesting that negative attributional style 'is not totally saturated with Lie score variance' (Corr and Gray, 1995, p.435).

3.5 A NOTE ON PERSONALITY AND INTELLIGENCE

Throughout this chapter it has become clear that personality factors are broadly implicated in learning and cognitive styles, and in performance of various kinds. In fact, this interlinking is rather more substantial, with some theorists – such as Cattell in the 1940s – suggesting that intelligence should be regarded as a component of a broader personality taxonomy. Even among contemporary theorists (e.g. Goldberg) there is some debate as to whether the fifth factor of the Big Five might not perhaps be one labelled 'intellect' (John, 1990). Thus it would appear that personality and intellectual functioning of whatever kind are closely connected according to some points of view. Indeed, it was Anastasi who remarked in her now classic text that:

> Personality and aptitudes cannot be kept apart. An individual's performance on an aptitude test, as well as his or her performance in school, on the job, or in any other context, is influenced by his or her achievement drive, persistence, value system, freedom from handicapping emotional problems, and other characteristics traditionally classified under the heading of 'personality'.
>
> (Anastasi, 1988, p.368)

As Anastasi (1988) notes, personality on its own is not entirely capable of predicting intellectual functioning, but it is a useful aid to understanding why individuals perform as they do on intelligence test measures. In addition, the influence is mutual. Thus individuals who perform at a high level are likely to be pleased with this outcome, which is in turn likely to enhance feelings of self-worth and self-esteem.

In an interesting recent development, Goff and Ackerman (1992) proposed that personality factors can predict 'typical intellectual performance', or one's 'intellectual engagement', in contrast to maximum intellectual performance. In other words, not only is it possible to predict actual outcomes (e.g. grade-point average, graduation rates, etc.), but one can also predict one's intellectual approach to a problem or the strategies that one is likely to use, and they suggest that intellectual abilities are dependent on a wide range of motivational, situational and dispositional factors. In their view, typical intellectual engagement consists of nine related personality constructs including, for example, hard work, absorption, introverted intellectual engagement, etc. (see Table 3.5 for details). These domains were found to link with the NEO personality factors as follows:

- *openness to experience*: associated with an interest in the arts and humanities, introverted intellectual engagement and extraverted intellectual engagement;
- *conscientiousness*: tends to be associated with hard work and perfectionism.

In conclusion, there are close associations between personality, learning and performance as measured in a variety of ways, including success at laboratory tasks, learning styles, ability and academic performance. What is clear is that individual differences have an important contribution to make to our understanding of human performance.

3.6 CONCLUSION

It is clear that personality factors play an important role in determining just how individuals learn new material, as well as their performance in a variety of tasks. For example, laboratory research has shown how extraversion affects one's performance on vigilance tasks and how one's level of anxiety is related to learning and performance. Moreover, these effects are not always as straightforward as they first appear. Type of task has an influence on outcome, as does whether one is a neurotic extravert or a neurotic introvert.

This chapter has also shown how recent research is increasingly beginning to adopt the Big Five personality taxonomy, particularly with respect to academic performance. The most consistent predictor of both academic performance and discipline choice would undoubtedly seem to be conscientiousness. Thus individuals with high levels of conscientiousness tend to study law, economics and the natural sciences, whilst low conscientiousness is

Table 3.5 Proposed dimensions of typical intellectual engagement

Dimension	Description
Typical intellectual engagement	Enjoys solving life's puzzles
Hard work	Prefers hard jobs to easy ones
Perfectionism	Seeks work requiring conscientious and exacting skills
Openness	Enjoys new untried activities
Absorption	Becomes oblivious to others when engaged in a task
Distractibility	Other activities are noticed when busy with tedious work
Extraverted intellectual engagement	Enjoys discussing things for long periods
Introverted intellectual engagement	Enjoys analysing own thoughts and emotions
Energy	Never too tired for a task, e.g. reading
Interest in arts and humanities	For example, poetry
Interest in sciences	Enjoys science
Interest in social science	For example, social unrest
Interest in technology	For example, shows an interest in technical problems

Adapted from Goff, M. and Ackerman, P. (1992) Personality – intelligence relations: assessment of typical intellectual engagement. *Journal of Educational Psychology* **84**, 540–1.

characteristic of history, psychology and education majors. Conscientiousness has also been linked to motivation to succeed in examinations. Future research needs to explore more thoroughly how the different facets of conscientiousness relate to academic and job performance.

Finally, a much neglected area concerns cross-cultural research on personality and performance. Given the slight variations that exist across cultures in the descriptions that are applied to the different personality domains, it might be wise to assess the role played by some of these personality domains in performance in non-western cultures.

REFERENCES

Aladjalova, N. and Arnold, O. (1991) The role of the slow controlling system of the brain in regulation of vigilance in introverts and extraverts: some effects of sleep deprivation. *Soviet Journal of Psychology* 12, 58–68.

Anastasi, A. (1988) *Psychological testing*, 6th edn. New York: Macmillan.

Anthony, W. (1973) The development of extraversion, of ability and the relation between them. *British Journal of Educational Psychology* **43**, 223–7.

Argyle, M. (1994) *The psychology of social class*. London: Routledge.

Boekaerts, M. (1996) Personality and the psychology of learning. *European Journal of Personality* **10**, 377–404.

Braden, J. (1995) Intelligence and personality in school and educational psychology. In Saklofske, D. and Zeidner, M. (eds), *International Handbook of Personality and Intelligence*. New York: Plenum Press, 621–50.

Brebner, J. and Cooper, C. (1985) A proposed unified model of extraversion. In Spence, J. and Izard, C. (eds), *Motivation, emotion and personality*. Amsterdam: Elsevier, 219–29.

Byrne, D.G. and Byrne, A. (1990) Adolescent personality, school type and educational outcomes: an examination of sex differences. In Heaven P. and Callan, V. (eds), *Adolescence: an Australian perspective*. Sydney: Harcourt Brace Jovanovich, 98–115.

Campbell, J. and Hawley, C. (1982) Study habits and Eysenck's theory of extraversion–introversion. *Journal of Research in Personality* **16**, 139–46.

Chapman, J. and Lawes, M. (1984) Consistency of causal attributions for expected and actual examination outcome: a study of the expectancy confirmation and egotism models. *British Journal of Educational Psychology* **54**, 177–88.

Child, D. (1989) The relationship between introversion–extraversion, neuroticism and performance in school examinations. *British Journal of Educational Psychology* **34**, 178–96.

Corr, P. and Gray, J. (1995) Relationship between attributional style and Lie scores in an occupational sample motivated to fake good. *Personality and Individual Differences* **18**, 433–5.

Crozier, W.R. (1997) *Individual learners: personality differences in education*. London: Routledge.

De Fruyt, F. and Mervielde, I. (1996) Personality and interests as predictors of educational streaming and achievement. *European Journal of Personality* **10**, 405–25.

De Raad, B. and Schouwenburg, H. (1996) Personality in learning and education: a review. *European Journal of Personality* **10**, 303–36.

Dorsey, M. and Jackson, A. (1995) Afro-American students' perceptions of factors affecting academic performance at a predominantly white school. *Western Journal of Black Studies* **19**, 189–95.

Drummond, R. and Stoddard, A. (1992) Learning style and personality type. *Perceptual and Motor Skills* **75**, 99–104.

Entwistle, N. (1972) Personality and academic attainment. *British Journal of Educational Psychology* **42**, 137–51.

Eysenck, H. (1967) *The biological basis of personality*. Springfield, IL: Charles C. Thomas.

Eysenck, H. (1971) Relation between intelligence and personality. *Perceptual and Motor Skills* **32**, 637–8.

Eysenck, H. and Eysenck, M. (1985) *Personality and individual differences: a natural science approach*. New York: Plenum.

Eysenck, H. and Gudjonsson, G. (1989) *The causes and cures of criminality*. New York: Plenum Press.

Eysenck, M. (1976) Extraversion, verbal learning and memory. *Psychological Bulletin* 83, 75–90.

Eysenck, M. (1981) Learning, memory, and personality. In Eysenck, H.J. (ed.), *A model for personality*. New York: Springer-Verlag.

Eysenck, M. (1988) Individual differences, arousal, and monotonous work. In Leonard, J. (ed.), *Vigilance: methods, models and regulation*. Frankfurt: Peter Lang, 111–18.

Ferrari, J. and Parker, J. (1992) High-school achievement, self-efficacy, and locus of control as predictors of freshman academic outcomes. *Psychological Reports* 71, 515–18.

Foon, A. (1988) The relationship between school type and adolescent self-esteem, attributional styles, and affiliation needs: implications for educational outcome. *British Journal of Educational Psychology* 58, 44–54.

Fry, P. and Coe, K. (1980) Achievement performance of internally and externally oriented black and white high-school students under conditions of competition and co-operation expectancies. *British Journal of Educational Psychology* 50, 162–7.

Furnham, A. (1992) Personality and learning style: a study of three instruments. *Personality and Individual Differences* 13, 429–38.

Furnham, A. (1995) The relationship of personality and intelligence to cognitive learning style and achievement. In Saklofske, D. and Zeidner, M. (eds), *International handbook of personality and intelligence*. New York: Plenum, 397–413.

Furnham, A. and Mitchell, J. (1991) Personality, needs, social skills and academic achievement: a longitudinal study. *Personality and Individual Differences* 12, 1067–73.

Furnham, A. and Medhurst, S. (1995) Personality correlates of academic seminar behaviour: a study of four instruments. *Personality and Individual Differences* 19, 197–208.

Furnham, A. and Bradley, A. (1997) Music while you work: the differential distraction of background music on the cognitive test performance of introverts and extraverts. *Applied Cognitive Psychology* 11, 445–55.

Furnham, A., Gunter, B. and Peterson, E. (1994) Television distraction and the performance of introverts and extraverts. *Applied Cognitive Psychology* 8, 705–11.

Gale, A. and Edwards, J. (1986) Individual differences. In Coles, M., Donchin, E. and Porges, S. (eds), *Psychophysiology: systems, processes and applications*. New York: Guilford Press, 431–507.

Gale, A. and Eysenck, M. (1992) *Handbook of individual differences: biological perspectives*. Chichester: Wiley.

Gallagher, D. (1996) Personality, coping, and objective outcomes: extraversion, neuroticism, coping styles and academic performance. *Personality and Individual Differences* 21, 421–9.

Goff, M. and Ackerman, P. (1992) Personality–intelligence relations: assessment of typical intellectual engagement. *Journal of Educational Psychology* 84, 537–52.

Goh, D. and Moore, C. (1978) Personality and academic achievement in three educational levels. *Psychological Reports* 43, 71–9.

Gray, J. (1981) A critique of Eysenck's theory of personality. In Eysenck, H. (ed.), *A Model for Personality*. Berlin: Springer Verlag, 246–76.

Green, D., Snell, J. and Parimanath, A. (1990) Learning styles in assessment of students. *Perceptual and Motor Skills* 70, 363–9.

Grigorenko, E. and Sternberg, R. (1995) Thinking styles. In Saklofske, D. and Zeidner, M. (eds), *International handbook of personality and intelligence*. New York: Plenum, 205–29.

Heaven, P. (1990) Attitudinal and personality correlates of achievement motivation among high-school students. *Personality and Individual Differences* 11, 705–10.

Honey, P. and Mumford, A. (1992) *The manual of learning styles*. Maidenhead: Peter Honey.

Howarth, E. and Eysenck, H. (1968) Extraversion, arousal, and paired-associate recall. *Journal of Experimental Research in Personality* 3, 114–16.

Humphreys, M. and Revelle, W. (1984) Personality, motivation, and performance: a theory of the relationship between individual differences and information processing. *Psychological Review* 91, 153–84.

Jackson, C. and Lawty-Jones, M. (1996) Explaining the overlap between personality and learning style. *Personality and Individual Differences* 20, 293–300.

Jindal, S. and Panda, S. (1982) A correlation study of achievement motivation, anxiety, neuroticism and extraversion of school-going adolescents. *Journal of Psychological Researches* 26, 110–14.

John, O. (1990) The 'Big Five' factor taxonomy: dimensions of personality in the natural language and in questionnaires. In Pervin, L. (ed.), *Handbook of personality theory and research*. New York: Guildford, 66–100.

Jones, J. (1990) Outcomes of girls' schooling: unravelling some social differences. *Australian Journal of Education* 34, 153–67.

Kline, P. and Gale, A. (1971) Extraversion, neuroticism and performance in a psychology examination. *British Journal of Educational Psychology* 41, 90–4.

Koelega, H. (1992) Extraversion and vigilance performance: 30 years of inconsistencies. *Psychological Bulletin* 112, 239–58.

Kolb, D. (1976) *Learning Style Inventory: technical manual*. Boston, MA: McBer.

Kolb, D. (1984) *Experimental learning*. Englewood Cliffs, NJ: Prentice-Hall.

Kossowska, M. and Necka, E. (1994) Do it your own way: cognitive strategies, intelligence, and personality. *Personality and Individual Differences* 16, 33–46.

Markham, R. and Darke, S. (1991) The effects of anxiety on verbal and spatial task performance. *Australian Journal of Psychology* 43, 107–11.

Matthews, G., Davies, D. and Lees, J. (1990) Arousal, extraversion, and individual differences in resource availability. *Journal of Personality and Social Psychology* 59, 150–68.

Messick, S. (1984) The nature of cognitive styles: problems and promise in educational practice. *Educational Psychologist* 19, 59–74.

Morgenstern, S., Hodgson, R. and Law, L. (1974) Work efficiency and personality. *Ergonomics* 17, 211–20.

Paspalanov, I. (1984) The relation of nAch to extraversion, emotional instability and level of anxiety in people of different social status and success. *Personality and Individual Differences* 5, 383–8.

Peterson, C. and Barrett, L. (1987) Explanatory style and academic performance among university freshmen. *Journal of Personality and Social Psychology* 53, 603–7.

Philbin, M., Meier, E., Huffman, S. and Boverie, P. (1995) A survey of gender and learning styles. *Sex Roles* 32, 485–94.

Prociuk, T. and Breen, L. (1974) Locus of control, study habits and attitudes and college academic performance. *Journal of Psychology* 88, 91–5.

Riding, R. and Douglas, (1993) The effect of cognitive style and mode of presentation on learning performance. *British Journal of Educational Psychology* **63**, 297–307.

Riding, R. and Wigley, S. (1997) The relationship between cognitive style and personality in further education students. *Personality and Individual Differences* **23**, 379–89.

Riding, R., Burton, D., Rees, G. and Sharratt, M. (1995) Cognitive style and personality in 12-year-old children. *British Journal of Educational Psychology* **65**, 113–24.

Rim, Y. (1991) Personality and attributional styles. *Personality and Individual Differences, 12,* 95–6.

Ross, M. and Fletcher, G. (1985) Attribution and social perception. In Lindzey, G. and Aronson, E. (eds), *Handbook of Social Psychology. Vol. 2.* New York: Random House, 73–122.

Rothstein, M., Paunonen, S., Rush, J. and King, G. (1994) Personality and cognitive ability predictors of performance in graduate business school. *Journal of Educational Psychology* **86**, 516–30.

Scott, W. and Scott, R. (1989) Family correlates of high-school adjustment: a cross-cultural study. *Australian Journal of Psychology* **41**, 269–84.

Sein, M. and Robey, D. (1991) Learning style and the efficacy of computer training methods. *Perceptual and Motor Skills* **72**, 243–8.

Spence, J. and Spence, K. (1966) The motivational components of manifest anxiety: drive and drive stimuli. In Spielberger, C.D. (ed.), *Anxiety and behavior.* London: Academic Press, 291–326.

Spielberger, C. (1966) The effects of anxiety on complex learning and academic achievement. In Spielberger, C.D. (ed.), *Anxiety and behaviour.* New York: Academic Press, 3–20.

Tullett, A. and Davies, G. (1997) Cognitive style and affect: a comparison of the Kirton adaption-innovation and Schutz's fundamental interpersonal relations orientation-behaviour inventories (KAI and FIRO-B). *Personality and Individual Differences* **23**, 479–85.

Wolfe, R. and Johnson, S. (1995) Personality as a predictor of college performance. *Educational and Psychological Measurement* **55**, 177–85.

4

Personality and Ideology

4.1 INTRODUCTION

It is self-evident that people differ markedly in the attitudes which they hold, and in their support for different ideologies, be they political, religious or philosophical. Even within the same family, it is acknowledged that members differ in their levels of religiosity, their support for different political parties and movements, their racial attitudes, and so forth. Further personality and individual difference factors (traits) are important in predicting one's ideological stance with respect to such issues as religion and politics. Such a view stands in contrast to social psychological and political theories that underplay or even ignore individual differences in particular personality traits.

The study of ideology by psychologists has a long and illustrious history. It is well known, for example, that Freud theorised about the role of religion in human existence, whilst other notable psychologists such as William James, G. Stanley Hall and Carl Jung also speculated about the psychological basis of religious beliefs (Spilka *et al.*, 1985). Likewise, psychologists have for many years been involved in attempting to understand political ideology, publishing their ideas in books that had a considerable impact on the field (e.g. Lasswell, 1930; Adorno *et al.*, 1950; Eysenck, 1954; Knutson, 1973). Indeed, there are a number of individual difference measures, such as the Right-Wing Authoritarianism Scale, that tap into ideological beliefs and have trait-like characteristics (Altemeyer, 1988).

Ideology refers to 'the shared understanding of the purpose and meaning of life' (Stone and Schaffner, 1988, p.28), whilst others see it as the 'representations and constructions of the world (which) serve to legitimate, maintain and reproduce the existing institutional arrangements' (Augoustinos and Walker, 1995, p.288). Ideology is an elusive concept and difficult to measure. It can be viewed from a number of different perspectives. One way to see ideology is as *system justification* (Augoustinos and Walker, 1995) – that is, to view it as a means to an end, as a way of asserting control and dominance over the populace. Ideology can also be viewed as consisting of religious views or political *belief systems* as evidenced by the attitudes and values of different political parties or groups.

This is the departure point of the present chapter. It will review work that examines the links between personality and two major forms of ideology, namely religious beliefs and politics. The latter section will discuss three constructs: tough-mindedness, authoritarianism and social dominance orientation. It is perhaps authoritarianism that has had the greatest impact on the work of psychologists. Finally, the chapter will end with a brief overview of the links between individual differences and voting intention, prejudice and social attitudes.

4.2 PERSONALITY AND RELIGIOUS IDEOLOGY

What does it mean to be religious? Argyle and Beit-Hallahmi (1975, p.1) define religion as 'a system of beliefs in a divine or superhuman power, and practices of worship or other rituals directed towards such a power'. Such beliefs and rituals can be manifested in many different ways, ranging from more traditional membership of an established church, saying private prayers or attending communal worship, to membership of far more informal groups.

It is clear from the above definition that being religious encompasses attitudes, beliefs and behaviour. It is therefore not surprising that psychologists since Freud have pondered whether religious beliefs can be explained in terms of psychological principles. As has already been made clear by Spilka *et al.*, religious experience is an important part of daily human life for many individuals – an important part of what can be referred to as 'psychological reality' (Spilka *et al.*, 1985, p.2). The practice of religion is intimately connected to human values, feelings, experiences and behaviours. This is probably true of the great monotheistic religions – Christianity, Islam and Judaism – as well as of other major (and minor) faiths.

For some psychologists, religion is viewed as a device which provides the individual with meaning for his or her daily life, as well as feelings of control and protection from anxiety (Argyle and Beit-Hallahmi, 1975; Spilka *et al.*, 1985). There is much conjecture in the literature that religion acts as a bulwark against the fear of death and the unknown, or as a buffer in times of stress. Religion, so it is argued, provides hope to the hopeless and strength to the fearful. Indeed, Freud suggested that religion functions to protect one from three different forms of anxiety, namely reality anxiety, moral anxiety and neurotic anxiety (Spilka *et al.*, 1985), and he described religion as a 'universal obsessional neurosis' (Pfeifer and Waelty, 1995) (see the work reported below on the links between neuroticism and religiosity).

Many religions serve to offer grand theories or explanations for some of the most fundamental questions of life, particularly the afterlife. Thus religion is particularly attractive to those seeking answers or certainty in a capricious world. It can provide a powerful sense of security as well as a sense of control. Instead of being anxious about what tomorrow may bring, believers can 'leave it to God'. Moral anxiety, Freud's second component, refers to one's feelings of guilt. The Judaeo-Christian point of view is that God is all-powerful and all-loving, but is also a jealous God. When people do wrong, or commit a sin, many of them feel guilty for having strayed from the narrow path. By turning to religion they can seek forgiveness and a cleansing of the soul. In this way they also seek to avoid God's wrath. Closely linked to these feelings of guilt is Freud's third component, namely neurotic anxiety.

Religion, it is argued, helps the individual cope with inner flaws and weaknesses (Spilka *et al.*, 1985), but this is also likely to lead to a religion that is rather inflexible and rigid. As Spilka *et al.* have stated, 'Too often a rigid, unbending, tyrannical faith results. Images of a threatening, demanding, punitive God to suppress unacceptable desires are also a common feature of such neurotically based religion' (Spilka *et al.*, 1985, p.14).

Freud also sought to explain religious behaviours in terms of father-projection (Argyle and Beit-Hallahmi, 1975). He saw a connection between one's earthly father and God (a divine or heavenly father) and one's views of one's earthly father thus determining to some extent one's attitudes toward religion. This seems to fit with the views of others (Spilka *et al.*, 1985) who argue that religiosity is nothing more than the manifestation of infantile gestures. Freud argued that religiosity is linked to the Oedipus complex, with family socialisation being an important feature in explaining religious beliefs. He therefore suggested that God is nothing more than an exalted father figure (Argyle and Beit-Hallahmi, 1975).

Religion may also satisfy a cognitive need (Argyle and Beit-Hallahmi, 1975; Spilka *et al.*, 1985). Religious beliefs order one's life by adding a degree of coherence, thereby accounting for a wide range of behaviours and phenomena. Religions are often behaviourally prescriptive, which makes the behaviour of religious people predictable, stable and consistent. Social psychologists (e.g. Festinger, 1957; Heider, 1958) have demonstrated that individuals have a need for cognitive consistency. Consequently, one adopts beliefs (either religious or not) that fit one's other beliefs, values and behaviours. However, it is worth noting that this approach does not adequately explain all religious behaviours, e.g. church membership or religious ritual (Argyle and Beit-Hallahmi, 1975).

Ryan *et al.* (1993) have recently suggested that individuals internalise religion in one of two ways, namely by identification or internalisation, and that both of these have implications for one's mental health. Identification refers to the fact that one adopts religious values as one's own, while internalisation (introjection) refers to the fact that religious values are only partially assimilated, and play a much more important *regulatory* role in one's life.

Based on a series of studies using different samples, support for these ideas has been obtained. Ryan *et al.* (1993) concluded that identification, but not introjection, is associated with positive mental health.

4.2.1 Development of Religious Beliefs

Fowler (1981) has proposed a stage theory of the development of faith (see Table 4.1), ranging from undifferentiated faith in infancy to Stage 6 faith – so-called universalising faith – as epitomised by people such as Mother Teresa of Calcutta, Gandhi, and others. Although these stages are noteworthy, so far as can be established they have not given rise to empirical research within mainstream personality and social psychology. Although this view is only speculative at present, it is quite likely that extraverts may function at a different stage of religious development to hostile, aggressive or neurotic individuals.

Vianello (1991) examined the relationship between religious beliefs and personality of 12- to 14-year-olds, and found evidence that younger adolescents assimilate religious ideas in a passive and uncritical way, whilst older adolescents are much more critical of religious dogma – that is, their religion is much more personalised than it is for younger people. Vianello (1991) found that, among 12-year-olds, 'search for security' was significantly related to endorsement of such views as 'God the judge', 'God the protector', and a 'personalized relationship with God'. However, among the older teenagers a critical attitude towards God was significantly associated with a capacity for synthesis, and for realistic, fertile and mature intelligence.

In a rare psychological study, Baird (1990) tracked college graduates for 20 years, assessing changes in the extent to which they endorsed religious values and beliefs. The values were measured with the aid of the Allport-Vernon-Lindzey (AVL) scale of values, as well as the religious orientation scale of the Omnibus Personality Inventory. Baird (1990) found that endorsement of religious values as measured by the AVL tended to decline over time, whilst there were also changes in the scores on the religious orientation measure. Respondents tended to become more liberal in their views over time, as evidenced by increasing rejection of fundamental and literal beliefs. Moreover, there was an increase in beliefs about 'general spirituality', with an accompanying general 'philosophical orientation' to life (Baird, 1990, p.481). Furthermore, those graduates who moved away from the region served by their college were found to be more liberal after 20 years than other students. Unfortunately, Baird (1990) drew few conclusions from his findings, but it does appear that college education and the later opportunities which this brings may serve to challenge the original religious ideas of individuals. However, it is not possible to rule out other influences on these religious beliefs, such as the ageing process and other life experiences.

Table 4.1 Stages of religious development

Stage	Characteristics
Undifferentiated faith (infancy)	This is a pre-stage. Caregivers engender trust, courage, hope and love in the individual
Stage 1: Intuitive-projective faith (2–6 years)	Influenced by the faith of others. A fantasy period where values are shaped by moods and examples of others. Imagination is very active and a good seed-bed for religious growth and development
Stage 2: Mythic-literal faith (schoolchild)	Child is able to distinguish fact from fantasy. Begins to adopt myths and beliefs of the wider community
Stage 3: Synthetic-conventional faith (puberty–adolescence)	Increasingly influenced by peers and media. Faith needs to fit into a more complex experience of the world, and forms the basis of a personal identity and value system. Clashes with authority figures are increasingly likely
Stage 4: Individuative-reflective faith (adult)	One adopts a unique identity not closely tied to significant others, and one develops an executive ego. Religious symbols can change their meaning for the individual
Stage 5: Conjunctive faith (midlife)	Goes beyond clear identities of Stage 4 and integrates conscious with unconscious. Re-integrates one's past. It seeks to unify paradoxes in experience and also recognizes limitations of group's symbols
Stage 6: Universalising faith (a rare experience)	These individuals (e.g. Gandhi, Mother Teresa, Martin Luther King) symbolise the human spirit. They can change the world for the better, but often have to suffer or even die for that

Source of information: Fowler, J.W. (1981) *Stages of faith: the psychology of human development and the quest for meaning.* San Francisco, CA: Harper & Row.

4.2.2 The Trait Perspective

More recently, there has been a resurgence of interest in the role of personality traits in religious life. This is not entirely surprising, given the view expressed earlier that for some individuals religion may have a neurotic basis. Several writers have adopted a trait perspective, with some locating religious beliefs within Eysenck's three-dimensional model of personality. For instance, one early view was that religiosity is closely linked to neuroticism, the argument being that neurotics are much more likely to be anxious, and hence to turn more easily to religion. Indeed, Bagley *et al.* (1979) have suggested that neurotic introverts are likely to have the highest religiosity scores, followed by neurotic extraverts, stable introverts and stable extraverts.

This suggestion is based on the view that introverts condition more easily than do extraverts. Moreover, Eysenck (Eysenck and Eysenck, 1985) has argued that neurotic introverts are more susceptible to conditioned states of anxiety than are neurotic extraverts, because extraverts have lower levels of arousal. It is suggested that neuroticism acts as an amplifying device because of its drive properties. This drive tends to multiply with habit, and certain behaviours (such as religious ones) are likely to be repeated if the individual scores high on the neuroticism dimension.

A more contemporaneous view suggests that low psychoticism (that is, tender-mindedness) rather than neuroticism or extraversion may be related to religious beliefs. This is due to the fact that impulsiveness items which once comprised the extraversion scale are now located within the psychoticism dimension (Francis and Pearson, 1985). Not surprisingly, this has changed the extent to which the major personality dimensions are related to different social attitudes and behaviours. As Francis (1992a, p.646) puts it, conditionability has now 'switched allegiance' from extraversion to psychoticism.

Recent empirical support for the view that religiosity is linked to either extraversion or neuroticism is limited. Several studies examining the links between neuroticism, extraversion and Eysenckian psychoticism have concluded that low psychoticism, not neuroticism, is linked to religiosity. In an earlier study, for example, Francis *et al.* (1983) assessed the links between personality and religiosity among 1715 English schoolchildren aged between 11 and 17 years. They noted that religiosity scores decreased across the age range, and that girls tended to be more religious than boys. However, no significant links between neuroticism and religiosity were observed. Instead, they concluded that introverts of different age groups are more religious than extraverts. These views were later qualified (Francis and Pearson, 1988), the authors concluding that due to changes in the operationalisation of (Eysenckian) extraversion, it is no longer associated with religiosity.

A later study of a US adult sample (Lewis and Maltby, 1995) examined the relationships between personality and attitudes towards Christianity, and concluded that low psychoticism, but not neuroticism or extraversion, were related to religious attitudes (Westman and Brackney, 1990). Recently, Wilde and Joseph (1997) also found that high P scores were significantly negatively related to attitudes to religion among Moslem students. No significant correlations were observed for N and E (see Box 4.1). Likewise, psychoticism has also been found to be implicated in religious *values*, such that those who endorse religious values and principles are less likely to be high P scorers (Heaven, 1990a).

Caird (1987) adopted a somewhat different approach to that followed by Francis *et al.* (1983). Rather than asking subjects to report their attitudes to religion, Caird (1987) followed the experiential approach by asking 115 undergraduate respondents to report their mystical experiences, in addition to completing the Eysenck Personality Questionnaire. There were no significant correlations between mystical experience and personality dimensions. Even after controlling for sex and age, none of the predictor variables were able to predict significantly scores on the mysticism measure.

What is it about the Eysenckian psychoticism (tough-mindedness) dimension that explains its negative relationship with measures of religious attitudes? The tough-minded personality can be described as aggressive, cold, impersonal, antisocial, unempathic and impulsive (Eysenck and Eysenck, 1985). Such individuals are also likely to be opposed to people in positions of authority, and to undervalue people in general. They favour impersonal sex, and have a predilection for movies with a high violence and horror content. They also have rather unusual artistic taste (Eysenck and Eysenck, 1976). At the same time, it is highly likely that high P scorers or those who score high on

BOX 4.1

Recently, Wilde and Joseph (1997) found that the personality correlates of attitudes toward Islam mirrored those of attitudes toward Christianity. That is, positive religious attitudes were significantly negatively related to Eysenck's P dimension. The results are based on the responses of 50 Moslem students attending the University of Essex. Religious attitudes were measured with the aid of the following inventory.

1. I find it inspiring to read the Qu'ran
2. Allah helps me
3. Saying my prayers helps me a lot
4. Islam helps me to lead a better life
5. I like to learn about Allah very much
6. I believe that Allah helps people
7. The five prayers help me a lot
8. The supplication (dua) helps me
9. I think the Qu'ran is relevant and applicable to modern-day living
10. I believe that Allah listens to prayers
11. Mohammed (peace be upon him) provides a good code of conduct for me
12. I pray five times a day
13. I fast the whole month of Ramadan
14. I observe my daily prayers in the Mosque

Source: Wilde, A. and Joseph, S. (1997) Religiosity and personality in a Moslem context. *Personality and Individual Differences* **23**, 899–900 (reprinted with permission).

openness to experience may be attracted to cults, or to other forms of worship.

The general consensus that high P scores are associated with low scores on measures of religious attitude is therefore not unexpected, and is consistent with what we already know about these individuals. For example, we know that they tend to be solitary types who are unlikely to endorse good interpersonal relationships and general politeness. They do not appear to be concerned with personal growth and inner harmony, nor do they care about a positive orientation to other people. They also lack social skills.

Pfeifer and Waelty (1995) recently assessed the possibility that psychopathology may predict religious commitment. Their sample consisted of a group of 44 psychiatric patients (that is, depressed and anxious individuals) as well as a matched control group. There were no significant differences in neuroticism between those who scored high and low on religious commitment, a finding which pertained to both the patient and non-patient groups. Moreover, general life satisfaction was positively related to religiosity in the patient group. A childhood fear of God was found *not* to be significantly related to neuroticism in the patient group, leading the authors to conclude that it is not religious commitment, but rather underlying psychopathology that explains neuroticism in a sample of religious patients.

Not surprisingly, describing oneself as religious is associated with a range of other attitudes, specifically beliefs about death. Thus being more religious is associated with not being afraid of death, and of viewing death as meaningful and quite natural. Religiosity is also associated with viewing death as a portal rather than as a wall (Westman and Brackney, 1990).

So far we have examined the personality characteristics of nominal believers. In the following section we shall examine the personality traits of committed churchgoers. One of the most active researchers in this area has been Francis who examined the personality profiles of student and adult church attenders (Francis, 1991a; Francis and Pearson, 1993), Anglican ordinands (Francis, 1991b) and clergy (Francis, 1992b). In the first study, over 800 regular student churchgoers in Cambridge completed the Eysenck Personality Questionnaire (Francis, 1991a). Table 4.2 shows the mean scores for this group on each of the personality dimensions, as well as normative data for other students and people aged 20–29 years of age. It is clear that male student churchgoers were significantly less extraverted than other groups of males. Male student churchgoers also had significantly lower scores on the P scale compared to the other male groups, as well as significantly lower Lie scale (social desirability) scores than the 20–29 years age group. However, there were no significant differences between the female groups on extraversion, psychoticism and neuroticism. Francis and Pearson therefore concluded that male churchgoers are much more likely than other males to have a 'feminine' personality profile, and that being religious may be more congruous for men with a 'feminine outlook' (Francis and Pearson, 1993, p.377).

Table 4.2 Mean personality scores for student churchgoers

Personality variable	Student churchgoers		Student norms		20–29 years age norms		t
	Mean	SD	Mean	SD	Mean	SD	
Male							
Extraversion	11.87	4.88	13.80	4.24	13.72	4.79	− 5.21*
Neuroticism	9.48	5.14	9.93	5.08	9.81	5.09	− 1.11*
Psychoticism	3.83	2.57	4.84	3.33	4.19	3.26	− 4.54*
Lie scale	5.18	3.02	—	—	6.50	3.88	− 6.40*
Female							
Extraversion	13.07	4.54	13.49	4.74	12.89	4.70	− 1.05
Neuroticism	11.16	4.74	12.16	5.85	12.87	4.99	− 2.19
Psychoticism	3.09	2.69	3.02	2.54	2.79	2.41	0.30
Lie scale	5.85	3.42	—	—	7.17	3.85	− 5.71*

*p < 0.01

Source: Reprinted from *Personality and Individual Differences*, **15**, Francis, L.J. and Pearson, P.R., The Personality characteristics of student churchgoers, Page No's. 373–80, Copyright (1993), with permission from Elsevier Science.

In another study using the Eysenck Personality Questionnaire, Francis (1991b) examined the personality profiles of 252 Anglican ordinands in England. The sample consisted of 155 men and 97 women of a wide age range. Male ordinands were significantly less extraverted than a normative group, and also scored significantly lower on the Lie scale. By contrast, female ordinands, when compared with the published norms, were significantly more extraverted and emotionally stable. They also tended to have elevated psychoticism scores, but lower scores on the Lie scale.

According to Francis (1991b), these results have several important practical implications for those entering the active ministry. For example, it is argued that Anglican priests and deacons appear to be quite different in their personality functioning from their parishioners, which is likely to lead to possible relationship problems between priests and those in their care. It is also clear that there are important differences between male and female clergy. This is not surprising given that female (Anglican) clergy are still fighting for general acceptance within the priesthood (Francis, 1991b). Moreover, it is apparent that male ordinands show a characteristically 'feminine' personality profile, while female ordinands display one that is more traditionally 'male' (for example, they are emotionally stable, score relatively high on the psychoticism measure, and have relatively high extraversion scores). Francis (1991b) suggests that this is problematical for the day-to-day functioning of the church in view of the particular roles that women have traditionally played within the church – that is, roles of subservience and subordination.

In further research, Francis (1992b) examined the relationships between personality and attitudes to religion among 112 clergy, who were representative of a wide age range and came from different Christian denominations. There were 92 males and 20 females in the sample. After controlling for sex differences, Francis (1992b) observed significant negative associations between attitudes to Christianity and psychoticism and neuroticism. Thus among Christian clergy, emotional stability is associated with increased religious faith.

In summary, what can one conclude about the relationship between religion (beliefs and behaviours) and personality functioning? First, researchers who have adopted a trait perspective are almost all agreed that Eysenck's P dimension is an important predictor of attitudes to religion. By inference, openness to experience from the Costa and McCrae system should be most clearly related to religious beliefs and behaviours. Secondly, in an important recent review of over 200 publications in this area, Gartner *et al.* (1991) concluded that research studies have produced mixed results, and that it is important to consider just how the variables were measured. For example,

Table 4.3 Relationships between mental health and religiosity

A. Religion is positively associated with mental health
- Religiosity associated with longevity
- Negative relationship between religiosity and suicide ideation
- Negative relationship between religiosity and drug abuse
- Religious involvement related to low alcohol use
- Religious commitment related to low levels of delinquency
- Church attendance negatively related to divorce
- Positive relationship between religious commitment and well-being
- Religiosity related to low levels of depression

B. The relationship between religion and mental health is ambiguous
- Religiosity and anxiety
- Religiosity and psychosis
- Religiosity and self-esteem
- Religiosity and prejudice
- Religiosity and intelligence/education

C. Religion is associated with psychopathology
- Religious conservatism related to F-scale authoritarianism
- Religious orthodoxy related to dogmatism and intolerance of ambiguity
- Religiosity related to suggestibility
- Some religious experiences may be mediated by temporal lobe activity

Source of information: Gartner, J., Larson, D.B. and Allen, G.D. (1991) Religious commitment and mental health: a review of the empirical literature. *Journal of Psychology and Theology* **19**, 6–25.

they suggest that in those studies which found a link between religiosity and psychopathology, the authors typically used so-called 'soft' variables (Gartner *et al.*, 1991) – that is, variables measured with the aid of paper-and-pencil inventories (Francis, 1991a, b, 1992a). On the other hand, studies which found a positive relationship between religiosity and mental health functioning used much more overt behavioural indices. Finally, those studies which have yielded ambiguous results might be explained by the fact that the researchers operationalised their variables in different ways. Some of the main trends observed by Gartner *et al.* (1991) are highlighted in Table 4.3. In conclusion, no studies have examined the relationships between religiosity and the Big Five factors. It is likely that religiosity will be significantly related to conscientiousness and agreeableness. It is also likely that adherents of the more 'fringe' religions or sects might score high on openness to experience. These predictions need to be tested.

4.3 PERSONALITY AND POLITICAL IDEOLOGY

The role of personality and individual difference factors in explaining socio-political attitudes has been a long and important one. Some of the factors reviewed below, particularly authoritarianism, have had a major influence in shaping psychological research into the nature and correlates of ideologies. Altemeyer (1981, 1988), Billig (1978), Duckitt (1992), Eysenck (1954), Eysenck and Wilson (1978), and Stone and Schaffner (1988) have all conducted important research in this field.

The first and major part of this section of the chapter will discuss two important psychological constructs that are deemed to be related to ideology, namely tough-mindedness and authoritarianism. This will be followed by a review of social dominance orientation. Finally, other individual difference variables that have been found to be related to ideology will be briefly noted.

4.3.1 Tough-mindedness and Ideology

Tough-mindedness (P, Psychoticism) is worthy of inclusion in a review such as this because it is the only individual difference explanation of ideology that is situated within a formalised theory of personality, namely Eysenckian theory (Eysenck and Eysenck, 1975).

In criticising the traditional left–right or conservative–radical continuum of socio-political beliefs, Eysenck (Eysenck, 1954; Eysenck and Wilson, 1978), in his book entitled *The Psychology of Politics*, postulated that socio-political beliefs are best understood by resorting to a two-dimensional scheme. By proposing a second continuum, namely tough-mindedness–tender-mindedness, which is orthogonal to the first, the Eysenckian scheme differs markedly in its function from other factors that are said to explain ideology, such as dogmatism (Rokeach, 1960), authoritarianism (Adorno *et al.*, 1950; Altemeyer, 1981; see below), and the frustration–aggression hypothesis (Dollard *et al.*, 1939). Whereas the first factor represents general conservative ideology consisting of one's social and political beliefs, the second (Eysenckian) factor is essentially a personality dimension, thus providing the 'psychological basis' for one's attitudes (Eysenck and Wilson, 1978, p.306).

Eysenck's (1954) description of his second dimension appears to be heavily influenced by the ideas of the German author Jaensch (1938; cited in Eysenck and Wilson, 1978), who describes different ideological 'types'. The tough-minded person is akin to Jaensch's J-type, characterised as 'masculine' with a preference for contact sports (e.g. football rather than tennis). This type is also described as 'soldierly', with an 'instinctive understanding of social reality' (Eysenck and Wilson, 1978, p.4). By contrast, the tender-minded person is viewed as being more introverted. According to the theory it is impossible to be 'just conservative' or 'just radical'. Rather, one is conservative or radical in a tough-minded or a tender-minded way (Eysenck and Wilson, 1978). Thus one may hold tough-minded conservative or tender-minded conservative views, but these are qualitatively quite different from each other. Whereas the former may include attitudes such as 'Martians should be prohibited from owning property', the latter could include such attitudes as 'abolish Sunday observance' or 'abolish religion'. Brand explained the Eysenckian position thus: 'What the racist and the radical, the Fascist and the Communist, lacked in similarity of their opinions, they made up in intractability, insensitivity and impoliteness' (Brand, 1981, p.12).

There appears to be some empirical support for the Eysenckian thesis. In one study by Eysenck and a doctoral student conducted just after World War Two (Eysenck and Coulter, 1972), it was found that fascists and communists in Britain were indistinguishable on the tough-mindedness factor. Using the T scale as an indicator of tough-mindedness, both of these political groups were found to be more tough-minded than members of a control group. Fascists were also found to hold their views more emphatically than communists, with both of these groups being more emphatic than members of a control group.

An important development in Eysenckian personality theory occurred in the 1970s with the inclusion of a third dimension, labelled psychoticism (P), also referred to as tough-mindedness (Eysenck and Eysenck, 1976). It is postulated that the personality factor P is orthogonal to the social attitude domain, and that P coincides with tough-mindedness. Thus, according to the revised Eysenckian position, P and to a much lesser extent extraversion are the factors that sustain adherence to ideology. P is the 'militant' spirit that underpins a collection of socio-political attitudes and beliefs, transforming them into an ideology. As Eysenck explains:

> The psychological basis of this common property of ideologues we would see in tough-mindedness (as far as social attitudes are concerned), and in the personality variable P (and possibly E) as far as personality is concerned. ... That this largely inherited personality configuration makes people emphatic, dogmatic, authoritarian and Machiavellian in the way they express their attitudes, and in the choice of attitudes which they adopt.
>
> (Eysenck and Wilson, 1978, p.306)

Heaven and Connors (1988) investigated whether individuals' political allegiance can be differentiated on the basis of their scores on a variety of measures, including the P scale. The sample consisted of over 180 Australian undergraduates who completed the Eysenck P scale as a measure of tough-mindedness (see Eysenck and Eysenck, 1975), together with a behaviourally valid measure of authoritarianism (Rigby, 1984) and a balanced measure of authoritarian attitudes (Ray, 1979). The analyses showed that the rightist and centrist groups were more likely to manifest authoritarian attitudes than the left-wing group. The leftist group was more likely to engage in anti-authority behaviours than either the rightist or centrist groups. Finally, as Eysenck (1954) would have predicted, the mean scores on the P scale measuring tough-mindedness were found not to differ significantly, suggesting that tough-minded types are found on both sides of the political divide.

The Eysenckian attitudinal scheme has not escaped criticism, nor has Eysenck's labelling of his third dimension as 'psychoticism', and it may be for these reasons that research into tough-mindedness and socio-political attitudes has been rather limited. In blistering attacks, Rokeach and Hanley (1956) and Christie (1956) accused Eysenck of miscalculation, omission and other errors. Perhaps the most telling blow was the suggestion by Rokeach and Hanley (1956) that, according to their recalculations of some of the original findings, communists were actually tender-minded on some of the items of the tough-mindedness inventory.

They argued that Eysenck's two-dimensional scheme must instead be seen as a religionism–humanitarianism taxonomy, with communists scoring low on the positive pole of religionism (e.g. 'going back to religion'), and endorsing the positive pole of the humanitarianism dimension (e.g. 'abolish the death penalty'). Communists would also reject the negative pole of the humanitarianism dimension (e.g. 'Coloured people are inferior'). Thus Rokeach and Hanley concluded that Eysenck's (1954) conception of tough-mindedness–tender-mindedness had 'no basis in fact' (Rokeach and Hanley, 1956, p.175).

In his critique, Christie (1956) noted the biased nature of some of Eysenck's samples stressing, for instance, the unrepresentativeness of his middle-class sample. A further problem for Christie (1956) was Eysenck's (1954) treatment of zero responses as tough-minded which, as Christie remarked, introduced a bias of unknown effect. Finally, Christie (1956) argued that the communists in Eysenck's (1954) sample did not respond to various items in the inventory on the basis of their being tough-minded, but rather on the basis of their falling somewhere on the conservatism–radicalism divide. In other words, 'tough-mindedness' was simply irrelevant as a valid construct for communists.

These were important criticisms of an approach that was essentially quite innovative, going as it does beyond the traditional radicalism–conservatism divide. Its attempt to incorporate personality with attitude was not only novel but important, yet was unable to weather some quite serious methodological and theoretical challenges. Consequently, further research into tough-mindedness and socio-political attitudes was quenched. It is interesting to note, in passing, that some years later Rokeach (1973) was to propose a two-dimensional scheme of ideology incorporating not personality as a projection of the attitude domain, but rather the values freedom and equality (see section 4.4.1).

4.3.2 Authoritarianism and Ideology

Published just before Eysenck's (1954) thesis about the role of tough-mindedness, *The Authoritarian Personality* (Adorno *et al.*, 1950) enjoyed slightly more success as a psychological explanation of socio-political ideology, and in particular racist ideology. None the less, authoritarianism as a psychological construct and its operationalisation in the F scale were also subjected to some severe criticism. However, as will be made clear below, authoritarianism has undergone a resurgence of late, and research into what is now referred to as right-wing authoritarianism (RWA) is to be found in contemporary social psychological literature (for reviews see, for example, Altemeyer, 1981, 1988; Duckitt, 1992).

Concerned at first with the factors giving rise to anti-Semitism, Adorno *et al.* (1950) viewed the authoritarian personality as a complex syndrome of behaviours and dispositions, including conventionalism, authoritarian submission, authoritarian aggression, projectivity, concern with sexual 'goings on', and so on (see Table 4.4). It was postulated that an individual's social attitudes are but an expression of deeply rooted personality characteristics, and that these inner impulses form the basis of the authoritarian personality syndrome. Based on empirical evidence, Adorno *et al.* (1950) observed that the authoritarian syndrome consisted of anti-Semitic, ethnocentric, and political and economic conservatism. Duckitt (1992) viewed the ideas expressed in the book as 'ambitious' and 'influential', while Billig went so far as to suggest that *The Authoritarian Personality* 'constitutes a major landmark in the history of psychology, as well as being the single most important contribution to the psychology of fascism' (Billig, 1978, p.36).

The early work of Adorno *et al.* (1950) was impressive, using as it did attitude questionnaires and projective techniques. One aspect of the original research involved the construction of the Fascist (F) scale as a measure of potential fascism, and what immediately attracted the attention of people

Table 4.4 Components of authoritarianism

Component	Description
Conventionalism	For example, supporting the norms established by the in-group (usually middle class)
Authoritarian submission	For example, being accepting and uncritical of the in-group
Authoritarian aggression	For example, not accepting those who violate conventional values and mores
Anti-intraception	For example, opposed to more creative individuals
Superstition and stereotype	For example, the tendency to respond dogmatically
Power and toughness	For example, seeing the world divided into the weak and the strong; likes to identify with the leader
Destructiveness and cynicism	For example, the tendency to be hostile towards the weak and members of out-groups
Projectivity	For example, a belief that there are dangerous forces out there trying to overthrow the established order
Sex	For example, intolerant of sexual expression

working in this area were the significant associations found between F-scale scores and measures of prejudicial attitudes. Although the ideas expressed by Adorno *et al.* (1950) were quite insightful, Billig (1978) has noted that, after the publication of the book, researchers showed little interest in the original intent of the authors, namely the conditions that create a fascist personality. Rather, as has been pointed out by several authors, researchers extracted the F scale and treated it as *the* measure of 'authoritarianism'.

Two properties of the F scale soon gave rise to some concern among researchers. One feature was the unilateral (or one-way) wording of the items of the scale (Christie *et al.*, 1958). Christie and colleagues noted that, although acquiescence may be indicative of authoritarianism, it is more likely that acquiescence on the F scale might be due to the ambiguous nature of many of the items. A second area of concern, identified by Titus (1968) and Titus and Hollander (1957), was the alleged inability of the F scale actually to predict authoritarian behaviour (see also Ray, 1976). As Titus (1968) suggested, it seemed quite likely that the F scale was nothing more than a measure of authoritarian attitudes, rather than authoritarian behaviour, and that this flaw explained the frequently observed significant relationships between the F scale and various measures of prejudicial attitudes.

Several other criticisms have been directed at the F scale. For instance, it is known that the F-scale items were selected because of their strong associations with anti-Semitism items (Adorno *et al.*, 1950; see also Altemeyer, 1981; Duckitt, 1992). Thus it is likely that the correlation between ethnocentrism and the F scale is not due to an underlying personality disposition. Moreover, the relationship between ethnocentrism and personality as measured by the Thematic Apperception Test (TAT) was established through intensive clinical interviews. As the scores of the subjects were known to the interviewers, this may have influenced the interpretation of the data (Krech *et al.*, 1962; Duckitt, 1992).

In line with Eysenck (1954), Shils (1954) suggested that, although authoritarians should be found on both sides of the political divide, that was not the case when using the F scale. In fact, communists tended to score lower on this measure than did fascists. Ray (1983) has supported an authoritarianism of the left, and Rokeach (1960) suggested that dogmatic individuals can be either 'left' or 'right', although this view has been disputed (see, for example, Stone, 1980).

As with Eysenck's (1954) tough-mindedness concept, the idea that 'authoritarianism' was somehow related to socio-political ideology soon lost favour, and lay dormant for many years (Taylor *et al.*, 1994) until it was resurrected in 1981 by Altemeyer.

4.3.3 Right-Wing Authoritarianism

In a major review of years of work on the nature and correlates of the F scale, Altemeyer (1981) concluded that one is surrounded by the 'wreckage' of research into authoritarianism. As he put it:

A major failing of the research we have just reviewed is that nearly all of the investigators who found positive results failed to determine if these results were attributable to the scale as a whole, or mainly to subsets of items with rather obvious connections to the criterion . . . it is rather stupefying to realise that we end up knowing so little. For we found not only that the theory is unconfirmed . . . but also that all of this research was incapable of testing the theory from the start. Why ever on earth, then, was most of it done?

(Altemeyer, 1981, p.80)

Altemeyer (1981, p.148) conceptualised right-wing authoritarianism in terms of authoritarian submission, authoritarian aggression and conventionalism. To be classified as a right-wing authoritarian, one has to manifest all of these dimensions. In a series of many studies spanning several years, Altemeyer (1981) constructed his right-wing authoritarianism (RWA) scale and tested its dynamics. The measure appears to have adequate psychometric properties, but more importantly it is distinct from the original F scale, the balanced F scale, the dogmatism scale and other similar inventories. Altemeyer (1981) reported significant associations between RWA scores and prejudice, punitiveness, and tolerance of government injustices against unconventional victims. Moreover, RWA adherents tend to be supporters of right-wing political parties rather than left-wing parties yet, surprisingly, they would support government action aimed at severely limiting the activities not only of fringe left-wing groups, but also of right-wing groups.

To date, Altemeyer's (1981, 1988) thesis has generated limited research. None the less, several major texts (e.g. Duckitt, 1992; Taylor *et al.*, 1994) acknowledge his role in breathing new life into an old idea.

Recently, Duckitt (1993) investigated the structure and correlates of the RWA scale among more than 200 white English-speaking university students in South Africa. He concluded that the RWA scale has excellent psychometric properties and is essentially one-dimensional. He found that high scores on the RWA measure were significantly associated with acceptance of parental religion, self-ratings as conservative, and acceptance of censorship and detention without trial. Individuals with high RWA scores also opposed the right of peaceful protest and were prejudiced as indicated by measures of blatant and subtle racism. Moreover, RWA adherents were much less likely to endorse interracial behaviours, manifesting instead interracial social distance. Finally, high RWA scores predicted support for right-wing political parties. In further research it was observed that RWA adherents in South Africa displayed anti-black and pro-white sentiments. Perhaps surprisingly, they also indicated a preparedness to tolerate infringements of civil liberties by a future black South African government. It was concluded that the respondents' authoritarian submission overrode their own self-interest (Duckitt and Farre, 1994).

To summarise, there is evidence that right-wing authoritarianism is related to political and racist ideology such that authoritarians support government policy and racist ideology. However, it is not clear to what extent these relationships are influenced by discrimination, or by the desire to 'fake good'.

4.3.4   Social Dominance Orientation

In a recent development, Pratto *et al.* (1994) proposed an individual difference variable capable of indicating the extent to which one believes that one's in-group should be dominant over other out-groups. They referred to this as social dominance orientation (SDO). High SDO individuals, so the authors reasoned, tend to accept hierarchy-enhancing legitimising myths – that is, they accept social inequities and profess beliefs which are likely to sustain such inequalities. Thus SDO is a crucial motivator that underpins ethnic and group inequalities. Sidanius (1993) argues that all human collectivities lead to the formation of social hierarchies which are group based with one hegemonic group at the top (e.g. whites in the USA). Typical statements in this inventory include the following: 'Some groups of people are simply not the equal of others'.

In a series of studies using 13 different samples, Pratto *et al.* (1994) found SDO to correlate significantly with political-economic conservatism, nationalism, patriotism, cultural elitism, anti-black racism, male gender, rape myths and sexist attitudes toward women. SDO adherents were also unlikely to support a range of policy initiatives including women's rights, gay and lesbian rights and racial equality, but were quite likely to endorse law and order policies, military programmes and chauvinism. In a study of a sample of US undergraduates, Sidanius and Liu (1992) found that SDO was better able than a general conservatism factor to explain significant relationships between support for the Gulf War and other prejudicial beliefs.

A central tenet of social dominance theory is behavioural asymmetry – that is, attitudes and behaviours reflect the social status of the group in question. This can manifest itself in several different ways, including out-group favouritism, asymmetrical in-group bias, self-handicapping, and ideological asymmetry (Sidanius, 1993, p.202). For example, white US undergraduates (high status) were found to be more opposed to cross-racial dating than were black US students (low status). Among high-status groups, therefore, there is a stronger relationship between SDO and political and social attitudes than there is among low-status groups.

How does SDO differ from authoritarianism? Whereas authoritarianism has traditionally referred to an individual difference factor explaining attitudes toward out-groups (e.g. attitudes toward minorities), SDO attempts to gauge what individuals think about intergroup relationships. In other words, whereas authoritarianism usually refers to within-group processes, SDO assesses intergroup relationships (Pratto *et al.*, 1994).

In a series of studies in three cultures (the USA, South Africa and Australia), Heaven *et al.* (1997) has found differing levels of support for the ability of both RWA and SDO to predict prejudice. For instance, among black female American undergraduates, anti-white prejudice was not predicted by either SDO or RWA, but rather by an identity as African-American. However, none of these predictors were significant for males. Among white South African students, anti-gay prejudice was best predicted by SDO and heterosexual identity, whilst among blacks SDO was a significant predictor of prejudice. Thus it would seem that the ability of factors such as SDO and RWA to predict prejudice may be a function of the types of prejudice being measured and the life experiences of the group expressing bigoted attitudes.

4.4 OTHER INDICATORS OF IDEOLOGY

This section will briefly note the relationships between other individual difference indicators of ideology and prejudice, social attitudes and voting behaviour.

4.4.1   Human Values, Voting Intention and Attitudes

The criticism levelled against Eysenck's (1954) concept of tough-mindedness as an explanation of socio-political beliefs has been discussed. Rokeach (1973) believed that one's endorsement of certain values, particularly freedom and equality, was predictive of political ideology, and that values function very much like individual difference factors. Whereas communists were said to endorse equality, but not freedom, capitalists were said to endorse freedom, but not equality. Socialists, it was argued, supported both freedom and equality, whilst fascists supported neither.

Previous attempts to differentiate political groups on the basis of the two-value model have proved unsuccessful. For example, in the UK and Australia it was found that left- and right-wing supporters differed in their endorsement of equality, but not in their endorsement of freedom (Cochrane *et al.*, 1979; Thannhauser and Caird, 1990).

Braithwaite (Braithwaite, 1982; Braithwaite and Law, 1985) has argued that Rokeach's model needs to be revised slightly to include the values 'national strength and order' and 'international harmony and equality', thereby replacing equality and freedom, respectively. According to Braithwaite (1997), these values represent core dimensions dealing with security and harmony issues, respectively. Whereas harmony deals with equality and the welfare of others, security is more concerned with order, competition and discipline. Harmony coincides with 'personal integrity', whilst security is concerned with the outcomes of one's behaviour.

This scheme has been found to be useful in differentiating between left- and right-wing voters in Australia, such that left-wing supporters endorsed international harmony and equality, but not national strength and order, whilst the position was reversed for right-wing supporters (Heaven, 1991). In addition, a belief in national strength and order among Australians is negatively related to support for income redistribution, a uranium-mining ban, aboriginal benefits, and job options for women, and it is positively related to support for crime control. This pattern of relationships was found to be reversed for international harmony and equality (Braithwaite, 1997).

However, it would appear that the cultural robustness of these findings may be limited to those societies with a well-established democratic tradition. Heaven *et al.* (1994) attempted to extend Braithwaite's (1982) model in a society moving towards democracy, namely South Africa. Prior to South Africa's historic all-race elections in 1994, a sample consisting of 593 black and white university students indicated the political party of their choice, and also completed a value inventory (Braithwaite and Law, 1985). The authors found that supporters of the various political parties could more easily be discriminated on the basis of their endorsement of international harmony and equality than on their endorsement of national strength and order. Thus it would seem that values do predict political ideology, but that the values which are involved may vary from one culture to another.

Are there links between values and personality factors? It would seem so. Furnham (1984) administered the Rokeach Value Survey and Eysenck's EPQ to 70 senior high-school students. He found that the neuroticism factor was best able to predict values compared to either the E or P factors. For example, neurotic introverts rated freedom and self-respect more highly than did other groups, and neurotics favoured inner harmony more than others. Extraverts rated an exciting life more highly than introverts.

In conclusion, it would appear that values function very much like individual difference factors, being able to predict ideology and showing predictable links to personality factors. Individuals who endorse security values have different political behaviours to those who endorse harmony values. These values doubtless shape a wide range of other ideological beliefs. Finally, neuroticism is an important personality factor that is able to discriminate support of different values.

4.4.2   Belief in a Just World and Prejudice

According to the just-world principle, we tend to view the world as essentially a fair and just place where people get what they deserve and deserve what they get (Lerner and Simmons, 1966). It has been suggested that belief in a just world is based on people's need for a sense of control over what happens to them, and that without this belief the world would seem to be arbitrary, with people at the mercy of uncontrolled forces (Lerner, 1965). It has been found that those individuals who score high on just-world measures tend to blame the poor for their plight (Furnham and Gunter, 1984), show very little sympathy for those living with HIV/AIDS (Connors and Heaven, 1990), are less sympathetic to feminist ideology (Wagstaff and Quirk, 1983), and derogate those on social security benefits (Furnham, 1982). Thus the tendency to 'blame the victim' is a self-serving attribution and functions to protect individuals from others' misfortune. By blaming the victim, we are able to rationalise societal inequalities by attributing the failings of individuals to their own dispositions, rather than to some weakness of social institutions (Furnham and Proctor, 1989).

There appear to be interesting and noteworthy sex differences in the ability of just-world beliefs to predict some forms of prejudice. For example, it has been found in Australia that just-world beliefs predict negative attitudes to those living with HIV/AIDS among men, but not among women (e.g. Connors and Heaven, 1990). Why should this be the case? It may be that traditional socialisation of women tends to promote caring and supportive attitudes, whilst the traditional socialisation of men promotes mastery, self-reliance and aggressiveness. Not surprisingly, therefore, men would be more likely to see those with HIV/AIDS as deviant, incompetent and dependent people who are undeserving of sympathy and therefore suitable for social distancing.

Belief in a just world fulfils an important need. It is related in a predictable fashion to various conservative social attitudes, and it is a useful individual difference variable for predicting one's ideological stance.

4.4.3 The Protestant Work Ethic

It is well established that Protestant work ethic (PWE) beliefs are related to ideological stance and achievement. For example, high-PWE individuals regard social security recipients as lazy and dishonest, whereas low-PWE individuals have quite the opposite view (Furnham, 1990). High- and low-PWE types also differ in the types of attributions that they make, with the former group tending to endorse 'blame the victim' attitudes, and the latter not. Perhaps unsurprisingly it has also been found that high-PWE individuals support right-wing political parties, whilst low-PWE people tend more towards the political left. High-PWE individuals are also more likely to endorse punitive suggestions (e.g. military conscription) for reducing unemployment compared to low-PWE people, who tend to endorse more compassionate alternatives (e.g. increased government spending) (Heaven, 1990b). Finally, high-PWE individuals support more right-wing economic views (e.g. profit, privatisation, etc.). By contrast, low-PWE individuals support left-wing economic views (e.g. the right to strike, support for picket lines, etc.) (Heaven, 1991).

In summary, PWE measures are very useful for predicting a wide range of political, social, and economic beliefs, supporting the view that links exist between the PWE and ideology. It is clear that PWE beliefs are part of a pattern of conservative social and economic beliefs (Heaven, 1991).

4.4.4 Personality and Social Attitudes

A central tenet of Eysenckian theory is that the factors psychoticism, extraversion and neuroticism predict social attitudes. For example, Eysenck (1972) has clearly demonstrated relationships between these factors and attitudes relating to sex. Neurotics, for instance, are much more likely to score high on attitude factors labelled inhibition, guilt and hostility, and to score much lower on factors relating to sexual satisfaction. Those scoring high on the P dimension are more likely to score high also on promiscuity, hostility, curiosity and pre-marital sex.

Although there is much evidence to suggest that social attitudes and behaviours are linked to personality (see, for example, Joe, 1974), others have argued to the contrary. Thus Orpen (1971) has suggested that cultural factors may be more important in explaining social attitudes, at least in South Africa during the apartheid years. Others (see, for example, Heaven and Connors,

1988) have found some attitudes to be linked to personality in members of only one sex.

Heaven (1992) demonstrated that the Eysenckian factors were linked to the social attitudes of 273 adult Australians. Extraversion was found to be significantly related to hedonism (in both sexes) and negatively related to religion/morality (in females only). Psychoticism was significantly negatively related to religion/morality (in both sexes), positively related to hedonism (in both sexes) and significantly negatively related to racial equality (in females only). There were no significant associations between neuroticism and social attitudes. Thus these results lend some support to the view (Eysenck and Wilson, 1978) that factors such as P and E are linked to social attitudes in a coherent fashion. Those with hedonistic and anti-morality views tend to be highly sociable and tough-minded, whereas racial equality tends to be endorsed by the tender-minded.

Riemann *et al.* (1993) used a group of students from a German university to construct a measure of current political issues. A principal-components analysis revealed four factors, namely general conservatism, social welfare and support for women's equality, liberalism and affirmation of technological progress, and finally affirmation of increases in taxation for environmental protection and the development of Eastern Europe. It was noted that conservatism was negatively related to openness to experience and positively related to conscientiousness. Openness to experience and agreeableness were positively related to the social welfare factor. Technological progress correlated negatively with neuroticism, agreeableness and extraversion. Support for taxation was positively related to openness to experience and agreeableness, but it was negatively related to extraversion.

These results show that openness to experience tends to be related to 'tender-minded' attitudes, such as support for welfare benefits, whilst conservatives are characterised by conscientiousness. Thus there are logical links between individuals' social attitudes and their personalities.

4.5 CONCLUSION

This chapter has discussed the role that psychologists have played in attempting to explain ideology. From this review it is clear that personality factors are heavily implicated in the religious, political, economic and other beliefs that we hold. For instance, it is apparent that people who are likely *not* to hold religious beliefs can more easily be described as 'tough-minded' rather than as 'tender-minded'. Thus there is some evidence to suggest a link between scores on Eysenck's P scale (psychoticism or tough-mindedness) and low scores on measures of religious attitudes. Furthermore, research into authoritarianism has shown links between high scores on this construct and negative attitudes toward racial groups and being favourably disposed toward government authorities. Although it is also possible to predict prejudice from knowledge of an individual's level of social dominance orientation, it would appear to be distinct from authoritarianism. None the less, it remains possible to characterise people who adhere to particular ideologies, and to define their personality functioning reasonably specifically.

One of the challenges that currently faces psychologists working in the area of ideology is to delineate further social dominance orientation. We noted that this individual difference variable has only recently been fully described (Sidanius, 1993; Pratto *et al.*, 1994), and the task that lies ahead is to explain exactly how it can be distinguished from other constructs such as right-wing authoritarianism. Moreover, it would seem that these factors may function differently from culture to culture, suggesting a possible avenue for future research.

REFERENCES

Adorno, T.W., Frenkel-Brunswik, E., Levinson, D.J. and Sanford, R.N. (1950) *The authoritarian personality*. New York: Harper.

Altemeyer, B. (1981) *Right-wing authoritarianism*. Winnipeg: University of Manitoba Press.

Altemeyer, B. (1988) *Enemies of freedom:Understanding right-wing authoritarianism*. San Francisco, CA: Jossey-Bass.

Argyle, M. and Beit-Hallahmi, B. (1975) *The social psychology of religion*. London: Routledge & Kegan Paul.

Augoustinos, M. and Walker, I. (1995) *Social cognition*. London: Sage.

Bagley, C., Verma, G.K., Mallick, K. and Young, L. (1979) *Personality, self-esteem and prejudice*. Westmead: Saxon House.

Baird, L. (1990) A 24-year longitudinal study of the development of religious ideas. *Psychological Reports* **66**, 479–82.

Billig, M. (1978) *Fascists: a social-psychological view of the National Front*. London: Academic Press.

Braithwaite, V. (1982) The structure of social values: validation of Rokeach's two-value model. *British Journal of Social Psychology* **21**, 203–11.

Braithwaite, V. (1997) Harmony and security value orientations in political evaluation. *Personality and Social Psychology Bulletin* **23**, 401–14.

Braithwaite, V. and Law, H. (1985) Structure of human values: testing the adequacy of the Rokeach value survey. *Journal of Personality and Social Psychology* **49**, 250–63.

Brand, C. (1981) Personality and political attitudes. In Lynn, R. (ed.), *Dimensions of personality*. Oxford: Pergamon Press, 7–38.

Caird, D. (1987) Religiosity and personality: are mystics introverted, neurotic, or psychotic? *British Journal of Social Psychology* **26**, 345–6.

Christie, R. (1956) Some abuses of psychology. *Psychological Bulletin* **53**, 439–51.

Christie, R., Havel, J. and Seidenberg, B. (1958) Is the F scale irreversible? *Journal of Abnormal and Social Psychology* 56, 143–59.

Cochrane, R., Billig, M. and Hogg, M. (1979) Politics and values in Britain: a test of Rokeach's two-value model. *British Journal of Social and Clinical Psychology* 18, 159–67.

Connors, J. and Heaven, P. (1990) Belief in a just world and attitudes toward AIDS sufferers. *Journal of Social Psychology* 130, 559–60.

Dollard, J., Doob, L., Miller, N.E., Mowrer, O. and Sears, R. (1939) *Frustration and aggression.* New Haven, CT: Yale University Press.

Duckitt, J. (1992) *The social psychology of prejudice.* New York: Praeger.

Duckitt, J. (1993) Right-wing authoritarianism among white South African students: its measurement and correlates. *Journal of Social Psychology* 133, 553–63.

Duckitt, J. and Farre, B. (1994) Right-wing authoritarianism and political intolerance among whites in the future majority-rule South Africa. *Journal of Social Psychology* 134, 735–41.

Eysenck, H. (1954) *The psychology of politics.* London: Routledge & Kegan Paul.

Eysenck, H. (1972) *Psychology is about people.* Harmondsworth: Penguin.

Eysenck, H. and Coulter, T. (1972) The personality and attitudes of working-class British communists and fascists. *Journal of Social Psychology* 87, 59–73.

Eysenck, H. and Eysenck, S. (1975) *Manual of the Eysenck Personality Questionnaire.* London: Hodder & Stoughton.

Eysenck, H. and Eysenck, S. (1976) *Psychoticism as a dimension of personality.* London: Hodder & Stoughton.

Eysenck, H. and Wilson, G. (1978) *The psychological basis of ideology.* Lancaster: MTP Press.

Eysenck, H. and Eysenck, M. (1985) *Personality and individual differences: a natural science approach.* New York: Plenum.

Festinger, L. (1957) *A theory of cognitive dissonance.* Stanford: Stanford University Press.

Fowler, J.W. (1981) *Stages of faith: the psychology of human development and the quest for meaning.* San Francisco, CA: Harper & Row.

Francis, L.J. (1991a) Personality and attitude towards religion among adult church-goers in England. *Psychological Reports* 69, 791–4.

Francis, L.J. (1991b) The personality characteristics of Anglican ordinands: feminine men and masculine women? *Personality and Individual Differences* 12, 1133–40.

Francis, L.J. (1992a) Is psychoticism really a dimension of personality fundamental to religiosity? *Personality and Individual Differences* 13, 645–52.

Francis, L.J. (1992b) Neuroticism and intensity of religious attitudes among clergy in England. *Journal of Social Psychology* 132, 577–80.

Francis, L.J. and Pearson, P.R. (1985) Extraversion and religiosity. *Journal of Social Psychology* 125, 269–70.

Francis, L.J. and Pearson, P.R. (1988) Religiosity and the short-scale EPQ-R indices of E, N and L, compared with the JEPI, JEPQ and EPQ. *Personality and Individual Differences* 9, 653–7.

Francis, L.J. and Pearson, P.R. (1993) The personality characteristics of student churchgoers. *Personality and Individual Differences* 15, 373–80.

Francis, L.J., Pearson, P.R. and Kay, W.K. (1983) Neuroticism and religiosity among English schoolchildren. *Journal of Social Psychology* 121, 149–50.

Furnham, A. (1982) Why are the poor always with us? Explanations for poverty in Britain. *British Journal of Social Psychology* 21, 311–22.

Furnham, A. (1984) Personality and values. *Personality and Individual Differences* 5, 483–5.

Furnham, A. (1990) *The Protestant work ethic*. London: Routledge.

Furnham, A. and Gunter, B. (1984) Just world beliefs and attitudes towards the poor. *British Journal of Social Psychology* 23, 265–9.

Furnham, A. and Proctor, E. (1989) Belief in a just world: review and critique of the individual difference literature. *British Journal of Social Psychology* 28, 365–84.

Gartner, J., Larson, D.B. and Allen, G.D. (1991) Religious commitment and mental health: a review of the empirical literature. *Journal of Psychology and Theology* 19, 6–25.

Heaven, P. (1990a) Religious values and personality dimensions. *Personality and Individual Differences* 11, 953–6.

Heaven, P. (1990b) Suggestions for reducing unemployment: a study of Protestant work ethic and economic locus of control beliefs. *British Journal of Social Psychology* 29, 55–65.

Heaven, P. (1991) The Protestant work ethic and economic beliefs. *Australian Psychologist* 26, 59–63.

Heaven, P. (1992) Social and economic beliefs in adulthood. In Heaven, P.C.L. (ed.), *Life-span development*. Sydney: Harcourt Brace Jovanovich, 242–64.

Heaven, P., Greene, R. and Stones, C. (1997) Psychological predictors of prejudice in three cultures. Paper presented to the Society of Australasian Social Psychologists, Christchurch, New Zealand, 16–19 April.

Heaven, P. and Connors, J. (1988) Politics and toughmindedness. *Journal of Social Psychology* 128, 217–22.

Heaven, P., Stones, C., Nel, E., Huysamen, G. and Louw, J. (1994) Human values and voting intention in South Africa. *British Journal of Social Psychology* 33, 223–31.

Heider, F. (1958) *The psychology of interpersonal relations*. New York: Wiley.

Joe, V.C. (1974) Personality correlates of conservatism. *Journal of Social Psychology* 93, 309–10.

Knutson, J.N. (ed.) (1973) *Handbook of political psychology*. San Francisco, CA: Jossey-Bass.

Krech, D., Crutchfield, R.S. and Ballachey, E.L. (1962) *Individual in society*. New York: McGraw-Hill Book Co.

Lasswell, H.D. (1930) *Psychopathology and politics*. Chicago: University of Chicago Press.

Lerner, M. (1965) Evaluation of performance as a function of performer's reward and attractiveness. *Journal of Personality and Social Psychology* 1, 355–6

Lerner, M. and Simmons, C. (1966) Observers' reactions to the 'innocent victim': comparison or rejection? *Journal of Personality and Social Psychology* 4, 203–10.

Lewis, C.A. and Maltby, J. (1995) Religious attitude and practice: the relationship with obsessionality. *Personality and Individual Differences* 19, 105–8.

Orpen, C. (1971) The relationship between extraversion and toughmindedness in a 'toughminded' culture. *Journal of Psychology* 78, 27–9.

Pfeifer, S. and Waelty, U. (1995) Psychopathology and religious commitment – a controlled study. *Psychopathology* 28, 70–7.

Pratto, F., Sidanius, J., Stallworth, L.M. and Malle, B.F. (1994) Social dominance orientation: a personality variable predicting social and political attitudes. *Journal of Personality and Social Psychology* **67**, 741–63.

Ray, J.J. (1976) Do authoritarians hold authoritarian attitudes? *Human Relations* **29**, 307–25.

Ray, J.J. (1979) A short balanced F scale. *Journal of Social Psychology* **109**, 309–10.

Ray, J.J. (1983) Half of all authoritarians are left-wing: a reply to Eysenck and Stone. *Political Psychology* **4**, 139–43.

Riemann, R., Grubich, C., Hempel, S., Mergl, S. and Richter, M. (1993) Personality and attitudes towards current political topics. *Personality and Individual Differences* **15**, 313–21.

Rigby, K. (1984) Acceptance of authority and directiveness as indicators of authoritarianism: a new framework. *Journal of Social Psychology* **122**, 171–80.

Rokeach, M. (1960) *The open and closed mind*. New York: Basic Books.

Rokeach, M. (1973) *The nature of human values*. New York: Free Press.

Rokeach, M. and Hanley, C. (1956) Eysenck's tender-mindedness dimension: a critique. *Psychological Bulletin* **53**, 169–76.

Ryan, R.M., Rigby, S. and King, K. (1993) Two types of religious internalization and their relations to religious orientations and mental health. *Journal of Personality and Social Psychology* **65**, 586–96.

Shils, E.A. (1954) Authoritarianism right and left. In Christie, R. and Jahoda, M. (eds), *Studies in the scope and method of 'the Authoritarian Personality'*. Glencoe, IL: Free Press, 14–29.

Sidanius, J. (1993) The psychology of group conflict and the dynamics of oppression: a social dominance perspective. In Iyengar, S. and McGuire, W. (eds), *Explorations in political psychology*. Durham, NC: Duke University Press, 183–219.

Sidanius, J. and Liu, J. (1992) The Gulf War and the Rodney King beating: implications for the general conservatism and social dominance perspectives. *Journal of Social Psychology* **132**, 685–700.

Spilka, B., Hood, R.W. and Gorsuch, R.L. (1985) *The psychology of religion: an empirical approach*. Englewood Cliffs, NJ: Prentice-Hall.

Stone, W.F. (1980) The myth of left-wing authoritarianism. *Political Psychology* **2**, 3–19.

Stone, W.F. and Schaffner, P.E. (1988) *The psychology of politics*, 2nd edn. New York: Springer-Verlag.

Taylor, S.E., Peplau, L.A. and Sears, D.O. (1994) *Social psychology*, 8th edn. Englewood Cliffs, NJ: Prentice-Hall.

Thannhauser, D. and Caird, D. (1990) Politics and values in Australia: testing Rokeach's two-value model of politics – a research note. *Australian Journal of Psychology* **42**, 57–61.

Titus, H.E. (1968) F-scale validity considered against peer nomination criteria. *Psychological Record* **18**, 395–403.

Titus, H.E. and Hollander, E.P. (1957) The California F-scale in psychological research: 1950–1955. *Psychological Bulletin* **54**, 47–64.

Vianello, R. (1991) Religious beliefs and personality traits in early adolescence. *International Journal of Adolescence and Youth* **2**, 287–96.

Wagstaff, G.F. and Quirk, M.A. (1983) Attitudes to sex roles, political conservatism and belief in a just world. *Psychological Reports* **52**, 813–14.

Westman, A.S. and Brackney, B.E. (1990) Relationships between indices of neuroticism, attitudes toward and concepts of death, and religiosity. *Psychological Reports* 66, 1039–43.

Wilde, A. and Joseph, S. (1997) Religiosity and personality in a Moslem context. *Personality and Individual Differences* 23, 899–900.

5

Personality and Close Relationships

5.1 INTRODUCTION

We have various social relationships with many different people – a neighbour, a child, a lover, a boss, to name just a few. Everyday life is characterised by intimate, close and passing relationships with other people, and the nature of these interactions has an important bearing on the quality of one's life. Some of these relationships are happy and cordial; others are strained and more formal. It is the nature of close and more intimate relationships, rather than other more mundane ones, that excites passion and is the subject of countless poems, novels and dramatic operas. As Lee (1976) notes, we are all eternal optimists who constantly seek that one, totally fulfilling love relationship. Some of us are even prepared to sacrifice all in order to find 'true' love. Thus we appear quite desperate for loving and lasting relationships, and constantly on the look-out for the 'perfect match', as the high divorce rate in most western cultures would attest.

Understanding the nature of close relationships is therefore a legitimate and important area of study for behavioural scientists. Are people with similar personalities attracted to each other, or do opposites attract? Are extraverts more easy and neurotics less easy to get along with? What are the personality correlates of sexual behaviour? How are attitudes to sex structured? Do we all love in the same way? Is it possible to study close relationships in ways that are considered scientific?

The questions that psychologists ask when studying close and romantic relationships are indeed varied, and to some extent reflect the different strategies that people use when they initiate (and try to maintain) a romantic relationship. When one first initiates a romantic relationship one supposedly needs to consider the following kinds of questions (Snyder, 1986). What would I hope to get out of this relationship, and how long term would I like this relationship to be? Both are important for the quality of the relationship. Another consideration deals with commitment. How committed am I to ensuring the success of this relationship? Finally, will our romantic relationship be a sexual one? Will I adopt a 'restricted' or 'unrestricted' (Snyder, 1986, p.71) sexual approach? How will my decision affect my partner, and what will it mean for our relationship? Doubtless these and many other considerations are shaped by our personality traits and cognitive abilities.

In recent years various psychologists (Cook and Wilson, 1979; Sternberg and Barnes, 1988; Hendrick, 1989) have begun to explore some of these questions, and it is on these issues that the present chapter will focus. The emphasis here will therefore be on close and intimate relationships, characterised by emotional intensity, rather than on other types of relationship, such as those that might exist between siblings or between employer and employee. Furthermore, there is little evidence to suggest that homosexuals love any differently to heterosexuals, so no distinctions will be drawn here between homosexual and heterosexual close relationships. In other words, we accept that homosexuals can experience erotic love as do heterosexuals, and that both are capable of a self-sacrificing form of love.

We shall begin by introducing psychoanalytic perspectives on love and attraction, followed by an examination of interpersonal attraction, different styles of love and their personality correlates, before discussing the nature of adult attachments. We shall also consider personality and some aspects of marriage before proceeding to consider sexual behaviour and attitudes to sex.

5.2 PSYCHOANALYTIC AND HUMANISTIC PERSPECTIVES

The contrast in style and content between the psychoanalytic and trait approaches to intimate relationships is indeed marked. Freud's ideas on love are found in his *Three Essays on the Theory of Sexuality* (reprinted in Strouse, 1974), and arose primarily – or so it would seem – through his experience of clients being attracted to their therapist, so-called transference love. Regarded as a form of infantile love, these situations provided Freud with the ideal opportunity for seeking to understand love relationships in the wider context (Lasky and Silverman, 1988). According to Freud, sexual life begins soon after birth, rather than after puberty, and most infantile expressions – such as crying, defecating and babbling – are expressions of this. He suggests that we are driven to obtain 'sexual pleasure' as evidenced by the sucking behaviour of young children. He points out that there are several erogenous bodily zones, each of which is capable of producing or providing pleasurable sensations. Included among these are the anal area and the genitals (Stafford-Clark, 1965).

Freud postulated that most human motivation is sexually driven – that is, 'sexuality' acts as a major force in nearly everything we do. He suggested that sexuality also underlies neuroses and deviant forms of behaviour, one such deviant behaviour form being homosexuality which, it was argued, has its roots in infancy. Infants, Freud suggested, believe that both sexes look alike, so homosexuality can therefore be considered to be an infantile form of sexuality in which adults feel sexually attracted to individuals of the same sex. As with other sexually deviant behaviours, homosexuality 'takes the place of a more complete sexual aim' (Stafford-Clark, 1965, p.99) and reflects inadequate and partial sexual maturity.

Erikson (1968) proposed his psychosocial stages of development, arguing that achieving intimacy with an important other person is an important milestone in early adulthood, and that this makes a significant contribution to identity development. In other words, intimacy is linked to our sense of who we are and acts as a buffer against emotional maladjustment. He referred to this stage as intimacy vs. isolation, and argued that it is vital that we form an intimate relationship, for the alternative is isolation. He explained his views in the following terms: 'Where a youth does not resolve such a commitment, he may isolate himself and enter, at best, only stereotyped and formalized interpersonal relations; or he may . . . seek intimacy with the most improbable of partners' (Erikson, 1968, p.167).

According to Fromm, love relationships satisfy important human needs such as fulfilling self-integrity, the escape from anxiety and being alone (Donelson, 1973). Love acts as a powerful drive that allows one to overcome the barriers that separate one from other objects or individuals. Fromm argued that a love relationship allows one to be in union with another person, while at the same time maintaining separateness from the other.

Maslow argued that we progress through a hierarchy of needs. At the lower end our needs are very basic and mostly concerned with physiological and safety issues, such as food, shelter, etc. At the other end they are uniquely human and encompass love and belonging, esteem and self-actualisation. Once one's basic needs are met, one can begin to satisfy the higher-order needs such as love and belonging. Not only does one seek love and friendship but, according to Maslow, one also has a need to *give* love (Cloninger, 1996).

Once one's needs have been met, one functions at a level which Maslow referred to as 'being motivation'. The alternative is to be at the 'deficiency motivation' level. It would seem that the same types of distinctions can be made with respect to love and belonging. He referred to B Love and D Love (being and deficiency, respectively), and whereas B Love is characterised by joy and being non-possessive, D Love is tormented by jealousy and anxiety (Cloninger, 1996).

Psychoanalytic and humanistic perspectives on love and close relationships are interesting and worth noting, yet have stimulated very little empirical research. Fromm was no doubt correct in saying that a close and loving relationship acts as a buffer against loneliness, yet this has done little to stimulate research or advance personality theory. In other words, although these theories deal with contemporary and important events (such as love), they go little way toward offering scientifically tested theories about the exact nature of close relationships.

5.3 INTERPERSONAL ATTRACTION

Why are we attracted to some people but not others? Some evidence would suggest that our preferences for others are structured such that personality attributes (e.g. being caring, honest or humorous) are viewed as being quite distinct from, and (usually) preferable to, other material attributes (e.g. has nice car, wears good clothes, etc.) (Smith, 1996), supporting reviews which consistently show that we desire mates who are dependable and emotionally stable. On the other hand, men have shown a preference for physical attractiveness when considering a *dating* partner (Felmlee, 1995), while other researchers (Byrne, 1961) have suggested that we are attracted to people with similar attitudes, although this view has been disputed (Ajzen, 1974). Yet others have proposed that we are attracted to those with traditional gender-typed characteristics (expressive qualities in women and instrumental qualities in men; see, for example, Brehm, 1992), but this suggestion, too, has been disputed (Green and Kenrick, 1994).

There are at least five theories of interpersonal attraction (Krueger and Caspi, 1993), which are summarised below.

- *The similarity hypothesis*: According to this view we are attracted to people who are similar to ourselves in attitude.
- *The ideal partner hypothesis*: This view states that we are attracted to individuals because they possess certain traits, such as kindness. It would seem that we have an ideal partner in mind and compare prospective partners with our ideal. Those that come closest to the ideal are viewed as most attractive.
- *The repulsion hypothesis*: This view states that we are repulsed by dissimilar others. Thus we tend to avoid or actively dislike those whose attitudes are dissimilar to our own.
- *The optimal dissimilarity hypothesis*: This theory suggests that we find people who are only slightly, but not totally, different to ourselves most attractive. Thus, we are aroused by what is novel and different, provided that it is not too dissimilar.
- *The optimal outbreeding hypothesis*: This view is based on the finding that some animals have shown a preference to breed with those who are somewhat different.

Krueger and Caspi (1993) found a certain amount of support for some of these views. Female respondents completed a temperament questionnaire and were then asked to make judgements about 5 hypothetical men whose personalities correlated by + 1.0, + 0.5, 0, 0.5 or 1.0 with that of the respondent. Support was found for the similarity and repulsion hypotheses – that is, respondents were attracted by those most similar to and repulsed by those most dissimilar to themselves. However, no support was found for the optimal dissimilarity hypothesis. Respondents were also likely to regard male partners who were more sociable, more active and less emotional as most pleasurable and arousing.

In an important extension of this research, Felmlee (1995) has recently shown that the characteristics which we view as important when selecting a dating partner are very often the same characteristics that lead to the breakup of that same relationship. She refers to this phenomenon as 'fatal attraction', and the characteristics involved in a fatal attraction can be grouped as follows. Partners are described as fun, caring, competent, have certain physical qualities, and are exciting. Consider the following, based on the responses of those who had recently broken a close relationship (adapted from Felmlee, 1995, p.303).

- *Fun*: You are initially attracted to someone because of their 'don't care' attitude. Later your partner seems to be lacking in maturity.
- *Caring*: You are initially attracted to someone who appears 'interested' in you, only to find later that he or she is very 'jealous and possessive'.
- *Competent*: You first regard someone as 'intelligent and confident', only later to note that they have an 'ego' problem.
- *Physical*: You are attracted to the physical qualities of an individual, but then discover that your relationship is 'based only on physical aspects'.
- *Excitement*: Someone is first viewed as 'strange' (in a positive sense), but is later regarded as 'flighty'.

These findings show how we reinterpret the personality traits of dating and romantic partners. As Felmlee explains:

> A fatal attraction can be viewed as a shift in the meaning of a relevant partner attribute ... such an inference suggests that individuals' changing interpretations of partners' qualities, rather than simply changes in the partner themselves, may play a significant role in the dissolution of romantic dyads.
>
> (Felmlee, 1995, p.307)

5.4 LOVE STYLES

'Being in love' is an experience that is unique to humans, yet there is no universally agreed upon definition of love (Ireland, 1988; Lasky and Silverman, 1988). None the less, it does seem to be generally accepted that love is something that exists beyond mere physical gratification, involving also the mind and heart (Lasky and Silverman, 1988). All of us have at some time experienced that unique bond which draws us very close to one other special person – an experience we might call 'love'. We certainly believe that we know when we are 'in love', because it is a 'transforming experience' (Aron *et al.*, 1995, p.1102), and songwriters allude to effects such as increased heart rate and 'tingling sensations'. We are all capable of loving, but do we all love in the same way?

Although, as we have seen (Lasky and Silverman, 1988), love has an important place in Freudian psychoanalysis, it is only relatively recently that social and personality psychologists have begun to expend considerable amounts of research energy on investigating the nature of close relationships, loving relationships and sexual behaviour. About 20 years ago Clark and her colleagues suggested that loving relationships can be described as either 'exchange' or 'communal' in nature (Clark and Mills, 1979). In exchange relationships, partners keep an account of all costs and benefits incurred, so the relationship therefore relies heavily on the principles of social exchange. In such a relationship one good deed deserves another, and a close watch is kept on exactly who does what and how much. Communal relationships are qualitatively different. The focus here is not on tight social exchange, nor is it on reward and cost, but rather on the needs of the partner. This form of relationship is therefore more self-sacrificing. You do something for your loved one without the expectation that a reward will necessarily be forthcoming. Although an exchange of benefits *might* occur in a communal relationship, the two types of relationship are distinguishable by their rules rather than by any actual benefit (Clark and Mills, 1979).

Although the personality correlates of these different types of relationship have yet to be investigated, it is possible to make tentative predictions. Thus it is highly likely that those who engage in self-sacrificing and communal relationships will be more agreeable than those who define their relationship as an exchange.

It is also possible to describe the love relationship as being either passionate or companionate (Walster and Walster, 1978). Passionate love refers to the shorter and more intense type of relationship, whereas companionate love refers to a more long-lasting and enduring relationship. Of course, it is possible for passionate love to evolve into companionate love, but this is likely to occur over the longer term. Lee (1976) has proposed a more complex taxonomy of love styles. Like others before him, he also describes passionate love, referring to this as *Eros*. These individuals sometimes experience 'love at first sight', which for some of Lee's (1976) participants endures for many years. Lee uses the following terms to describe Eros: 'gut reaction' as well as 'sweating', 'churning' and 'tightening of the stomach' (Lee, 1976, p.12).

Lee (1976) also delineates *Ludus*, a game-playing love which may entail deception and manipulation of the other person. These individuals, he suggests, do not take their emotions seriously. *Storge* refers to a merging of friendship and love, and it tends to be more enduring. Lee (1976) regards this love as 'natural affection', just as one might be drawn to a favourite relative. These styles are referred to as primary love styles, and he goes on to identify three main secondary styles. *Mania* is a possessive and dependent love, also indicating uncertainty about the self. Any indication of indifference from the other results in anxiety. *Pragma* is so-called 'shopping-list' or computer-matching love. It requires a compatible and committed partner, yet it need not necessarily be an exciting type of relationship (Lee, 1976). Finally, *Agape* is a

Table 5.1   The measurement of love styles

Love style	Sample item
Eros	Items deal with being attracted to each other quickly; love at first sight
Ludus	Items deal with being able to get over or cope easily with relationship breakdown
Storge	A long friendship ultimately leads to a lasting and good love relationship
Pragma	Items suggest that getting one's life 'in order' comes before a love relationship
Mania	Items refer to how excited one is about being in love
Agape	Items refer to a form of self-sacrificing love

Adapted from Hendrick, C. and Hendrick, S. (1986) A theory and method of love. *Journal of Personality and Social Psychology* **50**, 392–402.

selfless, all-giving love. The secondary styles are compounds of two primaries, although they are qualitatively quite different from either primary on its own.

Loving relationships can also be described in terms of passion, intimacy and commitment (Sternberg, 1986). For Sternberg, intimacy refers to how close two people feel they are, and the strength of the bond that keeps them together. Intimacy also refers to their concern for each other's happiness and well-being. Passion, as described above, is more concerned with romance and sexual attraction, while commitment implies cognitive functioning, and refers to the decision to persevere with or maintain an existing, loving relationship.

In an important development and extension of Lee's work (Lee, 1976), Hendrick and Hendrick (1986) constructed reliable and valid scales to measure the six love styles. This was a major research impetus for psychological inquiry, for it now became possible to examine correlations between love styles and personality attributes. Examples of the sub-scales are listed in Table 5.1.

5.4.1   Personality and Love Styles

Woll (1989) was of the view that personality traits are related to or 'can be integrated with' loving styles. In other words, individual differences are reasonably stable factors that help to shape one's loving style and, no doubt, one's whole experience of love. On the basis of his review of earlier work by

Lee (1976), Woll (1989) made the following predictions about the relationships between love styles and the major personality factors extraversion and neuroticism.

- *Pragma*:   Low N (Neuroticism).
- *Mania*:   High E, High N.
- *Agape*:   —
- *Ludus*:   High E (Extraversion).
- *Storge*:   —
- *Eros*:   High E, High N.

To what extent are these predictions satisfied? Using a rather small and restricted sample consisting of 88 American psychology undergraduates, Woll (1989) employed several personality inventories (the Personality Research Form (PRF), Sensation-Seeking, EPI, Locus of Control and Social Skills Inventory) to test his predictions. The main results are shown in Table 5.2, from which it is clear that not all of the predictions were met. (Given the large number of predictor variables, only associations at the 0.001 level are indicated here.)

Not all of Woll's (1989) hypotheses regarding E and N were supported, although several of the other results fit with our knowledge of the six love styles. For example, Ludus (game-playing) is seen to be associated with aggression and play, Mania (possessive and dependent) is associated with social cognition, and Agape (selfless) is associated with emotional sensitivity. Thus there appear to be predictable and logical links between personality dimensions and love styles.

Davies (1996) assessed the extent to which love styles relate to scores on Eysenck's EPQ. In this case the respondents were 127 UK undergraduates, and the results are in line with what we have come to expect of these personality

Table 5.2 Personality correlates of six loving styles

Pragma	Mania	Agape	Ludus	Storge	Eros
Cognitive structure (PRF)	Aggression (PRF)	Emotional sensitivity (PRF)	Disinhibition (SSI)		Dominance (PRF)
Aggression (PRF)	Social cognition (PRF)		Agression (PRF)		Order (PRF)
Social sensitivity	N (EPI)		Play (PRF)		
			E (EPI)		

Adapted from Woll, S. (1989) Personality and relationship correlates of loving styles. *Journal of Research in Personality* **23**, 480–505.

types (see Eysenck and Eysenck, 1985; Woll, 1989). For example, extraverts were found to endorse the Eros and Ludus love styles, whilst neurotics scored low on the Pragma but high on the Mania love styles. High P scorers endorsed Ludus, but did not endorse Storge and Agape love styles. In summary, extraverts (true to their sociable nature) emphasised the romantic and game-playing aspects of relationships, whilst neurotics emphasised possessive relationships (Davies, 1996). As one would expect, psychotics were not in favour of an all-giving and selfless type of relationship. Not only do these findings match our expectations of these personality profiles, but they also add to the validity of the love measures.

It is worth noting that Davies' (1996) findings regarding high P scorers support research by others who have observed that high P scorers are averse to physical closeness with another person, to merging minds with another, and to identifying with the achievements of others (Lester *et al.*, 1992).

Additional research by Davies (Mallandain and Davies, 1994) found evidence that positive self-esteem tends to be significantly positively related to Eros, but significantly negatively related to Storge and Mania. Impulsivity and emotionality were positively associated with Ludus and Mania. Further analysis of this data-set using canonical correlations revealed one significant canonical variate which suggested that low self-esteem and emotionality are linked to support for the Mania love style. In other words, low self-esteem and emotional types endorse a possessive and dependent love style, which again fits with our expectations of these personality types.

Do these results match our own *implicit* theories of the personalities associated with these love styles? To some extent they do. In an interesting study, Taraban and Hendrick (1995, pp.456–7) provided students with the love profiles of six fictitious individuals, and requested the students to provide their impressions of matching personalities. The Eros individual was described as being sexual, exciting, happy and loving (or high E), whilst the Ludus person was described as being inconsiderate, secretive and dishonest. This description of Ludus fits with our earlier findings of a link with aggressiveness.

The Storge individual was described as honest, loyal and mature, while the Pragma person was thought of as family-oriented, planning and careful, which tends to match the earlier finding of this person as scoring low on N. Mania individuals were described as jealous, possessive and obsessed (or with high N and low self-esteem), whilst Agape individuals were described as committed, caring and giving (or emotionally sensitive) (Taraban and Hendrick, 1995, pp.456–7). Therefore, there is considerable overlap between our implicit theories of the personalities associated with certain love styles and the results obtained from paper-and-pencil measures of the same.

Finally, it is important to consider that one ought to distinguish between state and trait measures of love styles. Mallandain and Davies (1994) suggest that as one's relationship undergoes change, or as one's experiences differ, so too might one's relative standing on the love scales change. These researchers argue that such state changes are more likely to affect scores on Eros and Mania, which will also affect relationships with other personality measures.

In conclusion, there are predictable links between personality traits and loving styles. Those who score high on measures of extraversion are more likely to manifest a romantic loving style, whilst the styles of P and N scorers are qualitatively quite distinguishable. There is still scope to investigate more closely the correlates of conscientiousness, openness to experience, and agreeableness, but these are expected to fit with what we know of these personality types. As the Eysencks once remarked, love and sex are central to a person's life, and it is no wonder therefore that personality traits play a crucial role in explaining this behaviour (Eysenck and Eysenck, 1985).

5.4.2 The Consequences of Falling in Love

Do we undergo a personality change when we fall in love? This is an interesting question; perhaps we change to become more like our partner. Very few researchers have attempted to examine this question, although one exception is the work by Aron et al. (1995). They define falling in love as 'the onset of a strong desire for a close, romantic relationship with a particular person; it is the transition from not being in love to being in love' (Aron et al., 1995, p.1102).

To date, most research on the personality changes that occur when we fall in love has been based on clinical samples rather than on members of the general population. According to one view, of which Erikson and Jung would be the chief proponents, falling in love is beneficial for identity development and personality integration (Aron et al., 1995). Longitudinal data collected by Aron et al. (1995) among a student sample indicates that falling in love has a significant effect on the contents of the self-concept (using labels such as freedom, happiness, etc.), as well as on the diversity of self-concept domains. These effects were maintained even after controlling for the respondents' mood status. It was also found that falling in love had a significant impact on feelings of self-efficacy and mean self-esteem scores using standard measures. In short, falling in love appears to have positive effects on the personality functioning and sense of identity of the individual. Moreover, these personality changes are quite substantial, and are not due to a mere change in mood.

5.5 ADULT ATTACHMENTS

Some researchers prefer to describe loving adult relationships in terms of attachments or interpersonal links rather than loving style. Much of this work has its genesis in the important developmental theory of Bowlby (1969), which will be briefly described.

Bowlby postulated that, for infants to survive, they must develop a range of behaviours that keep them close to their mother (or caregiver). These are referred to as attachment behaviours, and they consist of gestures and signals recognised by the parent. For instance, infants communicate through crying and smiling, to which the parent responds. Just *how* the parent responds will determine the later quality of the parent–child bond. Infants progress through various stages in this attachment process. According to Crain (1985) these stages are as follows.

Indiscriminate responding (from birth to about 3 months) This stage is characterised by an unselective form of responding – that is, crying or other forms of communication directed to most others.

Focusing on those who are familiar (from about 3 to 6 months) These individuals usually include the mother and father, followed by the siblings. The mother is usually the major attachment figure.

Active proximity-seeking (from about 6 months to 3 years) Young children actively seek out the major attachment figure. Thus they will try to crawl towards or stretch out to the parent, and are also visibly upset when removed from him or her.

Partnership behaviour (from about 3 years to end of childhood) As we get older and move into adolescence and then adulthood, we begin to break the close ties to our parents and form close attachments to others.

A major thesis of Bowlby (1969) is that the quality of our *current* adult attachments to a large extent mirrors that of our earlier attachments. A crucial determinant of the quality of the relationship is the parent's reactions when infants appear distressed. It is acknowledged that parents who respond in a warm, caring and positive way provide infants with the means to cope with future stressful and threatening situations (Mikulincer and Orbach, 1995). The image that we have of our parent–child bond serves as a blueprint and a guide for our future adult attachments. According to this argument, therefore, children who have positive and healthy attachments to their parents in childhood are likely to be able to form positive and healthy attachments to others as adults. This view – that there is a close connection between the quality of parent–child and adult–adult attachments – is held by some authors (Berk, 1993) but disputed by others (Buelow et al., 1996).

A major impetus for research into the nature of adult attachments was provided by Ainsworth et al. (1978) and operationalised by Hazan and Shaver (1987). Ainsworth argued that the primary caregiver plays a crucial role in determining the emotional adjustment of the young child. For instance, constantly interfering with the infant's desired behaviours can result in a child who is somewhat anxious and less inquisitive. Ainsworth argued that there are three styles of attachment, namely secure, anxious/ambivalent and avoidant. Whereas those who are secure in their attachment are willing to get close to others, and are not concerned about being 'abandoned' by a loved one, avoidant types find it uncomfortable being too close to others, do not completely trust others, and tend to be jealous. The anxious/ambivalent type feels that others do not get as close as he or she would like. These individuals are concerned that their loved one might not love them enough or, worse still, might abandon them. They also report experiencing 'extreme' sexual attraction and jealousy (see Hazan and Shaver, 1987, p.515).

5.5.1 Adult Attachments and Intrapersonal Processes

It is not unreasonable to expect attachment style to be significantly associated with the major personality dimensions, such as neuroticism and extraversion. Recent research by Shaver and Brennan (1992) supports this expectation. Using a measure of the Big Five personality dimensions (the NEO Personality Inventory (NEO-PI); Costa and McCrae, 1985), they found that avoidant types tended to be neurotic and to score low on extraversion, agreeableness and conscientiousness. Anxious individuals were found to be neurotic and to score low on agreeableness. Securely attached individuals were extraverted and agreeable, but scored low on neuroticism. Significant correlations were also observed for the facet scales of the NEO-PI, but only those with a very high level of significance ($P < 0.0001$) are shown in Table 5.3. It is clear that the different attachment styles are most strongly associated with the N and E facet scales, rather than with agreeableness, openness to experience or conscientiousness.

Evidence suggests that attachment style is also related to perceptions of the self and others (Hazan and Shaver, 1987). Thus secure types are more likely to endorse the view that they are easy to get to know and that most people would like them. They are trusting and hold the view that others are generally well intentioned. On the other hand, anxious/ambivalent types tend to express a lot of self-doubt, and believe that others misunderstand them or do not appreciate them. They also endorse the view that they are more willing than others to be involved in a long-term relationship. Secure types score lowest of all on measures of state and trait anxiety (Hazan and Shaver, 1987).

How do we regulate our levels of affect when coping with stressful events such as sad and anxiety-provoking memories? The evidence suggests that attachment styles play an important role in such situations. According to Israeli data (Mikulincer and Orbach, 1995), secure individuals are least anxious compared to ambivalent and avoidant types. With regard to defensiveness, avoidant respondents tend to be most defensive, and ambivalent individuals least so, whilst secure types usually show intermediate levels of defensiveness. In terms of memory recall, avoidant individuals show the lowest levels of accessibility to memories regarded as sad and anxiety-

Table 5.3 Attachment style and personality facets as measured by the NEO-PI

Attachment style	Personality facets
Secure	Hostility (− N)
	Depression (− N)
	Self-consciousness (− N)
	Vulnerability (− N)
	Warmth (E)
	Gregariousness (E)
	Positive emotions
Anxious/ambivalent	Anxiety (N)
	Depression (N)
	Self-consciousness (N)
	Vulnerability (N)
Avoidant	Hostility (N)
	Depression (N)
	Self-consciousness (N)
	Warmth (− E)
	Gregariousness (− E)
	Positive emotions (− E)
	Feeling (− O)

Adapted from Shaver, P. and Brennan, K. (1992) Attachment styles and the 'Big Five' personality traits: their connections with each other and with romantic relationship outcomes. *Personality and Social Psychology Bulletin* **18**, 536–45.

provoking, although they do not differ in the time it takes to recall sad, happy or anxious memories. By contrast, secure individuals tend to be significantly slower in recalling their anger-filled and sad memories compared to their happy and anxious ones. An analysis of the nature of recalled memories suggests that avoidant types display 'emotional shallowness', with ambivalent types being more intense and secure individuals scoring in the intermediate range.

Thus there are distinct differences between attachment typologies in personality functioning, such as anxiety and the types of memories that are recalled. For example, ambivalent individuals are anxious, do not repress unpleasant memories, and also access them relatively quickly. Findings such as these demonstrate crucial links between our pattern of attachment to others (that is, our relationship style) and our own inner self (Mikulincer and Orbach, 1995). As these authors suggest, there are:

'(vital) links between the interpersonal and intrapersonal spheres. It is evident that there is a parallelism between people's relationships with the social world and the make-up of their inner worlds. A working model of secure attachment seems to be manifested in openness to both intimate relationships and the emotional world.

(Mikulincer and Orbach, 1995, p.923)

It is worth noting that Collins and Read (1990) have modified Hazan and Shaver's (1987) approach to attachment style. Their critique centres on the view that respondents are normally asked to evaluate the whole description relating to each style, when in fact one may actually disagree with some aspects of the description. They have proposed a multi-item measure with three dimensions that are quite similar to the original, namely closeness (being comfortable with a close relationship), dependency (depending on others) and anxiety (feeling anxious about being abandoned). The evidence shows that these styles are related to depressive personality styles in predictable ways. For example, fear of closeness is significantly related to such factors as self-criticism and autonomy (Zuroff and Fitzpatrick, 1995).

5.5.2 Perceptions of Attachment to Parents

Employing several different measures, Heiss *et al.* (1996) suggested that four dimensions underpin students' perceptions of attachment to their parents. These are 'autonomous', 'insecure', 'dependence and concern' and 'attachment to father'. The first dimension incorporates a view of parents as encouraging independence and not being over-protective. The second dimension includes factors such as hostility and avoidant attachment. The third dimension reflects feelings of insecurity about the parental relationship, while the fourth reflects feelings of secure attachment with the parents.

What is significant from our view is that each of these dimensions relates significantly to personality measures in predictable ways, as summarised in Table 5.4. For example, Heiss *et al.* (1996) showed that an autonomous attachment style was positively related to trait affiliation, but that it was significantly negatively related to loneliness and lack of social self-confidence. They concluded that measures such as those discussed here are not capable of describing adult attachments in great detail, but rather that they serve only to describe attachments as being healthy or not, and to pass comment on the *general affective nature* of the relationship. None the less, the evidence shows that even such imprecise descriptions have important personality correlates.

In conclusion, we note that the types of relationships we have with others have strong links to our inner functioning, and that these links are logical and predictable. In other words, the quality of our relationships is neatly reflected in what we have come to expect of particular personality types. Indeed, it comes as no surprise to learn, for instance, that securely attached people are more agreeable, whilst avoidant types are more neurotic. Thus our close

Table 5.4 Dimensions of parental attachment and personality correlates

Dimension	Personality
Autonomy vs. protection	Loneliness (negative correlation)
	Affiliation
	Lack of social self-confidence (negative correlation)
Insecure attachment	Loneliness
	State-trait anxiety
	Self-critical depression
	Alienation
	Affiliation (negative correlation)
Dependence and concern	Dependency
	Assertion of autonomy (negative correlation)
Attachment to father	Affiliation (negative correlation)
	Efficacy
	Egocentricity (negative correlation)
	Alienation (negative correlation)

Source of information: Heiss, G., Berman, W. and Sperling, M. (1996) Five scales in search of a construct: exploring continued attachment to parents in college students. *Journal of Personality Assessment* **67**, 102–15.

relationships with others are quite closely shaped by our personal characteristics.

5.6 MARRIAGE

There is a growing literature on the personality correlates of partner choice, marital satisfaction and dissolution. Each of these will be succinctly addressed below.

5.6.1 Partner Choice and Marital Satisfaction

Based on work using the Big Five taxonomy (Botwin *et al.*, 1997), it would seem that we value agreeableness and openness/intellect most in our (prospective) partner. When asked to rank-order the most desirable traits, there is very little difference between what men and women rate as being most desirable – we all desire someone who is reliable, warm, fair, intelligent and knowledgeable. However, women do seem to be more selective than men. Dating women, more than dating men, want a partner who scores high on surgency and openness/intellect. Curiously, what women value/desire most so far as surgency is concerned is the facet dominance. In addition, newly-wed women are more exacting with respect to the remaining domains, namely agreeableness, conscientiousness and emotional stability. Among all respondents, agreeableness was found to be the best predictor of marital satisfaction and sexual satisfaction.

In a rare study, Hofstede (1996) examined the partner preferences of Asian women from eight different cities. The cities were characterised as 'masculine' (e.g. Tokyo) or 'feminine' (e.g. Bangkok, Seoul). Among those in so-called feminine cultures no differences were found between the desired characteristics of boyfriends or husbands. However, in the more masculine cultures some differences were noted. Boyfriends were preferred to have a sense of humour, to be intelligent and to show affection. Husbands were preferred to be healthy and to have wealth and understanding.

Although quite a large number of research studies have been conducted on marriage quality, relatively few have been concerned with the role of personality factors. Even fewer, it would seem, have based their work on recognised taxonomies such as the Eysenckian or Big Five factors. Likewise, longitudinal research has been scarce. Nevertheless, there is growing evidence that factors such as neuroticism and psychoticism are related to marital dissatisfaction.

Some evidence suggests that marital dissatisfaction is associated with high N levels in the female partner (Pond et al., 1963; Bentler and Newcomb, 1978). Perhaps not surprisingly, marital dissatisfaction and discord have been found to be related to high P levels in either the husband or the wife (Eysenck and Wakefield, 1981). Russell and Wells (1991) found modest levels of assortative mating between partners on N, P and Lie, and observed that marital dissatisfaction was related to differences on E, P and Lie, but not to differences on N. This finding seems to be at odds with the view that male–female differences should mirror those of the wider population if the marriage is to be experienced as satisfactory (Eysenck and Wilson, 1979). Thus one would expect females to have slightly higher N levels than their male partners. Finally, in one of the few good-quality longitudinal studies, Kelly and Conley (1987) found marital dissatisfaction to be associated with neuroticism in both partners and with low impulse control in the male partner (this study will be discussed in more detail later).

Russell and Wells (1994) conducted a study that is important because of its use of statistical modelling techniques. They were interested in the relationships between partners' personalities and marriage quality. The strongest correlations or levels of agreement were observed between partners' perceptions of the marriage quality – that is, happily married individuals tended to have contented partners. This was followed by partners' levels of neuroticism. Each had a negative influence on the marriage quality of the partner, thus refuting earlier suggestions that only the N levels of females are important. However, one should not assume a direct causal link between N and quality, as N levels in both partners were found to be correlated, and the marital quality of the one partner tended to be reflected in that of the other.

Table 5.5 Marital satisfaction as a function of respondent's and partner's affect

Respondent	Predictors
Wife	1. Wife's marital satisfaction positively related to her positive affect and negatively related to her levels of anger and sadness
	2. Husband's marital satisfaction positively related to wife's positive affect and negatively related to his wife's anger, whining and sadness
Husband	1. Husband's marital satisfaction positively related to his positive affect and negatively related to his sadness
	2. Wife's marital satisfaction positively related to husband's positive affect and negatively related to her levels of sadness

Adapted from Geist, R. and Gilbert, D. (1996) Correlates of expressed and felt emotion during marital conflict: satisfaction, personality, process and outcome. *Personality and Individual Differences* **21**, 49–60.

Marital dissatisfaction and discord are known to be associated with particular communication styles, the resolution of conflict, the management of affect, etc. Many of these behaviours are associated with marital satisfaction as well as the major personality domains not only of the respondent, but also of the partner (Geist and Gilbert, 1996). Table 5.5 summarises some of the main findings of a study of 56 married couples by highlighting the predictors of marital satisfaction. Although only the predictors of marital satisfaction are highlighted in the table, the results show that married dyads certainly appear to form a closely networked group where the behaviour of one individual has an impact on the marital satisfaction *and* the personality of the other (Geist and Gilbert, 1996).

5.6.2 Marital Dissolution

There are personality differences between those who are married and those who have divorced (the research seems to focus on divorce rather than separation). In an impressive sample of over 6000 UK adults, it was recently found that marital dissolution may be due more to the personality of the female rather than the male partner. Controlling for factors such as age and social class, the evidence showed that women whose relationship had dissolved had much higher extraversion and neuroticism scores than men (Cramer, 1993). Eysenck (1980) found that divorced men and women scored relatively high on the psychoticism dimension, while the differences between married and divorced women on the N scale were larger than the differences between married and divorced men. Presumably not all women who score high on measures of neuroticism will divorce. Thus the challenge for future research is to understand the exact circumstances under which some neurotic women decide to dissolve their marriage.

Luteijn (1994) distinguished men and women who divorced in terms of personality functioning. Based on his data for 51 heterosexual couples, men who divorced or who reported an unhappy relationship were more likely to be socially anxious, whereas women were more likely to score high on dominance. Men *and* women who reported an unsatisfying relationship were more likely to be neurotic and low in self-esteem.

Can one distinguish married individuals from divorcees on the basis of other lower-order personality traits? MacDonald *et al.* (1987) found that gender-role traits are significantly linked to marriage status. These researchers predicted that married couples would be more likely to accommodate each other by taking on traditional sex roles, with men assuming the more instrumental roles and women the expressive (or traditionally feminine) roles. Non-married subjects, it was predicted, would tend to be more androgynous. Their study of a rather small sample consisting of 183 women and 87 men revealed a significant association between length of time since the divorce and masculine (but not androgynous) scores. This would seem to suggest that, as the length of time since the divorce increases, male and female divorcees are more likely to be characterised by instrumental, but not expressive, gender-role traits (MacDonald *et al.*, 1987). As cause–effect relationships are not entirely clear from this research, longitudinal studies are required to track the changes in gender-role traits from pre- to post-marriage status.

5.6.3 Longitudinal Research

Following on from the above discussion, several longitudinal studies have demonstrated that links exist between emotional stability (or neuroticism) as assessed before marriage and marital satisfaction (e.g. Burgess and Wallin, 1953; Uhr, 1957, both cited in Kelly and Conley, 1987) or levels of psychological distress (Kurdek, 1991). However, it is likely that those personality factors which predict marital satisfaction after 10 years differ from those that predict marital satisfaction after, say, 20 or more years. Impulsive individuals, for example, are likely to divorce sooner rather than later. Moreover, researchers seem to operationalise their dependent variable in different ways, some focusing on marital satisfaction and others focusing on marital dissolution.

Research by Kelly and Conley (1987) attempted to obviate some of these methodological problems. Examining the antecedents of marital stability over a 50-year period (from the early 1930s to 1980), they found that men who divorced early had high neuroticism and low impulse control scores, whilst women who divorced early tended to be more neurotic than other women. Happily married couples tended to score low on neuroticism but high on impulse control. Moreover, males' composite scores of marital compatibility were predicted by the husband's neuroticism among the divorced and un-happily married group. Among women, the wife's level of neuroticism was a significant predictor. Thus these results suggest that personality factors such as neuroticism are important for predicting relationships that are under stress. However, as Kelly and Conley (1987) have stated, not all of these relation-ships will end in separation or divorce. There are other factors (e.g. religiosity, levels of conservatism, etc.) which serve to mediate these effects, and which determine whether a relationship will end in divorce or continue as an unhappy marriage.

An early study by Rockwell *et al.* (1979) examined the personality differ-ences between women born in the 1920s who remained married, and those who did not. The women were assessed in terms of their psychosocial development during their adolescent years. It was found that the divorced women had very strong heterosexual interests as teenagers, yet appeared to have good coping skills as youngsters. They appeared to adapt well to periods of uncertainty, although they were also more likely to be rebellious and non-conforming.

Using the MMPI, some researchers have uncovered significant differences between (ever) married and (ever) divorced individuals. For example, as early as 1966, Loeb found that the best predictor of divorce was the score on the Psychopathic deviate (Pd) scale 10 years earlier. Similar findings were obtained by McCrannie and Kahan (1986), who tracked medical students for over 20 years. They also found that Pd scores best predicted multiple divorce in their sample.

These two data-sets therefore suggest that individuals who divorce are more likely to be socially non-conforming, and to be impulsive, extraverted, sensation-seekers and risk-takers (McCrannie and Kahan, 1986). Just how do these traits lead to divorce? McCrannie and Kahan explain this as follows:

> Impulsivity, for example, may lead to shorter courtship and poor choice of spouse, resulting in greater likelihood of marital incompatibility and con-flict . . . greater stimulus-seeking tendencies may be associated with a lower boredom threshold . . . socially non-conforming tendencies may be asso-ciated with less desire and/or capacity to maintain intimate bonds.
> (McCrannie and Kahan, 1986, p.163)

Although research findings such as those reviewed here seem to suggest that certain personality traits are important in predicting divorce, Rockwell *et al.* caution against focusing too strongly on individual traits. As they explain:

> The life-course deprivations of early marriage (economic hardship, child-bearing pressures, etc.) undoubtedly override personal attributes in the causal process leading to separation and divorce. A comprehensive in-vestigation of marital outcomes must attend to the life histories of both partners and to characteristics of their evolving relationships.
> (Rockwell *et al.*, 1979, p.403)

This brief review has shown quite clearly how important personality factors are in explaining mate selection, marital satisfaction and marital dissolution. There are intricate and complex relationships between an individual personality (notably neuroticism), his or her marital satisfaction *and* that of his or her partner.

5.6.4 Comarital Sexual Relations

Some partners engage in sexual activity outside their primary relationship, an activity some researchers refer to as 'recreational sexual activity' (Wheeler and Kilmann, 1983). It is difficult to estimate the extent of this activity but, given the numbers of escort agencies in most large cities, it must be quite extensive.

Those who engage in comarital relationships have been found to have a high sex drive, and tend not to be too concerned about social taboos regarding their behaviour. Rather, they emphasise the positive aspects of such behaviour – citing, for example, increased sexual excitement (Wheeler and Kilmann, 1983). Wheeler and Kilmann compared two groups of couples, a comarital group and a matched control group, and found that although there were no differences in overall marital adjustment, there were some noteworthy differences in other areas. For instance, those engaging in comarital relationships were less likely to have good conflict resolution skills, and tended to interrupt each other more frequently. For the comarital group, sex outside the primary relationship did not interfere with the relationship, but improved it, with these individuals being more self-accepting and accepting of their partner.

5.7 SEXUAL BEHAVIOUR

Eysenck (1976) has formulated a number of specific hypotheses regarding the relationships between his three personality dimensions, E, N and P, and sexual behaviour. He predicted that:

1. Extraverts will have intercourse earlier than introverts.
2. Extraverts will have intercourse more frequently than introverts.
3. Extraverts will have intercourse with more different partners.
4. Extraverts will have intercourse in more different positions than introverts.
5. Extraverts will indulge in more varied sexual behaviours outside intercourse.
6. Extraverts will indulge in longer pre-coital love play than introverts.
   (Eysenck, 1976, pp.12–13)

What is the basis for these predictions? Differences in behaviour between extraverts and introverts are largely attributable to the functioning of the ascending reticular activating system (ARAS). The ARAS controls levels of physiological arousal, thus giving rise to what Eysenck (Eysenck and Eysenck, 1985) has referred to as his *arousal theory*. Several authors (e.g. Moruzzi and Magoun, 1949; Stelmack, 1981) have argued that the ARAS is linked to activity patterns as indicated by the EEG, as well as to psychological processes such as attention and orienting behaviour. In Eysenck's view, extraverts are generally under-aroused, whilst introverts tend to be over-aroused, which has important implications for their behaviour (Eysenck, 1976). Whereas extraverts are more likely to engage in thrill-enhancing behaviours, introverts are less likely to do so. Similarly, it can also be argued that extraverts are more likely than introverts to engage in varied and novel forms of sexual stimulation and to seek such stimulation more frequently.

The evidence tends to support Eysenck's (1976) predictions. For example, Giese and Schmidt (cited in Eysenck, 1976) studied the sexual behaviours of over 6000 German students. Using a short index of extraversion, they found clear differences in behaviour between high- and low-scoring extraverts. Extraverts were more likely than introverts to report having had four or more sexual partners over the past 12 months. On the other hand, introverts were more likely than extraverts to report only having had one sexual partner during a 12-month period. Extraverts were also far more likely to report having had intercourse by the age of 17 years than introverts, although introverts tended to masturbate more frequently than did extraverts. Finally, compared to introverts, male extraverts reported engaging in sexual intercourse using more than three different positions, although there were no significant differences between female introverts and extraverts.

Snyder and his colleagues have done much to initiate research into the relationships between self-monitoring and sexual behaviours (see, for example, Snyder *et al.*, 1986). Self-monitoring refers to how much people attend to the impression that they make on other people. High self-monitors are very aware of the impression that they have on others, and are keen to behave appropriately according to situational demands. Considerable empirical evidence suggests that self-monitoring is closely related to extraversion, with high self-monitors characterised as friendly, outgoing and talkative (Furnham, 1989), and it is therefore feasible that high self-monitors will, to a large degree, resemble extraverts with regard to their sexual behaviour. This is indeed the case.

Snyder *et al.* (1986) investigated the relationships between self-monitoring and sexual behaviour among a sample of university undergraduates. As predicted, high self-monitors were more favourably disposed towards casual sex, the number of foreseen partners, the number of 'one-night stands', the number of sex partners they had had in the last year, the number of sex partners they had had in their lifetime, and the frequency of sexual fantasy with a number of different partners. These results therefore support the view that high self-monitors are characterised by what Snyder *et al.* refer to as 'an unrestricted orientation toward sexual relations' (Snyder *et al.*, 1986, p.187). As these authors explain:

> (High self-monitors believe that) sexual relations need not be restricted to relationships in which they and their partners are psychologically close . . . if they were attracted to someone, they would feel comfortable and at ease engaging in sex with that person, even if they did not know him or her well.
>
> (Snyder *et al.*, 1986, p.181)

Other individual difference factors related to sexual behaviour are concerned with sex-role orientation, namely instrumentality and expressiveness. Leary and Snell (1988) noted that men and women differ with regard to sexual behaviour, such that men tend to become sexually active at a younger age, and also tend to be more sexually experienced than women. According to these authors, cultural and socialisation factors may be partly responsible for these differences, with males being more dominant or instrumental in their relationships and women being more nurturant or expressive.

In a study among undergraduates, Leary and Snell (1988) found that instrumentality in *both* sexes was significantly related to greater sexual activity. Thus for men and women, instrumentality was linked to ever having had sexual intercourse, the frequency of sexual intercourse, having had oral-genital sex, and experiencing nervousness about sex. Significant instrumentality–expressiveness interactions were also observed among females, such that high instrumentality–low expressiveness predicted the behaviours in question. Thus the authors were able to conclude that differences in sexual behaviour are partly due to dominant personality traits that are normally found to be characteristic of men and women.

Another individual difference factor shown to be linked with sexual behaviour is erotophobia–erotophilia (Fisher *et al.*, 1988). The sexual opinion survey said to measure this construct consists of three dimensions, namely open sexual display (e.g. 'I think it would be very entertaining to look at hard-core pornography'), sexual variety (e.g. 'Masturbation would be an exciting experience') and homoeroticism (e.g. 'Thoughts that I may have homosexual tendencies would not worry me at all').

As one would expect, erotophobia–erotophilia is linked to sexual behaviours and attitudes in predictable ways. Thus erotophobics are much more likely to experience sexual guilt and to be homophobic. Male and female erotophilics, on the other hand, are likely to masturbate more frequently and to have greater sexual experience than erotophobics. In addition, erotophilic men and women are more likely than others to engage in sexual behaviour during pregnancy than are erotophobics. Finally, links have been observed between erotophobia and sexual dysfunction, such as male erectile problems (Fisher *et al.*, 1988).

5.8 ATTITUDES TO SEX

Just as there are links between personality and sexual behaviours, so too links exist between personality and attitudes to sex, although the relevant research output in this regard has been very limited indeed. Given that cultural values regarding sexual matters probably vary quite considerably, there is considerable scope here for further study of cross-cultural differences in attitude.

One of the earlier studies in this area using standardised personality measures was conducted by Eysenck (1976). He surveyed over 800 adult UK respondents aged between 18 and 60 years, with a sample mean of about 30 years. Each respondent completed a 158-item survey on attitudes to sex in addition to measures of E, N and P. As a result, Eysenck (1976) uncovered 12 underlying dimensions to these attitudes, which are listed in Table 5.6. What is immediately apparent is the overlap between these Eysenckian dimensions and the three erotophobia–erotophilia factors referred to above. For example, Eysenck's permissiveness factor (Eysenck, 1976) seems quite similar to open sexual display (Fisher *et al.*, 1988).

Correlations were computed between personality scores and each of the individual attitude items (Eysenck, 1976), and it is possible to summarise the main trends as follows. Those men and women who scored high on the psychoticism scale were more in favour of impersonal sex and doing away with the institution of marriage. They were not opposed to their partner having sex with someone else, and believed that pornography should be freely available. These individuals displayed rather permissive attitudes towards sex, reflected in one of the attitude statements ('I believe in taking my pleasures where I can find them'). Curiously, these respondents also reported that they disliked others touching them, and that they felt nervous with people of the opposite sex (Eysenck, 1976).

As one would predict, individuals who scored high on the extraversion measure reported never having had a problem with sexual contacts, and having had strong sexual desires. They also reported having had their first sexual experience before introverts. High-scoring extraverts expressed their sexual feelings quite easily, and both men and women said they would take

Table 5.6 Structure of attitudes to sex among an adult sample

Attitudinal dimension			
1.	Permissiveness	7.	Sexual shyness
2.	Prudishness	8.	Impersonal sex
3.	Dominance–submission	9.	Aggressive sex
4.	Sexual digust	10.	Satisfaction
5.	Sexual excitement	11.	Neurotic sex
6.	Physical sex	12.	Pornography

Source of information: Eysenck, H. (1976) *Sex and personality.* London: Open Books Publishing Ltd.

part in an orgy if given the chance. Male extraverts sometimes felt like biting and scratching their sexual partner, whilst females reported making a lot of noise during intercourse, and were in favour of engaging in intercourse with the lights on. Unlike high P scorers, extraverts reported having discussed sexual issues with their parents (Eysenck, 1976).

Those who scored high on the neuroticism scale were marked by more disturbed attitudes to sex. According to Eysenck (1976), these individuals worried a lot about sex and believed that gaining sexual satisfaction was very important to them. They were also likely to become sexually excited very quickly, yet at the same time they were nervous about sex. In a sense, neurotics had an unsatisfactory sex life, both men and women reporting that something was 'lacking' in this area of their life. Both male and female neurotics had thoughts about aggressive sex, and seemed to prefer sex partners who were older than them.

Thus distinct and meaningful links can be drawn between attitudes to sex and individual personality functioning. These attitudes, like so many others discussed in this volume, are related to personality factors in quite predictable ways, thereby adding to our knowledge of the nature both of these attitudes and of particular personality types.

5.9 CONCLUSION

There can be no doubting the important ways in which personality traits and the nature of close relationships and loving styles go hand in hand. Personality has been shown to be logically related to attachment styles, marital dissolution, sexual attitudes and sexual behaviour. There is clear evidence that extraverts tend to be securely attached, that neurotic individuals tend to be anxious/ambivalent and avoidant, and that introverts manifest an avoidant attachment style. With regard to loving styles, there are also predictable and logical links to the major personality dimensions. At a clinical level, useful evidence is beginning to emerge about the influence of attachment style on the inner self and the recall of memory. Quite clearly, therefore, attachment style has implications for both interpersonal and intrapersonal functioning.

The evidence we have reviewed in this chapter indicates that personality factors are implicated in marriage dissolution. Factors such as impulsiveness, extraversion and sensation-seeking have been identified as being important. However, it is still not entirely clear whether these personality factors have the same effect on short-term *and* long-term relationships. Quite clearly the impact of personality on marriage dissolution is far more complex than has hitherto been suggested. Future research also needs to focus on personality and the dissolution of *de facto* relationships, which are increasingly common in many nations today. Notwithstanding the research challenges which remain to be addressed, psychologists have in a relatively short period of time done much to shed light on the interplay between personality and close relationships.

REFERENCES

Ainsworth, M., Blehar, M., Waters, E. and Wall, S. (1978) *Patterns of attachment: a psychosocial study of the strange situation.* Hillsdale, NJ: Erlbaum.

Ajzen, I. (1974) Effects of information on interpersonal attraction. *Journal of Personality and Social Psychology* **29**, 374–80.

Aron, A., Paris, M. and Aron, E. (1995) Falling in love: prospective studies of self-concept change. *Journal of Personality and Social Psychology* **69**, 1102–12.

Bentler, P. and Newcomb, M. (1978) Longitudinal study of marital success and failure. *Journal of Consulting and Clinical Psychology* **46**, 1053–70.

Berk, L. (1993) *Infants, children and adolescents.* Boston: Allyn & Bacon.

Botwin, M., Buss, D.M. and Shakelford, T. (1997) Personality and mate preferences: five factors in mate selection and marital satisfaction. *Journal of Personality* **65**, 107–36.

Bowlby, J. (1969) *Attachment and loss. Vol. 1. Attachment.* New York: Basic Books.

Brehm, S. (1992) *Intimate relationships.* New York: McGraw-Hill.

Buelow, G., McClain, M. and McIntosh, I. (1996) A new measure for an important construct: the attachment and object relations inventory. *Journal of Personality Assessment* **66**, 604–23.

Byrne, D. (1961) Interpersonal attraction and attitude similarity. *Journal of Abnormal and Social Psychology* **62**, 713–15.

Clark, M. and Mills, J. (1979) Interpersonal attraction in exchange and communal relationships. *Journal of Personality and Social Psychology* **37**, 12–24.

Cloninger, S. (1996) *Theories of personality: understanding persons,* 2nd edn. Upper Saddle River, NJ: Prentice-Hall.

Collins, N. and Read, S. (1990) Adult attachment, working models, and relationship quality in dating couples. *Journal of Personality and Social Psychology* **58**, 644–63.

Cook, M. and Wilson, G. (eds) (1979) *Love and attraction: an international conference.* Oxford: Pergamon.

Costa, P. and McCrae, R. (1985) *The NEO Personality Inventory.* Odessa, FL: Psychological Assessment Resources.

Crain, W. (1985) *Theories of development: concepts and applications,* 2nd edn. Englewood Cliffs, NJ: Prentice-Hall.

Cramer, D. (1993) Personality and marital dissolution. *Personality and Individual Differences* **14**, 605–7.

Davies, M. (1996) EPQ correlates of love styles. *Personality and Individual Differences* **20**, 257–9.

Donelson, E. (1973) *Personality: a scientific approach.* Pacific Palisades, CA: Goodyear Publishing.

Erikson, E. (1968) *Identity: youth and crisis.* New York: W.W. Norton & Co.

Eysenck, H. (1976) *Sex and personality.* London: Open Books Publishing Ltd.

Eysenck, H. (1980) Personality, marital satisfaction, and divorce. *Psychological Reports* **47**, 1235–8.

Eysenck, H. and Wilson, G. (1979) *The psychology of sex.* London: Dent.

Eysenck, H. and Wakefield, J. (1981) Psychological factors as predictors of marital satisfaction. *Advances in Behavior Research and Therapy* 3, 151–92.

Eysenck, H. and Eysenck, M. (1985) *Personality and individual differences: a natural science approach.* New York: Plenum.

Felmlee, D. (1995) Fatal attractions: affection and disaffection in intimate relationships. *Journal of Social and Personal Relationships* 12, 295–311.

Fisher, W., Byrne, D., White, L. and Kelley, K. (1988) Erotophobia–erotophilia as a dimension of personality. *Journal of Sex Research* 25, 123–51.

Furnham, A. (1989) Personality correlates of self-monitoring: the relationship between extraversion, neuroticism, Type A behaviour and Snyder's self-monitoring construct. *Personality and Individual Differences* 10, 35–42.

Geist, R. and Gilbert, D. (1996) Correlates of expressed and felt emotion during marital conflict: satisfaction, personality, process, and outcome. *Personality and Individual Differences* 21, 49–60.

Green, B. and Kenrick, D. (1994) The attractiveness of gender-typed traits at different relationship levels: androgynous characteristics may be desirable after all. *Personality and Social Psychology Bulletin* 20, 244–53.

Hazan, C. and Shaver, P. (1987) Romantic love conceptualized as an attachment process. *Journal of Personality and Social Psychology* 52, 511–24.

Heiss, G., Berman, W. and Sperling, M. (1996) Five scales in search of a construct: exploring continued attachment to parents in college students. *Journal of Personality Assessment* 67, 102–15.

Hendrick, C. (ed.) (1989) *Close relationships.* Newbury Park, CA: Sage.

Hendrick, C. and Hendrick, S. (1986) A theory and method of love. *Journal of Personality and Social Psychology* 50, 392–402.

Hofstede, G. (1996) Gender stereotypes and partner preferences of Asian women in masculine and feminine cultures. *Journal of Cross-Cultural Psychology* 27, 533–46.

Ireland, W. (1988) Eros, agape, amor, libido: concepts in the history of love. In Lasky, J. and Silverman, H. (eds), *Love: psychoanalytic perspectives.* New York: New York University Press, 14–30.

Kelly, E. and Conley, J. (1987) Personality and compatibility: a prospective analysis of marital stability and marital satisfaction. *Journal of Personality and Social Psychology* 52, 27–40.

Krueger, R. and Caspi, A. (1993) Personality, arousal, and pleasure: a test of competing models of interpersonal attraction. *Personality and Individual Differences* 14, 105–12.

Kurdek, L. (1991) Marital stability and changes in marital quality in newly wed couples: a test of the contextual model. *Journal of Social and Personal Relationships* 8, 27–48.

Lasky, J. and Silverman, H. (1988) *Love: psychoanalytic perspectives.* New York: New York University Press.

Leary, M. and Snell, W. (1988) The relationship of instrumentality and expressiveness to sexual behavior in males and females. *Sex Roles* 18, 509–22.

Lee, J. (1976) *The colors of love.* Englewood Cliffs, NJ: Prentice-Hall.

Lester, D., Martin, R., Serrecchia, T. and Sgro, J. (1992) The desire to lose one's identity. *Personality and Individual Differences* 13, 1351–2.

Loeb, J. (1966) The personality factor in divorce. *Journal of Consulting Psychology* 30, 562.

Luteijn, F. (1994) Personality and the quality of an intimate relationship. *European Journal of Psychological Assessment* **10**, 220–23.

McCrannie, E. and Kahan, J. (1986) Personality and multiple divorce: a prospective study. *Journal of Nervous and Mental Disease* **174**, 161–4.

Macdonald, N., Ebert, P. and Mason, S. (1987) Marital status and age as related to masculine and feminine personality dimensions and self-esteem. *Journal of Social Psychology* **127**, 289–98.

Mallandain, I. and Davies, M. (1994) The colours of love: personality correlates of love styles. *Personality and Individual Differences* **17**, 557–60.

Mikulincer, M. and Orbach, I. (1995) Attachment styles and repressive defensiveness: the accessibility and architecture of affective memories. *Journal of Personality and Social Psychology* **68**, 917–25.

Moruzzi, G. and Magoun, H. (1949) Brain stem reticular formation and activation of the EEG. *Electroencephalography and Clinical Neurophysiology* **1**, 455–73.

Pond, D., Ryle, A. and Hamilton, M. (1963) Marriage and neurosis in a working-class population. *British Journal of Psychiatry* **109**, 592–8.

Rockwell, R., Elder, G. and Ross, D. (1979) Psychological patterns in marital timing and divorce. *Social Psychological Quarterly* **42**, 399–404.

Russell, R. and Wells, P. (1991) Personality similarity and quality of marriage. *Personality and Individual Differences* **12**, 407–12.

Russell, R. and Wells, P. (1994) Personality and quality of marriage. *British Journal of Psychology* **85**, 161–8.

Shaver, P. and Brennan, K. (1992) Attachment styles and the 'Big Five' personality traits: their connections with each other and with romantic relationship outcomes. *Personality and Social Psychology Bulletin* **18**, 536–45.

Smith, S. (1996) Dating-partner preferences among a group of inner-city African-American high-school students. *Adolescence* **131**, 79–90.

Snyder, M. (1986) *Public appearances, private realities: the psychology of self-monitoring.* New York: W.H. Freeman.

Snyder, M., Simpson, J. and Gangestad, S. (1986) Personality and sexual relations. *Journal of Personality and Social Psychology* **51**, 181–90.

Stafford-Clark, D. (1965) *What Freud really said.* Harmondsworth: Penguin.

Stelmack, R. (1981) The psychophysiology of extraversion and neuroticism. In Eysenck, H. (ed.), *A model for personality.* Berlin: Springer, 38–64.

Sternberg, R. (1986) A triangular theory of love. *Psychological Review* **93**, 119–35.

Sternberg, R. and Barnes, M. (eds) (1988) *The psychology of love.* New Haven, CT: Yale University Press.

Strouse, J. (1974) *Women and analysis: dialogues on psychoanalytic views of femininity.* New York: Dell Publishing Co.

Taraban, C. and Hendrick, C. (1995) Personality perceptions associated with six styles of love. *Journal of Social and Personal Relationships* **12**, 453–61.

Walster, E. and Walster, G. (1978) *A new look at love.* Reading, MA: Addison-Wesley.

Wheeler, J. and Kilmann, P. (1983) Comarital sexual behavior: individual and relationship variables. *Archives of Sexual Behavior* **12**, 295–306.

Woll, S. (1989) Personality and relationship correlates of loving styles. *Journal of Research in Personality* **23**, 480–505.

Zuroff, D. and Fitzpatrick, D. (1995) Depressive personality styles: implications for adult attachment. *Personality and Individual Differences* **18**, 253–65.

6

Personality and Crime

6.1 **INTRODUCTION**

According to most news reports, crime rates appear to be rising in nearly every society, particularly industrialised societies and those with a large gulf between rich and poor. One cannot open a newspaper or watch the evening television news without some report of a criminal act somewhere accompanied by intense speculation as to the personality of the criminal and, occasionally, his or her victim. Even more disturbing are the increasing numbers of young children who are suspected of involvement in violent crime, even murder. It is not surprising, therefore, that psychologists along with criminologists, sociologists, lawyers, police and politicians are increasingly being called upon to comment on such incidents and to provide an explanation for what has occurred.

Psychologists have come a long way in understanding the psychological processes associated with different criminal acts. It was commonly held in the 1700s and 1800s that criminal behaviours could best be explained in terms of one's 'free will' (Hollin, 1989) – that is, individuals somehow *chose* to engage in crime. Retribution by the law was usually swift and severe. Contemporary psychological research and theorising now recognises that a range of genetic, social and personality factors interact in explaining antisocial acts; there are strong and varied forces at work that shape the criminal behaviours of individuals. Recent advances in the measurement of different personality traits together with advanced computer technology and statistical procedures (e.g. structural equation modelling) have sharpened our research methodologies and analytical tools to such an extent that our understanding of the psychology of crime and the personality of the criminal has increased considerably.

The present chapter reviews important recent research into the personality correlates of crime, including also more specific crimes such as drink-driving, violent crimes such as rape, and crimes against property. It will soon be clear to the reader that most of the published work, rather than being psychoanalytic, has been conducted from a trait perspective. In this regard, numerous studies using standardised personality inventories have examined the role of established personality factors in explaining criminal behaviours. However, we shall begin with a brief review of the contribution of psychoanalytic theory.

6.2 PSYCHOANALYTIC PERSPECTIVES

The psychoanalytic approach to understanding crime and delinquency is embedded in the functioning of the id and ego and, as will be pointed out below, the emotional experiences of the individual as a child. One's inner dynamic forces predict whether one will engage in criminal activity or not (Hollin, 1989). Driven by the so-called pleasure principle (or id), the young person is essentially asocial and strives simply to attain pleasure and enjoyment. However, with the development of the reality principle (or ego), most of us will follow established rules and norms, although in a minority of individuals this is not always the case. For them, socialisation has not been effective, and delinquent and antisocial tendencies continue to be a hallmark of their behaviour, situated as it is outside established boundaries of what is regarded as acceptable behaviour.

According to this perspective, therefore, criminal behaviour is viewed as the result of a conflict between the ego and the superego, or intrapsychic conflict (Asch, 1974), and is not necessarily linked to a particular personality type (such as low self-esteem or high levels of extraversion). Even those with a 'well-developed superego', as Asch (1974, p.161) calls it, can engage in criminal behaviour, thereby 'acting out forbidden impulses' (Asch, 1974, p.162).

These themes are also taken up by Healy and Bronner (1936; cited in Hollin, 1989). In their view, *sublimation* is important in understanding criminal behaviour. What this means is that instincts guide behaviour; our emotions and thoughts are driven by instinctual impulses such that criminal behaviours are an *acting out* process. We are *driven* to commit unacceptable behaviours, and Hollin explains this tendency in the following terms:

> Thus the criminal act, it is argued, results from inner unsatisfied desires and dissatisfactions; these unsatisfied wishes, in turn, stem from a failure to experience strong emotional ties with another person, usually a parent.
>
> (Hollin, 1989, p.35)

Several other psychoanalytic explanations which have been put forward to explain criminality are discussed by Hollin (1989), and these are listed in Table 6.1. They include impulsive behaviours and parental approval of

Table 6.1 Psychoanalytic explanations for criminal behaviour

Individual unable to control impulsive and pleasure-seeking behaviour

---

There is unconscious parental approval of non-normative behaviours. This results in an underdeveloped superego with seemingly little control over antisocial impulses

---

Acting out feelings of oppression and helplessness

Source of information: Hollin, C. (1989) *Psychology and crime: an introduction to criminal psychology.* London: Routledge, 35.

deviant behaviour. In the latter example, the superego appears to be functioning in a negative sense, condoning unacceptable behaviours (see also Kaplan, 1976).

Martins (1991) also highlights the role of instincts by suggesting that crime and delinquency are best explained in terms of complex instinctive drives which do not appear to be responsive to education. Also implicated are certain environmental factors, notably disturbed mother–infant relationships. He suggests that criminals suffer from heightened levels of 'anxiety of a traumatic nature', which is unlikely to recede, despite the individual's fantasies of invincibility. Thus criminals are viewed as anxious types who have experienced disturbed mother–child relationships, and who are driven to criminal behaviour.

The importance of disturbed mother–infant relationships in the aetiology of criminal behaviour is also noted by Adler (1982). One consequence of such a disturbed relationship is immaturity (as in the case of delinquents) and mood swings. Such individuals have a sense of 'incompleteness', and suffer from unrealistic expectations. Because of their disturbed mother–infant relationship, these individuals are fearful of being 'abandoned', 'rejected' or 'dropped', and long 'to be held and contained' (Adler, 1982, p.283). As Adler (1982) explains, some individuals engage in criminal behaviours because they are deliberately provoking the justice system into 'containing' them.

Does the psychoanalytic perspective differentiate between various categories of crime, such as violent and non-violent? It would appear so. According to Asch (1974), extreme violence is explained as an impulsive search for self-esteem. By engaging in mindless violence or destruction, the perpetrator is simply demonstrating his or her disregard for the superego or societal restrictions.

To date, these views have proved difficult to test empirically. Some of the elements purportedly related to crime have proved difficult to operationalise, whilst Vold (1958) has suggested that it is well nigh impossible to generalise beyond the specifics of any one individual. Another criticism levelled against the psychoanalytic approach concerns its emphasis on instincts and drives, and the suggestion that some behaviours are the product of a biological force (Indira, 1987).

6.3 THE SOCIAL–COGNITIVE APPROACH

Although this approach is clearly linked to intellectual functioning, it also appears to subsume a number of personality traits – including, for instance, impulsiveness (Hollin, 1989). In short, the social–cognitive approach suggests that individuals do not always *understand* the consequences of their actions. Thus it follows that they may act impulsively, that they may fail to think about their behaviour, that they may fail to consider the outcomes of their behaviour (for themselves or others), and they may fail to think about alternative responses. Research findings with regard to the importance of factors such as impulsiveness tend to be equivocal, although it is generally assumed that a high level of impulsivity is characteristic of delinquent and criminal types (e.g. Binder, 1988).

It is firmly held by some that criminal activity depends in part on an individual's cognitive abilities. According to Hollin (1989), one key feature that distinguishes criminals from others is the inability of the former to distinguish clearly between a variety of different social stimuli. In other words, the following are missing from their repertoire of behaviours (Hollin, 1989, p.49):

- the ability to decide on suitable behaviours for different occasions;
- the ability to generate possible solutions to problems;
- the ability to consider the consequences of one's actions;
- the ability to plan to achieve different outcomes.

Also implicated in the social–cognitive approach is the view that (some) criminals actually do think about what they are about to do. Thus the criminal is viewed as a 'rational decision-maker' (Hollin, 1989, p.50) who decides, because a house appears to be momentarily unattended, to enter with the intent of committing a burglary. In cases such as these criminals have taken advantage of what is for them a favourable situation, and have exploited it for their own purposes.

6.4 PERSONALITY FACTORS AND DELINQUENCY

Research studies spanning many years have shown quite conclusively that personality factors are related to a wide range of antisocial, criminal and delinquent behaviours (e.g. Rutter and Giller, 1983; Eysenck and Eysenck, 1985; Farrington, 1986, 1992; Binder, 1988; Eysenck and Gudjonsson, 1989). The vast majority of research in the area of delinquency has been cross-sectional in nature and has sought to examine the links between criminality and the three major higher-order personality factors of extraversion (E), neuroticism (N) and Eysenckian psychoticism (P). Several other trait variables or lower-order factors have also been identified, including low self-esteem, impulsiveness, venturesomeness, aggression and hostility. We shall first discuss the higher-order factors before considering some of the lower-order variables.

In his early work, Eysenck first saw criminality as being related to tough-mindedness, both having a basis in extraversion (for a recent review see Gudjonsson, 1997). More recently, however, Eysenck has proposed that E, N and P are predictive of criminality, with P being the strongest correlate (see Eysenck and Eysenck, 1970; Eysenck and Eysenck, 1985; Eysenck and Gudjonsson, 1989). Respondents who score high on measures of extraversion are said to be stimulus hungry and to engage in thrill-enhancing behaviours. The reason for this lies in the functioning of the ascending reticular activating system which controls one's level of physiological arousal. It has been shown that extraverts tend to score low on arousal, and hence will seek out novel and venturesome activities. By contrast, introverts tend to be highly aroused, and they therefore avoid too much social contact or novel stimuli. It has also been suggested (Eysenck and Eysenck, 1985) that a link exists between arousability and conditionability. Because extraverts are under-aroused, they are less likely to condition easily or to learn new and more acceptable (i.e. less delinquent) behaviours.

Neuroticism is linked to criminal and delinquent behaviours through anxiety (Eysenck and Eysenck, 1985). Neurotics also tend to be anxious, and high anxiety functions very much like a drive which multiplies with habit. In other words, someone who engages in delinquent behaviours is likely to persist with such activities if they also happen to score high on N. Finally, there is abundant evidence to suggest that P is strongly linked to delinquent and criminal activities. For example, it is well established that high-P individuals are also aggressive, uncaring, troublesome, inhumane and insensitive to the needs and feelings of others, and tend not to experience feelings of guilt. They also appear foolhardy and have a preference for strange and unusual things (Eysenck and Eysenck, 1970). Howarth (1986) argued that high-P individuals are impulsive and tend not to be co-operative. They are also rigid and lack sensitivity. Claridge (1981) suggested that this dimension is closely allied to overt aggressiveness and impulsivity. For these reasons, it is perhaps not surprising that the P measure is well able to discriminate between criminals and non-criminals (Eysenck and Gudjonsson, 1989). As these authors point out, 'Criminality is related to certain dimensions of personality, in particular that labelled psychoticism, which is apparent in all age groups and under all conditions studied' (Eysenck and Gudjonsson, p.88).

6.4.1 Empirical Evidence: E, N, P and Delinquency

A report by Furnham and Thompson (1991) lists several studies which have examined Eysenckian theory in relation to delinquency. Although it was not intended to be an exhaustive review of all research, it cited 29 studies which found evidence for the importance of at least one of E, N and P, and 8 studies which did not. Attempting to explain equivocal findings in this area, Furnham and Thompson (1991) have suggested the following:

- that N and criminality are often positively linked in prison populations, but not in others.
- that E, N and P may predict some crimes, but not others.
- that N may predict criminality in older rather than younger populations.

In this section we shall focus on quite diverse studies in terms of methodologies and measuring instruments used, but for a more exhaustive review the interested reader should consult Eysenck and Gudjonsson (1989).

A study of Australian 14-year-olds showed that the P factor plays an important mediating and additive role in explaining delinquency (Heaven, 1994). For instance, P was found to exacerbate the effect of venturesomeness among both males and females. That is, P increased the likelihood that venturesome individuals would engage in delinquent acts, whilst among females P was found to mediate the effect of perceptions of negative family communication. In other words, an increase in self-reported delinquency was associated with negative family communication, and the effect was mediated by P. Thus it is clear that P fulfils an important and quite complex function in explaining delinquency.

One study of a sample of 210 non-delinquent UK adolescents is noteworthy. It evaluated three competing theoretical positions, namely the role of personality factors, anomie (or alienation) and social skills as predictors of scores on a measure of self-reported delinquency (Furnham, 1984). It is suggested that anomie occurs when an individual is thwarted by societal constraints from striving to attain reasonable goals. Such constraints may include poverty or lack of educational opportunities. With regard to social skills, it has been argued that those who engage in delinquent acts do so simply because they lack appropriate social skills. Furnham (1984) observed that self-reported delinquency correlated most strongly with P, followed by N, anomie, E and social skills. Thus psychoticism correlated most strongly with delinquency for this sample, thereby supporting the views of Eysenck (Eysenck and Gudjonsson, 1989).

Although it was conducted several years ago, a study of UK and Canadian respondents is noteworthy, as it evaluated the relative importance of several personality inventories, including the EPI, EPQ, 16PF and High School Personality Questionnaire (Rushton and Chrisjohn, 1981). It was concluded that both E and P, but not N, are reliably linked to delinquency. More recently, Farrington (1992) has also questioned the exact role of N. In his view, it depends on whether one is referring to 'official' or self-reported delinquency. 'Official' offenders are most often characterised by high N and low E scores, whereas self-reported offenders are characterised by low N and high E scores. However, both forms of delinquency are related to the P factor.

The extent to which self-reported delinquency is predicted by the factors E, N and P appears to vary from one study to another and also depends on the age of the respondents and the exact measures used to gauge personality. For instance, it has been argued that N is not an important predictor among younger respondents, although E is (Eysenck and Gudjonsson, 1989). Yet in a study of university undergraduates, Furnham and Thompson (1991) found P to be a significant correlate, but not N or E. Eysenck and Eysenck (1985) have also noted that the E scores of incarcerated individuals tend to be rather low, although this is not altogether surprising. With regard to the personality measures that are used, findings with respect to the influence of E appear to be equivocal. Earlier versions of Eysenck's E scale contained impulsiveness and sociability items (Eysenck and Eysenck, 1969), whereas newer forms of the inventory include mainly sociability items. This change has therefore had an effect on the strength of the association between E and self-reported delinquency.

BOX 6.1

Measuring self-reported delinquency

There are several scales which purport to measure self-reported delinquency, a recent example being by Mak (1993). This instrument assesses the frequency of occurrence of a range of different behaviours over the last 12 months, and possesses adequate internal consistency. It also successfully discriminates adjudicated delinquent from non-delinquent children, and includes the following dimensions:

1. cheat (e.g. cheating on games machines);
2. status (e.g. buying alcohol; drinking alcohol);
3. fight (e.g. fighting with a weapon);
4. vehicle (e.g. stealing a bicycle);
5. drugs (e.g. using LSD);
6. theft (e.g. engaged in shoplifting);
7. harm (e.g. blackmailing someone);
8. driving (e.g. drink-driving);
9. disturb (e.g. vandalising school property).

Source: Mak, A. (1993) A self-report delinquency scale for Australian adolescents. *Australian Journal of Psychology* **45**, 75–9.

6.4.2 Delinquency and the Big Five Personality Dimensions

Very little research has been concerned with the relationships between self-reported delinquency and the so-called Big Five personality factors. One exception appears to be a recent study by Heaven (1996a), who reported two sets of results. In the first, over 200 high-school students completed measures of vandalism/theft and interpersonal violence as well as domain measures of N, E, openness to experience (O), conscientiousness (C) and agreeableness (A).

Neither O nor E were significantly related to either form of delinquency for males and females. The C factor was significantly negatively related to vandalism for both sexes, while N was significantly related to vandalism/theft for males and to interpersonal violence for females. Factor A was significantly negatively related to both delinquency measures for males, and was significantly negatively related to interpersonal violence for females.

A second study examined the importance of some of the facet scales of the NEO domains (Costa and McCrae, 1992). On this occasion, the respondents were 90 university undergraduates (Heaven, 1996a). The main results from two multiple regression analyses are shown in Table 6.2. The best predictors of interpersonal violence were excitement-seeking (E) and trust (A), while the best predictors of vandalism/theft were self-discipline (C), excitement-seeking and trust. Thus individuals who engage in delinquent behaviours appear to be driven by a need for excitement-seeking and low levels of trust in others. It is therefore possible to conclude that the five-factor description of personality, as measured by the NEO inventory, is a useful taxonomy for conducting research into social behaviours such as delinquency. The delinquency scores correlate with the personality domains in the expected directions, and do not contradict Eysenck's theory.

Table 6.2 Multiple regression analyses of delinquency measures

Variable	R^2	β	t
Interpersonal violence			
E – Excitement-seeking	0.05	0.22	2.05*
A – Trust	0.16	– 0.33	– 3.36*
A – Altruism	0.19	– 0.19	– 1.65
A – Compliance	0.19	– 0.04	– 0.43
Vandalism/theft			
C – Self-discipline	0.08	– 0.29	– 2.80*
E – Excitement-seeking	0.15	0.25	2.52*
A – Trust	0.24	– 0.30	– 3.09*
A – Altruism	0.24	– 0.08	– 0.75

*$p < 0.05$

Source: Reprinted from *Personality and Individual Differences*, **20**, Heaven P., Personality and self-reported delinquency: analysis of the 'Big Five' personality dimensions, Page No's. 47–54, Copyright (1996), with permission from Elsevier Science.

6.4.3 Delinquency and Other Personality Traits

Many studies have examined the links between delinquency and scores on other personality inventories such as the MMPI. Weaver and Wootton (1992) found that delinquents could be differentiated from normative groups on the basis of their MMPI scores, with delinquents being classified as more pathological on the following subscales: social responsibility, alcoholism, familial discord, persecutory ideas, psychomotor acceleration, staid-personal rigidity, and depression and apathy. Delinquents seem unwilling to take or incapable of accepting responsibility for their own actions – one cannot rely on them, nor are they trustworthy. According to Weaver and Wootton (1992), they lack integrity and do not experience a sense of responsibility towards the group (or family) to which they belong. However, they are keen to explore other values and behaviours. Moreover,

> Such persons are socially extroverted and exhibitionistic, have difficulty concentrating, and may have a history of behaviour problems in school. They describe their home and family situations as being unpleasant, lacking in love, understanding, and support. Family members are seen as being critical, quarrelsome, and as refusing to permit adequate freedom and independence.
>
> (Weaver and Wootton, 1992, p.551)

Reviews of the literature suggest that criminal acts are also related to a wide range of personality traits or facets which have usually been studied in isolation. These include, for example, anger/hostility, venturesomeness (Heaven, 1993), assertiveness, low conventionality (e.g. Binder, 1988), aggression, anxiety, low self-control (e.g. Feldman, 1977), low self-esteem (Rice, 1992), impulsiveness, negative attitudes to authority (e.g. Rigby *et al.*, 1989), sensation-seeking, low empathy (Eysenck and Gudjonsson, 1989) and locus of control (e.g. Shaw and Scott, 1991).

Of interest is the suggestion that personality factors may mediate the effects of other variables (such as perceptions of the family) on delinquency. In a study of Australian adolescents, Shaw and Scott (1991) found that the respondents' locus of control mediated the relationship between perceptions of parental discipline style and self-reported delinquency. In other words, punitive parenting and parental love withdrawal were significantly associated with heightened delinquency, with these effects being mediated by an external locus of control. On the other hand, self-reported delinquency tended to decrease in combination with an inductive (non-punitive) parental discipline style. This effect was mediated by an internal locus of control (for contradictory findings see Peiser and Heaven, 1996).

One study of 386 high-school students (Heaven, 1993) assessed the relationships between delinquency and several personality factors, including self-esteem, trait anger, venturesomeness, attitudes to authority and dysfunctional impulsiveness, as well as psychoticism and extraversion. Interesting sex differences were observed. It was found that both psychoticism and extraversion were significant predictors of self-reported delinquency for both males and females. However, whereas the other traits were directly related to delinquency for males, this was not the case for females. In fact, psychoticism was found to mediate the effect of the other traits for girls. It was concluded that psychoticism was found to act as a conduit, thereby channelling the effects of the other traits on delinquency for girls.

Coolidge *et al.* (1992) asked the parents of non-violent juvenile offenders to judge the personality of their offspring. Compared with a matched control group, the delinquents were judged to be significantly more antisocial, passive-aggressive, self-defeating, dependent and histrionic. They were also rated as depressed, and scored in the pathological direction on a neuropsychological index which included measures of planning, attention problems, motor co-ordination and hyperactivity. Thus these results point to distinct neuropsychological impairment in this group, as well as to indices of emotional maladjustment (Coolidge *et al.*, 1992).

So far, much of the review presented here has focused on the personalities of what could be described as 'normal-range' youth. What about incarcerated youth? Hollander and Turner (1985) assessed the personality characteristics of 200 consecutively incarcerated male juvenile offenders aged between 12 and 19 years. About one-third of them had a personality disorder (schizotypal, paranoid or borderline; see Table 6.3), whilst almost 20 per cent had a specific developmental and/or attention deficit disorder. Almost 50 per cent of the offenders had IQ scores below 85. It is worth noting that most of the juveniles came from stressed and disorganised families. Almost 75 per cent of

Table 6.3 Personality symptoms of 200 incarcerated male juvenile offenders

Borderline symptoms	Schizotypal symptoms
Excessive use of drugs and alcohol	Mood swings
Manipulativeness	Recurrent auditory experiences
Instability in interpersonal relationships	Bizarre behaviour
Feelings of boredom and emptiness	Deviant communication patterns
Assaultiveness	
Unrealistic career expectations	

Source of information: Hollander, H. and Turner, F. (1985) Characteristics of incarcerated delinquents: relationship between development disorders, environmental and family factors, and patterns of offense and recidivism. *Journal of the American Academy of Child Psychiatry* **24**, 225.

the boys came from non-intact families. Thus the extent to which such external factors interact with personality dispositions also needs to be borne in mind and more carefully examined.

6.4.4   Longitudinal Predictors of Self-Reported Delinquency

Of the relatively few longitudinal studies that have been conducted into the causes of delinquency, most are quite limited in terms of the number of independent variables included or their theoretical underpinning. Thus, for example, some have examined the impact of early disruptive behaviours on delinquency at age 14 years (Tremblay *et al.*, 1992) or scores on the Child Behaviour Checklist as a predictor of delinquency (Bank *et al.*, 1993). Other studies, although impressive in size (e.g. Glueck and Glueck, 1950), have tended to focus on non-personality factors. For instance, the Gluecks focused their study on family factors identifying predictors such as family cohesiveness and the nature of the relationships between parents and offspring.

One research project which included, among others, the role of personality factors and that can be considered to be a classic in this area was conducted by Farrington (West and Farrington, 1973; Farrington, 1986). In this study, over 400 English boys who came from several different primary schools in the London area were tracked for several years. The boys were described as predominantly urban working-class youngsters, and were traced from 8 to 25 years of age. It was concluded that several factors measured in the early years were able to predict later criminal behaviour. Naturally, some of the variables measured pertained to social psychological influences, such as parental supervision and convictions, poor parental behaviour, and the respondents' unstable job record, although some personality factors were also deemed to be important.

Convictions at the age of 10–13 years were best predicted by earlier 'troublesomeness', while convictions at age 17–20 years were predicted by teacher-rated aggressiveness at age 12–14 years, and by the respondents' level of neurotic extraversion at age 16 years. Self-reported delinquency at 18 years of age was predicted by teacher-rated aggressiveness at 12–14 years, and by neurotic extraversion at 16 years. Convictions at age 21–24 years were predicted by an anti-establishment attitude at age 18 years, and by hostile attitudes to the police at age 14 years. Thus there appear to be clearly identifiable personality factors, evident in early childhood, that predict later antisocial and criminal behaviours. As Farrington notes:

> It seems clear that the causes of adult criminal convictions can be traced back to childhood. ... The kinds of youths who were convicted or who admitted large numbers of delinquent acts were identified as troublesome, daring, dishonest, and aggressive by their teachers, peers, and parents from an early age.

(1986, pp.373, 382)

Jessor *et al.* (1995) recently examined the effects of protective and risk factors on the later development of problem behaviours, including delinquency. Over 2000 respondents were surveyed over a period of 3 years. Risk factors included low self-esteem, feelings of hopelessness, having friends who engaged in risky behaviours, and so on. Protective factors included a positive attitude to school, intolerance of deviance, having positive relationships with adults, and having friends who were models of conventional behaviour. Of significance from our perspective is the finding that protective factors were found to be very important in moderating the long-term development of problem behaviours. Indeed, protective factors overwhelmed factors such as low self-esteem and feelings of hopelessness.

Lane (1987) was interested in the ability of the Eysenckian dimensions P, E and N to predict criminality over a 5-year period among 60 schoolchildren. As expected, high P scores predicted later convictions, while *low* N scores were also able to differentiate criminally prone children from others. Unfortunately, Lane (1987) appears to have used rather unsophisticated data analysis techniques, and very little information is given about the nature of the sample, the drop-out rate; and so on. Thus we must interpret his findings more cautiously. Likewise, Putnins (1982) traced two groups of young people for a 12-month period. In the first case he found that boys who were later apprehended for offences scored significantly higher than the non-offenders at Time 1 on the P scale and on a measure of criminal propensity (C). In the second group, which consisted of adjudicated delinquents, it was found that recidivists scored significantly higher than non-recidivists on the P and C scales.

A study using more sophisticated analytical techniques was conducted recently by Heaven (1996b). It included measures of delinquency, extraversion, self-esteem and psychoticism, and involved tracking 282 14-year-olds over a 2-year period. Using structural equation analyses, the best longitudinal predictor of later delinquency was found to be psychoticism at Time 1, with extraversion and low self-esteem (both at Time 1) having very little impact. Although the importance of the P factor supports previous findings, the total effect was rather small. It was found that the three personality factors at Time 1 together explained just over 16 per cent of the variance in the delinquency scores at Time 1, but only about 6 per cent of the variance in delinquency scores at Time 2. In other words, the results suggest that, over time, the impact of personality on the maintenance of delinquency scores appears to be rather limited.

How are we to explain these findings? Heaven (1996b) suggests that future research needs to incorporate personality *facets* rather than personality *domains* as predictors. These could include factors such as excitement-seeking and trust (see above) or impulsiveness, venturesomeness, and so on. It is possible that factors such as extraversion are too broad and insensitive to capture the full nuances of longitudinal change – something which the lower-order factors might accomplish.

In summary, there can be no doubt that personality factors such as Eysenck's P, E and N domains are related to criminal behaviours and delinquency, but that their effects vary across different age groups and types of criminal behaviour. It would seem that the effect of P on delinquency is strongest, and some longitudinal research using structural equation modelling suggests that the personality effects, in total, may be relatively small. Clearly much more work needs to be done on assessing the interaction between personality and external factors such as family life, peer pressure, group norms, and so on. Indeed, evidence also suggests that physiological factors (e.g. heart rate) may be implicated in the personality–behaviour link (e.g. Maliphant *et al.*, 1990). This kind of research needs to be undertaken increasingly if we are to achieve a much more comprehensive understanding of the psychology of criminality.

6.5 PERSONALITY AND RECIDIVISM

Although it has been suggested by many psychologists that personality factors are important in explaining recidivism, not all of the evidence supports this view. For example, it has been argued that a previous history of criminal activity is as good an indicator of further detention as other factors (e.g. McGurk *et al.*, 1978). In this study by McGurk *et al.*, recidivists were found to be younger rather than older, and to have had more previous convictions. These authors followed up 315 detainees, all of whom were male. In total there were 191 recidivists, who tended to have lower arithmetic and reading ability than non-recidivists, and were also more likely to manifest extra-punitive hostility, as measured by the Hostility and Direction of Hostility Questionnaire (HDHQ), and to disregard rules and to be more suspicious, as measured by the 16PF. Not surprisingly, they also tended to be non-conformers.

More recent work among child molesters by Hanson *et al.* (1993) also demonstrated the relative importance of non-personality factors in predicting recidivism. This study examined the recidivism rates of almost 200 child molesters who were released from prison over a 16-year period. The best predictors of re-conviction were the following:

- not being married;
- having had a prior sexual conviction;
- admitting to previous offences.

In addition, those who committed offences against young boys were at greater risk of recidivism than were those who had offended against young girls or who had committed incest. The authors also examined the relationships between recidivism and personality factors as measured by the MMPI and the EPI. Of 60 relationships, only four were found to be significant, which is only a slightly higher incidence than would be expected by chance. Based on these findings, therefore, Hanson *et al.* (1993) question the ability of personality factors to predict recidivism. Clearly, more work is needed to clarify the interaction between personality factors and the variables mentioned above.

Scores on the MMPI subscales do not appear to be capable of predicting recidivism among drink-drivers. Craig and Dres (1989) found that three MMPI scales explained only 10 per cent of the variance predicting recidivism. By contrast, Weaver and Wootton (1992) found evidence that recidivism for *other* types of offences was predicted by scores on the MMPI subscales among a sample of 401 adjudicated male juvenile delinquents. They found significant differences on several scales, as shown in Table 6.4.

Weaver and Wootton also found that some MMPI scales differentiated between youths who engaged in serious and less serious offences. Those who engaged in serious crime scored towards the pathological end of the following scales: social responsibility, ego strength, control and social status. Those who were engaged in less serious offences scored toward the pathological end of the following scales: narcissism–hypersensitivity and family problems. This suggests that these individuals tended to experience family problems and were sensitive about themselves. As the authors put it: they were 'perhaps more sensitive about themselves and not yet as (hardened) as their counterparts who were engaging in more serious crimes' (Weaver and Wooton, 1992, p.550).

Ingram *et al.* (1985) examined the recidivist rates among 52 male volunteers from several different sources, including a US State Penitentiary. The sample included 20 blacks and 32 whites who were matched for age, IQ and socio-economic status. Important differences were noted on the MMPI subscales and the Problem-Solving Inventory between recidivists and non-recidivists, including some significant racial differences. These are summarised in Table 6.5. However, it is important to note that although some significant differences were observed between groups, not all of the results are readily

Table 6.4 MMPI subscales differentiating recidivist youths from non-recidivist youths (*n* = 401)

- MacAndrew alcoholism
- Psychopathic deviance
- Social responsibility
- Amorality
- Mania
- Authority problems
- Authority conflict
- Social impertubability
- Manifest hostility
- Persecutory ideas

Source of information: Weaver, G. and Wootton, R. (1992) The use of the MMPI special scales in the assessment of delinquent personality. *Adolescence* **27**, 545–54.

Table 6.5 Differences between black and white recidivists and non-recidivists on the MMPI and PSI

Black recidivist	Score higher on the Confusion (F) scale than white recidivists or black non-recidivists; score higher on Lie (L) scale than white non-recidivists
Black non-recidivists	Score higher on the Lie scale than black recidivists, white recidivists and white non-recidivists; score higher on the Social Responsibility (RE) scale than black recidivists
White recidivists	Score higher on Lie scale than white non-recidivists; score higher on the Social Responsibility scale than white non-recidivists
Non-recidivists	Score higher on the Dominance (Do) scale than recidivists
Recidivists	Score higher on the Impulsivity scale of the PSI than non-recidivists

Source of information: Ingram, J., Marchioni, P., Hill, G., Caraveo-Ramos, E. and McNeil, B. (1985) Recidivism, perceived problem-solving abilities, MMPI characteristics, and violence: a study of black and white incarcerated male adult offenders. *Journal of Clinical Psychology* **41**, 425–32.

interpretable. For instance, all of the groups fell within the normal range on the Lie (L) scale, while all of them fell within the totally irresponsible range of the Social Responsibility (RE) scale.

McGurk *et al.* (1983) traced Borstal inmates aged between 15 and 21 years for 3 years. On the basis of respondents' scores on the 16PF, HDHQ and Psychological Screening Inventory at the time of admission, the authors identified four personality types: withdrawn (representing 25.9 per cent of the sample), disturbed (30.9 per cent), normal (33.7 per cent) and truculent (9.4 per cent). The characteristics of each sub-type are described in more detail in Table 6.6. Recidivism rates were lowest (64 per cent) among the withdrawn group, but highest (87 per cent) among the normal group. This finding can be explained in terms of Eysenckian theory (Eysenck and Gudjonsson, 1989), which suggests that extraversion is predictive of criminality. Individuals in the 'normal' group were described as 'least expressive and outgoing', shy and timid.

Research on the personality profile of recidivist drink-drivers has tended to yield conflicting results. On the one hand, there is evidence that multiple offenders tend to score higher on the depression scale (scale 2) of the MMPI than non-multiple offenders (e.g. Sutker *et al.*, 1980; Hartz and Retzlaff, 1987). Yet Hartz and Retzlaff (1987) observed that all of the scores obtained in their study fell within the normal range, suggesting that multiple offenders cannot be classified as clinically depressed.

Table 6.6 Personality types identified among young Borstal inmates

Type	Description
Withdrawn	Self-sufficient, sober, taciturn, shy, timid; low on expressiveness; not outgoing
Normal	Relaxed, controlled, self-assured; has a 'normal' PSI profile
Disturbed	High levels of general hostility; self-critical, tense and alienated
Truculent	High levels of extrapunitive and acting out hostility; scores high on assertiveness, expediency, suspiciousness and happy-go-lucky approach; also socially non-conformist

Source of information: McGurk, B., McEwan, A. and McGurk, R. (1983) Personality types and recidivism among Borstal trainees. *Personality and Individual Differences* **4**, 116–7.

Ram (1987) compared the EPQ scores of murderers with non-murderer recidivists in Bangalore, India. It was observed that the recidivists scored significantly higher on the E and N scales, whereas the murderers scored significantly higher on the P dimension. These results are consistent with Eysenckian predictions (e.g. Eysenck and Gudjonsson, 1989).

In conclusion, it is possible to use personality descriptions to differentiate between recidivists and non-recidivists. Exactly which personality factors are important will undoubtedly vary from one behaviour to another. None the less there seem to be clear and predictable patterns. For instance, some individuals appear to have authority problems, manifest some hostility and tend to be impulsive. Some have also been described as 'self-assured', if not outgoing, to some extent. Thus these results are consistent with what we know about those who score high on P and E.

6.6 THE PERSONALITIES OF OFFENDERS

6.6.1 Drink-Drivers

Given the general levels of mobility of most individuals who reside in industrialised nations, it is not surprising that many studies have examined the personalities of those who drink and drive. Such individuals are not only a danger to themselves, but also pose a risk to other road users. Those who have been apprehended for drink-driving offences have generally been described as heavy drinkers who tend to drink in order to reduce levels of tension. Compared to control subjects, they also tend to be more depressive, to have low self-esteem, and to be emotionally unstable and hostile (e.g. Selzer *et al.*, 1967; Selzer and Barton, 1977).

Some writers have identified different sub-types of drink-drivers, thereby questioning conventional wisdom that drink-drivers are a homogenous group. For instance, Steer *et al.* suggested the existence of the following types in the USA:

- white men with a large proportion of non-drinking fathers; individuals in this group appear capable of controlling their behaviour;
- black men with a large proportion of non-drinking fathers;
- mainly white men who tend to use psychotropic drugs; they also have drinking fathers;
- a racially mixed group with high N scores and a history of heavy alcohol use;
- respondents with high scores on measures of impulsiveness and alcohol-related offences;
- respondents who score high on indices of alcohol impairment; they tend to be recidivist drink-drivers;
- respondents who are psychologically and physiologically addicted to alcohol manifesting psychiatric symptomatology.

(Steer *et al.*, 1979)

Donovan and Marlatt (1982) used attitudinal and personality measures to determine the existence of sub-types of drink-drivers. All of the respondents in their study were males attending an alcohol educational programme following their arrest for drink-driving. The authors were able to identify five sub-types, although only three appear to have direct relevance to our discussion. The first group was characterised by depression, low assertiveness, low emotional adjustment and high external control. The second subtype was characterised by aggressive drivers who were speed competitive. They also tended to score higher on measures of sensation-seeking, hostility and depression, whilst also being characterised as irritable, emotionally unstable and externally controlled. Members of the third sub-type tended to drive in order to reduce tension, but were more internally controlled and less depressive than the previous group. Based on the above evidence, therefore, it would seem that drink-drivers tend to be emotionally unstable and depressive, and to drive to reduce tension.

6.6.2 Motor Car Theft

Cookson (1994) surveyed 538 male inmates of a correctional facility for young offenders. Almost 50 per cent of the respondents had been convicted of motor car theft, while about 64 per cent reported being a passenger in a car which they knew had been stolen. Of those who had taken a car without permission, most were aged between 14 and 16 years. Each respondent completed the revised form of the EPQ as well as a measure of impulsiveness.

Those classified as habitual car thieves were found to score significantly higher than other inmates on psychoticism and impulsiveness. Cookson (1994) interprets these results as being in line with what we know about high-scoring P individuals. The respondents included in this study were young and probably ill-trained in driving skills. It is also likely that car thieves usually tend to drive fast and take unnecessary risks, reflecting their high levels of psychoticism and impulsiveness.

6.6.3 Violent Crime

Is it possible to discriminate between those delinquents who commit assaultive crimes and those who do not? Weaver and Wootton (1992) found that the following MMPI scales discriminated between these groups: imperturbability (Ma3), masculinity–femininity (Mf) and poignancy (Pa2). The assaultive group also scored in the pathological direction on the following scales: social responsibility (Re), family discord (Pd1) and psychomotor acceleration (Ma2).

Heilbrun (1979) developed a specific measure of psychopathy using the psychopathic deviate (Pd) scale of the MMPI and the socialization scale of the California Psychological Inventory (CPI). He detected important mediation effects between psychopathy and intelligence and their relationship to violent crime (including murder, rape, manslaughter and assault). Psychopathy, when combined with low intelligence, was found to be the predictor of violent crime, compared to psychopathy and high intelligence. These results led Heilbrun (1979) to suggest that members of the former group are poorly socialised and do not have the necessary cognitive abilities to regulate their own behaviour adequately or to engage in alternative, more acceptable and less impulsive behaviours.

Raine (1993) has postulated that individuals who commit extreme forms of interpersonal violence, such as murder, are characterised by borderline personality disorder. This may include unstable interpersonal relationships, affective instability, anger and impulsivity. He tested his hypothesis on a sample of 37 white long-term UK prisoners, some of whom were serving sentences for murder or manslaughter. It was found that some borderline traits, notably affective instability and unstable/intense relationships, discriminated between these prisoners and others. Significant group differences were also observed for total borderline scores, with the experimental group scoring in the direction of greater pathology.

Some support for these views emanates from the work of Labelle *et al.* (1991), who assessed the psychological characteristics of 14 adolescent murderers (13 males and one female). Only five individuals had not yet had contact with a psychiatrist, and 10 subjects had records of antisocial behaviour, theft, attempted murder, violence against property, and so on. The authors also found evidence of a wide range of disorders, which are listed in Table 6.7. These included neuropsychological damage, organic impairment

Table 6.7 Psychological characteristics of 14 adolescent murderers

Number presenting	Description
Neurological testing	
3	Neurophysical impairment
1	Subtle organic impairment
1	Impairment of fronto-temporal area
2	Abnormal EEG ratings
1	Temporal lobe epilepsy
1	Febrile convulsions
DSM-III-R diagnoses	
2	Major depression
2	Adjustment disorder
4	Personality disorder
1	Mild developmental disability
1	Organic personality sexual disorder

Source of information: Labelle, A., Bradford, J., Bourget, D., Jones, B. and Carmichael, M. (1991) Adolescent murderers. Canadian Journal of Psychiatry **36**, 583–7.

and abnormal EEG readings, while some individuals also presented with substance use disorder, personality disorder, major affective disorder or adjustment disorder.

6.6.4 Rape

Kalichman (Kalichman *et al.*, 1989; Kalichman, 1990) assessed the personalities of 127 incarcerated male rapists using the MMPI and the Multiphasic Sex Inventory. These researchers were able to discriminate the following subtypes.

- Sociopathic types with low impulse control. For these individuals rape is frequently committed in the course of some other criminal behaviour. They score high on Pd and Ma.
- Unstable, hostile and dangerous types. These individuals tend to be antisocial and aggressive, and their act is driven more by hostility than sexuality. They are identified by their scores on Hs, D, Pd, Pa and Sc.
- Distrustful types with poor relationships. These individuals tend to be socially alienated, have low impulse control, and are dissatisfied with others and themselves. For them, rape is one way of demonstrating dominance over others. They score high on Pa and Pt.
- Severely disturbed types. These individuals are characterised by confused thought processes and major psychological and social disturbance.

They are sadistic, and their sexual arousal is enhanced in the presence of a suffering victim.

(Kalichman *et al.*, 1989, pp.169–80)

6.6.5 Crimes Against Property

Included in this group are people who engage in such crimes as theft, arson and burglary. People who commit robbery have been described by Goma (1995) as antisocial sensation-seekers. This study, which was designed to discriminate between a range of quite different groups, concluded that individuals who were committed for armed robbery tend to score significantly higher on measures of disinhibition, susceptibility to boredom, and thrill- and adventure-seeking of the sensation-seeking scale, as well as on neuroticism, psychoticism, impulsiveness and susceptibility to reward. They also scored lower on the socialisation scale of the CPI. Following Zuckerman *et al.* (1988), Goma (1995) refers to these individuals as impulsive unsocialized sensation-seeking types.

Cornell *et al.* (1996) differentiated between instrumental aggression and reactive or emotional aggression. Whereas instrumental aggression is regarded as 'purposeful and goal directed' (Corenell *et al.*, 1996, p.783), reactive aggression very often occurs as a result of prior frustration. In other words, instrumental aggression is a deliberate act, such as a planned robbery or assault, although most of the respondents in the study reported here were apprehended for robbery or burglary.

Using the Screening Version of the Psychopathy Checklist, Cornell *et al.* (1996) examined which items discriminated best between instrumental violent, reactive violent and non-violent offenders. Those labelled 'instrumental aggressives' scored significantly higher on the following indices: pathological lying, callousness, parasitic lifestyle, poor behaviour control, promiscuous sexual behaviour, lacking realistic goals, impulsivity, irresponsibility and criminal versatility. Thus instrumental aggressives who commit acts such as robbery or burglary are reminiscent of high-scoring P individuals (see Eysenck and Eysenck, 1975). According to Cornell *et al.*, such individuals lack the following:

well-internalized social standards and associated feelings of concern and respect for others that otherwise would inhibit the offender . . . the presence of extreme impulsivity or anger might override these inhibitions and drive them to act aggressively to achieve their instrumental objectives.

(Cornell *et al.*, 1996, pp.788–9)

The following scales on the MMPI have been found to discriminate between young people who commit crimes against property and those who do not (Weaver and Wootton, 1992): psychopathic deviance (Pd), authority problems (Pd2), MacAndrew alcoholism, social responsibility (Re) and amorality (Ma1). The offender group also scored in the pathological direction on the following scales: social responsibility (Re), persecutory ideas, social alienation (Sc1A), ego inflation (Ma4), family problems and depression and apathy (TSC4). By contrast, research using the 16PF has been less successful in identifying those individuals who commit crimes against property (Tammany *et al.*, 1990). According to this report, these respondents tended to score relatively low on the 16PF intelligence scale compared to others, such as drug traffickers. No other personality markers were found using the 16PF.

6.7 CONCLUSION

The evidence we have reviewed here is very encouraging in terms of the ability of standardised personality measures to predict criminal acts. It is clear that most of the research in this context has been conducted with the EPQ and the MMPI, and the results tend to fit an underlying pattern of behaviour that is recognisable from one criminal behaviour to another. Although the measures used in many of the studies cited here explain only a modest proportion of the variance in criminal behaviour, they none the less do so reasonably consistently from sample to sample. Thus, for example, there is compelling evidence which suggests that Eysenck's P factor is closely linked to criminal behaviours, whereas the MMPI has also proved useful in establishing different profiles of criminal sub-types, such as those found among rapists.

Most of the research reviewed here, as in the other chapters, is cross-sectional in nature. In order to consolidate the advances already made in this area, researchers should be encouraged to undertake more longitudinal research. For instance, future research could examine how personality interacts with other psychosocial and psychophysiological factors in predicting criminal and delinquent behaviours over time. It might well be that personality in early childhood may 'set up' someone for a life of crime, but by the late teenage years other social psychological factors assume more prominence in maintaining criminal behaviour (see Heaven, 1996b). Research is therefore needed in which respondents are traced from early childhood into adulthood.

In conclusion, personality factors are integral to a scientific understanding of the nature of criminality. Different forms of criminal behaviour are related to different personality factors, thus highlighting the complex interplay between personality and crime.

REFERENCES

Adler, G. (1982) Recent psychoanalytic contributions to the understanding and treatment of criminal behaviour. *International Journal of Offender Therapy and Comparative Criminology* 26, 281–7.

Asch, S. (1974) Some superego considerations in crime and punishment. *Journal of Psychiatry and Law* 2, 159–81.

Bank, L., Duncan, T., Patterson, G. and Reid, J. (1993) Parent and teacher ratings in the assessment and prediction of antisocial behaviors. *Journal of Personality* **61**, 693–709.

Binder, A. (1988) Juvenile delinquency. *Annual Review of Psychology* **39**, 252–82.

Claridge, G. (1981) Psychoticism. In Lynn, R. (ed.), *Dimensions of personality: papers in honour of H.J. Eysenck.* Oxford: Pergamon Press, 79–109.

Cookson, H. (1994) Characteristics of young motor thieves in custody. *Personality and Individual Differences* **16**, 353–6.

Coolidge, F., Reilman, B., Becker, L., Cass, V. and Coolidge, R. (1992) Emotional problems and neuropsychological symptoms in juvenile non-violent offenders. *Journal of Personality and Clinical Studies* **8**, 7–13.

Cornell, D., Warren, J., Hawk, G., Stafford, E., Oram, G. and Pine, D. (1996) Psychopathy in instrumental and reactive violent offenders. *Journal of Consulting and Clinical Psychology* **64**, 783–90.

Costa, P. and McCrae, R. (1992) *Revised NEO Personality Inventory (NEO-PI-R) and NEO Five-Factor Inventory (NEO-FFI).* Odessa, FL: Psychological Assessment Resources Inc.

Craig, R. and Dres, D. (1989) Predicting DUI recidivism with the MMPI. *Alcoholism Treatment Quarterly* **6**, 97–103.

Donovan, D. and Marlatt, G. (1982) Personality subtypes among driving-while-intoxicated offenders: relationship to drinking behavior and driving risk. *Journal of Consulting and Clinical Psychology* **50**, 241–9.

Eysenck, H. and Eysenck, S. (1975) *Manual of the Eysenck Personality Questionnaire.* London: Hodder & Stoughton.

Eysenck, H. and Eysenck, M. (1985) *Personality and individual differences: a natural science approach.* New York: Plenum.

Eysenck, H. and Gudjonsson, G. (1989) *The causes and cures of criminality.* New York: Plenum Press.

Eysenck, S. and Eysenck, H. (1969) The dual nature of extraversion. In Eysenck, H. and Eysenck, S. (eds), *Personality structure and measurement.* London: Routledge & Kegan Paul, 141–9.

Eysenck, S. and Eysenck, H. (1970) Crime and personality: an empirical study of the three-factor theory. *British Journal of Criminology* **10**, 225–39.

Farrington, D. (1986) Stepping stones to adult criminal careers. In Olweus, D., Block, J. and Radke-Yarrow, M. (eds), *Development of antisocial and prosocial behavior.* Orlando, FL: Academic Press, 359–84.

Farrington, D. 1992) Juvenile delinquency. In Coleman, J. (ed.), *The school years: current issues in the socialization of young people,* 2nd edn. London: Routledge, 123–63.

Feldman, M. (1977) *Criminal behaviour: a psychological analysis.* Chichester: John Wiley.

Furnham, A. (1984) Personality, social skills, anomie and delinquency: a self-report study of a group of normal non-delinquent adolescents. *Journal of Child Psychology and Psychiatry* **25**, 409–20.

Furnham, A. and Thompson, J. (1991) Personality and self-reported delinquency. *Personality and Individual Differences* **12**, 585–93.

Glueck, S. and Glueck, E. (1950) *Unravelling juvenile delinquency.* Cambridge, MA: Harvard University Press.

Goma, M. (1995) Prosocial and antisocial aspects of personality. *Personality and Individual Differences* **19**, 125–34.

Gudjonsson, G. (1997) Crime and personality. In Nyborg, H. (ed.), *The scientific study of human nature: tribute to Hans J. Eysenck at Eighty.* Oxford and New York: Pergamon, 142–654.

Hanson, R., Steffy, R. and Gauthier, R. (1993) Long-term recidivism of child molesters. *Journal of Consulting and Clinical Psychology* **61**, 646–52.

Hartz, G. and Retzlaff, P. (1987) Minnesota Multiphasic Personality Inventory profiles of enlisted air force and army men arrested for driving while intoxicated: a comparison of single- and multiple-incident offenders. *Military Medicine* **152**, 187–9.

Heaven, P. (1993) Personality predictors of self-reported delinquency. *Personality and Individual Differences* **14**, 67–76.

Heaven, P. (1994) Family of origin, personality, and self-reported delinquency. *Journal of Adolescence* **17**, 445–59.

Heaven, P. (1996a) Personality and self-reported delinquency: analysis of the 'Big Five' personality dimensions. *Personality and Individual Differences* **20**, 47–54.

Heaven, P. (1996b) Personality and self-reported delinquency: a longitudinal analysis. *Journal of Child Psychology and Psychiatry* **37**, 747–51.

Heilbrun, A. (1979) Psychopathy and violent crime. *Journal of Consulting and Clinical Psychology* **47**, 509–16.

Hollander, H. and Turner, F. (1985) Characteristics of incarcerated delinquents: relationship between development disorders, environmental and family factors, and patterns of offense and recidivism. *Journal of the American Academy of Child Psychiatry* **24**, 221–6.

Hollin, C. (1989) *Psychology and crime: an introduction to criminological psychology.* London: Routledge.

Howarth, E. (1986) What does Eysenck's psychoticism scale really measure? *British Journal of Psychology* **77**, 223–7.

Indira, R. (1987) The psychoanalytic theory as a basis for understanding criminal behaviour. *Indian Journal of Behaviour* **11**, 29–32.

Ingram, J., Marchioni, P., Hill, G., Caraveo-Ramos, E. and McNeil, B. (1985) Recidivism, perceived problem-solving abilities, MMPI characteristics, and violence: a study of black and white incarcerated male adult offenders. *Journal of Clinical Psychology* **41**, 425–32.

Jessor, R., Van Den Bos, J., Vanderryn, J., Costa, F. and Turbin, M. (1995) Protective factors in adolescent problem behavior: moderator effects and developmental change. *Developmental Psychology* **31**, 923–33.

Kalichman, S. (1990) Affective and personality characteristics of MMPI profile subgroups of incarcerated rapists. *Archives of Sexual Behavior* **19**, 443–59.

Kalichman, S., Craig, M., Shealy, L. *et al.* (1989) An empirically derived typology of adult rapists based on the MMPI: a cross-validation study. *Journal of Psychology and Human Sexuality* **2**, 165–82.

Kaplan, E. (1976) Recidivism, crime, and delinquency: a psychoanalyst's perspective. *Journal of Psychiatry and Law* **4**, 61–104.

Labelle, A., Bradford, J., Bourget, D., Jones, B. and Carmichael, M. (1991) Adolescent murderers. *Canadian Journal of Psychiatry* **36**, 583–7.

Lane, D. (1987) Personality and antisocial behaviour: a long-term study. *Personality and Individual Differences* **8**, 799–806.

McGurk, B., Bolton, N. and Smith, M. (1978) Some psychological, educational and criminological variables related to recidivism in delinquent boys. *British Journal of Social and Clinical Psychology* **17**, 251–4.

McGurk, B., McEwan, A. and McGurk, R. (1983) Personality types and recidivism among Borstal trainees. *Personality and Individual Differences* **4**, 165–70.

Mak, A. (1993) A self-report delinquency scale for Australian adolescents. *Australian Journal of Psychology* **45**, 75–9.

Maliphant, R., Hume, F. and Furnham, A. (1990) Autonomic nervous system (ANS) activity, personality characteristics and disruptive behaviour in girls. *Journal of Child Psychology and Psychiatry* **31**, 619–28.

Martins, C. (1991) The psychodynamic basis of delinquency (abstract). *Revista Brasileira de Psicanalise* **25**, 175–84.

Peiser, N. and Heaven, P. (1996) Family influences on self-reported delinquency among high school students. *Journal of Adolescence* **19**, 557–68.

Putnins, A. (1982) The Eysenck Personality Questionnaires and delinquency prediction. *Personality and Individual Differences* **3**, 339–40.

Raine, A. (1993) Features of borderline personality and violence. *Journal of Clinical Psychology* **49**, 277–81.

Ram, P. (1987) A comparative study of murderers and recidivists using Eysenck's Personality Inventory. *Indian Journal of Clinical Psychology* **14**, 100–101.

Rice, F. (1992) *The adolescent: development, relationships, and culture.* Boston, MA: Allyn & Bacon.

Rigby K., Mak, A. and Slee, P. (1989) Impulsiveness, orientation to institutional authority and gender as factors in self-reported delinquency among Australian adolescents. *Personality and Individual Differences* **10**, 689–92.

Rushton, J. and Chrisjohn, R. (1981) Extraversion, neuroticism, psychoticism and self-reported delinquency: evidence from eight separate samples. *Personality and Individual Differences* **2**, 11–20.

Rutter, M. and Giller, H. (1983) *Juvenile delinquency: trends and perspectives.* Harmondsworth: Penguin.

Selzer, M. and Barton, E. (1977) The drunken driver: a psychosocial study. *Drug and Alcohol Dependence* **2**, 239–53.

Selzer, M., Payne, C., Westervelt, F. and Quinn, J. (1967) Automobile accidents as an expression of psychopathology in an alcoholic population. *Quarterly Journal of Studies on Alcohol* **28**, 505–16.

Shaw, J. and Scott, W. (1991) Influence of parent discipline style on delinquent behaviour: the mediating role of control orientation. *Australian Journal of Psychology* **43**, 61–7.

Steer, R., Fine, E. and Scoles, P. (1979) Classification of men arrested for driving while intoxicated, and treatment implications. *Journal of Studies on Alcohol* **40**, 222–9.

Sutker, P., Brantley, P. and Allain, A. (1980) MMPI response patterns and alcohol consumption in DUI offenders. *Journal of Consulting and Clinical Psychology* **48**, 350–55.

Tammany, J., Evans, R. and Barnett, R. (1990) Personality and intellectual characteristics of adult male felons as a function of offense category. *Journal of Clinical Psychology* **46**, 906–11.

Tremblay, R., Masse, B., Perron, D. and Leblanc, M. (1992) Early disruptive behavior, poor school achievement, delinquent behavior, and delinquent personality: longitudinal analyses. *Journal of Consulting and Clinical Psychology* **60**, 64–72.

Vold, G. (1958) *Theoretical criminology.* New York: Oxford University Press.

Weaver, G. and Wootton, R. (1992) The use of the MMPI special scales in the assessment of delinquent personality. *Adolescence* 27, 545–54.

West, D. and Farrington, D. (1973) *Who becomes delinquent?* London: Heinemann.

Zuckerman, M., Kuhlman, D. and Camac, C. (1988) What lies beyond E and N? Factor analyses of scales believed to measure basic dimensions of personality. *Journal of Personality and Social Psychology* 54, 96–107.

7

Personality and Work

7.1 INTRODUCTION

It is self-evident to any manager, if not to all psychologists, that the personality of employees, along with their ability, has a powerful influence on their work output and satisfaction. Indeed, many people assume that they can be 'understood' from their (chosen) occupations – 'you are what you do'. Absenteeism, productivity and morale, lying and cheating are all seen to be a function of characteristics of individuals, not especially of organisational factors (such as supervisor style or corporate culture). There is a scattered, but growing, research literature looking at personality as it relates to vocational choice, work motivation, productivity, satisfaction, work and stress, as well as absenteeism, accidents, etc. (Bernadin and Bownas, 1985; Furnham, 1992; Lanyon and Goodstein, 1997). More recently, it has been suggested that career change, innovation and creativity in the workplace and work-team performance are also logically related to personality traits, as well as to such factors as training outcomes. The studies are of a highly variable quality, but where the traits are theoretically expected to relate to a particular work behaviour, *and* where that behaviour is reliably measured by aggregated data, it does seem clear that personality traits are one important factor in determining work outcome.

Hogan (1990) notes that the behaviourist critique of the 1970s, which argued that traits rarely predict much of the behaviour displayed at work, has been repudiated. However, he does note that traditional personality psychology was rooted in clinical practice and intended to explain disordered behaviour. Therefore, much of it seems of little relevance to organisational and occupational psychology. Yet modern personality theory is concerned with the dynamics of everyday behaviour, including that in the workplace. He agrees that it is impossible to define personality in terms of any single dimension, and that five seems to be a minimum, although of course not all superfactors necessarily relate to all facets of behaviour at work.

The best studies in this area are inevitably longitudinal studies with multiple measures of traits and job experience. For instance, Van den Berg and Feij (1993) found that emotional stability and extraversion measured at the time of recruitment predicted self-reported job experiences (satisfaction, tension, propensity to leave and self-appraised performance 18 months to 2 years later). Indeed, they found non-neuroticism to be the best predictor of overall job experience.

Yet as Nicholson has argued:

> the essential value and sophistication of current thinking about the structure of personality is thrown away if reduced to arguments about the predictive validity of single dimensions to particular jobs or situations . . . likewise, situations need to be seen as profiles of potentiality, on to which personality dispositions might reasonably be supposed to map. Thus, how persons fit teams or cultures is more complex and fruitful territory than simple, bureaucratic questions such as whether extraverts are better salespeople than introverts.
>
> (Nicholson, 1996, p.199)

Likewise, Adler (1996) argues that work behaviour is an ideal 'life arena' in which to test personality models, as well as to understand the psychological nature of work.

It is not surprising, therefore, that personality and ability tests have been used in selection since before World War One (Holloway, 1991; Furnham, 1992a). Even before World War One, the use of psychometric tests was advocated for selection at work (Musterberg, 1913). In that conflict, both America and Britain used primitive personality tests, and in the 1920s various institutions and corporations were formed to promote the use of (personality) psychology in business. A great deal of this work was what we would today call *vocational psychology*, and involved fitting people to the job (Muscio, 1919). Essentially, two activities went on, namely guidance to appropriate jobs after a job specification and 'person analysis', and selection of the people best fitted to do the job.

Furnham (1997) has, in fact, described what occupational psychologists do in the simple epithet 'Fit the person to the job; fit the job to the person'. Schneider (1996) has noted that choices – of potential employee and employer – in the hope of an ideal fit are modified and attenuated by many other factors. There has been a recent resurgence of interest in personality testing in the workplace (Furnham, 1997). This is due to two major causes – first, impressive development and a general consensus in the area of personality measurement, and secondly, the powerful need for selectors in areas of high job turnover in order to help select and retain good workers.

There is a growing body of evidence that personality measures are logically and statistically significantly related to successful job performance (Day and Silverman, 1989; Hogan and Hogan, 1989). Data have come from studies in diverse sectors ranging from insurance claim examiners (Arneson *et al.*, 1993) to sewing-machine operators (Krilowicz and Lowery, 1996). Both managers and researchers acknowledge that it is a combination of personality, aptitude (ability) and vocational interest factors that predict job performance and satisfaction. Furthermore, these different factors may relate quite specifically to particular dimensions of work success (Gellarty *et al.*, 1991).

Various small-scale developments in the applied world of personality testing occurred between the wars, but it was at this stage that many important pure theoretical and methodological developments were taking place. After World War Two, studies were often small-scale and piecemeal. Furthermore, many were never published because they were commissioned by companies who believed that if their competitors saw the results, they would copy them, so rendering their research worthless in terms of competitive advantage. The problem for any researcher in this area is to get a company who actually regularly and reliably measures multiple work outputs to give it to a psychological researcher who may wish to relate it to personality data that needs to be collected.

Validation of a psychological test is relatively straightforward. However, the problem for the applied personality researcher lies not so much in the choice of good psychometric measures as in obtaining a sensitive, robust and reliable measure of work performance. Perhaps this is best illustrated in the basic selection model.

Figure 7.1 shows how one might validate a selection instrument (be it a personality or ability test, or any other measure). Having conducted a job analysis and considered the results (step 1), two questions need to be considered, namely what test to use, and which aspect of the job to measure. Thus, for example, one might choose an extraversion questionnaire for sales personnel and select as the criteria either (or both) sales revenue (or profit) or customer responses (step 2).

Step 3 involves administering the instrument(s) and then measuring the performance on the chosen criteria, noting both unusual circumstances that may affect the outcome (such as seasonality), and also the influence of others (in the work-team) on the performance criterion (or criteria). Step 4 involves correlating the two or, better still, doing some multivariate statistics (regression analysis) and determining which of several characteristics (age, work experience, gender, etc.) other than – but as well as – the factors measured in the selection instrument predict performance. If the relationship is statistically significant and psychologically meaningful, the selection instrument may be used. If not, one has to start again with another instrument (steps 5 and 6).

Although there is no shortage of tests and instruments with which one may choose to predict occupational behaviour or work performance, the usual problem is finding a good performance criterion. Very few organisations keep regular, reliable data on the performance of their employees (such as productivity, absenteeism, and so on). Indeed, it comes as a surprise to most researchers who attempt to validate instruments and help organisations with

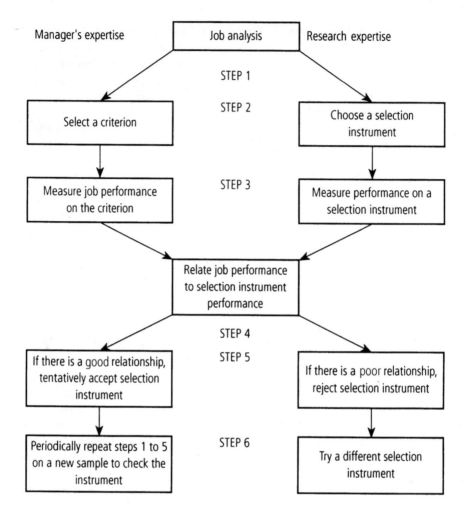

Figure 7.1 Basic selection model.

selection that the latter have little in the way of performance records which they can use.

However, many researchers have listed the kinds of occupational measures that could prove useful. Hough (1992), in her various studies, has been able to define and record various job performance data, as listed below.

1. *Overall job performance*: overall job performance ratings, promotion vs. demotion, overall suitability, fired vs. not fired.
2. *Technical proficiency*: measures of technical competency, knowledge of one's line of work.
3. *Irresponsible behaviour*: poor attendance, counter-productive behaviour, number of disciplinary actions, not following directions, being absent without authorisation, use of drugs (including alcohol) on the job.

4. *Sales effectiveness*: amount sold, sales goals attained, supervisory ratings of sales effectiveness.
5. *Creativity*: number of patents, peer and/or supervisory ratings of innovativeness and creativity.
6. *Teamwork*: ratings of co-operativeness with other co-workers/team members, ability to work with others in joint efforts, quality of interpersonal relationships, constructive interpersonal behaviour.
7. *Effort*: measures of hard work, initiative, work energy, extra effort, working long hours under adverse conditions.
8. *Combat effectiveness*: survival in combat, reaction to life-threatening situations.

Many reviewers have pointed out that examination of modern textbooks on work psychology reveals that little serious attention is given to the study of personality traits as a major (or even minor) determinant of work (O'Brien, 1986; Hough, 1997). There is much interest in topics such as leadership, motivation, satisfaction and stress, but very little in how stable traits influence choice of work or productivity, the psychological functions of work for different employees, or how, if at all, work shapes personality. As O'Brien has noted, in much work psychology the individual is treated as a component of a system or organisation whose goals are to be predicted and maximised. 'It is hard, therefore, to avoid a suspicion that organisational psychologists are only interested in the effects of work on people to the extent that these effects can be shown to affect their subsequent performance' (O'Brien, 1986, p.2). Unless we know about the psychological functions of work for the individual, and the particular organisation demands and constraints on work output, it is difficult to understand fully how personality predicts work behaviour. Other reviewers, like Raymark *et al.* (1997), have identified 12 specific behaviours, related to the Big Five, that may be used in selection. They include general leadership (leading, taking control), interest and negotiation (mediating, resolving disputes), achievement striving (ambition), a friendly disposition, sensitivity and interest in others, co-operative/collaborative work tendencies, general trustworthiness, adherence to the work ethic, thoroughness and attentiveness to detail, emotional stability, desire to generate ideas and a tendency to think things through.

Very few personality psychologists take into consideration structural variables, yet it is obvious that productivity and satisfaction are powerfully moderated by power, communication and political forces in the organisation, as well as by group norms and the state of the market economy at large. Thus both the personality and the organisational structure, jointly and probably interactively, determine work output and may change over time. Many researchers also fail to take into consideration other relevant factors such as a person's experience (how they have been managed), as well as other individual factors such as intelligence, home support structure and motivation. Equally, very few personality theorists are happy to consider the possibility that work experiences might – over time – actually influence personality. Thus the conscientious worker, if they are never rewarded and sometimes even punished for their dedication and determination, may lose both of the latter. It is both possible and likely that organisational structure changes personality structure, which in turn influences organisational structure.

7.2 REVIEWS OF WORK CRITERIA VALIDITY

Both work psychologists and also many managers want to know whether personality (e.g. traits, variables) predicts work performance. More specifically, they want to know *which* personality traits (e.g. extraversion, conscientiousness) predict which *work-related* behaviour (e.g. absenteeism, morals, satisfaction), and under what particular conditions. Researchers also wish to understand the process or mechanism whereby this occurs. Equally importantly, they want to know how much variance is accounted for by the above personality factors (and, naturally, what other factors account for the variance).

Every so often, a hard-working researcher does the scientific community a major service by undertaking a critical review of the use of tests in the workplace. Most of these reviewers now attempt a meta-analysis of the data published in papers, which they critically review in order to look for clear patterns in the many and highly varied studies published. Ghiselli and Barthol (1953) reviewed 113 studies reported between 1919 and 1953. The validities ranged from 0.13 to 0.36, the mean being 0.22. Although the authors wisely attempted to exclude data for measured traits that were clearly unrelated to the job, it seems that no thorough job analysis was performed, and hence some of the weaker correlations may well be due to traits that are not relevant to specific jobs. Secondly, and most importantly, it is likely that many of the personality questionnaires that were being used at the same time were psychometrically poor, with few reliability or validity statistics.

The first thorough report on the validity of personality tests was made by Ghiselli and Brown (1955) over 40 years ago. They were interested in the prediction of occupational success by means of various types of tests (intelligence, spatial, motor and personality). The types of results they typically noted are set out below.

	Intelligence	Personality
Managerial staff	0.37	0.18
Foreman	0.27	0.15
Salesman	0.32	0.36
Sales clerk	− 0.10	0.35

Considering work proficiency in various occupations, they reported the following.

	Intelligence	*Personality*
General clerk	0.38	0.29
Recording clerk	0.25	0.19
Computing clerk	0.16	0.13
Protected occupations	0.26	0.24
Service occupations	0.07	0.16
Vehicle operation	0.14	0.26

Given the nature of test development at this time, these results look most impressive. About 10 years later, Ghiselli (1966) undertook a second review which provided evidence of the validity of personality measurement (see Table 7.1).

It is aggregated data and it shows that the best predictor of work-related behaviour was 0.24. It should be noted, because it is crucially important, that the reviewers only considered studies in which the personality trait measure seemed to be relevant to the work variable.

However, other reviews up until the late 1980s were much less positive about the role of personality traits in predicting job/work performance.

Table 7.1 The observed validities of occupational aptitude tests (criterion: job proficiency)

Type of job	Type of predictor				
	Intellectual abilities	Spatial and mechanical	Perceptual accuracy	Personality[a]	Interest
Executives	0.29	0.18	0.24	0.27	0.31
Foremen	0.24	0.23	0.14	0.15	0.15
Clerks	0.27	0.20	0.27	0.24	0.12
Sales clerks	− 0.10	—	− 0.05	0.35	0.23
Commission sales	0.31	0.07	0.21	0.24	0.31
Protective services	0.23	0.16	0.17	0.24	− 0.01
Personal services	0.03	—	− 0.10	0.16	—
Vehicle operators	0.14	0.20	0.36	—	0.26
Trades and crafts	0.19	0.23	0.22	0.29	− 0.13
Industrial occupations	0.16	0.16	0.18	0.50	0.14
Median validity	0.21	0.19	0.20	0.24	0.15

[a] Only those results where the trait seemed pertinent to the job in question were included in this summary (Ghiselli, 1966, p. 21).

Source: adapted from Ghiselli, E.E. (1966) *The validity of occupational aptitude tests.* New York: John Wiley & Sons (Tables 3.1 to 3.8, pp. 34–56).

Between 1965 and 1985, there were 8–10 meta-analyses using different tests and outcome measures. Validities ranged from 0.10 to 0.60, with most being in the range 0.15–0.25. Some reviewers did not even list personality traits and valid predictors of job performance (Hunter and Hunter, 1984). The review of Guion and Gottier (1965), like others published in the 1960s, seemed gloomy and damning. Their conclusion was often repeated: 'it is difficult in the face of this summary to advocate, with a clear conscience, the use of personality measures in most situations as a basis for making employment decisions' (Guion and Gottier, 1965, p.160). However, many subsequent reviewers have pointed out serious flaws in their review method (Tett *et al.*, 1991).

Early meta-analyses were criticised on various grounds (Van den Berg and Feij, 1993). First, all of the results were collapsed across personality dimensions, occupations and work outcome criteria. Secondly, situational factors such as organisational culture, management style and job content were neglected. Thirdly, the criteria were often problematic, being based primarily on supervisor ratings. Multiple independent but related, rather than composite, data are the ideal (but infrequently used) criteria.

Schmitt *et al.* (1989), investigated the assessment tools used in North America between 1964 and 1984, and showed that personality tests were most widely used, followed by aptitude tests, peer evaluation, assessment centres, physical tests and job samples. With 32 personality scale validities, and using performance ratings as the criterion, they found a mean correlation of 0.21, which compared favourably with measures of general cognitive ability (0.22) and special aptitude scales (0.16).

Because of increasing interest in both the structure of personality dimensions (in particular, the five-factor model) and the validation of the personality tests through work-related criteria, a number of important and comprehensive reviews and meta-analyses appeared in the 1990s. The first of these was by Barrick and Mount (1991), who looked at the relationship between the Big Five personality variables and job proficiency, training proficiency and personnel data in widely varying occupational groups (police, sales, etc.). They expected to find at least two correlates in all jobs, namely *conscientiousness*, because it assesses persistent, playful, careful, responsible and hardworking traits important in all jobs, and *neuroticism*, because it assesses worrying, nervousness, self-pity, etc., which tend to inhibit rather than facilitate work-task performance and other dimensions that they thought would predict performance in particular jobs. Thus in management and sales ('people-type' jobs), extraversion and agreeableness would be important. Furthermore, some dimensions of personality were thought to be related only to particular aspects of the job. Thus openness to experience was thought to relate more to training than to performance criteria.

In total they reviewed 117 studies, which were carefully selected to fulfil exact criteria. As predicted, they found that conscientiousness – a manifestation of a strong sense of purpose, obligation and persistence – was strongly predictive of work proficiency across all of the data. On the whole, the other predictors were confirmed, although they found less evidence that neuroticism was a good predictor of poorer work, notably for technical reasons.

They also distinguished between objective and subjective work criteria, the former relating to such factors as sales figures, productivity counts, etc., and the latter usually involving ratings by others. Personality tests appear to predict ratings better than objective measures, either for methodological reasons (item overlap) or else because ratings measure replication, which is a good summary of a person's personality.

Tett *et al.* (1991a) argued that many previous reviews were based on an exploratory approach and not a confirmatory one. Furthermore, for various reasons older review methods tend to inflate some statistical correlations while deflating others.

Using a different type of meta-analysis, Tett *et al.* (1991a) identified higher average correlations between personality and job efficiency than the Barrick and Mount (1991) review. They included 494 studies that together examined over 13,000 people, and they found a corrected mean personality scale validity of 0.29, and an even higher validity (0.38) when examining studies that conducted a job analysis to attempt to determine which personality dimensions should actually be related to the particular job. According to their very careful analysis, personality traits were clearly better predictors of work-related behaviour under the following conditions:

1. in confirmatory rather than exploratory studies – that is, when the expected relationships (in terms of theory) were examined, as opposed to all of those available;
2. where job analysis was used to select predictions – that is, where jobs were examined in detail and the requirements linked logically to personality theory;
3. for recruits rather than incumbents, doubtless because there are a greater number of variables in recruits, and the effects of socialisation and non-retention have not operated;
4. in military rather than civilian samples, possibly because it is easier to define job requirements in the former;
5. in published articles rather than doctoral dissertations, no doubt because of the quality of research.

This review has been subject to criticism on methodological grounds (Ones *et al.*, 1994), which of course demanded and received a reply (Tett *et al.*, 1991b). Re-analysis showed slightly lower correlations, but they were still respectably high ($r = 0.24$).

In a UK study, Robertson and Kinder (1993) were also concerned with the poor validity of 0.15 reviewed by the analysis of Schmitt *et al.* (1984). Following the critique of others, they used confirmatory criterion-related measures – that is, they examined the correlations they expected would be related to 12 different work judgements (e.g. decision-making ability, managing staff, etc.). They found the average mean sample (based on 20 samples) of around 1500 people to be 0.20 for the personality variables, but with higher values (up to 0.33) for specific work-related criteria such as creativity and judgement. Interestingly, they found that ability measures were unrelated to the trait measures, and accounted for similar amounts of variance to the personality tests.

Looking exclusively at studies performed in the European Community, Salgado (1997) conducted a meta-analysis of 36 studies on the relationship between personality and job performance. He found that conscientiousness (true validity 0.25) was the best predictor, followed by emotional stability (true validity 0.19). Openness to experience and agreeableness were valid predictors of training proficiency, and extraversion was a good predictor in certain professional groups.

7.3 PERSONALITY TRAITS AND WORK-RELATED BEHAVIOUR

There have been some interesting and important, albeit piecemeal, studies of trait correlates of work-related behaviour. Many of them have tested quite specific hypotheses. For instance, Furnham (1992a) found six rather different approaches to examining the relationship between personality and work-related behaviour:

- the classic personality theory approach, which validated the theory with work-related dependent variables;
- classic occupational psychology, in which researchers attempted to find personality/individual difference correlates of a particular work-related behaviour in which they were interested (e.g. absenteeism, accidents);
- developing or adopting a work-specific personality measure that specifically asked about behaviour at work;
- looking at the concept of fit between personality structure/needs and job constraints/demands;
- longitudinal studies of people at work, showing how personality variables at selection can predict work variables many years later;
- biographical or case-history research on particular individuals or groups.

Furnham (1992a) argued that not all personality variables predict occupational variables. Furthermore, other factors such as ability, motivation and biographical variables inevitably, both alone and in interaction with personality variables, do determine behaviour. It is also important to note that organisational factors, such as the way in which organisations are structured and the selection policies and practices pertaining to them, can powerfully influence the effects of personality, often by suppressing them.

The notion that introverted workers are better able than extraverted ones to handle routine work activities was investigated by Cooper and Payne (1967) in a study conducted in the packaging department of a tobacco factory, where the work was repetitive and light. Job adjustment, as assessed by two supervisors, was negatively related to extraversion, and those workers who left the job within 12 months following testing were significantly more extraverted than those who remained. Neuroticism was also implicated, being related to poor job adjustment and to frequency of non-permitted absence. They wrote:

> Beginning with the withdrawal indices, we find that the only appreciable correlations are with length of service and non-permitted absence. The more extraverted workers in this study have shorter periods of service to their credit than the less extraverted (more introverted); this finding may be taken as evidence that the more extraverted individuals will withdraw permanently from work of a routine nature. Non-permitted absence offers further interesting support for the withdrawal assumption. The correlation between extraversion and surgery attendance, although in the expected direction, is probably too small to merit serious attention. Surprisingly, certified sickness absence is almost completely unrelated to extraversion; it would be tempting to account for this non-relationship on the basis of certified sickness requiring a visit to a doctor and subsequent submission of a medical certificate to the employer, all of which may not be considered worth the effort when there exists the alternative of taking one or two days uncertified absence (i.e. non-permitted absence) with virtually no trouble at all. However, such an explanation is not in keeping with an unpublished finding of Taylor, that extraversion scores for 194 male oil refinery workers correlated 0.22 with sickness absence.
>
> (Cooper and Payne, 1967, p.112)

Because extraverts condition poorly and introverts condition readily, extraverts are less able to tolerate tasks of a routine nature, since inhibition accumulates and inhibits sustained task performance. Moreover, because extraverts are under-aroused, they seek arousal and do not function as well as introverts with a minimal or sensory variation input.

Savage and Stewart (1972) found that 100 female card-punch operators in training showed negative correlations between extraversion and supervisor ratings of output per month, although there was no relationship between this personality variable and drop-outs from the programme. Hill (1975) also compared the behaviour of introverts and extraverts on a monotonous task and found, as predicted, that extraverts tend to build more variety into their responses on a monotonous task than introverts.

Logically, extraverts are more likely than introverts to prefer occupations that involve social contact. There is therefore a danger that introverted workers may become over-aroused if their jobs involve considerable extra-organisational contact and a relative absence of routine. Blunt (1978) argued that introverted managers would thus tend to choose positions involving relatively routine duties (e.g. finance, production or technical management), whereas extraverted managers would be more likely to seek jobs in sales, marketing or transport. The results were broadly as postulated, except for the finding that transport managers were less extraverted and production managers were more extraverted than predicted.

In a study of personality correlates of job preference and satisfaction, Sterns *et al.* (1983) found that extraverts preferred jobs with higher levels of cognitive task demands, pace of task demands, cognitive closure, extrinsic rewards and intrinsic rewards. Neuroticism, on the other hand, was negatively related to each of these preferences except for extrinsic awards. Extraverts were less satisfied with the clerical work itself, the supervision and their co-workers than introverts. It should be pointed out that these subjects were non-managerial civil service clerical employees in a job that would suit stable introverts more than extraverts.

The arousal and conditionability process that is part of Eysenck's theory means that it is possible to test some obvious ideas about the suitability of particular personality types for specific jobs. Fairly impressive findings were obtained among *training pilots* by Jessup and Jessup (1971), who tested would-be pilots with the Eysenck Personality Inventory (EPI) early on in their course, and discovered that the subsequent failure rate varied considerably as a function of personality. Specifically, 60 per cent of the neurotic introverts failed compared to 37 per cent of the neurotic extraverts, 32 per cent of the stable extraverts and only 14 per cent of the stable introverts. Thus high levels of neuroticism had a much greater adverse effect on introverts than on extraverts. They note that they expect introverted cadets to learn better, both in the aircraft and in the lecture room, than extraverts. Jessup and Jessup concluded:

> The comparative failure of the specifically neurotic introvert may be tentatively explained as follows. High arousal in the visceral system is associated with high N; high cortical arousal with low E. Given that there is no optimal level of arousal for learning to fly, and that this is a particularly stressful optimum, the learning of the stable introvert on the other hand profits from cortical arousal with suffering from additional visceral arousal.
>
> (Jessup and Jessup, 1971, p.120)

Similar findings were reported by Reinhardt (1970), who carried out a battery of personality tests of a sample of the US Navy's best pilots. Their mean score on the neuroticism scale of the Mandsley Personality Inventory (MPI) was only 11, compared with a mean of 20 among American college students. Okaue *et al.* (1977) divided the extraversion and neuroticism of military pilots into three categories (high, average and low) on each dimension. Of the sample of 75 pilots, 38 individuals fell into the stable extravert category, with the highest frequency in any of the other eight categories being only 8. In research with military pilots in the UK, Bartram and Dale (1982) found a tendency for successful pilots to be more stable and extraverted than those who failed flying training. They had data on over 600 pilots from the Army Air Corps (AAC) and the Royal Air Force. The consistent findings that neuroticism is negatively related to flying success make intuitive sense. Flying can obviously be stressful, with a single mistake proving fatal. In such circumstances, pilots who are especially susceptible to stress are likely to perform less well than those who are more stable. This association prompts a number of questions. Do all aviators have this personality pattern? Are military pilots pre-selected with respect to it, or do military flying training regimes filter out those who do not have it?

More recently, Bartram (1995) obtained 16PF and EPI data from 528 male army applicants for flying training. He found the applicants to be highly 'self-selected', being much more emotionally stable and more extraverted than the general population. He found both questionnaires predictive, with single validities in the range 0.20 to 0.30. He concluded:

> In conclusion, the results of this study provide further support for the role of personality measures in predicting flying training outcome. While the effects found are relatively small, they are consistent with expectations and earlier research. Even quite small increments in validity (or $r = 0.10\text{--}0.20$) will result in very substantial cost-benefit in flying training – and in subsequent operational flying. Personality variance is relatively independent of that which is otherwise assessed during selection (primarily ability and motivation). As a result, measures of personality can potentially yield useful increases in the overall validity of the selection process for flying training.
> (Bartram, 1995, pp.234–5)

Hörman and Maschke (1996) showed that commercial airline pilot success could be predicted with 73.8 per cent accuracy by a similar checkflight and flying experience. However, when the personality variables were also included, the correct classification of pilots increased to 79.3 per cent. Some studies showed personality traits to be modest but significant predictors of job performance. Furnham and Miller (1997) reported a study in which nearly 250 telephone sales employees completed the EPI, and their scores were related to periods of sick leave, total number of days of sick leave over a 1-year period, supervisor's performance, and potential rating. These results demonstrate modest but significant personality trait correlates of two work-related measures. Whilst there were no personality or demographic correlates of total number of days of sick leave taken, there were significant predictions of the number of (presumably short) periods of absence. Younger extraverts appeared to take more sick leave. This may be due to boredom, as the telesales staff sit in a large, open-plan room all day, never leaving their building. Young people, and particularly extraverts, rather than being prone to illness may 'take the odd day off' to do other things. In this sense, they may be an unreliable group for this type of selling.

Yet, as predicted, the extraverts were rated as higher performers and as having more potential than introverts. This is to be predicted as a consistent finding in the sales literature (Furnham, 1992a; Furnham and Coveney, 1996). Extraverts are more sociable and responsive, more comfortable dealing with strangers (customers), and enjoy the variety of contacts that telesales brings. Furthermore, neuroticism was negatively correlated with supervisor ratings of potential, although the correlation narrowly missed the level of significance when the scores were partialled out.

In a related study, Furnham *et al.* (1998) asked just over 200 telephone sales staff to complete the Eysenck Personality Inventory (EPI) and the Learning Styles Questionnaire (LSQ). These two measures were correlated with each other, as well as with two supervisor rating scores (actual performance and development potential), based on extensive electronically logged performance records and other data. Personality and learning styles were logically inter-correlated, as in previous studies. Personality variables (extraversion and neuroticism) and certain learning styles (reflector and pragmatist) were statistically significant predictors of rated performance. They noted that, according to Honey and Mumford (1982), reflector learners are careful, thoughtful, thorough and methodical. However, they do have a tendency to hold back from direct participation, and they are indecisive, averse to risk-taking and unassertive. It is no wonder that these characteristics are consistently negatively related to performance among telesales personnel. It therefore appears to be a good 'select-out' or negative predictor.

Theorists, according to Honey and Mumford (1982), are logical, rational, disciplined and objective, and good at asking probing questions. Yet they do tend to have a low tolerance for uncertainty, disorder and ambiguity, and are full of 'shoulds', 'oughts' and 'musts'. Again, the finding that theorists are positively related to rated performance and development is unsurprising, given that telesales staff have to obtain and log specific information regarding particular policies.

Other studies, which looked at Jungian measures of personality (Myers-Briggs Type Indicator; MBTI), have been much less successful in predicting work-related behaviour (Furnham and Stringfield, 1993).

Personality trait dimensions have also been found to predict 'negative' occupational variables. There has been some interest in the relevance of personality to performance under rather monotonous conditions. It might be predicted that under-aroused extraverts would find it more difficult than introverts to maintain performance over time. Extraverts showed a greater deterioration than introverts in driving performances over a 4-hour period (Fagerström and Lisper, 1977). However, their performance improved more than that of the introverts when someone talked to them or the car radio was turned on.

Shaw and Sichel (1970) compared the personality characteristics of accident-prone and safe South African bus drivers (see Fig. 7.2). Most of the accident-prone drivers were neurotic extraverts, whereas the safe drivers were

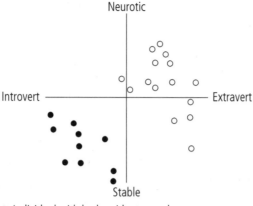

○ Individual with bad accident record
● Individual with good accident record

Figure 7.2 Personality differences between accident-prone and safe bus drivers (adapted from Shaw and Sichel, 1970).

predominantly stable introverts. As might have been expected, it is the impulsiveness component of extraversion rather than the sociability component that is more closely related to poorer driving and greater accident proneness (Loo, 1979).

A number of studies have examined the relationship between personality (particularly extraversion and neuroticism) and accidents (particularly motor car accidents) (Furnham and Saipe, 1993). Despite various methodological difficulties and differences, the results are fairly consistent. Venables (1956) found, as predicted, that driver consistency is related to neuroticism and extraversion in some groups. Presumably erratic and inconsistent behaviour is closely associated with accidents.

Fine (1963) argued that since extraverts are assumed to be less socialised than introverts, it is reasonable to assume that they should be less bound by prescribed rules of society regarding motor vehicle operation. It was therefore postulated that they would incur more traffic accidents and violations than introverts (Fine, 1963, pp.95–6). A study conducted on 937 college students showed, as predicted, that extraverts had incurred more accidents and traffic violations than introverts.

Similarly, Craske (1968), who investigated 70 men and 30 women being treated after accidents in a minor trauma clinic, found a highly significant correlation between extraversion and accidents among the men, but not among the women. Moreover, the positive correlation between accidents and extraversion was not significantly altered by examining severe and minor accidents. A closer examination of the actual test items related to accidents showed that the few extraversion questions which significantly related to accident repetition tended to be related to impulsiveness rather than sociability, while the three neuroticism questions were all concerned with guilt or depression. Schenk and Rausche (1979) also found that neuroticism was closely associated with driving accidents.

Hansen (1989) examined biodata, personality and cognitive correlates of accidents in a causal model. Looking at 362 chemical industry workers, Hansen postulated that traits of social maladjustment, various aspects of neurosis, cognitive ability, employee age and actual job experience would have independent causal effects on accidents, even when risk was partialled out. A social maladjustment scale was constructed from the Myers-Briggs Type Indicator (MBTI) which, together with a measure of (neurotic) distractibility, was clearly linked with accidents. Both scales, although correlated, demonstrated independent causal relationships to accidents, suggesting that two major factors were at work. Hansen believes that the central psychological question of psychologists should be changed from 'What personality or cognitive trait is related to accidents?' to 'What is the strength of the causal impact that trait anxiety has on accidents?'

Booysen and Erasmus (1989) have done a sterling job in reviewing personality factors associated with accident risk. No less than 43 traits (many of them related) have been examined with regard to their relationship to accidents. In a conceptual factor analysis, they suggested that two factors were relevant, namely recklessness (extraversion, domineering, aggressive, sensation-seeking) and anxiety-depression. They then administered the 16 Personality Form (16PF) to nearly 200 bus drivers, who were divided into three groups depending on their previous involvement in accidents and the degree of severity of the accidents in which they had been involved. A stepwise multiple regression showed that four factors – dominance, carefreeness, emotional sensitivity and shrewdness – accounted for between 10 and 12 per cent of the variance.

Thus there appears to be sufficient evidence that personality variables do relate to all kinds of accidents in all kinds of populations. They appear to be able to account for about 10 per cent of the variance, a finding which is certainly not to be dismissed. The two orthogonal factors that appear to be the best predictors of accidents are clearly extraversion/sensation-seeking/A-type behaviour, and neuroticism/anxiety/instability – which, of course, is clearly in accordance with Eysenck's (1967a) theory.

7.4 NEUROTICISM AND JOB SATISFACTION

A number of studies have suggested that neurotics are less productive and satisfied than non-neurotics. In a natural experiment, Organ (1975) observed neurotic and non-neurotic business students as they took structured or

Table 7.2 Correlation between the four personality measures and the eight job satisfaction factors ($n = 88$)

Job satisfaction factor	Personality scale			
	Psychoticism	Extraversion	Neuroticism	Lie
1. Supervision	− 0.17*	0.01	− 0.12	0.15
2. Nature of work	− 0.21*	− 0.11	− 0.14	0.32***
3. Amount of work	− 0.01	0.10	− 0.33***	0.28**
4. Working conditions	− 0.05	0.10	− 0.08	0.10
5. Co-workers	− 0.19*	0.05	− 0.31***	0.21*
6. Pay	0.01	0.20*	− 0.29**	0.36***
7. Future with the organisation	− 0.007	0.04	− 0.01	0.01
8. Overall job satisfaction	− 0.03	0.18*	− 0.06	0.10

*$P < 0.05$, **$P < 0.01$, ***$P < 0.001$.

Source: Reprinted from *Personality and Individual Differences*, **7**, Furnham, A. and Zacherl, M., Personality and job satisfaction, Page No's. 453–5, Copyright (1986), with permission from Elsevier Science.

'ambiguous' examinations under high or low pressure. Predictably, the neurotics reported much more emotional stress in the ambiguous examination than the non-neurotics.

Furnham and Zacherl (1986) examined the relationship between personality and job satisfaction as measured by a multidimensional scale. The results are shown in Table 7.2. Both the psychoticism and neuroticism scales correlated negatively with all of the subscale scores, while both extraversion and the Lie scale correlated positively with all of the subscale scores. Individuals with high psychoticism scores (tough-minded) tended to be significantly less satisfied with their supervisors, the nature of the work and their co-workers than people with low psychoticism scores (tender-minded).

Individuals with high neuroticism scores (unstable neurotics) tended to be significantly less satisfied with the amount of work that they were required to do, with their co-workers, and with their pay. However, it was the Lie scale – a measure of desirability – which in fact yielded the strongest correlation. The fact that neuroticism is consistently negatively correlated with the job satisfaction factors suggests that neurotics in general experience less job satisfaction than non-neurotics. This may be because they are less productive, or alternatively their poor satisfaction might lead to poorer productivity. Whatever the direction of causality, it seems that neurotics make less satisfied employees than non-neurotics.

Levin and Stokes (1989) looked at the trait of 'negative affectivity' (NA), which for them is a combination of anxiety, irritability, neuroticism and self-depreciation. They argue as follows:

High NA individuals have ongoing feelings of distress and nervousness. They tend to dwell on their mistakes, disappointments and shortcomings, and to focus more on the negative aspects of the world in general. In contrast, low NA individuals appear to be more satisfied, self-secure and calm, and to focus less on, and be more resilient in response to, life's daily frustrations and irritations.

(Levin and Stokes, 1989, p.753)

In both laboratory and 'natural' experiments, they found that negative affectivity (neuroticism) was related to lower job satisfaction. They argue that non-neurotics may be denying or repressing various frustrations, disappointments and problems, or that the cognitive processes of neurotics lead them to perceive the world more negatively. It would seem wise for organisations to screen out extreme neurotics and those with negative affectivity.

Perone *et al.* (1979) found similar correlations when examining satisfaction with real and simulated jobs. They found that neuroticism and sensation-seeking were negatively correlated with satisfaction, indicating that dissatisfaction is symptomatic of general emotional maladjustment.

Thus it seems that neuroticism is a highly undesirable trait in the workplace. Yet there is fairly consistent evidence that neuroticism is correlated with academic success. McKenzie (1989) has reviewed two possible explanations for this. First, neuroticism only correlates positively with success in highly selected groups – particularly those selected for intelligence. Secondly, neuroticism only correlates positively with achievement in people who have appropriate coping strategies and superego strength. There is in fact evidence for both of these theories, suggesting that if neuroticism is 'moderated' by intelligence and appropriate coping skills, it will not seriously inhibit achievement.

7.5 PERSONALITY AND DISTRACTIBILITY AT WORK

Eysenck (1967a) has argued that introverts and extraverts differ in terms of their level of cortical arousal. Individuals who are classified as introverts have been shown to have a lower optimum arousal threshold, and therefore do not need much stimulation before they pass their optimum functioning level. Those who are classified as extraverts have higher optimum arousal thresholds, and therefore tend to seek arousal-stimulating situations. Gray (1964) linked these categories with the Russian ideas of strong (extravert) and weak (introvert) nervous systems.

Vermonlayeva-Tomina (1964) found that individuals with a strong nervous system tended to learn more in distracting situations than those with a weak nervous system. This study therefore postulates that introverts would be more negatively affected and extraverts more positively affected by the introduction of extra stimulation, e.g. music, into their work environment.

It has been demonstrated that, when studying in a library, introverts were significantly more likely to choose a place to work away from the bustle of certain areas, while the extraverts were more attracted to the latter as a workplace (Campbell and Hawley, 1982). This finding provides further evidence of the regulation of arousal differences between introverts and extraverts (see also section 3.2).

Morgenstein et al. (1974) found that extraverts actually performed better in the presence of distractions than they did in silence, while introverts showed a deficit in performance. Their subjects were asked to attend to, and remember, a number of words from a long list that was read out to them, whilst they were being read a passage by the same voice. They were given the means of controlling the balance of sound between the word list and the passage, but the greater this difference, the more the words to be remembered were distorted. The study posed three questions. Is the preference for distortion or distraction related to the personality dimension of introversion/extraversion? Do the two groups of subjects differ in their performance on the task? How did the subjects arrive at their preferred balance? They found that extraverts make extravagant sweeping movements in their effort to find a balance, while introverts make much fewer and smaller adjustments. This finding was consistent with Eysenck's theory that the introvert's nervous system is over-damped. There was a trend for introverts to avoid distraction when the personality dimension was compared with choice of distortion/distraction, and they did not perform the task as well, although the effect was not statistically significant. They concluded:

> It would seem that the extroverted subjects do not merely prefer to be in the company of others, but that their work efficiency actually improves in the face of distractions, while the solitary preferences of the introverts are reflected in their reduced efficiency of work when distracted. Paying heed to such preferences, as measured by the Eysenck Personality Inventory, is therefore not only a method of increasing contentment at work by means of personnel selection, but should also result in improved efficiency of output.
>
> (Morgenstein et al., 1974, p.220)

Various studies have examined the distracting effects of television on cognitive processing. Recent research on television distraction effects reported significant performance decrements for several measures, namely spatial problem-solving, mental flexibility and reading comprehension as a function of television. These results are consistent with the idea that background television influences performance by causing cognitive processing limits to be exceeded on complex tasks. Furnham et al. (1994) conducted a study on the effects of the presence of an operating television on introverts and extraverts who were completing reading comprehension tasks. As predicted, they found a significant interaction between the personality dimension and the treatment effect. In other words, the introverts and extraverts performed equally well with the television switched off, but the extraverts performed better than the introverts when the television was switched on.

More recently, Furnham and Bradley (1997) looked at the distracting effects of 'pop music' on introverts' and extraverts' performances on various cognitive tasks. It was predicted that there would be a main effect for music, and an interaction effect with introverts performing less well in the presence of music. Introverts and extraverts were given two tests, namely a memory test (with immediate and delayed recall) and a reading comprehension test, which were completed either while pop music was being played, or in silence. The results showed that there was a detrimental effect on immediate recall in the memory test for both groups when music was played, but no main effect in the other condition. However, two of the three interactions were significant. After a 6-minute interval the introverts who had memorised the objects while pop music was being played had a significantly lower recall than the extraverts in the same condition, and also than the introverts who had observed the objects in silence. The introverts who completed a reading comprehension task when music was being played also performed significantly less well than these two groups. These findings have implications for the study habits of introverts when they need to retain or process complex information.

The results of these studies are relevant to all individuals who work in a communal area, be it an open-plan office or a student work-room. Some people may thrive on background noises, while others (the extreme introverts) will find it immensely debilitating. This consideration is important for management who wish to optimise the output of their work-force and minimise the space in which they work.

7.6 THE GENETIC DETERMINANTS OF JOB SATISFACTION

Eysenck has always been interested in the biosocial 'model of man' and behaviour genetics. He has consistently stated that there is a significant amount of the variance in IQ and personality scores that is directly attributable to inheritance. However, it was not until recently that behaviour geneticists seriously examined the possibility that work behaviours are genetically determined.

Arvey *et al.* (1989) investigated 34 monozygotic twins reared apart in order to look at the genetic and environmental components of job satisfaction. They were quite clearly provoked by the article by Staw and Ross (1985), who noted:

> Job attitudes may reflect a biologically based trait that predisposes individuals to see positive or negative content in their lives. . . . Differences in individual temperament . . . ranging from clinical depression to a very

positive disposition could influence the information individuals input, recall and interpret within various social situations, including work.

(Staw and Ross, 1985, p.471)

There is, they argue quite correctly, no reason to believe that genetic factors do not affect job satisfaction, and they therefore examined 34 monozygotic twins (reared apart), who were (on average) just over 40 years old. They completed a multidimensional questionnaire on job satisfaction, and the results showed a significant heritability of intrinsic and general, but not extrinsic and overall, satisfaction. They also provided clear evidence that there is a genetic component in terms of the job that is sought and held by an individual, although the fact that members of the sample held similar jobs cannot account for the heritability coefficient being significant.

However, the authors note that the genetic factor accounted for about 30 per cent of the variance, which is not an overwhelming result, but does not necessarily imply that all of the remaining variance is due to the environment. The authors argue that intellectual capacity (which has been shown to have a strong hereditary component) probably accounts for the similarity between the jobs chosen by the twins. They argue that these results have two major implications. First, workers bring to jobs dispositions that are more difficult to modify than was previously acknowledged. Thus job enrichment and other satisfaction-increasing programmes might miss the mean levels of satisfaction for workers, but the rank order is preserved. Secondly, future satisfaction may be predicted from current satisfaction, i.e. it can be used as a criterion for prediction.

These results, like the whole issue, will remain extremely contentious, not so much because of the methods used, but because of the socio-political implications of these results for selection and, more importantly, for organisational and structural attempts to improve job satisfaction (and hence perhaps general satisfaction). Hans Eysenck would certainly express no surprise at these results. Moreover, he would doubtless fully understand the implications of these findings for achieving job satisfaction.

7.7 SENSITIVITY TO REWARDS AND PUNISHMENT, AND JOB SATISFACTION

The motivational differences between extraverts, who are motivated to seek rewards, and introverts who are motivated to avoid punishment, have been examined by Gray (1973) who, in rotating Eysenck's two factors along a 45-degree axis, has presented one of the most coherent challenges to that theory. Gray's challenge to his former supervisor is well known, but its organisational implications have been less considered.

Gray's theory asserts that extraverts will respond more readily to reward, while introverts react primarily to punishment. Although extraverts will react positively to an achieved reward and introverts will react positively to an applied punishment, both extraverts and introverts perceive reward and punishment in terms of possible current or future realisations. The extravert is motivated to gain a promised reward, whereas the introvert is motivated to avoid a threatened punishment. Moreover, the over-application of the principle tends to lessen the intended effects, dampening the motivational qualities of reward and punishment. Because the extravert is motivated by opportunity to gain reward, too much rewarding reinforcement tends to create a sating effect on the extravert's desire to achieve. Similarly, since the introvert is motivated by a need to avoid punishment, too many threats or actual enforcement of the negative reinforcement places the introvert in the position of being unable to avoid punishment, and so he or she becomes immobilised and the motivational effect of punishment is consequently decreased. The motivational effects of reward and punishment are not mutually exclusive – an extravert does not wish to be punished, and will react to negative reinforcement, and all introverts want to be rewarded and are motivated by positive reinforcement.

There are two crucial factors in this theory: first, the tendency of the extravert or introvert to perform more satisfactorily in the face of either reward or punishment, and secondly, the degree of extraversion or introversion in a given personality. The more extraverted the individual, the greater the sensitivity they have towards promises of reward, while a person closer to the introversion end of the continuum would display greater sensitivity towards threats of punishment.

The practical application of Gray's theory to occupational settings is appealingly obvious, and we can now more effectively apply the carrot-and-stick principle in socialising human behavioural responses. It becomes apparent that it would be a waste of time to try to motivate an extravert with threats of dire punishment (such as sacking or no pay rise), and equally unsuccessful would be attempts to entice an introvert with the promise of pay and benefits. To exact the highest level of performance from individuals, motivators must encourage the extravert with potential rewards and prompt the introvert with judicial use of punitive threats. Thus extraverted organisations, like those involved in selling, could best motivate and satisfy their staff by providing regular but varied rewards. Equally, a primarily introverted organisation, like many bureaucracies, could best shape or motivate staff by the threat of sanctions.

Gray's theory concerning sensitivity to signals of reward and punishment attempts to explain individual differences in extraversion and introversion, but also deals with neuroticism. Just as extraversion and introversion can be viewed on a continuum scale, so too can individuals be evaluated on a continuum of stability–neuroticism.

The degree of neuroticism heightens an individual's sensitivity to reward or punishment. The introvert, sensitive to punishment, who displays high levels of neuroticism becomes more sensitive to both reward and punishment, with the greatest increase being towards punishment. That is, the neurotic introvert becomes more concerned with reward, but is even more anxious about punishment than the low-neuroticism introvert. As neuroticism increases, the extravert (sensitive to reward) becomes more sensitive to both reward and punishment, with high increases in reward sensitivity. Although extraverts and introverts increase in sensitivity to reward and punishment as the level of neuroticism increases, each shows the highest increase in sensitivity towards that trait which is commonly attributed to extraversion or introversion.

Thus an extraverted neurotic, being highly sensitive to reward, is less socialisable in terms of legal, organisational norms, and more likely to become maladaptive or difficult. Given moderate levels of extraversion, high-N (neurotic) individuals are usually more responsive to control techniques than low-N (stable) individuals. Whether reward or punishment is the controlling factor, the over-socialised individual will respond readily and may tend to become over-controlled, while under-socialised individuals may show little or no response to control measures. Consequently, the low-N (stable) individual may necessitate the use of rigid control and severe disciplinary measures (Wakefield, 1979).

Empirical support for this thesis has come from various sources. Gupta (1976) used a linguistic task to show that extraverts condition more readily to reinforcement and introverts condition more readily to punishment. Gupta used two experimenters. Although all of the subjects were male, one experimenter was male and the other was female. When the word 'good' was vocalised by the female, the young male extraverts showed a more significant response differential than when the word was spoken by the male experimenter. Gupta concluded that the encouraging word spoken by the female appeared to be sufficiently rewarding, while it appeared probable that the more explicit reward was required from the male. 'The strength of conditioning is to a certain extent determined by the individual's subjective attitude towards the person who administers the reinforcement' (Gupta, 1976, p.50).

Similarly, Wakefield *et al.* attempted to apply Gray's theory to educational settings. They argued that achievement in the elementary classroom can be improved by applying differential modes of reinforcement to extraverts and introverts. Extraverts should be rewarded with extensive praise and consistently encouraged by reminders of potential rewards commensurate with competent performance. Introverts, on the other hand, should be judicially exposed to threats of punishment and made continually aware of the negative sanctions resulting from unsatisfactory performance.

McCord and Wakefield (1981) postulated that (1) introverts show better arithmetic achievements than extraverts when exposed to higher levels of teacher-presented punishment in the classroom, and (2) a reversal would occur in which extraverts would achieve arithmetic advantages in classroom situations where teacher-presented rewards were prevalent. They related the reward-to-punishment ratio to teachers, the personality of children and the arithmetic performance of elementary-school pupils. They found that extraverts do meet expectations of higher achievement than introverts in classrooms where there is a predominance of teacher-presented reward, but when the gap between reward and punishment predomination narrows, introverts show higher achievement levels.

Boddy *et al.* (1986) gave introverts and extraverts two tasks to perform, namely a computer game involving initiation of cursor movements on a VDU to find a hidden target, and a task involving recoding of decimal numbers and letters, and performing calculations. As predicted, extraverts performed better under positive than negative reinforcement, while introverts performed better under negative than positive reinforcement. In a study looking at reactions to punishment, Patterson *et al.* (1987) found that extraverts fail to pause following the punishing of errors, but that longer pausing following punishment predicted better learning from punishment for both introverts and extraverts. They note:

> In the presence of reward incentive, extraverts are more prone to facilitate their approach behaviour than to elicit interruption and reflectivity. Without adequate reflection, extraverts fail to associate punishment with the incorrect response and are therefore less likely to inhibit that response on subsequent occasions. In contrast to stable extraverts, whose disinhibited reaction to punishment appears to depend on the presence of cues for reward, the reaction of neurotic extraverts appears to be less situationally determined. To the extent that this disinhibited reaction to punishment interferes with learning and subsequent inhibition, we might expect that stable extraverts' insensitivity to punishment will be more situation specific than neurotic extraverts.
>
> (Patterson *et al.*, 1987, p.570)

A number of attempts have been made to devise measures of Gray's theory. For instance, Torrubia and Tobena (1984) devised a 'susceptibility to punishment' scale which showed predictable and satisfactory correlations with Eysenck's measure. However, Wilson *et al.* (1989) were less successful. They devised a five-dimension measure – approach, active avoidance, passive avoidance, extinction and fight/flight – which, although it showed satisfactory internal consistency, did not correlate with the Eysenckian dimensions as postulated.

Given the nature of this theory, what are the implications for organisational behaviour? Furnham (1992a) has speculated that the organisational incentives (e.g. performance related to pay, promotion possibilities) and prohibitions (e.g. potential sacking, fining) work differently for different people within the organisation. Extravert organisations (that is, those that are dominated by extraverts) can motivate and shape staff by having small (but incremental and worthwhile) incentives that act as reinforcements. The more regular, consistent and public these are, the better. 'Sales-person of the month' and annual awards for efficiency, tact, customer relations, etc. are likely to be more successful with extraverts. Introverted organisations (that is, those that are dominated by introverts and highly sensitive to potential sanctions and punishments) could be used to shape, or at least prevent, various kinds of behaviours. Thus threats of imminent job loss, compulsory retirement and working half-time are likely to make introverts work harder than extraverts. Organisations dominated by extraverts would do well to maintain a 'culture' where people give each other open, honest and regular positive feedback for work well done, while introverted cultures would have ways to remind people regularly that stepping out of line or under-performing will be punished. The obvious major implication of this work is that management systems devised to regulate the behaviour of employees should be sensitive to major individual differences. The carrot and the stick should both be available, but they will not have an equal effect on all employees.

7.8 MODELS

There are various models of how personality influences work. Consider O'Brien's (1986) model, shown in Fig. 7.3.

He notes that personality influences both job change and different responses to different jobs. Although the model does not show this, he is also aware that work structures and job context do influence, if not change, personality and general adjustment.

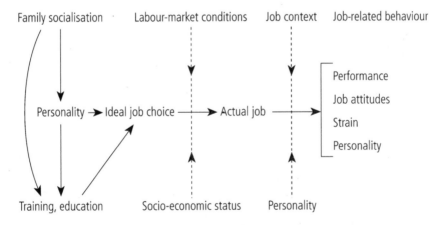

Figure 7.3 The relationship between personality, job choice and job content. Labour market conditions and socio-economic status moderate the relationship between job choice and the job actually obtained. Job-related behaviour is directly determined by job content, but is moderated by job context as well as by personality. Reproduced from O'Brien, G. (1986) *The psychology of work and unemployment*. Chichester: John Wiley. Copyright John Wiley & Sons Limited. Reproduced with permission.

7.9 THE BIG FIVE AT WORK

For nearly 15 years, the Big Five, or their predecessors (Neuroticism Extraversion Openness; NEO) have been related to work issues, particularly issues of selection and performance (Cortina *et al.*, 1992), but also the profile of particular groups (Dykeman and Dykeman, 1996). There have been a number of 'one-off' studies looking at FFM correlates of work-related behaviour in particular jobs. Thus Grant (1995) found conscientiousness, extraversion and proactivity to be predictors of success in real estate agents. Salgado and Rumbo (1997) found neuroticism to be a negative predictor and conscientiousness a positive predictor of job performance in financial service managers. Costa *et al.* (1984) demonstrated clear, logical relationships between personality and vocational interests, noting that because the latter did not measure neuroticism, the two measures should be complementary. They also note that as vocational interests and personality are highly stable across adulthood, each must play an important role in choosing and changing careers at all ages. Gottfredson *et al.* (1993) found that the Big Five measures related to Holland's six interest models. Thus social and enterprising vocational preferences were likened to extraversion, and conventional preferences to conscientiousness. Costa *et al.* (1995) argued that the Big Five can supplement measures of vocational interests and abilities, especially calling attention to the client's strengths and weaknesses in adjustment and motivation. In a recent review of the Big Five as predictors of job performance in the European Community, Salgado (1997) found that conscientiousness and emotional stability were valued predictors across job criteria and occupational groups. He concluded that:

> the Five Factor Model provides the following important advantages: (a) it is a very parsimonious taxonomy; (b) it is a framework for integrating results of many studies carried out to investigate the relationship between personality and work behaviours; and (c) it advances understanding of job performance by offering some personality dimensions related to all jobs and criteria.
>
> (Salgado, 1997)

Furnham *et al.* (1997) recently validated the FFM using assessment centre ratings as the dependent variable. Conscientiousness and extraversion were the most consistent correlates, and agreeableness was the least consistent. Judge *et al.* (1997) found that extraversion and conscientiousness predicted absenteeism, particularly the latter, stressing once again the importance of this factor as a predictor of work-related behaviour.

What critics argue is that the Big Five do not represent an adequate taxonomy for predicting important work criteria (Hough, 1992). Some have argued that the Big Five are too heterogeneous and incomplete to predict work criteria such as job proficiency, training success, educational success, and commendable and law-abiding behaviour. Thus Hough (1992) splits extraversion into affiliation, potency and achievement, and adds rugged individualism (decisive, action-orientated, independent, unsentimental) and locus of control. She also provides evidence of the relationship between these nine personality factors and work-related behaviours. Not surprisingly, achievement and locus of control seem to be particularly powerful measures. Others have claimed that the available psychometric evidence attests to its utility in the prediction of job performance. Costa (1996) has argued that his Big Five measure, which measures traits at both broad, superordinate and narrower, specific levels is useful in vocational, industrial and organisational settings.

Hough and Schneider (1996) evaluated the FFM against five criteria:

1. that traits have been replicated – this has been done across times and samples (including cross-cultural samples), self and peer data, and across adjective and questionnaire measures;
2. that the test is comprehensive – whilst covering much of the area, it is argued that other possible factors (e.g. masculinity/femininity) need to be included;
3. that the factors have external correlates – all of the factors have this;
4. that the five factors are 'source traits with underlying causal structures' that can be invoked to make informed predictions – that has been achieved;
5. that the FFM description consists of multiple level traits.

They note that 'the relevance of personality to industrial/organisational psychology is no myth, it is an undeniable and scientifically exciting reality' (Hough and Schneider, 1996, p.76).

Mount and Barrick (1995), in a very comprehensive review of the implications of the FFM for human resource management, propose that there is a pressing need for a theory of work development. They argue, as have many others in the area, that correlations in the range of 0.20 between Big Five traits and work-related behaviour increase to around 0.45 when composite measures of personality scales *and* work behaviour are used, and when the two are conceptually related. In answering the question 'Is there a functional personality at work?' they believe that there is sufficient evidence of a combination of three FMM factors – conscientiousness, agreeableness and emotional stability – that are powerfully predictive across many work domains.

Recent studies have shown that the Big Five are significant predictors of training success. Thus Collar *et al.* (1996) reported that flight attendants' success during a 6-week training programme was significantly related to extraversion, openness, agreeableness and conscientiousness. Rothstein *et al.* (1994) found that the Big Five were not related to graduate business school students' written work, but that they were in part related to grade-point average and classroom performance. Extraversion and openness were negatively related to rated classroom performance and agreeableness.

7.10 FREUDIAN PERSPECTIVES

Freud's views on work are mainly to be found in his book entitled *Civilisation and Its Discontents*. His views on this topic appear to be somewhat contradictory. O'Brien (1986) believes that Freud's view of work is pessimistic because he regarded it as a necessity induced by scarcity and the need to survive. The formal structure of work in society also prevented the uninhibited satisfaction of the fundamental sexual and aggressive instincts. Work structures imposed rules of conduct which required employees to live by a reality and not by the more desirable pleasure principle. The physical environment and pre- and proscribed contact with co-workers were ordered by imposed rules which prevented immediate gratification of instinctual impulses and thus strengthened the ego. Because of these external controls, work for men was not a pleasurable activity because human beings exhibit an inborn tendency towards carelessness, irregularity and unreliability at work.

Yet according to Freud there was also a positive side of work, because it provided meaning and structure in life. This structure had a positive function for the individual in that it allowed him or her to learn and adapt to the real world, and thus contributed to a state of maturity. Adult maturity is achieved when a person's ego strength is strong enough to direct their activities so that their instincts are satisfied in a socially acceptable form. Furthermore, they would not be overwhelmed by external or internal unconscious libidinal demands which, if accepted, would lead to high levels of anxiety. However, these general functions of work could be accompanied by the potential negative effects of neurotic attachment to work. Freud had a hydraulic view of energy or libido, whereby the quantity of libido is fixed, and if a person invests a lot of energy in work, then that much less energy is available for love and personality activity. Traditional Freudians assert that the overt function of work is self-preservation, and that its covert or latent function is as an integrated ego activity that prevents direct or indirect satisfaction of sexual and aggressive instincts. Freudians, through the case studies of particular cases (e.g. someone with a work compulsion), hope to describe the largely unconscious but very complex meaning of work for individuals. Neo-Freudians have been interested not so much in personality structure as in the psychological functions of work for individuals.

Based on her work dating from the 1930s, Jahoda (1982) has developed a theory based on the idea that psychological distress is produced in the unemployed by the deprivation of the latent functions of work. These are similar to the reality and ego functions specified by Freud (O'Brien, 1986). They include the following.

- *Work structures time.* Work structures the day, the week, and even longer periods. The loss of a time structure can be very disorientating.
- *Work provides regularly shared experiences.* Regular contact with non-nuclear family members provides an important source of social contact.
- *Work provides experience of creativity, mastery and a sense of purpose.* Work, even not particularly satisfying work, gives some sense of mastery or achievement. Creative activities stimulate people and provide a sense of satisfaction.
- *Work is a source of personal status and identity.* A person's job is an important indicator of his or her personal status in society. Furthermore, it is not only to the employed person that the job gives certain status, but also to his or her family. The employed person is therefore a link between two important social systems – family and home.
- *Work is a source of activity.* All work involves some expenditure of physical or mental effort. Whereas too much activity may induce fatigue and stress, too little results in boredom and restlessness, particularly among extraverts. Others have pointed to additional obvious functions that work fulfils, such as a source of relationships outside the nuclear family, as well as (more obviously and prosaically) a source of income and control.

This 'deprivation theory' has had its critics. Fryer (1986) has offered three kinds of criticism. The first is pragmatic – the theory is very difficult to test. The second is methodological – one cannot be sure which deprivations are caused by unemployment, or how; people who are *not* deprived do not necessarily enjoy, appreciate or acknowledge this state. The final criticism is empirical – the theory does not take into account changes over time and undivided differences in reaction.

In a sense, Jahoda (1982) argues that people are *deprived*, while Fryer (1986) argues that institutions *impose* things on people (such as stigma). Furthermore, whereas the former underplays individual choice and personal control, the latter tends to underplay social identity and interdependence of people at work. Note that neither Freud nor Jahoda paid particular attention to individual differences, or indeed whether work experience ever shaped personality. Yet it is not difficult to see the application of Freudian personality theory at work. Thus because *oral* characters are sociable, talkative, sarcastic, argumentative, etc., they should be drawn to oral occupations (Kline, 1984). Thus they are likely to be dentists, lawyers, preachers, radio commentators, etc. If they choose to play musical instruments, they would be more likely to play woodwind or brass instruments than strings or percussion. They may be interested in food products (cooks) or, if they are fixated at the oral, breast/bottle-feeding stage, they may choose and thrive in occupations which in part fulfil this need. *Anal* characters, whose traits include orderliness, obstinacy, parsimony and self-control, should – if the theory is correct – be attracted to occupations such as accountancy, librarianship, safety-checking and banking.

Despite these interesting speculations derived from psychoanalytic theory, there have been few attempts to test them, in part because of the poor nature of personality test measures of Freudian traits. Therefore ideas about the psychological function of work must remain of most importance for psychoanalytic output. However, this does not prevent those with psychoanalytic interests from speculating about behaviour at work. For instance, Rohrlich (1980) has identified a high level of aggression in the workplace, particularly the terms used in everyday language: '*tackling* new problems'; '*grappling* with new ideas'; '*wrestling* with the data'; '*sinking one's teeth* into work'; '*making a killing* on the stock-market'; 'choosing people with more *punch*'. It is suggested that work provides a sense of self, feelings of security, victorious feelings of competence, power and self-respect when interacting with the external world, the conquest of time and the feeling of progress. However, where there is an imbalance between work and love, unfortunate psychopathological consequences are likely to occur. These include the following:

1. *addiction to work* – due to a predilection for skill development (and discomfort with emotion, fantasy and spontaneity); a need for order and analysis; an opportunity to manipulate and control the environment; an obsession with achieving future goals; the need for efficiency and effectiveness. Various types of work addicts are identified;
2. *angry and hostile* – work provides a socially acceptable means of discharging aggressive energy;
3. *ashamed* – has low self-esteem and can only salvage a sense of self-worth in the workplace;
4. *competitive* – work provides a forum for scoring against the world and winning the game;
5. *defensive* – work protects one from unpleasant feelings and helps one to avoid needs, desires and wishes that cause pain;
6. *friendless and lonely* – work functions to bind people into larger groups, beyond the nuclear family, and to give a sense of belonging;
7. *guilty* – some work harder and harder to repudiate the pleasure they derive from their work;
8. *latent homosexual* – enjoys being kept in submission by other men or enjoys the hypermasculinity of the environment;
9. *narcissist* – compulsively depends on work to compensate for an otherwise unremitting sense of inadequacy;
10. *obsessive* – work provides an ideal environment for organising, categorising and defining;
11. *passive dependent* – in the workplace people are taken care of and told what to do;
12. *pre/post-psychotic* – lose their bearings after work where personal relationships are diffused and leisure time too vague;

13. *impotent* – work provides an area for flirtation and pseudo-intimacy.

> Work confirms and defines the self; loving dissolves and obliterates it. Work is structure and order; love is freedom. Work is oriented to the future, to goals; love demands the present. Work is domination and mastery; love is receptivity and submission. Work is mind; love is feeling.
>
> (Rohrlich, 1980, pp.231–2)

7.11 SELF-THEORISTS

From Marx to Maslow, the self-theorists believe that if work is good – allowing people to use and learn new skills, to make responsible decisions, etc. – then individuals will develop a healthy self-esteem and sense of personal control. Equally, they will feel alienated, separated from their true selves and have dysfunctional low self-esteem if their work is menial, boring, degrading or stressful. All of the self-actualisation theories are characterised by a belief that a dominant motive for all behaviour at work, and elsewhere, is to express individual skills and capacities in the fullest possible way (O'Brien, 1986).

Maslow's theory is, without doubt, the best known. He argued that workers could self-actualise if their work positively used their capacities, gratified their needs, and was committed to values such as truth, uniqueness, wholeness, perfection and self-sufficiency. However, there are serious problems with these theories, most notably in how various concepts are defined and measured. Most importantly, though, these are not individual differences or personality theories. The assumption is that job satisfaction, and possibly productivity, results for *all* people in the same way. Despite an interest in needs, many of the self-theorists do not have a sophisticated theory of individual differences and how they influence choice of and productivity in particular jobs.

Of course the evidence for this comes from case histories, not from large-scale empirical research, and may therefore simply represent a small group of people who are not happily adjusted, but are nevertheless hard-working.

Oates (1971) claimed to have invented the neologism 'workaholic', meaning the addiction to work and the compulsion or uncontrollable need to work incessantly. However, unlike other forms of addiction which are held in contempt, workaholism is frequently lauded, praised, expected and even demanded. According to Oates (1971), signs of this 'syndrome' include boasting about one's hours of work, invidious comparisons between oneself and others concerning the amount of work achieved, inability to refuse requests for work, and general competitiveness.

Machlowitz (1980) has defined workaholics as people whose desire to work long and hard is intrinsic, and whose work habits almost always exceed the prescriptions of the job they do and the expectations of the people with whom, or for whom, they work. She quotes Galbraith on the first page of her book, who noted that 'No ethic is as ethical as the work ethic'. Throughout her book she assumes that the workaholic is the embodiment of the Protestant Work Ethic (PWE).

According to Machlowitz (1980), all true workaholics share six traits, some of which are more paradoxical than stereotypic. Workaholics are intense, energetic, competitive and driven, they have strong self-doubts, they prefer labour to leisure, they can – and do – work any time and anywhere, they make the most of their time, and they blur the distinctions between business and pleasure.

All workaholics have these traits, but may be subdivided into four distinct types as follows.

- *The dedicated workaholic.* These are quintessentially the single-minded, one-dimensional workaholics frequently described by lay people and journalists. They shun leisure and are often humourless and brusque.
- *The integrated workaholic.* This type does integrate outside features into their work. Thus although work is 'everything', it does sometimes include extracurricular interests.
- *The diffuse workaholic.* This type has numerous interests, connections and pursuits which are far more scattered than those of the integrated workaholic. Furthermore, they may change jobs fairly frequently in pursuit of their goals.
- *The intense workaholic.* This type approaches leisure (frequently competitive sport) with the same passion, pace and intensity as work. They become as preoccupied by leisure as by work.

To some extent it is thought that workaholism is an obsessive-compulsive neurosis characterised by sharp, narrowed, focused attention, endless activity, ritualistic behaviours, and a 'strong desire to be in control'. However, the aetiology of this 'syndrome' is seen to lie in childhood, where workaholism is fairly easily recognised. Machlowitz (1980) argues that some children are driven from within, but others are pushed by their parents, e.g. by reinforcement – that is, the parents threaten to withdraw love if ever-increasing expectations are not fulfilled:

> Seeing paternal love as contingent on achievement instead of unconditional surely spurs progress, but it may also be the source of self-doubts ... success is self-perpetuating, but the promise of failure is even more propelling and compelling.
>
> (Machlowitz, 1980, pp.41–2)

Furthermore, parents may encourage workaholism by providing a model for their children. However, because the parents are so busy they may be poor parents in that they are inattentive or simply exhausted when at home. To find workaholics at play may simply be an oxymoron. Machlowitz (1980) suggests a number of reasons why workaholics shun vacations and time off. For example, they have never had a good experience of holidays, either because they have expected too much or they chose the wrong type; as their jobs are their passion they do not feel that they need to get away from it all; traditional forms of recreation seem like a waste of time and are incomprehensible to them; the preparation for and anxiety that precedes taking a holiday are more trouble than they are worth; and, finally, workaholics are afraid that they would lose complete control over their jobs if they left for a holiday.

More recently, Spence and Robbins (1992) found that workaholics scored high on work involvement, but low on work enjoyment, whereas work enthusiasts scored high on both. They found that workaholics score high on perfectionism, non-delegation of responsibility, job stress and, interestingly, health complaints. The latter may be an indicator of the neurotic side of workaholism.

7.12 CONCLUSION

There has been a recent resurgence of interest in personality testing for personnel selection. Many of the early methodological objections about response distortion (Hough *et al.*, 1990), social desirability (Ones *et al.*, 1996) and bandwidth fidelity trade-offs (Hogan and Roberts, 1996) have been resolved. Further studies over the past 20 years have shown unequivocally that personality is 'implicated' in a very wide range of work-related behaviours such as absenteeism, employee reliability, satisfaction, variability and motivation. The period when organisational and occupational psychologists looked at personality variables as alternative or weak predictors at work seems to be over.

There is now an emerging consensus about the use of personality theory at work. First, traits not only need to be measured reliably, but also require measurement at the right level of specificity. That is, higher-order traits may be too wide or 'fat' to pick up sensitive differences. Thus the 'warmth' or 'positive emotions' primary factor of extraversion may be positively associated with service orientation, while 'excitement-seeking' may not. Therefore it is important that careful attention is paid to the *predictor* variable (what trait to measure and at what level, whether to use self or other reports, etc.).

More importantly, it remains crucial to obtain an accurate, sensitive, aggregated measure of the *criterion* variable, e.g. leadership and personal discipline, counter-productive behaviour, creativity, sales effectiveness, training success. Once the measure has been determined, it becomes possible to specify the predictor measure. Using personality batteries against poorly measured work criteria leads to both disappointment and bad science. It is precisely such an approach that leads to personality theory developing a poor reputation with organisational psychologists.

REFERENCES

Adler, S. (1996) Personality and work behaviour: exploring the linkages. *Applied Psychology: An International Review* 45, 207–24.

Arneson, S., Millikin-Davies, M. and Hogan, J. (1993) Validation of personality and cognitive measures for insurance claims examiners. *Journal of Business and Psychology* 7, 459–73.

Arvey, R., Bouchard, T., Segal, N. and Abraham, L. (1989) Job satisfaction: environmental and genetic components. *Journal of Applied Psychology* 74, 187–92.

Barrick, M. and Mount, M. (1991) The Big Five personality dimensions and job performance: a meta-analysis. *Personnel Psychology* 44, 1–26.

Bartram, D. (1995) The predictive validity of the EPI and 16PF for military flying training. *Journal of Occupational and Organizational Psychology* 68, 219–30.

Bartram, D. and Dale, H. (1982) The Eysenck Personality Inventory as a selection test for military pilots. *Journal of Occupational Psychology* 55, 287–96.

Bernadin, H. and Bownas, D. (1985) *Personality assessment in organisations.* New York: Praeger.

Blunt, P. (1978) Personality characteristics of a group of white South African managers. *International Journal of Psychology* 13, 139–46.

Boddy, I., Carver, A. and Rowley, K. (1986) Effects of positive and negative verbal reinforcement on performance as a function of extraversion–introversion. *Personality and Individual Differences* 7, 81–8.

Booysen, A. and Erasmus, J. (1989) Die verband tussen enkele persoonlikheidsfaktore en botsingrisiko. *South African Journal of Psychology* 55, 321–9.

Campbell, J.B. and Hawley, C.W. (1982) Study habits and Eysenck's theory of extraversion–introversion. *Journal of Research in Personality* 16, 139–46.

Collar, D., Miller, M., Doverspike, D. and Klawsky, J. (1996) Comparison of factor structures and criterion-related validity coefficients for two measures of personality based on the five-factor model. *Journal of Applied Psychology* 81, 694–700.

Cooper, R. and Payne, R. (1967) Extraversion and some aspects of work behaviour. *Personnel Psychology* 20, 45–7.

Cortina, J., Doherty, M., Schmitt, N., Kaufman, G. and Smith, R. (1992) The 'Big Five' personality factors in the IPI and MMPI: predictors of police performance. *Personnel Psychology* 45, 119–40.

Costa, P. (1996) Work and personality: use of the NEO-PI-R in industrial/ organisational psychology. *Applied Psychology: An International Perspective* 45, 225–41.

Costa, P., McCrae, R. and Holland, J. (1984) Personality and vocational interests in an adult sample. *Journal of Applied Psychology* 69, 390–400.

Costa, P., McCrae, R. and Kay, G. (1995) Persons, places and personality: career assessment using the revised NEO personality inventory. *Journal of Career Assessment* 3, 123–39.

Craske, S. (1968) A study of the relation between personality and accident history. *British Journal of Medical Psychology* 41, 399–404.

Day, D. and Silverman, S. (1989) Personality and job performance: evidence of incremental validity. *Personnel Psychology* 42, 25–36.

Dykeman, C. and Dykeman, J. (1996) Big five personality profiles of executive recruiters. *Journal of Employment Counselling* 33, 77–86.

Eysenck, H. (1967a) *The biological basis of personality.* Springfield, IL: Thomas.

Eysenck, H. (1967b) Personality patterns in various groups. *Occupational Psychology* 41, 249–50.

Fagerström, K. and Lisper, H. (1977) Effects of listening to car radio, experience and personality of the driver on subsidiary reaction time and heart rate in a long-term driving task. In Michael, R. (ed.), *Vigilance.* New York: Plenum.

Fine, B. (1963) Introversion–extraversion and motor vehicle driver behaviour. *Perceptual and Motor Skills* 12, 95–100.

Fryer, D. (1986) Employment deprivation and personnel agency during unemployment. *Social Behaviour* 1, 3–27.

Furnham, A. (1992a) *Personality at work.* London: Routledge.

Furnham, A. (1992b) Personality and learning style. *Personality and Individual Differences* 13, 429–38.

Furnham, A. (1997) *The psychology of behaviour at work.* Hove: Psychology Press.

Furnham, A. and Zacherl, M. (1986) Personality and job satisfaction. *Personality and Individual Differences* 7, 453–5.

Furnham, A. and Saipe, J. (1993) Personality correlates of convicted drivers. *Personality and Individual Differences* 14, 329–36.

Furnham, A. and Stringfield, P. (1993) Personality and occupational behaviour. *Human Relations* 46, 827–48.

Furnham, A. and Coveney, R. (1996) Personality and customer service. *Psychological Reports* 79, 675–81.

Furnham, A. and Bradley, A. (1997) Music while you work: the differential distraction of background music on the cognitive test of performance of introverts and extraverts. *Applied Cognitive Psychology* 11, 445–55.

Furnham, A. and Miller, T. (1997) Personality, absenteeism and productivity. *Personality and Individual Differences* 23, 705–8.

Furnham, A., Gunter, B. and Peterson, E. (1994) Television distraction and the performance of introverts and extraverts. *Applied Cognitive Psychology* 8, 705–11.

Furnham, A., Crump, J. and Whelan, J. (1997) Validating the NEO Personality Inventory using assessors' ratings. *Personality and Individual Differences* 22, 669–75.

Furnham, A., Jackson, C. and Miller, T. (1998) *Personality, learning and work performance.* Unpublished paper.

Gellarty, I., Paunonen, S., Meyer, J., Jackson, D. and Goffin, R. (1991) Personality, vocational interest, and cognitive predictors of managerial job performance and satisfaction. *Personality and Individual Differences* 12, 221–31.

Ghiselli, E. (1966) *The validity of occupational aptitude tests.* New York: John Wiley.

Ghiselli, E. and Barthol, P. (1953) The validity of aptitude inventories in the selection of employees. *Journal of Applied Psychology* 37, 18–20.

Ghiselli, E. and Brown, C. (1955) *Personnel and industrial psychology.* New York: McGraw-Hill.

Gottfredson, G., Jones, C. and Holland, J. (1993) Personality and vocational interests. *Journal of Counselling Psychology* 40, 518–24.

Grant, J. (1995) The proactive personality scale and objective job performance among real estate agents. *Journal of Applied Psychology* **80**, 532–7.

Gray, J. (1964) Strength of the nervous system and levels of arousal: a reinterpretation. In Gray, J. (ed.) *Pavlov's typology*. Oxford: Pergamon, 289–366.

Gray, J. (1973) Causal theories of personality and how to test them. In Royce, J. (ed.), *Multivariate analysis and psychological theory*. New York: Academic Press.

Guion, R. and Gottier, R. (1965) Validity of personality measures in personnel selection. *Personnel Psychology* **18**, 135–64.

Gupta, B. (1976) Extraversion and reinforcement in verbal operant conditioning. *British Journal of Psychology* **67**, 47–52.

Hansen, C. (1989) A causal model of the relationship among accidents, biodata, personality and cognitive factors. *Journal of Applied Psychology* **74**, 81–90.

Hill, A. (1975) Extraversion and variety-seeking in a monotonous task. *British Journal of Psychology* **66**, 9–13.

Hogan, J. and Hogan, R. (1989) How to measure employees' reliability. *Journal of Applied Psychology* **74**, 273–9.

Hogan, J. and Roberts, B. (1996) Issues and non-issues in the fidelity bandwidth trade-off. *Journal of Organisational Behaviour* **17**, 627–37.

Hogan, R. (1990) Personality and personality measurement. In Dunnette, M. and Hough, L. (eds), *Handbook of industrial/organisational psychology*. Paola Alto, CA: Consulting Psychologists Press.

Holloway, W. (1991) *Work psychology and organisational behaviour*. London: Sage.

Honey, P. and Mumford, A. (1982) *The manual of learning styles*. Maidenhead: Honey.

Hörman, H-J. and Maschke, P. (1996) On the relation between personality and job performance of airline pilots. *International Journal of Aviation Psychology* **6**, 171–8.

Hough, L. (1992) The 'Big Five' personality variables – construct confusion: descriptive versus predictive. *Human Performance* **5**, 139–55.

Hough, L. (1997) Personality at work: issues and evidence. In Hakel, M. (ed.), *Beyond multiple choice: evaluating alternatives to traditional testing for selection*. Hillsdale, NJ: Erlbaum.

Hough, L. and Schneider, R. (1996) Personality traits, taxonomies, and applications in organisations. In Murphy, K. (ed.), *Individual differences and behaviour in organisations*. San Francisco, CA: Jersey Bass, 31–88.

Hough, L., Eaton, N., Dunnette, M., Kamp, J. and McCloy, R. (1990) Criterion-related validities of personality constructs and the effects of response distortion on those validities. *Journal of Applied Psychology* **75**, 501–95.

Hunter, J. and Hunter, R. (1984) Validity and utility of alternative predictors of job performance. *Psychological Bulletin* **96**, 72–98.

Jahoda, M. (1982) *Employment and unemployment: a social–psychological analysis*. Cambridge: Cambridge University Press.

Jessup, G. and Jessup, H. (1971) Validity of Eysenck's Personality Inventory in pilot selection. *Occupational Psychology* **45**, 111–23.

Judge, T., Martocchio, J. and Thorensen, C. (1997) Five-factor model of personality and employee absence. *Journal of Applied Psychology* **82**, 745–55.

Kline, P. (1984) *Psychology and Freudian theory*. London: Methuen.

Krilowicz, T. and Lowery, C. (1996) Evaluation of personality measures for the selection of textile employees. *Journal of Business and Personality* **11**, 55–61.

Lanyon, R. and Goodstein, L. (1997) *Personality assessment.* New York: Wiley.

Levin, I. and Stokes, J. (1989) Dispositional approach to job satisfaction: role of negative affectivity. *Journal of Applied Psychology* **74**, 752–8.

Loo, R. (1979) Role of primary personality factors in the perception of traffic signs and driver violations and accidents. *Accident Analysis and Prevention* **11**, 125–7.

McCord, R. and Wakefield, J. (1981) Arithmetic achievement as a function of introversion–extraversion and teacher-presented reward and punishment. *Personality and Individual Differences* **2**, 145–52.

McKenzie, J. (1989) Neuroticism and academic achievement: the Furneaux factor. *Personality and Individual Differences* **10**, 509–15.

Machlowitz, M. (1980) *Workaholics.* New York: Mentor.

Morgenstein, S., Hodgson, R.J. and Law, L. (1974) *Work Efficiency and Personality Ergonomics* **17**, 211–20.

Mount, M. and Barrick, M. (1995) The big five personality dimensions: implications for research and practice in human resources management. *Research in Personnel and Human Resources Management* **13**, 153–200.

Muscio, B. (1919) *Lectures on industrial psychology.* Easton: Hive.

Musterberg, H. (1913) *Psychology and industrial efficiency.* Boston, MA: Houghton Mifflin.

Nicholson, N. (1996) Towards a new agenda for work and personality. *Applied Psychology: An International Review* **45**, 189–215.

Oates, W. (1971) *Confessions of a workaholic.* New York: World Publishing Co.

O'Brien, G. (1986) *The psychology of work and unemployment.* Chichester: John Wiley.

Okaue, M., Nakamura, M. and Niura, K. (1977) Personality characteristics of pilots on EPPS, MPI and DOSEFU. *Reports of Aeromedical Laboratories* **18**, 153–200.

Ones, D., Mount, M. and Hunter, J. (1994) Personality and job performance: a critique of the Tett, Jackons & Rothstein (1991) meta-analysis. *Personnel Psychology* **47**, 147–156.

Ones, D., Viswesvaran, C. and Reiss, A. (1996) Role of social desirability in personality testing for personnel selection: the red herring. *Journal of Applied Psychology* **81**, 660–79.

Organ, D. (1975) Effects of pressure and individual neuroticism on emotional responses to task–role ambiguity. *Journal of Applied Psychology* **60**, 397–400.

Patterson, C., Kosson, D. and Newman, J. (1987) Reaction to punishment, reflectivity, and passive avoidance learning in extraverts. *Journal of Personality and Social Psychology* **52**, 565–75.

Perone, M., De Waard, R. and Baron, A. (1979) Satisfaction with real and simulated jobs in relation to personality variables and drug use. *Journal of Applied Psychology* **64**, 660–68.

Raymark, P., Schmidt, M. and Guion, R. (1997) Identifying potentially useful personality constructs for employee selection. *Personnel Psychology* **50**, 720–36.

Reinhardt, R. (1970) The outstanding jet pilot. *American Journal of Psychiatry* **127**, 732–6.

Robertson, I. and Kinder, A. (1993) Personality and job competence: the criterion-related validity of some personality variables. *Journal of Occupational and Organisational Psychology* **66**, 225–44.

Rohrlich, J. (1980) *Work and love: the crucial balance.* New York: Summit.

Rothstein, M., Paurison, S., Rush, J. and King, G. (1994) Personality and cognitive ability predictors of performance in graduate business schools. *Journal of Educational Psychology* **86**, 516–30.

Salgado, J. (1997) The five-factor model of personality and job performance in the European Community. *Journal of Applied Psychology* **82**, 30–43.

Salgado, J. and Rumbo, A. (1997) Personality and job performance in financial service managers. *International Journal of Selection and Assessment* **5**, 91–100.

Savage, R. and Stewart, R. (1972) Personality and the success of card-punch operators in training. *British Journal of Psychology* **63**, 445–50.

Schenk, J. and Rausche, A. (1979) The personality of accident-prone drivers. *Psychologic und Poaxis* **23**, 241–7.

Schmitt, N., Gooding, R., Noe, R. and Kirsch, M. (1984) Meta-analysis of validity studies published between 1964 and 1982 and the investigation of study characteristics. *Personnel Psychology* **37**, 407–22.

Schneider, B. (1996) Whither goest personality at work? *Applied Psychology: An International Review* **45**, 289–96.

Shaw, L. and Sichel, H. (1970) *Accident proneness*. Oxford: Pergamon.

Spence, J. and Robbins, A. (1992) Workaholism: definition, measurement, and preliminary results. *Journal of Personality Assessment* **58**, 160–75.

Staw, B. and Ross, J. (1985) Stability in the midst of change: a dispositional approach to job attitudes. *Journal of Applied Psychology* **70**, 469–80.

Sterns, L., Alexander, R., Barrett, G. and Dambrot, F. (1983) The relationship of extraversion and neuroticism with job preferences and job satisfaction for clerical employees. *Journal of Occupational Psychology* **56**, 145–55.

Tett, R., Jackson, D. and Rothstein, M. (1991a) Personality measures as predictors of job performance: a meta-analysis review. *Personnel Psychology* **44**, 703–37.

Tett, R., Jackson, D., Rothstein, M. and Reddon, J. (1991b) Meta-analysis of personality and job performance relations. *Personnel Psychology* **47**, 157–72.

Torrubia, R. and Tobena, A. (1984) A scale for the assessment of 'susceptibility to punishment' as a measure of anxiety. *Personality and Individual Differences* **5**, 371–5.

Van den Berg, P. and Feij, J. (1993) Personality traits and job characteristics as predictors of job experience. *European Journal of Personality* **7**, 337–57.

Venables, P. (1956) Car driving consistency and measures of personality. *Journal of Applied Psychology* **40**, 21–4.

Vermonlayeva-Tomina, L.B. (1964) *Pavlov's typology*. Oxford: Pergamon.

Wakefield, J. (1979) *Using personality to individualize instruction*. San Francisco, CA: Edward.

Wilson, E., Barrett, P. and Gray, J. (1989) Human reactions to reward and punishment: a questionnaire examination of Gray's personality theory. *British Journal of Psychology* **80**, 509–15.

8

Personality and Leisure

8.1 INTRODUCTION

There is a surprising paucity of literature on the relationships between personality and leisure. Neither personality theorists nor leisure researchers appear to have been particularly interested in why certain people choose, excel at, become addicted to, or indeed are bored, frightened or bewitched by particular leisure activities. However, lay people, particularly in their role as selectors, have long been interested in leisure. Thus a great number of job applicants are asked about their leisure activities at interview, and some may in fact have been required to list them on their application form. What the majority of interviewers appear to assume is that because most leisure pursuits are relatively unconstrained and 'freely chosen', one gains a privileged insight into personality needs and traits by inferring what satisfactions various activities fulfil (Furnham, 1990, 1994). This intuition may indeed be true (Brandstätter, 1994). Thus risk-taking sensation-seekers choose paragliding and bungy-jumping, logical, competitive introverts enjoy bridge and chess, and socially inadequate obsessionals are attracted to train- and plane-spotting. As Neulinger noted:

> Leisure seemed the ideal place to investigate personality dynamics. Leisure may be compared to a Rorschach card on to which we project our fantasies, wishes and dreams. In what area of life can one better determine behaviour that is, or ought to be, primarily determined by the person's desires and motives.
>
> (Neulinger, 1978, p.ix)

Leisure provides many varying opportunities to fulfil psychological needs ranging from enjoying nature, reducing tension and escaping physical stressors to social recognition, skill development and excitement-seeking. Leisure can distort time experiences and reduce anxiety and constraints. Through total involvement one can have the pleasurable experience of forgetting oneself and/or having a narrower but richer focus of attention.

Many writers have provided a long list of 'leisure facts' and statistics that give some insight into leisure motivations (Neulinger, 1978; Argyle, 1996). Certainly the data on leisure suggests that there are considerable demographic correlates, particularly those preferred factors of age, sex and social class. Whilst leisure is probably much less sex-linked than used to be, there remain strong sex differences. As age relates to such factors as wealth and physical fitness, this means that leisure preferences also show clear age relationships. Leisure preference is also clearly related to many social class correlates, such as education, income and occupation.

Religious beliefs, race differences, nationality and health status are clearly related to leisure-time pursuits and preferences. Certainly there are also cultural and subcultural differences in attitudes to leisure.

The study of the relationship between personality and leisure is complex, and this is partly to do with the definition of both variables. It is also difficult to try to predict leisure behaviour from personality traits, because any given activity may fulfil different needs for different people, or even for the same person at different times or in different conditions. Yet various individual difference variables have been considered in relation to leisure, including attribution style, mental health, motives, needs, traits, self-esteem and self-perception.

Shivers (1981) has argued that leisure can be conceived of in seven quite distinct ways:

- leisure as *recreation* – a time set aside for creativity and learning; a symbol of cultural achievement and educational betterment;
- leisure as *pleasure* – a source of happiness and moderate hedonism; leisure is a time of opportunity to avoid ennui and maximise preferred enjoyment;
- leisure as *rejuvenation* – leisure provides the necessary physiological and psychological stimulation and variety to return to work, which must be the primary arena for self-realisation;
- leisure as a *state of being* – leisure is a self-perceived state of freedom that can only be defined in its own terms and not by activities performed;
- leisure as *function* – leisure can be thought of in terms of the functions it fulfils, such as relaxation, diversion, experience-broadening; it is essentially freedom from a certain number and kind of obligation;
- leisure as *social stratification* – leisure is the unrestrained and conspicuous spending of time/money by one class in order to live up to the concepts of others; it is the unproductive use of time, and evidence of the pecuniary ability to afford a life of idleness;
- leisure as *time* – it is the discretionary or free time of any individual; it is the time not required to maintain biological functions, economic worth and socio-cultural obligations. Leisure is choice.

Shivers (1981) notes the many problems linked to inadequate conceptual-isation of leisure:

> Traditional definitions of recreation have been founded on five concepts. They include when recreation occurs (in leisure), why recreation occurs (prime motive), how recreation occurs (freedom of choice), what occurs (activity), and in what context it occurs (virtue). On those bases restrictive meanings have been applied to prevent many human activities from being termed recreational in either quality or connotation. . . . In both the past and the present, recreation has been viewed as the antithesis of work and labour. It has been thought of as value derived, contributing to mental health, physical well-being, creativity, personality development, satisfaction, self-assertion, pleasure and so on. . . . Thus it has been explained as everything from the universal panacea to mere sports and games or physical exercise and art.
>
> (Shivers, 1981, p.180)

The definition of both sport and leisure remains highly problematic. Neulinger (1978) has contrasted classical and twentieth-century definitions of leisure. He attempted a denotative and connotative definition of leisure, and stressed such factors as discretionary time and activity as well as a particular state of mind as being the essential characteristics of leisure. Although a number of definitions exist, they are somewhat vague, contradictory and nebulous. Yet as Stockdale (1986) has noted, it is difficult to develop a coherent theoretical framework or body of knowledge if no clear, con-sensually held definition of leisure exists. She writes:

> Some researchers take the easy way out; they pay lip service to the definitional problems and focus on easily measurable aspects, such as frequency of participation in activities which the majority regard as leisure. This frequently leads to a focus on more formal leisure activities and the neglect of informal, private or inactive pursuits. Moreover, it perseverates an implicit view of leisure as defined by researchers rather than by the individual consumer.
>
> (Stockdale, 1986, p.7)

8.2 HISTORY OF LEISURE

The arts and sciences and even technology developed out of the creative and imaginative use of leisure-time. Cave paintings may be one of the first (and still surviving) forms of art. Dancing, drama and child's play are documented as very early forms of recreational pastimes. Sports and games were very popular in ancient Rome. Hunting and fishing were popular in Renaissance Europe when there appeared a clear distinction between the leisure-time pursuits of the aristocracy and those of the common labourer. Fifteenth-century Calvinism condemned leisure as idleness equated with mischief and the devil's work.

The decrease in the number of working hours has naturally witnessed a great change in the amount and type of leisure activities that are engaged in and enjoyed. Leisure for the masses is essentially a twentieth-century concept. In pre-industrial times, work was not competitive and it was performed at a 'leisurely pace'. It often allowed people to stamp their individuality on their product or process, and it frequently provided for extensive social intercourse. During the industrial revolution and up until the Second World War, much work was tedious, humdrum, and neither intrinsically nor often even extrinsically satisfying. Leisure was often compensatory.

The economics of leisure shows that leisure activities are clearly related to national wealth, as many require materials and services that have to be paid for. Urbanisation also led to the growth of public recreational agencies. Since the Second World War, particularly in the developed Western countries, leisure has been accepted as both necessary and healthy. Cultural prejudices and religious taboos have broken down, and leisure is now seen as not only essential for personal satisfaction but also coincidentally stimulating the economy and providing a large number of jobs.

Puritanism and the Protestant work ethic in Europe, America and its colonies have had, and still do have, an intensely controlling and channelling influence on human energy and endeavour. Weber pointed out that the work ethic accepted sport and leisure if (and only if) it served a rational purpose, namely physical efficiency. Much sport was thought to be frivolous and brutal. Furthermore, it encouraged disrespect for the Sabbath and a negation of spiritual duties, and it was believed to encourage gambling, and to sow the seeds of its own destruction.

However, the paradox of the work ethic was also evident in sport (Furnham, 1990). As Calhoun (1994) noted, puritanism produced a workaholic mentality that increased production and created leisure and affluence, thus generating a market for commercial sport rather than 'fun and games'. Thus modern competitive, commercial sport (and leisure as a whole) is at the same time both an escape from modern industrialism and an expression of it. In a mobile urban world, sport provided roots. It became divided into amateur and professional sport, although there are many contradictions within amateur sport. As a business, professional sport exercises an influence that extends far beyond its actual size. However, for the puritans it is held that sport trains young people for competitive society. Sport is also intimately related to social stratification and social mobility.

Furnham (1990) argued that Calvin's view was that, for the most part, leisure was a form of idleness (synonymous with mischief and the devil's work). Calvin considered dancing, gambling and card games to be immoral, but did not disapprove of all recreational activities. If leisure activities recuperated power or kept one more fit to sustain the physical and mental faculties required at work, they were to be tolerated. Thus, just as there was a deserving and non-deserving poor, so there was good and bad leisure.

Mudrack (1992) has demonstrated how work ethic beliefs can still motivate people at work and leisure. He found that work ethic endorsement was positively related both to the frequency with which employees visited their company's fitness centre, and to the perception that exercise provided work-related benefits. Thus on-the-job fitness and leisure facilities may be more a component of work than of leisure attitudes. One could define attitudes to work and leisure as either broadly in favour or broadly against.

Four possible combinations exist which may be categorised thus:

- *AB*: work hard/play hard – the idea that both work and leisure are desirable characteristics and that, no doubt when properly distinguished, both should be highly enjoyable;
- *AD*: puritan – the idea that work (in all its forms) is good, and equally that leisure (whatever form that takes) is bad;
- *CB*: hedonist/idle rich – this position is largely against all forms of work (particularly if they are not immediately enjoyable or worthwhile), but in favour of most (particularly preferred) forms of leisure;
- *CD*: alienated – people who are against work and leisure seem particularly alienated, perhaps with concomitant feelings of powerlessness, normlessness and meaninglessness.

Clearly, the strict Calvinistic position is AD, although it is quite conceivable that work ethic believers could endorse AB. It all depends on the nature of leisure-time pursuits. No doubt all Protestant Work Ethic (PWE) believers would be against idle, self-indulgent leisure, such as drinking, but would be in favour of educational or health-promoting leisure. Indeed many leisure pursuits, such as do-it-yourself work, amateur science and fitness-training, seem to be the very embodiment of work ethic virtues. Due to the fact that both leisure behaviours and beliefs are very diverse, it is difficult to reach any simplistic conclusion. However, depending on the nature of the leisure-time activity, it is quite conceivable that it could be strongly approved of by those who endorse the work ethic.

It may well be, though, that a leisure ethic has replaced the work ethic. Many writers have talked about the new leisure ethic which states that 'to leisure' is by far the greatest virtue, namely to develop one's potential in discretionary time (Neulinger, 1978). Although it is not entirely clear what this new ethic stands for, some empirical work had to be done in this field. Thus Buchholz (1976) attempted to measure what he termed the *leisure ethic*, which regards work as a means to personal fulfilment primarily through its provision of the means to pursue leisure activities. According to Buchholz, the leisure ethic is defined thus:

> Work has no meaning in itself, but only finds meaning in leisure. Jobs cannot be made meaningful or fulfilling, but work is a human necessity to produce goods and services and enable one to earn the money to buy them. Human fulfilment is found in leisure activities where one has a choice regarding the use of his time, and can find pleasure in pursuing activities of interest to him personally. This is where a person can be creative and involved. Thus the less hours one can spend working and the more leisure time one has available the better.
>
> (Bucholz, 1976, p.1180)

Thus the leisure ethic may be seen as the positive opposite of the work ethic. People who do not endorse the work ethic may or may not endorse the leisure ethic, but it is unlikely that individuals will endorse both the work ethic and the leisure ethic. Hence one may predict a sizeable significant negative correlation between the work ethic and the leisure ethic.

What is the relationship between work and leisure? Since Wilensky (1960), it has been customary to divide the relationship between leisure and work into three possibilities: Spillover–leisure is an extension of work, so therefore they are similar, the demarcation is weak and work is the person's central interest. Compensation–leisure is an opposition to work, in which leisure is set apart from and counterposed to work. Neutrality–leisure is somewhat different, and while the demarcation is not strong, the individual is probably more interested in leisure. This relationship has been generated by research and theorising.

Parker (1972, 1983) has attempted to look at the consequences of these three relationships, which he calls extension, opposition and neutrality, in a range of job relationships (see Table 8.1). Each of these possibilities, particularly the first two, suggests a wide variety of hypotheses that may be tested, e.g. work satisfaction is correlated with leisure satisfaction, types of work are correlated with leisure activities, the degree of role involvement in leisure.

Kabanoff and colleagues (Kabanoff, 1980; Kabanoff and O'Brien, 1982) have attempted an empirical and theoretical analysis of the relationship between work and non-work. They proposed a task attribute analysis in which people described their jobs in terms of five task attributes, namely autonomy, variety, skill utilisation, pressure and interaction. Leisure activities could be rated on the same dimensions. Thus it was possible to test which model – compensation, generalisation or segmentation – applied to which attribute. A variety of patterns emerged, although the general lack of correlations between attributes of people's work and leisure activities suggests that segmentalist ideas tend to be correct. Furthermore, both sex and socio-economic factors affected the relationship. Kabanoff (1980) suggests that four distinct work/leisure patterns exist:

- *passive generalisation* – low levels of both work and leisure attributes (predominantly males with low income, low education and intrinsic work motivation);

- *supplemental compensation-* – low levels of an attribute in work, but a high level in leisure (predominantly older, low income, internally controlled, low extrinsically work-motivated people);
- *active generalisation* – high level of an attribute in both work and leisure (tend to be better educated, high income, intrinsically rather than extrinsically motivated people);
- *reactive compensation* – high levels of an attribute at work and a low level in leisure (predominantly males, job centred, with intrinsic motivation).

Because they acknowledge that both work and leisure are multidimensional, it could be that both compensation and the spill-over hypothesis are operating at the same time. Hence similar effects may arise from different causes, and vice versa. Intervening variables, such as one's position in the life cycle, as well as one's personality may change the nature of the relationship between work and leisure.

Table 8.1 Types of work–leisure relationship and associated variables

Work–leisure relationship variables	Extension	Opposition	Neutrality
Content of work and leisure	Similar	Deliberately different	Usually different
Demarcation of spheres	Weak	Strong	Average
Central life interest	Work	—	Non-work
Imprint left by work on leisure	Marked	Marked	Not marked
Work variables			
Autonomy in work situation	High	—	Low
Use of abilities (how far extended)	Fully ('stretched')	Unevenly ('damaged')	Not used ('bored')
Involvement	Moral	Alienative	Calculative
Work colleagues	Include some close friends	—	Include no close friends
Encroachment of work on leisure	High	Low	Low
Typical occupations	Social workers (especially residential)	'Extreme' (e.g. mining, fishing)	Routine (e.g. clerical and manual)
Non-work variables			
Educational level	High	Low	Medium
Duration of leisure	Short	Irregular	Long
Main function of leisure	Continuation of personal development	Recuperation	Entertainment

There has been considerable research on the relationship between and the differences in the attributes associated with leisure and work (Tinsley *et al.*, 1993). Some have argued that central concepts such as *control* essentially differentiate between yet also link the two concepts (Hoff, 1986).

Other researchers have conducted specific studies which have yielded fascinating results. Thus Kaun (1991) examined the longevity of creative artists and found that writers tend to die young. He developed a theory based on the interaction of the effects of work and leisure on health. Writing provides little immediate pleasure and often much pain. The process is difficult, and the product is not immediate and is often very long in completion. The leisure/recreational pursuits of many writers – drinking, smoking and drug-taking, casual morality and risky sports – are often a way both to exorcise a stuffy middle-class background and also to reduce the 'pain of writing'. It is of course these factors which lead to early death. Hence we have work problems leading to leisure activities which are linked to early death. Moreover, this relationship between work and leisure is mediated by personality factors.

8.3 LEISURE RESEARCH

The measurement of leisure activities is usually conducted in one of three ways, based on the amount of time used in a variety of activities, the amount of money spent on them, and finally the amount of interest expressed in them. Hence there are various time or money budget studies, free-time activity surveys and diary studies, as well as questionnaires designed to examine the meaning of leisure and attitudes to leisure. However, nearly all of these approaches run into the problems first of what activities to include and exclude in a list of possible leisure pursuits that is to be both comprehensive and parsimonious, and secondly of how to categorise leisure. The following is a typical list: watching television; visiting friends or relatives; working around the yard or in the garden; reading magazines; reading books; going pleasure-driving; listening to records; going to meetings or other organisation activities; special hobbies; going out to dinner; participating in sports; playing cards, checkers, etc.; none of those listed; spending time at the drugstore, etc.; singing or playing a musical instrument; going to see a sports event; going to watch movies at a cinema; going to drive-in movies; going to dances; going to a play, concert or opera; going to lectures or adult education classes.

Others have attempted to categorise the wide range of leisure/free-time activities into specific categories as follows:

- *work related* – overtime, travel to work, moonlighting;
- *adult education* – classes, courses, research and reading;
- *housework* – cooking, cleaning, repairs;
- *organisational 'work'* – volunteer, religious, PTA;

- *child care* – general care, homework, entertaining;
- *social entertainment* – theatre, parties, sports, nightclubs, social visits;
- *shopping* – everyday vs. luxury needs, personal needs, family needs;
- *active leisure* – sport, music, travel, walking, games;
- *personal needs* – washing, dressing, sleep/naps, medicinal care;
- *passive leisure* – radio, television, records, reading.

However, there is still no comprehensive yet parsimonious classification of leisure activities, a situation which inevitably inhibits good research in this area. Once again we have the problem encountered in the literature on the personality at work, and on personality and consumption, namely difficulties in obtaining a reliable and robust measure of the dependent variable – in this case leisure.

Play and recreation which express the same idea are highly personalised. People play with devotion, energy and passion. For some theorists, play is an instinct, yet not only are there very subtle differences in the concept, but also it is not clear if, and whether, conceiving of leisure as an instinct helps one define or understand it more clearly.

Recreation and leisure are defined by their consummatory nature. Chosen activities have the power to hold and maintain an individual's attention so that time is forgotten. What is lost at work and in other frustrating experiences, namely well-being, equilibrium and a sense of proportion, can be gained through preferred leisure activities. To partake in any preferred leisure activity is to do something for its own sake, to be totally involved, and to be able to express one's capacities, potentials and values (Neulinger, 1978).

Neulinger (1978) reported a study in which he asked ordinary people (American adults) what leisure meant to them. Over 75 per cent mentioned discretionary time, and 20 per cent mentioned discretionary activity. Only 5 per cent believed that leisure was a state of mind. Many felt that leisure was good for health, variety and self-actualisation, and for self-reflection.

Free time is not necessarily leisure time, but is largely a function of the nature and type of employment that a person has. However, non-work time includes time spent travelling to work, and the numerous other duties and responsibilities that people have. Thus the number of hours spent on the job or in job-related activities may reflect the amount of free time available, but cannot then be measured as pure leisure time.

Empirical studies on leisure motivation have identified a number of related motives to take part in leisure activities (Manfredo *et al.*, 1996). Leisure and sports researchers are eager to point out the psychological benefits of leisure. Thus Driver *et al.* (1990) argued that leisure experiences had direct effects on psychological needs which impacted on both physical and mental health through to life satisfaction and personal growth. They found that leisure had eight identifiable social benefits, including the following:

1. *self-expression* – to use creative talents and undertake novel activities;
2. *companionship* – to engage in playful but supportive relationships;

3. *power* – to control social situations and be the centre of attention;
4. *compensation* – to experience something new, fresh or unusual;
5. *security* – to make long-term commitments free of bothersome change;
6. *service* – to be of assistance to others;
7. *intellectual aestheticism* – to have intellectual stimulation;
8. *solitude* – to do things alone without feeling threatened.

In their theory of the leisure experience, Tinsley and Tinsley (1986) set out 21 propositions, most with specific corollaries all of which refer to processes and individual differences. However, no systematic personality factors are stated, although they are implied.

8.4 PERSONALITY TRAITS AND LEISURE

Iso-Ahola (1976) argued that the literature can be easily categorised into two quite different approaches, namely the *trait* approach, which insists that personality exists in the individual being observed, and the *attributional* approach, which claims that personality is in the eye of the beholder. The attributional approach is seen to have various components. These include the process by which people attribute personality factors to others on the basis of their knowledge of their sport/leisure preferences, attribution errors in the perception of the amount of freedom people have to choose their leisure, and how participants explain the causes of success and failure in their own and others' leisure behaviour. Thus while the trait approach is predominantly biological in conception, the attributional approach is essentially cognitive. Whilst there remains some interest in the attributional approach, most research has concentrated on trait correlates of leisure preference and success.

In their highly comprehensive, critical and thoughtful review of the relationship between sport and personality, Eysenck *et al.* (1982) list a number of important conclusions. Based on Eysenck's three well-defined dimensions of personality – extraversion, neuroticism and psychoticism – a number of findings are apparent. Both average and superior sports enthusiasts tend to be extraverted, no doubt because of their higher pain thresholds, sensation-seeking, assertiveness and speed of reaction. On the other hand, sports enthusiasts tend to score low on neuroticism (with no attendant anxiety) but high on psychoticism, doubtless because of the aggressiveness, egocentricity and competitiveness associated with tough-mindedness. Moreover, body type (most frequently mesomorphic) is related to both personality and sports performance. Eysenck *et al.* also conclude that the effects of sport and competition on personality are not known. State as well as trait measures of mood are good correlates of sporting behaviour. They note that competence in sport has a strong genetic component, accounting for between 70 and 90 per cent of the variance, and that behaviour modification and therapy could be of considerable importance in leading to higher levels of achievement in sport. They note:

> We may conclude that there are undoubtedly fairly close relationships between personality, on the one hand, and sporting activity on the other. These relationships must always be qualified by the *level of activity* reached by the competitor, by the particular *type of sport* indulged in, and even by *particular parameters* within a given sport. ... Putting these approaches together, the whole field is ready for research of an altogether higher quality than has been characteristic of the past two or three decades. There is already enough evidence available to show that the rewards will be considerable.
>
> (Eysenck *et al.*, 1982, p.49)

Nias (1985), who examined the relationship between personality and recreational behaviour, stressed the importance of classifying interests, not all of which are usually described as sports. Various taxonomies are available, depending largely on the nature (i.e. the number, detail and type) of items selected for analysis *and* the statistical method chosen. After examining half a dozen or so studies, he concludes:

> Personality has been shown to be related to interest preferences, but at a rather low level. Perhaps because of the specific nature of interest factors, it is expecting too much for general personality dimensions to show anything other than tenuous relationships to them. A more fruitful approach might be to relate specific personality traits to the interest factor.
>
> (Nias, 1985, p.285)

Nias (1985) was clearly influenced by need theory, and was concerned with the motives people have for pursuing specific interests. He also points out a genetic component of interest preference, as well as the notion of family influence on interest development. Finally, he points out that the current state of the literature does not allow for accurate 'leisure guidance' along the lines of vocational guidance, but that research is moving in that direction.

There have been a number of studies using the Eysenck paradigm. Furnham (1981) investigated the relationship between personality (extraversion and neuroticism) and preference with regard to social and leisure activities. On two leisure factors, namely 'social interaction' (visiting friends and relatives, going to the movies, discos, dances and parties) and 'physical pursuits' (active hobbies, going for walks, playing board games), extraverts were shown to participate significantly more than introverts. Neuroticism was unrelated to either of these two leisure scales. On a free-time activity scale, introverts displayed a significantly higher interest in order (organisation, arrangement, precision, neatness and planned action), and were less inclined to express affiliative needs (group involvement, interaction and co-operation activity). Non-neurotics tended to emphasise achievement and understanding in free-time activities more than neurotics. However, Furnham (1982) found that

Eysenck's P(sychoticism) scale (which measures tough-mindedness) and L scale (which measures social desirability) were not as clearly related to activity preferences as extraversion and neuroticism.

In a study examining the relationship between leisure pursuits and personality among adults, Nias (1985) showed that the trait extraversion was associated with drinking, talking with friends, and watching adventure and crime films (social activities). Again, neuroticism was unrelated to recreational interests. This is consistent with other findings that individuals with a marked preference for leisure activities are inclined to be outgoing, self-assured, versatile, expressive, enthusiastic and energetic.

The concept of arousal-seeking can be found in many different conceptions of personality. Thus in arousal theory the concept is that paratelic dominance is closely related to classic ideas of arousal-seeking. Various studies have shown that this variable is related to sport preference and participation. Thus Kerr (1991) found that Australian surfers and sailboarding groups were more arousal-seeking than weight-training groups, that Dutch parachutists and motor-cycle racers scored higher on arousal-seeking than marathon runners, and that UK glider pilots scored higher than the general population. Kerr and Cox (1991) reported different levels of arousal – related to extraversion and neuroticism – and general sports playing ability and success.

However, it is the classic trait concepts of extraversion and neuroticism that seem to be particularly predictive of leisure pursuits. As Brandstätter (1994) found, using time-sampling diaries, during leisure (and work) extraverts preferred high-stimulation social situations. Egloff and Gruhn (1996) showed that extraversion and neuroticism were linked to preference for, and success in, endurance sports. Tri-athletes and long-distance runners were more extraverted and reported fewer physical complaints. Extraverts trained more, tended to be more successful, and tended to set themselves clearer goals than introverts. Certainly their results suggest that personality may influence attitudes to training, managing negative affect, and goal-setting, which in turn influences success in a particular sport.

Kirkcaldy, in a critical evaluation of the contribution of traits to sports, reported that:

> despite some inconsistencies, a certain degree of generalization can be tentatively proposed. For instance, extraversion–introversion emerges as a trait associated with an *interest* in sport participation . . . the implication of extraversion with sport fits in well with the description of the extravert as active and vigorous, relishing the demands of strenuous activity and exercise. They are impulsive and pursue varied interests as a means of satiating their *stimulus hunger.* They prefer being with others rather than alone, enjoying participation in parties and other social gatherings.
>
> (Kirkcaldy, 1985, p.257)

The importance of extraversion as a determinant of leisure preference has been substantiated across various age groups. In a large-scale study of the recreational interests of secondary-school children, Nias (1985) revealed that the magnitude of the correlations observed between leisure interests and personality variables was generally small for predictive purposes, but was consistent with theoretical expectations. For example, extraversion was related to interests in pop music and sport. Kirkcaldy (1985) found that, among male adolescents, the primary 16PF trait affectothymia was positively correlated with 'team-oriented' leisure activities. Tough-mindedness was related to a preference for athletics and sports of a 'competitive' nature.

In a West German study involving 162 older adults aged 58–90 years old, Angleitner (1977) reported that sport and gymnastic recreational pursuits, reading popular colour magazines, and visits to the theatre, concerts and 'coffee-shops' were significantly correlated with those 16PF primaries associated with extraversion, but not with the secondary factor, namely emotionality.

Kirkcaldy and Furnham (1991) found that extraversion appears to be more influential in differentiating recreational interest preferences than neuroticism. Extraverts were particularly drawn towards activities of a social, playful kind – consistent with their needs for social interaction – as well as to dynamic, competitive, combat-oriented sports, in contrast to introverts, who tended to avoid such activities. There was no indication that extraverts were more inclined to express an interest in traditional team sports (e.g. football, ice-hockey, basketball and handball) as opposed to single sports (Kirkcaldy, 1985). Neurotics appear to be less interested in competitive sports, although the magnitude of the relationship was not significant.

In total, about one-third of the variance in leisure interests is explained by traits. It seems that leisure does not involve pure choice, but often expresses personality needs. However, as already mentioned, the selection of leisure pursuits is further restricted by other factors such as age (veterans are unlikely to pursue certain sports), geography (individuals may live too far away from mountain ranges to take part in climbing or skiing), money (limited finances prevent involvement in golf, ballooning, etc.), gender, class, ethnicity and health (Furnham, 1981).

Vealey (1989) has updated a review by Martens (1975) of the sport and personology literature published between 1950 and 1970. Martens (1975) categorised the literature as experimental (10 per cent), correlational (89 per cent) and clinical (1 per cent), and found evidence of methodological problems (poor operationalisation of variables, poor sampling, inappropriate instrumentation and biased statistical analysis) as well as interpretative errors (improper inferences to causal relationships from correlational data, unsupported generalisation, and improper prediction of sports success from clinical personality assessment). Vealey's (1989) review update has four aims: to examine paradigmatic trends from 1974 to 1989; to examine predominant methodologies; to identify the primary objectives of sport personality research; and to identify what we know about the role of personality in sport, based on sports personality research. The methodology involved a content analysis of 11 prominent journals carrying articles on personality and sport research. He found that 68 per cent of the studies were correlational, 28 per cent were experimental and 4 per cent were clinical. The research settings ranged from survey methodology (26 per cent) to field studies (25 per cent), laboratory experiments (23 per cent), field surveys (15 per cent) and field experiments (11 per cent). A statistical analysis of the content analysis showed that the trait approach decreased markedly from 1974 to 1981, whereas the cognitive approach showed a marked increase during this time period. Moreover, the trait-state approach increased from the early 1970s, but this approach never achieved great popularity.

Vealey (1989) answered his four questions thus. First, classic trait approaches have declined in favour of trait-state fit, such that individuals with different dispositions are seen to react to situations with state responses that contribute to their behavioural responses. Secondly, methodologically the field has become more balanced, with fewer correlational and more experimental studies, yet there remain serious problems (univariate as opposed to multivariate designs and analyses, and the misuse of psychological theories and measures). Thirdly, research remains equally divided between questions about structure (description) and dynamics (prediction), with a small percentage of researchers interested in modification (intervention). Finally, most progress has been made in areas characterised by established theoretical bases in attribution research, self-confidence, anxiety and modification.

8.5 PERSONALITY AND SPORT

The research literature on sport and personality is as extensive and diverse as it is theoretically and methodologically problematic. The literature is also highly multidisciplinary, being simultaneously the province of physiologists, psychologists, sport scientists and sociologists, all of whom have different models, agendas and preferences. Attempts have been made to link physiology, morphology, fitness levels, genetics and personality traits to interest and excellence in sport (Davis and Mogle, 1994). These researchers believe that a major problem for researchers is attempting to differentiate the attitudes of non-athletes as well as those who may be described as 'elite' or 'high performers' from the others.

Davies (1989) argues, quite rightly, that myths and over-simplistic viewpoints exist in the area of psychological sport. Many factors, such as technical ability and skill, speed of movement, physical fitness, persistence, anticipation, concentration and temperament, combine to determine excellence in sport. He lists (somewhat arbitrarily) and discusses eight 'psychological' factors that are thought to influence sporting behaviour, namely personality and adjustment, past experience of tournament play, availability of psychological support and counselling, social pressures, consistency, confidence and concentration, mental preparation, and motivation. Davies (1989) believes that all self-report measures of personality encounter problems because of dissimulation, also because people are not always able to report accurately on their nec However, he is convinced of the importance of neuroticism in predicting and explaining sports performance:

> It does seem to be the case that on balance sportsmen who compete at international level are extroverted and emotionally stable. They tend to be dominant, tough-minded, self-assured, self-confident, and with a high capacity to endure the pressures of others' competitive sport. They are temperamentally robust. . . . Research also shows that extraverts are less adversely affected by distracting stimuli such as, for example, the noise and movement of the crowd, and tend to enjoy performing in the company of others rather than in seclusion. On the other hand, however, extraverts are likely to be at a disadvantage in sports in which the emphasis is on accuracy. . . . For such sports as rifle-shooting and archery, which call for calm, slow and deliberate preparation, the quick impulsive nature of the extravert is therefore likely to be a handicap.

(Davies, 1989, p.145–6)

For 30 years there has been a constant stream of papers on personality and achievement in sport. Researchers have chosen, almost randomly it seems, a great variety of personality tests, some with solid foundations and good psychometric properties, and others with little or no evidence of validity or reliability. This makes comparison between studies very difficult. However, one personality scale – namely *sensation-seeking* – has attracted a fair amount of attention. Zuckerman's (1979) sensation-seeking scale has been used successfully a number of times to predict leisure preferences and participation. The high sensation-seeker displays a need for varied, novel sensations, and appears willing to take physical and social risks to gain those experiences, and it is fairly easy to test specific hypotheses.

Thus Babbitt *et al.* (1990) found participation in aerobic exercise classes (measure of attendance and motivation) was related to low rather than high levels of sensation-seeking. On the other hand, Campbell *et al.* (1993) examined sensation-seeking among white-water canoe and kayak paddlers and found that their scores (particularly the thrill- and adventure-seeking subscale) were higher than comparative norms. Wagner and Houlihan (1994) found, as predicted, that high-glider pilots had much higher sensation-seeking scores than others. Schroth (1995) found that athletes scored higher than non-athletes, contact sport athletes scored higher than non-contact-sport athletes, and male athletes scored higher than female athletes. Gilchrist *et al.* (1995) found, as predicted, that people who chose adventure holidays had higher sensation-seeking scores than those who did not, particularly on the thrill- and adventure-seeking subscale.

Sensation-seeking has also been shown to relate to television preferences. Rowland *et al.* (1989) found sensation-seeking was related to uses of, preferences for, and attitudes to television viewing. Thus high sensation-seekers combined television viewing with other activities, while low sensation-seekers preferred fewer distractions, although sensation-seekers seemed to have more regular television-viewing habits. Potts *et al.* (1996) did find that sensation-seeking related to programme-viewing preferences. Compared to low scorers, high scorers watched more music videos, daytime talk shows, stand-up comedy programmes, documentaries and animated cartoons, but fewer news programmes and drama series. Forabosco and Ruch (1994) found that ratings of different types of humour were clearly related to sensation-seeking.

Studies have shown that other factors as well as sensation-seeking are important predictors in sports interest and participation (Franken *et al.*, 1994). Clearly the most specific type of leisure activity specified the obvious relevance of sensation-seeking to it. As well as sensation-seeking, there have been a host of other studies which have shown a theoretically predictable link between personality and sports preference and achievement.

Davis and Mogle (1994) compared four groups (each containing 30 subjects) of elite athletes, sub-elite athletes, recreational sport enthusiasts and a non-athlete control group on various arousal measures. They found that personality factors such as extraversion, psychoticism and thrill-and-adventure seeking are more related to *interest* (and recreational participation) in sport than to *success* in sport. They note that the sociability factor in extraversion may be negatively related to sporting success because of the long hours of repetitive, solitary training that are required for success in most sports. It seems that personality traits *per se* do not powerfully discriminate between different levels of athletic skill. However, they may be closely related with regard to sports spectators and recreational athletes.

Sports scientists in the 1960s were particularly interested in the relationships between sport and personality. Hundreds of 'one-off' studies have been published on the personality traits of different types of athletes and sports players – between 'superior' or exemplar and 'regular' players, and between coaches and fans of various sports. Some focus on aggression, attempting to argue how sport controls and 'catharsises' aggression and violence (Kenyon, 1968). Others have attempted to show how personality changes as a function of exercise, social contact or competition. Still other enthusiasts have demonstrated not only how trait and state anxiety affects sports performance, but also how training and success in sport reduce anxiety.

Whilst some researchers concentrated on trait differences, others were more interested in cognitive style, self-perception or – as some quaintly put it – 'winner attitude'. Perhaps inevitably, studies on sport motivation seem to be more speculative and naive, and less experimental. Other topics which have attracted research are the psychological problems of superior/gifted athletes, sport and emotional health, socio-interaction between athlete and spectator, personality and motor learning, and the social psychology of sport and play.

Research conducted 30 years ago traditionally used established trait measures (e.g. the 16 Personality Factor Questionnaire; 16PF) and compared gifted
and non-gifted men and women. Some of these studies were relatively
psychometrically sophisticated, using regression and discriminant analysis
(Kane, 1968), and they showed how personality factors appear to be able to
account for about 20 per cent of the explained variance.

Naturally, one implication of the personality and leisure/sport performance
literature is the idea that *training methods* are devised to suit the needs of
particular personalities. Furthermore, individuals may be helpfully channelled
into activities for which they are best suited because of their personality. Thus
unstable introverts may be advised to try cross-country running – if, of course,
they are physiologically suited to it. Because of their adverse reactions to
failure, unstable individuals may be advised not to take part in certain
competitive sports where feedback of results is constant and public.

How sports people are *rewarded* is also potentially important. If extraverts
are more motivated by promise of reward, and introverts by threat of
punishment, this has important implications for coaching sportsmen and
women.

Definitions and categorisations are important (Dowd and Innes, 1981;
Eysenck *et al.*, 1982; Kirkcaldy, 1985) because both personality and sport are
multifaceted, and it is quite possible that some dimensions of the former are
related to some (but by no means all) dimensions of the latter. Eysenck *et al.*
(1982) make two basic distinctions regarding sport, namely individualistic vs.
team sport and outstanding vs. average performance. Various other dimensions are possible, e.g. ball vs. non-ball sport, amount of physical contact,
extent to which endurance is important, and the nature of the skill involved
(e.g. perceptual motor vs. cognitive). However, just as there is considerable
disagreement about how to classify or taxonomise personality and individual
differences, so there appears to be considerable disagreement about how to
group sports. If the beginning of any 'science' is clear, careful and salient
taxonomisation, it may explain some of the theoretical problems in this
area.

One problem for the personality theorist is that individuals do not appear
to possess a general ability to learn sports skills, and thus generalisation
between personality and sport becomes very problematic. Although it is
probably true that, on average, gifted and successful sportspeople tend to be
emotionally stable, tough-minded, self-controlled, disciplined, self-assured
and relaxed, there are always exceptions. Thus extraverts may do better in
some sports (e.g. rugby) than in others (e.g. archery).

Eysenck *et al.* (1982) concluded from their overview that sportspeople tend
to be *extraverted*. This seems to be as true of outstanding performers as of
average performers, physical education students, and others who perform at a
much lower level than Olympic champions in various sports. There are many
different possible explanations for this, including high pain thresholds,
sensation-seeking, assertiveness and competitiveness, and generally a lack of

cortical control and inhibition of ongoing behaviour and immediate reactions.

There is a tendency for athletes, particularly outstanding ones, to score low on neuroticism, and to suffer less from anxiety than do non-sportsmen and women. The reason for the negative relationship between excellence in sport and anxiety–neuroticism probably lies in the *drive stimulus qualities* of anxiety, which distract the athlete from his or her appointed task. The outstanding athlete clearly needs to be relaxed, unemotional and not prone to phobias, depression or anxiety attacks.

Very successful athletes seem to have *higher scores on P(sychoticism)* than do less successful sportsmen or women or non-sporting individuals. The reason for the relationship between P and success in sport is probably related to the aggressiveness of the high P scorer, their egocentricity and their general competitiveness. It is possible that these qualities may be less apparent in team sports, but there are few data to support the hypothesis as yet.

The effects of sporting activities on personality remain unclear, but it is suggested that sporting activities may have a beneficial effect on personality, particularly in reducing depression and anxiety. The effects of competition on personality are also not known, and there are many theories, which are equally unsupported by good evidence.

Driving a car may be regarded as a sporting activity, and is quite definitely related to personality in the sense that both *extraversion* and *neuroticism* (and sensation-seeking) are positively related to accident proneness. The combination of high N and high E is uniquely favourable for the occurrence of driving accidents.

Sexual activity, too, may be regarded as a sport, such activity being carried out in many cases for amusement, and being physical in nature. *Extraversion* has been found to be the personality component most commonly correlated with different types of sexual activity, such as early sexual activity involving many different partners, and activity indulged in frequently. *Neuroticism* appears to have a negative influence on sexual activity, being associated with frigidity, impotence, lack of orgasmic capacity, and other disorders.

State measurements of mood correlate strongly with athletic performance and sporting activity, more so than do traits. Anxiety in particular has been found to be so related when state (mood) rather than trait measures are taken. The same is true of feelings of energy and competitiveness.

Most personality and sport studies have used groups which are too heterogeneous to yield clear-cut results. It has been found that even in apparently homogeneous groups, such as pistol or rifle shooters, different types of shooting are correlated with quite different personality traits, by depending on such factors as time allowed for reaction to the stimulus, etc. Where little time is allowed, *extraverts* excel, but where much time is allowed, *introverts* do quite well. Thus different personality traits may be associated with soccer, depending on whether one is a defensive or attacking player.

Physical skills learning, and the cognitive strategies which are being developed, are also related to personality. An integration of this experimental approach with the study of sport-type situations could be of considerable importance in throwing new light on the relationship between sport and personality. We still know little about the cognitive strategies used by sportsmen and women.

Genetic factors are known to determine both personality and physique. It has also been shown that competence in many different sporting activities has a strong genetic component. This finding does not suggest that training cannot help individuals to improve their performance, but it does suggest that selection for sport in general, and for specific types of sport in particular, should take account of both personality *and* physique, as well as personal motivation.

Eysenck *et al.* (1982) believe that behaviour modification, i.e. the application of psychological principles to learning and improvement in sport, could be of considerable importance in leading to higher levels of achievement in sport. The technique of behaviour therapy (including desensitisation, flooding and modelling) could be of considerable use in reducing anxiety, in so far as this interferes with optimum performance. However, the relative isolation of psychology from sport may be changing, with a growing interest in sports psychology.

8.6 THE EFFECTS OF SPORT AND LEISURE ON PERSONALITY

Whereas personality has nearly always been treated as the independent variable in sport psychology by examining personality differences in preference for or effectiveness in specific sports, some research has considered personality as the dependent variable. Depending on the personality theory or model adhered to, it is possible that various physical and social consequences that occur in sport and leisure could change certain aspects of personality functioning.

Dienstbier (1984) has proposed four possible mechanisms for personality change as a function of sport exercise:

> *Physiological changes* – sports exercise can affect many physiological systems, including hormonal, which (it) is known has influential effects on mood and emotions. If we define temperament as a long-term tendency toward certain moods or emotional dispositions, it is apparent that we should expect to see some effect upon such a measure after extreme training. Thus there seems a strong probability that changes in depression, anxiety and positive moods and emotions should follow directly (with no additional mediators) from physiological changes induced through running.

> (Dienstbier, 1984, p.250)

Self-perception of changes – there appear to be potential self-concept and self-esteem consequences of sport that reduce body fat, redistribute weight, increase energy levels and lead to a more youthful appearance (*cf.* Tucker's article). The amazing distances a healthy individual may be able to run after only a few months of training therefore can lead to an increased sense of one's ability to master challenges and to attain goals that seemed remote only months earlier. One's entire belief system about the degree to which one's life is self-determined or internal (versus other or fate-determined, or external) may be influenced by such significant successes.

(Dienstbier, 1984, p.257)

Socializing and life-style changes – dedication to a particular sport or leisure activity brings with it life-style changes in such things as eating, drinking, smoking, sleeping and resting; in short, life-style. Life-style changes mean different interaction patterns with different individuals who may have a substantial effect on personality functioning.

(Dienstbier, 1984, p.257)

Expectations – expectations and values may change as a function of being exposed to peers and coaches who share a quite different pattern of expectation about health, diet, and exercise. Gradually these new values and expectations are associated so as to change personality functioning.

(Dienstbier, 1984, p.258–9)

Although all of the above effects are possible, they are far from easy to demonstrate, and the research evidence is patchy and problematic. Dienstbier (1984) has listed six control features which one would need to set in place in order to demonstrate some causal relationship between exercise sport (leisure pattern) and personality. Studies need to be longitudinal in order to tease out cause and effect, non-sport control groups must be involved in the before–after design, the control group should be engaged in some systematic activity capable of giving some of the same psychological benefits as the sport, the control group needs to be involved in a socially engaging activity, changes in lifestyle need to be covaried out in analysis to ensure that this is not the cause of change, and the control group needs to be given similar expectations of personality change. It is only when these various criteria are met that it is in any way possible actually to demonstrate personality change as a function of sport leisure.

This means that the extant literature is difficult to evaluate (Dienstbier, 1984). For instance, Folkins and Sime (1981) concluded that there are no global changes in personality test scores after fitness training. However, others have reported more favourable results. For example, Jasnoski and Holmes (1981) used the 16PF to demonstrate that subjects became more imaginative, less shy and more apprehensive after a 15-week aerobic training programme.

A major problem with this research field, like so many in the area of sport and personality, is theoretical naivety. Few researchers appear to have considered personality theory, or indeed theories, and evaluated them (and the instruments designed to measure personality) in terms of validity, veridicality and reliability. Once this has been done, a judicious rather than random choice of test and theory may be made, and more robust findings shown. Secondly, it seems fairly naive to expect changes to occur so soon after 'short, sharp, shock' exposure to sport and exercise. Whether the changes are physiological or cognitive, they are likely to take place over fairly lengthy periods of time, and then only minimally. Whether sporting activity changes the sympathetic nervous system functioning or expectations and values, these alterations occur slowly and gradually, and would presumably decay or revert to previous levels of functioning once the activity ceased.

8.7 PERSONALITY AND TRAVEL

Why are some people inveterate travellers and tourists (regularly and by choice going abroad to exotic, 'far-away' countries), while others are not only content to stay at home, but feel most unhappy breaking their daily routine?

Various attempts have been made to taxonomise tourist behaviours. Thus Pearce (1982) listed 15 possible 'traveller categories' which clustered into five groups, namely exploitative travel, pleasure-first travel, high-contact travel, environmental travel and spiritual travel. He did not do so, but it is not difficult to see how one might speculate that specific personality traits are associated with each of these roles – with extraverts preferring high-contact travel, individuals who score highest on openness to experience preferring spiritual travel, etc.

Various market research initiatives have attempted to examine vacation preferences and personality. Thus the Canadian Government Travel Bureau posited particular relationships (see Table 8.2). The results were hardly surprising, and tended to be descriptive rather than analytical. However, as Mayo and Jarvis (1981) point out, these types of findings certainly have implications for how travel agents may market their products. Thus they distinguish between psychocentric (inhibited, unadventurous, concerned with self) and allocentric (outgoing, curious, self-confident) individuals – clearly an introversion–extraversion distinction. Thus, from a North American perspective, the allocentric choose Africa and the Pacific Rim and the psychocentric choose safe and well-publicised resorts at home. However, they argue that travel itself encourages people to become less psychocentric and that, over time, destinations become more or less popular to each type as they are more or less visited. They also note how psychographic (or lifestyle) research can help us to understand travel behaviour (Gunter and Furnham, 1992).

Table 8.2 Personality traits and Canadian vacation travel

Personality/vacation type	Personality characteristics
Vacation travellers	Reflective, active, sociable, outgoing, inquisitive, confident
Vacation non-travellers	Reflective, passive, restrained, serious
Non-vacationers	Anxious
Auto vacationers	Reflective, active, sociable, outgoing, inquisitive, confident
Air vacationers	Very active, very confident, reflective
Train vacationers	Reflective, passive, aloof, non-social, apprehensive, dependent, emotionally unstable
Bus vacationers	Dependent, apprehensive, sensitive, hostile, belligerent, unrestrained
Domestic vacationers	Outgoing, active, carefree
Foreign vacationers	Confident, trusting, reflective, impulsive, brave
Male vacationers	Reflective, brave
Female vacationers	Impulsive, carefree, brave
Visit friends/relatives	Passive
Visit 'vacation spots'	Active, sociable, reflective
Sightseers	Reflective, sensitive, emotionally unstable, unrestrained, passive
Outdoor activities	Brave, active, asocial, apprehensive, moody
Winter vacationers	Active
Spring vacationers	Reflective
Autumn vacationers	Emotionally stable, passive

Source: Canadian Government Travel Bureau (1971) *1969 Vacation Trends and Recreation Patterns*. (Ottawa, Canada: Canadian Government Travel Bureau).

Mayo and Jarvis (1981) have found evidence of five different types of leisure traveller:

- the *peace-and-quiet traveller* (introverted, reflective, family oriented);
- the *overseas traveller* (self-confident, sociable, movers-and-shakers);
- the *historian traveller* (puritan, intellectual, family committed);
- the *recreational vehicle traveller* (home and work centred);
- the *travel now/pay later traveller* (optimistic, impulsive).

The relationship between personality and preferred travel destination, method of getting there, preferred activity on holiday and experiences remains a seriously neglected research area.

8.8 FREUDIAN PERSPECTIVES

It is not difficult to speculate about how Freudians might perceive leisure. Choice of leisure should fulfil particular conscious and unconscious needs. Clearly, some leisure activities have more 'potential' than others to fulfil complicated psychological needs. Thus amateur dramatics is richer than gardening, and painting is richer than squash. What would make psychoanalytic insight different to common-sense or pseudo-Freudian insight is the paradoxical theme underlying many psychoanalytic ideas, e.g. the gambler who plays to lose, the altruist who gives to inflict pain, or the comic who is depressed.

In addition to unconscious need fulfilment, leisure may fulfil various Freudian personality types. Thus oral characters may find many recreations ideal for their needs, e.g. debating, wine-tasting, cooking, etc. The anal character may enjoy hobbies that fulfil his or her needs for parsimony, order and frugality, especially collecting, etc.

Kline (1984) often illustrates Freudian ideas with reference to sport. In considering the defence mechanism of repression, whereby threatening material is forced back into the unconscious, he notes:

> The repressed impulse seeks expression and such expression, often sublimations or in permissible moderate forms, may be of the following kind: an excessive interest in body contact, sports, wrestling, boxing, football. Notice how in football matches after a goal is scored players actually embrace. In a rugby scrum men put their heads between the legs of other men. Indeed, in rugby players other defence mechanisms can be seen. For example, denial and reaction-formation, which we will illustrate later. Indeed, the whole aura of rugby is homosexual: the emphasis on toughness and virility; the importance attached to the changing rooms, usually with communal baths; the exaggerated concern with heavy drinking which destroys inhibition and allows outward expression of affection – drinking men often put their arm around their companion; and the banishment of women (of whom homosexuals are afraid, in Freudian theory) from the

whole fraternity of rugby players. Again it is no coincidence that rugby is the favoured game of the British public schools which, with their regime of single-sex boarding education, would be expected to foster homosexuality.

(Kline, 1984, p.22)

Again with *denial* (the unconscious denial of an unconscious impulse), he notes:

To take our rugby playing example, rugby players deny their homosexuality. Rugby songs are heavily sexual but there are almost never homosexual references. Indeed, the emphasis put on heterosexuality, the sexually attractive player who can lay any girl he desires, is a form of denial.

(Kline, 1984, p.23)

Even with *reaction-formation* (feeling and acting in ways quite opposite to the denial impulse), he writes:

The emphasis on heterosexual virility is really a reaction-formation. His avowed jeering contempt of homosexuals, pansies, queers, poofters, queens, is a reaction-formation. The spinster who devotes her life to her mother at the expense of her own has never come to terms with her Oedipal guilt. Hate becomes love.

(Kline, 1984, p.23)

However, Freudians do not appear to have written about leisure directly, except of course through the case histories of specific individuals.

8.9 SELF-THEORISTS

Self-concept, self-image and self-worth are concepts which it is not difficult to relate to leisure. Mayo and Jarvis (1981) note that travel – both business and pleasure – is a visible and highly symbolic activity. 'As a symbol, travel can communicate a great ideal about an individual: success, achievement, sophistication, worldliness. The opportunity to travel, therefore, can be extremely important in reinforcing certain types of image' (Mayo and Jarvis, 1981, p.122). It has been suggested that people 'place-drop' just as they 'name-drop' – that is, they use travel and other leisure activities for impression management.

Self-theorists have pointed out that work loses its capacity to serve as a basis for self-esteem and identity formation, even while a person is still at work. If work leads to a loss of self, then leisure may compensate for this (see Section 8.2). In this sense you are not what you do (occupation), but how (when and why) you play.

Furthermore, leisure is often used to reduce the gap between the real self and the ideal self. People often attempt to express who they are and what they aspire to be through leisure-time activities. Neulinger (1978) noted two self-actualisers with regard to leisure, namely a preference for the acquisition of knowledge and/or skills (*intellectual self-actualiser*), or a preference for making or being with friends and/or coming closer to the community (*social self-actualiser*). The following are hypothetical descriptions of such types.

The intellectual self-actualiser   This person enjoys tackling difficult tasks and achieving high standards in their leisure activities; their primary concern is not with relaxation or play. Both their work-day and Sunday are in part devoted to adult education or occupational training. Their preferred free-time activities are music and reading, and engaging in voluntary work. With regard to arts and crafts, they prefer writing to cabinet-making, and their musical taste runs to opera rather than musicals. They prefer to attend a lecture or opera rather than a musical, the circus or a movie. When watching television, they are likely to view political discussion and news rather than comedy shows or sports events.

The social self-actualiser   This person enjoys being with people and co-operating in common activities with them during their leisure. They place little emphasis on tackling difficult tasks or gaining recognition for their accomplishments; they do not engage in activities for the enjoyment of aesthetic feelings and sensuous impressions. Both their work-day and Sunday are devoted to social entertainment and other social life. They feel that society should encourage activities which emphasise social interactions. Engaging in sport is not one of their preferred free-time activities, nor are arts and crafts. Given the option of stretching out and doing nothing under various conditions, they are least likely to choose to do so in a gently drifting boat. Their preferred type of music is musicals, and this is also the kind of event they would be most likely to attend.

There is a surprising dearth of serious research from the self-theorists on leisure, sport and travel, no doubt for some of the reasons discussed above.

8.10 CONCLUSION

Because leisure, travel and sport offer many free choices (within certain economic, geographical and other constraints), it is unsurprising that there is a strong relationship between personality and sport and leisure. There is ample evidence for the existence of logical and consistent trait correlates of leisure preference and sporting success. Indeed, there is evidence that traits discriminate quite well within specific leisure categories. Thus Marchant-Haycox and Wilson (1992) found quite distinct personality profiles for four groups of performing artists (musicians, singers, actors and dancers) while Buttsworth and Smith (1995) found personality differences between brass-, string- and keyboard-playing musicians. Personality has even been shown to be linked to how and when people use television remote-control devices.

The problem for research in this area has been how to decide what to measure. Is personality related to leisure preference or sporting success, or both? Some variables are easier to measure reliably than others. Secondly, research on sport has not always focused sufficiently on behavioural differences within different sports. Thus in cricket there may be personality differences between bowlers, batsmen, all-rounders and wicket-keepers. It is only after one has conducted a careful behavioural and motivational analysis of a sport or the particular features of a sportsperson's position or role that one can develop sufficiently sophisticated hypotheses to test for personality differences. Nevertheless there is impressive evidence that personality traits, particularly extraversion, are related to choice of leisure activity. Other personality factors are also important – neuroticism is often a strong correlate of competitive leisure activity failure, while conscientiousness (as manifested by the work ethic) is related to choice of leisure activity.

There is no doubt that other factors in addition to personality mediate the choice of leisure activity. There is also evidence of a reciprocity effect, whereby the leisure activity may change personality. Hopefully the rise of sport psychology as a serious research area means that qualitatively and quantitatively better research will be undertaken in this important but neglected area of personality research.

REFERENCES

Angleitner, A. (1977) Persönlichkeit und Freizeitverhalten. Ergebnisse und Folgerungen. In Schmitz-Scherzer, R. (ed.), *Aktuerlle Beiträge zur Freiztforschung. Praxis der Sozialpsychologie. Vol. 7.* Darmstadt, 1977.

Argyle, M. (1966) *The social psychology of leisure.* Harmondsworth: Penguin.

Babbitt, T., Rowland, G. and Franken, R. (1990) Sensation-seeking and participation in aerobic exercise classes. *Personality and Individual Differences* 11, 181–3.

Brandstätter, H. (1994) Pleasure of leisure – pleasure at work: personality makes the differences. *Personality and Individual Differences* 16, 931–46.

Buchholz, R. (1976) Measurement of beliefs. *Human Relations* 29, 1177–88.

Buttsworth, L. and Smith, G. (1995) Personality of Australian performing musicians by gender and by instrument. *Personality and Individual Differences* 18, 595–603.

Calhoun, D. (1994) *Sport, culture and personality.* Champaign-Urbana, IL: Human Kinetics.

Campbell, J., Tyrell, D. and Zingaro, M. (1993) Sensation-seeking among white water canoe and kayak paddlers. *Personality and Individual Differences* 14, 489–91.

Davies, D. (1989) *Psychological factors in competitive sport.* London: Falmer Press.

Davis, C. and Mogle, J. (1994) Some personality correlates of interest and excellence in sport. *International Journal of Sport Psychology* 25, 1–13.

Dienstbier, R. (1984) The effect of exercise on personality. In Sachs, M.I. and Buffone, G.W. (eds), *Running as therapy.* London: University of Nebraska Press.

Dowd, R. and Innes, J. (1981) Sport and personality: effects of type of sport and level of competition. *Perceptual and Motor Skills* 53, 79–89.

Driver, B., Tinsley, H. and Manfredo, M. (1990) The paragraphs about leisure and recreation experience preference scales. In Driver, B., Brown, P. and Peterson, G. (eds), *Benefits of leisure*. Pennsylvania: Ventura Publishing, 263–6.

Egloff, B. and Gruhn, J. (1996) Personality and endurance sports. *Personality and Individual Differences* **21**, 223–9.

Eysenck, H., Nias, D. and Cox, D. (1982) Sport and personality. *Advances in Behaviour Therapy* **4**, 1–56.

Folkins, C. and Sime, W. (1981) Physical fitness training and mental health. *American Psychologist* **36**, 373–89.

Forabosco, G. and Ruch, W. (1994) Sensation-seeking, social attitudes and humour appreciation in Italy. *Personality and Individual Differences* **16**, 515–28.

Franken, R., Hull, R. and Kierstead, J. (1994) Sport interest as predicted by the personality measures of competitiveness, mastery, instrumentality, expressivity and sensation-seeking. *Personality and Individual Differences* **17**, 467–76.

Furnham, A. (1981) Personality and activity preference. *British Journal of Psychology* **20**, 57–68.

Furnham, A. (1982) Psychoticism, social desirability and structure selection. *Personality and Individual Differences* **3**, 43–51.

Furnham, A. (1990a) *The Protestant work ethic*. London: Routledge.

Furnham, A. (1990b) Personality and demographic determinants of leisure and sports preference and performance. *International Journal of Sport Psychology*, **21**, 218–36.

Furnham, A. (1994) *Personality at work*. London: Routledge.

Gilchrist, H., Povey, R., Dickinson, A. and Povey, R. (1995) The sensation-seeking scale: its use in a study of the characteristics of people choosing 'adventure holidays'. *Personality and Individual Differences* **19**, 513–16.

Gunter, B. and Furnham, A. (1992) *Consumer profiles*. London: Routledge.

Hoff, E.-H. (1986) Subjective theories of work, leisure and controls. In Debus, G. and Scroff, H.W. (eds), *The psychology of work and organization*. Amsterdam: North Holland, 311–19.

Iso-Ahola, S. (1976) On the theoretical link between personality and leisure. *Psychological Reports* **39**, 3–10.

Jasnoski, M. and Holmes, F. (1981) Influence of initial aerobic fitness, aerobic training and changes in aerobic fitness of personality functioning. *Journal of Psychosomatic Research* **25**, 553–6.

Kabanoff, B. (1980) Work and non-work: a review of models, methods and findings. *Psychological Bulletin* **88**, 60–77.

Kabanoff, B. and O'Brien, G. (1982) Relationships between work and leisure attributes across occupational and age groups in Australia. *Australian Journal of Psychology* **34**, 165–82.

Kane, J. (1968) Personality and physical ability. In Kenyon, G. (ed.), *Contemporary psychology of sport*. Chicago: Athletic Institute, 131–41.

Kaun, D. (1991) Writers die young: the impact of work and leisure on longevity. *Journal of Economic Psychology* **12**, 381–91.

Kenyon, G. (ed.) (1966) *Contemporary psychology of sport*. Chicago: Athletic Institute.

Kerr, J. (1991) Arousal-seeking in risk sport participants. *Personality and Individual Differences* **12**, 613–16.

Kerr, J. and Cox, T. (1991) Arousal and individual differences in sport. *Personality and Individual Differences* **12**, 1075–85.

Kirkcaldy, B.D. (1985) The value of traits in sport. In Kirkcaldy, B.D. (ed.), *Individual differences in movement*. Boston, MA: MTP Press.

Kirkcaldy, B.D. and Furnham, A. (1991) Personality and sex differences in recreational choices. *Sportwissenschaft* **20**, 43–56.

Kline, P. (1984) *Psychology and Freudian theory: an introduction*. London: Methuen.

Manfredo, M., Driver, B. and Tarrant, M. (1996) Measuring leisure motivation: a meta-analysis of the recreation experience preference scale. *Journal of Leisure Research* **28**, 188–213.

Marchant-Haycox, S. and Wilson, G. (1992) Personality and stress in performing artists. *Personality and Individual Differences* **13**, 1061–8.

Martens, R. (1975) The paradigmatic crisis in American sport personology. *Sportwissenschaft* **1**, 9–24.

Mayo, E. and Jarvis, L. (1981) *The psychology of leisure travel*. Boston, MA: CBI.

Mudrack, P. (1992) 'Work' or 'leisure': the protestant work ethic and participation in an employee fitness program. *Journal of Organizational Behaviour* **13**, 81–8.

Neulinger, J. (1978) *The psychology of leisure*. Springfield, IL: C.C. Thomas.

Nias, D. (1985) Personality and recreational behaviour. In Kirkcaldy, B. (ed.), *Individual differences in movement*. Lancaster: MTP Press.

Parker, S. (1972) *The future of work and leisure*. London: Granada.

Parker, S. (1983) *Leisure and work*. London: George Allen.

Potts, R., Dedmon, A. and Halford, J. (1996) Sensation-seeking, television-viewing motives, and home television-viewing patterns. *Personality and Individual Differences* **21**, 1081–4.

Rowland, G., Fouts, G. and Heatherton, T. (1989) Television-viewing and sensation-seeking: uses, preferences and attitudes. *Personality and Individual Differences* **10**, 1003–6.

Schroth, M. (1995) A comparison of sensation-seeking among different groups of athletes and non-athletes. *Personality and Individual Differences* **18**, 219–23.

Shivers, J. (1981) *Leisure and recreation concepts: a critical analysis*. Boston: Allyn & Bacon.

Stockdale, J. (1986) *What is leisure?* London: Sports Council & ESRC.

Tinsley, H. and Tinsley, D. (1986) A theory of the attributes, benefits and causes of leisure experience. *Leisure Sciences* **8**, 1–45.

Tinsley, H., Hinson, J., Tinsley, D. and Holt, M. (1993) Attributes of leisure and work experiences. *Journal of Consulting Psychology* **40**, 447–57.

Vealey, R. (1989) Sport psychology: a paradigmatic and methodological analysis. *Journal of Sport and Exercise Psychology* **11**, 216–35.

Wagner, A. and Houlihan, D. (1994) Sensation-seeking and trait anxiety in hang-glider pilots and golfers. *Personality and Individual Differences* **16**, 975–9.

Wilensky, H. (1960) Work careers and social integration. *International Social Science Journal* **12**, 543–60.

Zuckerman, A. (1979) *Sensation-seeking: beyond the optimal level of arousal*. New York: Wiley.

9

Personality and Consumption

9.1 INTRODUCTION

Do people with different personalities have different patterns of consumption? Is there a clear empirical and theoretically based relationship between personality, saving and shopping, personal possessions and the preference for, as well as purchasing of, art, music and poetry products? Are some traits particularly associated with conspicuous consumption? Is the purchasing of particular brands related to personality? Indeed, is shopping pathology, manifested in such behaviours as shop-lifting and compulsive buying, a function of personality?

Of all the areas examined in previous chapters, research in this area appears to be the most piecemeal and least sophisticated. It is not surprising that personality as a central analytical construct has been largely abandoned in marketing (Albanese, 1990), yet is regarded as fundamentally important by economic psychologists (Maital, 1982). The reason for this paradoxical state of affairs lies in both theory development and research practice. Many market specialists are desperately out of date with regard to personality theory or choosing good personality measures for their research. They also find it difficult to obtain reliable measures of consumer behaviour – that is, reliable evidence of a person's multiple purchasing of a product or one brand in preference to another over time. Given the poor measurement of both variables and the somewhat unsophisticated nature of the theorising and hypothesis-testing in this area, it is not surprising that the results are so equivocal and weak.

Engel *et al.* (1995) argue that earlier failures when using personality theory to predict consumer behaviour have stimulated three related areas of research:

- a focus on brand personality – the consistent response evoked by consumers when presented with a brand. Personality terminology is used to *describe* brand attributes and to explain their appeal to certain groups;
- an increasing interest in information-processing variables (e.g. learning styles, need for cognition) rather than traits which supposedly better predict consumer decision-making (Sproles and Sproles, 1990).
- an interest in personal values and beliefs that, in part, express the goals of individuals. Thus ecology/green values vs. conservative values may be more predictive of particular product avoidance than are personality traits.

Hawkins *et al.* (1996) have stressed the importance of affect, i.e. emotional states and consumption. Certainly with regard to advertising they believe that emotional content affects attention, memory and evaluation. Thus sensitivity to affective stimuli (determined in part by neuroticism) should be a predictor of various forms of consumer behaviour.

Although shopping is a normal and routine experience, there are some individuals who are compulsive shoppers. The condition has been recognised for 100 years – indeed Kraepelin wrote about 'buying maniacs'. Pathological shopping is characterised by chronic, repetitive purchasing, in response to some negative emotion, which is difficult to stop and which has harmful consequences. Some researchers consider that it is similar to alcohol and drug addiction. Compulsive buyers tend to be anxious, depressive and obsessional with low self-esteem. Clothing and shoes are common purchases. Interestingly, the items are frequently given away, returned or stored, and often remain unwrapped (Black, 1996). Researchers in the area of compulsive shopping point out that little is known about the aetiology or onset of the disorder, the situations that prompt buying, or the natural history of the disorder. However, they do acknowledge that there is considerable psychiatric morbidity, suggesting that compulsive shopping may be a sign of other serious psychiatric disorders (Black, 1996).

Personality variables *per se*, therefore, have not attracted as much interest recently as other individual factors such as *mood* (Moore *et al.*, 1995), *values* (Richin and Dawson, 1992), *attitudes* (Holbrook and Schindler, 1994) and *lifestyle* (Gutman and Mills, 1982; Gunter and Furnham, 1992). Mood or affect intensity and sensitivity are clearly important, both in responding to advertisements and in decision-making about purchases. When in a naturally good mood, or on having their mood changed by in-store characteristics (e.g. music, lighting, smells), it does seem that people are more likely to buy. Values, too, are important, particularly those related to materialism and possessions, which do predict what kind of purchases individuals make. Inevitably, attitudes to objects must be related to consumption, albeit in conjunction with many other factors, including personality.

Many marketing specialists segment their markets using personality terminology, i.e. they talk about brands and buying types in terms of *traits*, or they explain the process whereby individual differences are systematically related to purchasing decisions. Competition and secrecy mean that few publish or disclose the data upon which they base their consumption types. However, one suspects that this is done more by intuition and the 'case-study method' than by a careful theoretically or methodologically based method. In fact, many companies have tried to describe product-using types more in terms of lifestyle analysis than according to personality traits.

It is very common for lay people to infer personality traits from the possessions that people acquire, or indeed even flaunt. You are what you eat, drive or wear. Freudian ideas of symbolism (e.g. the phallic red motor car) are well known to lay people, who believe that because possessions are carefully chosen, often to make a public statement, they reveal a lot about the actual (and desired) personality of the possessor.

Possessions are thus an extension of the self – special objects (e.g. jewellery, clothing), transitional objects, objects to do with magic, science and religion, memory-laden objects (e.g. gifts, photographs) as well as rare and mysterious objects and collections are particularly important to people. As Belk (1991) has noted, with regard to special objects, people are unwilling to sell at market rates or even discard. They will buy these items with little regard to price, they are completely non-substitutional, and they can cause powerful and direct feelings of elation and depression. Many become personified. It is not surprising, therefore, that both lay people and personality theorists believe the acquisition and display of special objects and possessions must be related to personality factors.

Ideas about personality and personal possessions are most clearly linked with *self-theorists*, who regard possessions as self-presentational and related to personal identity. There is an interesting but scattered literature on topics as varied as preference for clothes, cars, food and home furnishings, all of which have been shown to be related to self-image. In addition, there is a rich literature which suggests that observers make reliable (if not valid) inferences about the personality characteristics of others (Burroughs *et al.*, 1991). These findings would be more interesting for the trait theorist, however, if it was clearly demonstrated that preference for the purchase or even the display of personal possessions was correlated with robust and reliable trait measures. Self-rating involves problems of projection, elevation and shared stereotypes. Trait-measured questionnaires are not immune to problems, but are overall better predictors of social behaviour.

Bell *et al.* (1991) believed that they could, in part, solve the problem of being unable to demonstrate empirically the intuitively plausible effects of personality variables on consumption. They argued that products had two distinct types of symbolism, namely aesthetic or hedonic value (e.g. music, art, clothes) vs. social or status-enhancing value. They argued (and attempted to demonstrate) that personality traits influence the 'ideal self-impression' which people attempted to make, which in turn influenced the social impression they wished to create and that, along with a general liking factor based on an aesthetic response, it could be predicted whether or not individuals wanted to own certain products.

Freudian and neo-Freudian ideas have also inspired research in this area. Furthermore, marketing specialists seem particularly intrigued by the use of (largely scientifically rejected) projective technique. Psychoanalytic theory has served as the conceptual basis for the motivation research movement that was the precursor to lifestyle studies. Consumer behaviour is often the result of unconscious consumer motives, which can be determined only through indirect assessment methods that include a wide assortment of projective and related psychological techniques. However, this approach is no longer commonly used in marketing, mainly due to failed attempts to apply Freudian concepts in the past. In the USA, Webster and Von Pechmann (1970) used a replication of the Mason Haire (see Section 9.2) shopping list, which yielded results different to those of the original research based on psychoanalysis – instant coffee users were no longer perceived as psychologically different to drip grind users.

One source of marketing ideas derived from psychoanalytic theory is Klein's work on orality and the oral character (Klein, 1983). For instance, oral characters are said to be more likely to be both smokers and vegetarians. Oral optimists supposedly tend to prefer soft, milky foods, whereas oral pessimists favour hard, spicy and bitty foods. Certainly being able to categorise people into Freudian types such as oral, anal and phallic offers a rich (albeit somewhat unlikely) collection of hypotheses about market segmentation.

Cohen (1968) found that compliant types prefer brand names and use more mouthwash and toilet soaps, that aggressive types tend to use a razor rather than an electric shaver, use more cologne and aftershave lotion, and buy Old Spice deodorant and Van Heusen shirts, and that detached types seem to be least aware of brands. However, Cohen admitted to picking and choosing from his data. Cohen's compliant-aggressive-detached (CAD) test of Horney's classification scheme has been used in marketing research elsewhere (Kernan, 1971). Cohen and Golden (1972) found correlations between CAD, Eysenck's introversion–extroversion variable and Riesman's inner and outer direction variables. Noerager (1979), in a study assessing the reliability and validity of CAD as a marketing measurement, concluded that further development and refinement were necessary. However, the relative demise of Freudian psychology, at least in academic circles, has meant that few serious studies have been inspired by psychoanalytic researchers.

Psychoanalytic 'research' came up with the following extraordinary ideas in the 1950s (Assael, 1987), which may have put off more serious researchers from getting involved in this area.

- Men dislike air travel because of posthumous guilt (the anticipation of leaving a wife a widow).
- Sweet consumption is a source of guilt because of childhood associations with reward and punishment.

- Men sometimes resist giving blood because this is associated with a loss of potency.
- Power tools provide men with a feeling of omnipotence and manliness.
- Consumers resist using plastic wraps because of a lack of control over the product.

In this chapter we shall, as always, concentrate on trait literature and attempt to examine the evidence for traits being related to various patterns of consumption.

9.2 PERSONALITY AND BRAND CHOICE/USAGE

It seems intuitively obvious that personality should be systematically (and powerfully) related to consumer behaviour – the choice, purchase and long-term vs. short-term use of products (Plummer, 1985). Certainly, the most celebrated American study of brand choice was that of Evans (1959), who used 15 traits from the Edwards Personal Preference Schedule (EPPS) to determine whether he could distinguish between the owners of Ford and Chevrolet cars. He thought Ford owners would be independent, impulsive, masculine and self-confident, whereas Chevrolet owners would be conservative, thrifty and prestige conscious. He found some differences (he could classify people accurately for 63 per cent of the time based on the personality scores), but when his data were later re-analysed to test specific hypotheses, various clear differences did emerge. Westfall (1962) attempted a replication and was able to distinguish those individuals who had convertibles.

This conclusion has been disputed by several writers who re-analysed Evans' data. For example, Kuehn (1963) was able to raise the predictive accuracy to 90 of 140 by subtracting the 'need affiliation' score from the 'need dominance' score. Marcus (1965) was able to correctly predict 91 of 140 by graphically comparing these two need scores. Both Kuehn's and Marcus's re-analyses showed that the two EPPS scores correctly identified most Ford owners, but were less effective in identifying Chevrolet owners. They also showed that the two personality variables were efficient determining factors if the middle range of the distribution was eliminated. These results led other researchers to suggest that there is a need to organise the various influences on the purchase decision so that conditions can be identified when personality or situational variables are most likely to come significantly into play.

Foxall (1980) provided a useful summary of five major studies conducted between 1959 and 1967 (see Table 9.1). He argued that, of the evidence which he reviewed, it appeared that personality alone could account for between 5 and 10 per cent of brand choice. Other studies conducted at much the same time looking at the purchase and use of convenience foods, those who preferred store vs. national brands, and the specific types of banking institutions, all failed to yield consistent personality trait discriminations (Wells and Beard, 1973).

Foxall and Goldsmith (1989) have argued that it is time to have another look at the relationship between personality and consumer research. They noted that it was in the 1950s that (American) advertisers and marketers first suggested that personality might play a role in product purchase.

In a notorious early experiment, Haire (1950) used a projective technique to investigate why women were reluctant to buy instant coffee when it was first introduced. He constructed two shopping lists which were identical, except that one included 'regular' coffee and the other included instant coffee. Housewives were then asked to describe the type of woman who would be most likely to have developed each shopping list. The housewife who included instant coffee in the list was characterised as lazy and a poor planner. These findings supposedly demonstrated that many women had a deep-seated fear of buying products such as instant coffee or instant cake mixes out of a concern

Table 9.1 Personality and product choice: some examples. Reproduced with permission from Foxall, G. (1980) *Consumer behaviour: a practical guide.* London: Croom Helm.

Product/brand	Traits	Results
Fords/Chevrolets	Achievement, deference, exhibition, autonomy, affiliation, intraception, dominance, abasement, change, heterosexuality, aggression	Allowed correct prediction of 13% more buyer's choices than chance alone would predict
Car types	Activeness, vigour, impulsiveness, dominance, stability, sociability, reflectiveness	'No personality differences between Ford and Chevrolet owners.' Low activity related to low convertible ownership
Magazines	Sex, dominance, achievement, assistance	Less than 13% of purchase behaviour variance explicable in terms of personality for magazines or cigarettes
Cigarettes	Dominance, aggression, change, autonomy	
Toilet tissue	45 traits	Personality of no value predicting brand loyalty, number of units purchased or colour of tissue
Private brands	Enthusiasm, sensitivity, submissiveness	Less than 5% of purchase variance explained by these three traits; other traits of no value

that their husbands would feel they were avoiding their traditional role as homemakers. As a result of the study, instant coffee was subsequently advertised in a family setting portraying the husband's approval. Note that this study did not look at actual trait differences between consumers of different products, but at observational attributes, not unlike stereotypes. The idea that psychological factors can and do play a powerful (and slightly mysterious) role in consumer choice looks naive today. However, the psychoanalytically derived measures used to measure the (real, unconscious and predictive) motivation of consumers proved not to do so for various reasons, including the psychometric properties of the instruments, and the size and representativeness of the sample used, let alone the theory upon which the idea was based.

The psychoanalytically derived research was soon replaced with personality trait tests, some of which were well constructed. However, they fared no better.

> Those studies that yielded significant findings were limited in generality to a single brand or product class or by the social or economic composition of the study's sample, and as a practical matter the trait measure usually 'explained' less than 10% of the variance in the dependent variables. No other behavioural science concept was so decisively written off by both academic and commercial consumer researchers by the mid-1970s.
>
> (Foxall and Goldsmith, 1989, p.114)

They suggest that the main reasons for the personality predictive failure up to this time were as follows:

- unrealistic expectations of how the tests would perform (expecting traits alone to account for far too much of the variance);
- inappropriate use of clinically derived tests (not using tests that reliably measure major 'normal' traits);
- neglect of the situation in which the tests were administered;
- tests were not carefully chosen or hypotheses developed (not being sufficiently aware of personality processes);
- the reliability of the dependent variable (single-item responses or instances of behaviour) was low or unknown (this has always been a major problem in the area);
- the levels of generality/specificity of the independent variable (personality traits) and the dependent variable (consumer behaviour) needed to be, but never were, the same – buying was highly specific, and traits were very general.

Recent research has used better measures of traits that are obviously theoretically relevant to consumer behaviour, and researchers are also more careful about the validity of the dependent measure – the consumption itself. As was pointed out in Chapter 1, multiple measures of behaviour are always more reliable than one-off measures.

For Lastovicka and Joachimsthaler (1988), the key to improving the predictability of personality tests lies in examining the reliability of the dependent variable, namely the consumer behaviour itself. They note the irony of the fact that marketing managers have little interest in predicting single purchasing acts (as opposed to repeat purchasing), yet measure single acts in research. If multiple behavioural consumer acts are recorded, and if correlational attenuations are performed depending on behavioural measurement reliability, the personality–consumer behaviour relationships can be significantly increased.

Kassarjian and Sheffet (1991) reviewed over 300 studies on personality and consumer behaviour published up to 1990. They note that the equivocal results of previous studies are often due to poor measurement, both of personality and of consumer behaviour. They also mention that in consumer research studies many carefully psychometricised instruments are adapted, revised and restructured, and it is unclear what damage this does to the validity and reliability of instruments. They also point out that few studies have developed clear, theoretically justified hypotheses to test.

It is therefore perhaps testimony to the robustness of the relationship between personality and consumer behaviour that so many poorly constructed studies *still* show that personality accounts for 5 to 10 per cent of the variance. If good studies show that this amount is doubled to 20 per cent, it is indeed remarkable. Too often personality traits are rejected as unimportant determinants of consumer purchasing because of the highly unrealistic expectations of the consumer researchers.

A great deal of research has been conducted on the relationship between personality and consumer behaviour. It has been suggested that there may be a relationship between:

- personality and foreign vs. local products;
- personality and store (shop) choice;
- personality and 'green'/environmentally friendly products;
- personality and brand loyalty;
- personality and susceptibility to persuasion by advertising;
- personality and consumer movement involvement.

Over 25 years ago Kassarjian (1971) reviewed the previous 15 to 20 years of enthusiastic but piecemeal studies on personality and consumer behaviour. He found the results that were obtained equivocal and the methodologies that were employed weak. Schiffman and Kanuk (1983) have listed six reasons why extant studies did not reveal the (presumably existent) relationship between personality traits and consumer behaviour:

(1) they were based on convenient multi-trait rather than specifically selected single-trait personality tests, (2) they employed personality tests designed for diagnosis of social adjustment problems rather than identifying the range of normal–healthy behaviour, (3) they had no *a priori* hypotheses that proposed a relationship between the traits under study and specific

consumer behaviour, (4) they focused on single brand choices rather than on more general product category usage patterns, (5) they focused on consumers' brand choice rather than on the dimensions of the decision process leading to the choice, and (6) they assumed that the personality–consumer behaviour relationship is consistent across situations, rather than influenced by the particular situation.

(Schiffman and Kanuk, 1983, p.93)

Similarly, account must be taken of the conditions under which variables such as price and convenience are stronger determinants of choice than personality. For example, Brody and Cunningham (1968) provide evidence that personality is a better predictor of choice of products when consumers perceive the products to differ in significant ways and are confident that at least one product will fulfil their requirements.

Self-evidently, demographic factors, especially sex, age, education, income and social class, are powerful predictors of everyday consumption. It is quite possible that these factors *interact* with personality, but few of the early studies tested interaction effects. According to Wilkie (1990), recent research has improved greatly because of three trends: first, studying behaviour *patterns* rather than single purchasing decisions; secondly, focusing on consumption rather than general needs; and thirdly, taking into account cognitive, physiological and self-concept factors as well as trait factors.

Despite the unimpressive results obtained from early research on personality and consumer behaviour, more recent studies employing measures that are empirically better and theoretically grounded offer more promise for the future. Among the measures that can be tentatively identified at this point as likely to be useful in market segmentation are internal–external locus of control and self-monitoring. In most cases, reliable and valid measures already exist with which to measure these constructs. However, it will be necessary to specify quite precisely what aspects of consumer behaviour are involved. For example, different personality characteristics may be related to shop and supermarket use, information-seeking and appraisal of new products, exposure to different media, willingness to innovate, and brand loyalty. Again, stable patterns of consumer behaviour, and behaviours about which consumers feel more subjectively certain, are likely to be more strongly related to personality than are 'one-off' factors, and knowledge of the salient aspects of personality should lead to much more effective segmentation strategies in the future.

9.3 STUDIES USING SPECIFIC TRAIT MEASURES

Both reviews by Kassarjian (Kassarjian, 1971; Kassarjian and Sheffet, 1991) attempted to examine the results of studies by considering research conducted on different personality questionnaires. This will be summarised below.

9.3.1 Gordon Personality Profile

Tucker and Painter (1961) used the Gordon Personality Profile and the Sales and Marketing Personality Index, which included questions on the use of headache remedies, cigarettes, chewing gum, deodorants, mouthwash and other items commonly purchased by college students. Their results showed a relationship between product use and personality traits, accounting for about 10 per cent of the variance. This relationship included both *frequency* of use of particular products and *preference* for different brands of a single product.

Sparks and Tucker (1971) found sociability, emotional stability and irresponsibility to be predictors of cigarette smoking, alcohol drinking, shampoo use and early fashion adoption. They found that a combination of sociability, cautiousness and emotional stability was related to use of headache remedies, mouthwash and aftershave lotion, and late fashion adoption. Other studies 'show interesting relationships but are by no means startling' (Kassarjian and Sheffet, 1991, p.285).

9.3.2 Edwards Personal Preference Schedule (EPPS)

The EPPS has been used in numerous studies of consumer behaviour. Its popularity in measuring customer behaviour can be traced back to Evans' landmark study (1959). Kopenen (1960) found that among a sample of 9000 people cigarette smoking was positively related to sex, dominance, aggression and achievement needs among males, and that it was negatively related to order and compliance needs. He also found differences between filter and non-filter smokers, and observed that these differences were made more pronounced by heavy smoking. In addition, there seemed to be a relationship between personality variables and readership of three specified magazines.

Using the same data in a study of purchase of coffee, tea and beer, Massy *et al.* (1968) concluded that personality accounted for only 5 to 10 per cent of the variance in purchases. In another study, Claycamp (1965) presented the EPPS to 174 subjects who held savings accounts in banks or savings and loans associations. The personality variables predicted better than demographic variables whether an individual was a customer of a bank or a savings and loan association.

In a study of the relationships between personality and consumer decision processes, Brody and Cunningham (1968) argued that the 'low-level' relationships found by previous research could have been caused by inadequate theoretical frameworks, rather than by the inability of personality measures to predict consumer behaviour. They offered a conceptual model by which the significant sets of factors which affect consumer decision-making could be identified. This model contained four types of variables: *personal system* variables (e.g. conscious and unconscious needs), *social system* variables (e.g.

membership and reference groups), *exogenous* variables (e.g. relative price and purchase convenience) and *risk-reducing* variables (e.g. trusted retail outlets and brands). Categorising the multiplicity of variables known to affect consumer behaviour into these four groups, they argued, makes them more manageable when analysing their role in a given purchase situation. Brody and Cunningham (1968) suggested that the consumer decision process could be further simplified if the relative influences of each variable system were regarded as a function of the person's perception of the choice situation. They proposed that three perceptions in particular may act as filters to determine the group of variables with the greatest weight:

- the perceived performance risk of the decision – to what extent the person thinks that different brands perform differently in ways that are important;
- specific self-confidence – how certain the person is that the chosen brand will perform as expected;
- the perceived social risk – the extent to which the person thinks that other people will judge them by their brand decision.

When combined, therefore, the filtering and classification systems indicate where to look for explanatory variables. Reaction to high perceived risk with regard to a brand is largely dependent on a subjective judgement of perceived risk.

Brody and Cunningham (1968) tested their theory by examining the ability of the EPPS to predict brand choice among coffee drinkers. One personality variable among males (need for dominance) and four personality variables among females (need analysis, need dependence, need depreciation and consistency) emerged as significant predictors of brand loyalty. Just 3 per cent of the variance was accounted for by the total set of variables, with demographic variables accounting for over 50 per cent of that.

They also re-analysed their data, within their theoretical framework, which identified those conditions under which personality variables are most likely to be important, namely conditions of high perceived performance risk and high specific self-confidence. Researchers had earlier found that consumers tended to concentrate a high percentage of their purchases on one brand. Guided by this framework, Brody and Cunningham found that, as the above conditions became more pronounced with regard to brand purchases decision, personality variables increasingly explained large amounts of the variance in predicting brand loyalty. In the most extreme case, where consumers concentrated 100 per cent of their purchase on their favourite brand, EPPS variables explained 48 per cent of the variance. The results were even better when comparisons were run across groups, showing high degrees of purchase concentration with different brands. It is a pity that this important study was so overlooked.

9.3.3 Californian Personality Inventory (CPI)

Robertson and Myers (1969) and Bruce and Wilt (1970) developed measures for innovativeness and opinion leadership in the areas of food, clothing and appliances. A total of 18 traits on the CPI were regressed on to this measure, but little variance was accounted for (the proportion of variance accounted for was 4 per cent for clothing, 5 per cent for food but 23 per cent for appliances). The findings supported previous studies on innovation and opinion leadership that show a fairly minimal relationship between personality variables and behaviour towards new products. Boone (1970) attempted to relate the variables on the CPI to the consumer innovator on the topic of community antenna television systems.

9.3.4 The Big Five

Recognising the Big Five model as an important recent taxonomy of global personality traits, Mooradian and Oliver (1996) looked at personality traits and shopping motives. After a careful reading of the personality literature, they derived nearly 20 testable hypotheses (see Table 9.2).
Most of the hypotheses were supported.

> Neuroticism was directly related to Diversion, Self-gratification, Physical Activity, and Sensory Stimulation motives. Neuroticism was also inversely correlated with Pleasure in Bargaining. Extraversion was linked with Social Experiences Outside the Home, Communication with Others Having Similar Interests, Peer Group Attraction, and Status and Authority motives. Extraversion was *not* significantly related with Pleasure in Bargaining. Openness to Experience was correlated with Sensory Stimulation and Learning About New Trends. Agreeableness was inversely related to Pleasure in Bargaining. Unexpectedly, Agreeableness was *not* related to Social motives (and *was* positively related with Pleasure in Bargaining). Conscientiousness was directly related to Pleasure in Bargaining and Learning motives, and inversely with Self-gratification.
>
> (Mooradian and Oliver, 1996, p.588)

They argue that these results may help retailers to understand their customers. Yet they did not recognise that the motives they examined focused more on experiential and social motives, whereas functional and utilitarian motives were relatively ignored. Whilst the correlational studies are important, they can never replace studies on actual behaviour – that is, the Big Five predictors of actual, regular consumption (i.e. purchasing and using) patterns.

9.4 CONSUMERISM-BASED PERSONALITY TRAITS

In an attempt to overcome the shortcomings associated with applying standardised personality instruments originally developed for clinical purposes to marketing, some researchers have attempted to develop personality measures within a marketing context, which therefore have more relevance to the assessment of consumer behaviour.

Worthing *et al.* (1973) used scales from Jackson's (1967) Personality Research Form (PRF), which were intended for a wide variety of situations, including consumer behaviour. The PRF offers measures on five factors, namely affiliation, aggression, dominance, exhibitionism and social recognition. Worthing *et al.* found that affiliation and aggression related to use of cigarettes, beer, headache remedies, mouthwash and men's dress shorts.

Earlier, Fry (1971) not only took advantage of the consumer-based personality measures provided by the Jackson Personality Research Form, but also utilised the conceptual framework of Brody and Cunningham (1968), which was devised to identify the conditions under which personality variables are most likely to affect consumer behaviour (cigarette brand preferences). In

Table 9.2 Summary of postulated relationships between the five-factor model and specific shopping motives. Reproduced with permission of authors and publisher from: Mooradian, T. A., and Olver, J. M. "Shopping motives and the Five Factor Model: an integration and preliminary study." *Psychological Reports*, 1996, 78, 579–592. © Psychological Reports 1996

Global trait	Shopping motives
Neuroticism	Diversion – to get out of the house, kill time Sensory – excitement, enjoyment of hustle and bustle Self-gratification – pampering, picking up spirits Physical – exercise Bargaining – enjoyment of the negotiation process
Extraversion	Social – opportunity for social interaction Communication – talking to salespeople and other shoppers Peer – spending time with friends Status – being pampered, being treated with respect Bargaining – see above
Openness to experience	Sensory – see above Learning – learning about new products Diversion – see above Self-gratification – see above
Agreeableness	Social – see above Bargaining – see above
Conscientiousness	Self-gratification – see above Learning – see above Bargaining – see above

total, 10 personality variables were investigated, namely achievement, affiliation, aggression, autonomy, dominance, femininity, change, sentience, social recognition and self-confidence. The femininity scale was taken from the CPI. Together with socio-economic variables, personality variables accounted for between 20 and 30 per cent of the variance in cigarette brand choices. In particular, the study found that a respondent's sex, social class and self-confidence were moderately important predictors of brand selection. Fry concluded that personality variables as measured by standard tests appear to have considerable potential for improving our understanding of the psychological basis of brand choice. However, this is only true when research is guided by an appropriate theoretical perspective. Vitz and Johnson (1965), using the masculinity scale of both the CPI and the Minnesota Multiphasic Personality Inventory (MMPI), hypothesised that the more masculine a smoker's personality, the more masculine would be the image of his regular brand of cigarettes. The correlations were low, but statistically significant, and the authors concluded that the results provided moderate support for product preference as a predictable interaction between the consumer's personality and the product's image.

Kassarjian and Sheffet (1991) have suggested that less clinical and more 'market-oriented', 'product-specific' instruments should be developed for research in this field, in order to improve the predictability. Hence the interest in and development of measures of trait aspects of vanity (Netemeyer *et al.*, 1995) and nostalgia (Holbrook, 1993). However, there are serious pitfalls in this approach. It could lead to the proliferation of measures that are unrelated to each other and only tangentially related to major traits in personality theory (see Chapter 1). Furthermore, although the product-specific measures may show greater consumer behaviour validity, this could equally well be due to item overlap. That is, if the 'personality questionnaire' contains questions about specific product use or preference, then it is not surprising if it predicts product use. One ends up with neat tautology and no understanding of process. A much better approach is to explore a consumer issue – such as compulsive buying – through a series of well-chosen and established measures (O'Guinn and Faber, 1989).

Shop-lifting or compulsive stealing from shops has also been linked to addictive behaviour. To be defined as legal theft, shop-lifting must be conscious, deliberate and willingly committed. Researchers have found an association between eating disorders and shop-lifting, where nearly 20 per cent of patients have stolen food during the bulimic phase of their illness. Bridgeman and Slade (1996) have offered various case-history-based explanations of the link between the two. One possible explanation is that fasting leads to food craving and an urgent need for food, which triggers off a compulsive drive to obtain and consume food, hence stealing food from shops. Alternatively, bingeing and purging can lead to disorientation and chaotic and disorganised behaviour, which in turn leads to shop-lifting. There seems to be no doubt, therefore, that pathological consumption manifested in such behaviours as compulsive buying or shop-lifting is clearly linked to other pathologies which may themselves be linked to personality differences.

The idea of developing trait measures based on consumerism is a good one, and would no doubt increase the predictive validity of tests. However, there are two pitfalls in this approach. First, it could be a licence to develop many unrelated product-specific trait measures that are not based on personality theory. Secondly, it could easily result in item overlap and tautology, rather than providing an explanatory process whereby some individuals consume certain products rather than others.

9.5 RECENT DEVELOPMENTS

Various ideas in psychology, some very old and others relatively new, have attracted researchers who are interested in personality and consumption choice. Four of them will be briefly discussed here.

9.5.1 Self-Concept

Many researchers have been attracted to 'self psychology' and the many self-concepts (e.g. self-image, ideal-self) which they assume may make for better predictive validity of consumer choice. According to Kassarjian and Sheffet (1991), self-confidence was the most commonly investigated concept until the 1970s.

A number of somewhat pretentious-sounding self-theories have been proposed to aid understanding of the relationship between consumption and the self-concept (Soloman, 1996):

- symbolic self-completion – the idea that products provide a social crutch to make one more masculine, sophisticated, arty, etc.;
- self-image congruence models – the idea that products are chosen to match the perceived self. People choose brands of cigarettes, cars, beer, soap, etc., because of the congruity between the perceived product (e.g. rational/emotional, rugged/delicate) and the self-concept;
- extended self – favourite, treasured products are invested with meaning, personalised and kept for long periods of time.

For many, all of these theories could be expressed by the simple epithet 'You are what you wear' or 'You are what you use.'

Self-concept theory has provided essentially two perspectives in its application to marketing problems. First, the discrepancy between self and ideal self is perceived as a measure of dissatisfaction. This measure not only reveals the degree of overall discontent with the self, but also pinpoints on which attributes this discontent occurs most strongly. This indicator of dissatisfaction could be related to product usage patterns, particularly with regard to products which purport to offer the consumer a brand of self-improvement.

White (1967) employed a measure of discrepancy between self and ideal self, according to which high discrepants were dissatisfied with their self-image and wished for major and unrealistic change, middle discrepants were somewhat dissatisfied and wanted to improve themselves, but in a more realistic way, and low discrepants had accurate and often harsh notions of themselves, with little tolerance for fantasy. These categories were related to ownership of cars, and it was found that a significant proportion of the middle discrepants owned cars which they had had for 2 years longer, on average, than the other two groups. These findings suggested that car ownership was greater among consumers with a more realistic, somewhat better adjusted self-perception.

Dolich (1969) studied this relationship for beer, cigarettes, bar soap and toothpaste, and found that respondents tended to prefer brands which they rated as similar to themselves on both the actual and ideal dimensions. Several studies have shown the same relationship for cars. An owner's perception of his or her car is consistent with his or her image of others with the same car (Grubb and Hupp, 1968).

Other research has revealed that the relationship between brand and self-image is somewhat more complicated because consumers change their self-image according to the situation they are in. For instance, consumers may have different impressions of themselves in social and business contexts. There is another dimension of self-concept and its application to marketing. Self-image may not only affect the products that consumers choose, but also the products that are chosen frequently as opposed to infrequently. Certain products may have symbolic value, sometimes referred to as 'badge' value – they say something about us and the way we feel about ourselves. Products are thus bought to make a self-enhancing statement. Yet products also move in and out of fashion, and thus the inability to enhance self-concept may be very fickle.

9.5.2 Self-Monitoring

One of the most promising developments in the 'self' literature has been the work of Snyder (1974, 1987), according to whom self-monitoring is the tendency to notice cues for socially appropriate behaviour and to modify one's behaviour accordingly. Individuals can be classified into two groups with regard to their level of self-monitoring. Those who score high on the trait of self-monitoring are characterised by sensitivity to social cues indicating socially appropriate behaviour, and by using those cues to modify self-presentation. Low self-monitors are thought to be relatively insensitive to social cues, and tend to maintain a consistent self-presentation across different situations. High self-monitors emphasise the public self and, like actors, seem to be asking 'What role should I be playing in this situation?' Low self-monitors are more interested in their personal value systems and private realities. The central question asked by the low self-monitors is 'How can I look like the person I truly am?'

Snyder (1987) distinguished between the hard and soft sell in advertising – the former being about quality (e.g. intrinsic merit, functional value) and the latter about image. He argued and demonstrated that high self-monitors rated image-oriented advertisements and products as more appealing and effective, and would be willing to pay more for the product. By contrast, low self-monitors reacted more favourably to product quality-oriented advertisements. He also showed that the same principle applied when encouraging a person not to consume a product. Thus high self-monitors may be put off smoking because of the consequences of bad breath and smelly clothes, while low self-monitors may be more concerned with health consequences (e.g. coughing, sore throat).

Snyder notes:

> Thus, high self-monitoring consumers may be the ones who purchase the sleek, flashy, sporty-looking car (even if its performance and handling characteristics are far from sports-car calibre), the ones who use the toothpaste that makes their teeth look the whitest (even if there is the suggestion that, over a long enough period of time, its abrasive content may threaten the enamel of their teeth), and the ones who pour the 'super premium' beer, that special imported beer that says something about its drinker's status (even if it tastes no different than the less expensive domestic brands). Such consumers may be choosing *form* over *function*.
>
> By contrast, low self-monitoring consumers may be the ones who purchase the nutritious breakfast cereal (even if it isn't the one endorsed by the Olympic gold medal winner), the ones who use the mouthwash that is purported to kill the most bacteria (even if it does leave their breath with that faint medicinal odour), and the ones who choose the energy-efficient refrigerator (even though it's not available in the most trendy platinum-toned, designer-styled finish). They may be choosing *function at the expense of form*.
>
> (Snyder, 1987, p.106)

More recently, Browne and Kaldenberg (1997) found that high self-monitors were more involved with clothing as a product category than low self-monitors. High self-monitors, being more fashion conscious, are more apt to switch brands when situations and/or fashions change, and hence are less brand-loyal. This seems to be a promising area for further research.

9.5.3 Innovation Behaviour and Consumer Choices

In a programmatic series of studies, Foxall and associates looked at personality correlates of the uptake of new innovative products. Using a measure that distinguishes an individual as an adaptor (confining problem-solving to familiar frames of reference) or an innovator (seeking new and different solutions to problems), they set about testing specific hypotheses concerning the choosing of new products. They postulated that innovators tend to be more extravert, less dogmatic, more tolerant of ambiguity, radical, flexible, assertive, expedient, undisciplined and sensation-seeking than adaptors, so it was predicted that they would make more innovative consumer product choices. Unfortunately, many of the relatively straightforward hypotheses were not confirmed. However, they did attempt to 'explain away' the contradictory findings by noting that innovators are, by definition, not product-loyal (Foxall and Goldsmith, 1989). These researchers believed that if one took into account a particular brand/product and the continuity of purchasing, the adaptor–innovator trait could still be a useful predictor of behaviour. However, a trait psychologist or psychometrician might believe otherwise. The clever attempts to rescue this dimension from the pile of other failed trait measures do not look very convincing.

9.5.4 Variety-Seeking/Optimising Stimulation and Consumer Behaviour

There has been a fairly long-standing interest in arousal concepts (Raju, 1980) as predictors of consumer behaviour. One assumption is that stimulation level (clearly introversion–extraversion) is related to uptake of new, novel or even risky products. The idea of stimulation-seeking and stimulation-avoiding is central to the major personality dimension of extraversion, and may be of central interest to personality theorists who are trying to predict consumer behaviour.

Steenkamp and Baumgartner (1992) have noted that an individual's optimum stimulation level should theoretically be linked to exploratory consumer behaviour such as curiosity, variety-seeking, risk-taking and innovative behaviour. From a comprehensive review they set out to test and confirm a number of hypotheses in this area. These were that, compared to individuals with low optimum stimulation levels, individuals with high optimum stimulation levels will:

- generate more curiosity-motivated responses to advertisements;
- experience more tedium during repeated exposure to the same advertisement;
- exhibit more variety-seeking behaviour when examining products;
- make more risky choices;
- be more likely to gamble for higher stakes;
- be more likely to try out new brands.

These authors note that the effect size was consistent with other studies in the area. The results would not surprise trait theorists, as extraversion, sensation-seeking and other related concepts have been shown to be related to curiosity motivation, variety-seeking and risk-taking behaviours in many situations.

9.6 PERSONALITY AND AESTHETIC PREFERENCE

Is a preference for (and purchasing of) art, music, poetry and even architecture related to personality? Could personality variables be used to predict purchasing of art, attendance at music concerts, or the style of decorating one's room?

A substantial amount of research has been devoted to the relationship between personality characteristics and aesthetic preference (Peel, 1945; Cardinet, 1958; Child, 1962; Juhasz and Paxson, 1978; Litle and Zuckerman, 1986), including one of the earliest studies of aesthetic preferences, conducted by Burt (1933), involving an assortment of picture postcards which his subjects were required to rank in order of preference. Factor analysis of the correlations between ratings indicated first, a general factor of aesthetic judgement which was applicable to all of the subjects and secondly, bipolar factors for different types of artistic preference, which appeared to be related to individual differences in personality.

Eysenck (1940, 1941) extended this line of research, using a wide variety of pictorial stimuli and extracting two factors from the intercorrelation between preferences. He named these the 'T' factor (a general factor of *good taste*) and the 'K' factor (a bipolar factor which tended to separate preference for *modern*, impressionistic, colourful art from older, more *traditional* and less colourful artwork). Eysenck found indications that the 'K' factor might be associated with several other kinds of psychological variables, namely extraversion/introversion, radicalism/conservatism, youth/age, colour preference/form preference and preference for bright colours/preference for subdued colours. A number of subsequent studies have also found a general factor and a bipolar factor in aesthetic judgements and preferences (Peel, 1945).

Child (1965) conducted a fairly extensive study with 138 male students, looking at the relationships between a large number of personality and cognitive measures, and the students' aesthetic judgements of 120 pairs of pictures which had been chosen so that members of each pair were the same in type and subject matter, but differed in aesthetic value. Among the variables he found to be positively related to aesthetic judgement were tolerance of complexity, intuition rather than sensation, perception rather than judgement, anxiety, verbal aptitude, and visual preference for subdued colours, abstract designs, and Baroque over Classical art. In addition, a negative correlation with aesthetic judgement was found for viscerotonia (love of comfort and relaxation).

Preference for abstract and modern art compared with traditional, representational art has perhaps been the most widely investigated area recently. Preference for abstract art has been found to be associated with personality characteristics that include conservatism (Wilson *et al.*, 1973), sensation-seeking (Tobacyck *et al.*, 1981; Furnham and Bunyan, 1988), field dependence (Tobacyck *et al.*, 1981) and aesthetic value as opposed to religious value

(Knapp and Wulff, 1963). Some studies have looked at personality and preferences relating to the pictorial and emotional content of paintings, such as tension in paintings (Zuckerman *et al.*, 1993) and aggressive content (Tobacyck *et al.*, 1981).

A study by Juhasz and Paxson (1978) looked at preference for cubist and surrealist paintings in relation to locus of control. They predicted that the highly controlled painting style of cubism would be associated with a belief in internal control, whereas preference for the more uncontrolled surrealist paintings would be related to an external locus of control. The results obtained were consistent with this hypothesis.

The personality construct of sensation-seeking (SS) has been developed by Zuckerman and defined as an individual's desire to seek varied, novel, complex and intense sensations and experiences, and the willingness to take physical, social, legal and financial risks for the sake of such experience. The most widely used form of the SS scale is Form V (Zuckerman *et al.*, 1978), which consists of 40 forced-choice items and was the measure used in this study. Factor analysis of the scale by Zuckerman *et al.* (1978) identified four behavioural components within the construct of sensation-seeking. 'Thrill and adventure seeking' (TAS) is expressed by a desire to engage in physically risky sports and other activities, such as parachuting and skiing. The component of 'experience seeking' (ES) relates to the seeking of new sensations and experiences through the mind and senses, and through social non-conformity. The third factor is 'disinhibition', which concerns the seeking of sensations from social activities such as social drinking and sex. The fourth component is 'boredom susceptibility', which is expressed by an intolerance of repetitive and monotonous experiences and situations.

A number of studies have found associations between sensation-seeking and preferences in art and other imagery. Zuckerman *et al.* (1970) showed that low sensation-seekers displayed a greater preference for simple, symmetrical designs, whereas high sensation-seekers preferred complex, asymmetrical designs that were suggestive of movement. With regard to preferences for different styles of formal art, there is evidence that sensation-seeking is positively related to a liking for abstract paintings. Tobacyck *et al.* (1981) asked 210 students to make preference ratings of 40 slides of paintings that had been selected to form eight a priori categories. The results indicated that sensation-seeking was associated with a greater liking for abstract futurist cubist paintings by Boccioni, and for abstract impressionistic paintings by Pollock. A significant positive correlation was also found between sensation-seeking and representational paintings depicting aggressive scenes. Furnham and Bunyan (1988) provided further support for the association of sensation-seeking and a liking for abstract art. A set of 20 slides of paintings was classified into four groups as combinations of simple/complex and abstract/representational, and 60 subjects made preference ratings of the slides. The sensation-seeking total score (assessed by the SSS Form V) was found to be significantly negatively correlated with a liking for complex representational paintings and significantly positively correlated with a liking for complex abstract paintings. The representational/abstract nature of the paintings was found to be more strongly related to preferences of high or low sensation-seekers than whether the paintings were simple or complex.

Preference differences relating to content, as well as style, have also been found for sensation-seekers, although it appears that, on the whole, content is less influential than the style and complexity of the art. Zuckerman *et al.* (1993) conducted two studies concerning sensation-seeking and attitudes towards a selection of nineteenth-century nature paintings which varied with regard to artist, style, complexity and tension. An interaction was found between sensation-seeking and the tension component. High and low sensation-seekers did not differ in their preference for paintings with low tension, but the high sensation-seekers had a more favourable opinion of the paintings of medium and high tension than the low sensation-seekers. However, the most salient influence was again the degree of abstractness or representation. Complexity was not found to be relevant in this experiment either. Zaleski (1984) asked subjects to choose the pictures they liked most from a set of 21 paintings depicting images that were either positively emotionally arousing (e.g. celebratory scenes), negatively emotionally arousing (e.g. scenes of death) or neutral. The results showed a significant difference in the distribution of the first-choice picture among the three picture categories for high compared to low sensation-seekers.

More recently, Furnham and Avison (1998) looked at preference for surreal (vs. representational) paintings. Whilst extraversion, neuroticism, openness and tolerance of ambiguity were not clearly related, two of the sensation-seeking scales were. Experience-seeking clearly predicted a liking for surreal art, whereas boredom susceptibility was clearly related to a dislike of traditional representational art. It certainly seems that sensation-seeking is the most subtle but powerful personality predictor of aesthetic preference.

What about the fundamental traits of extraversion and neuroticism? Child (1962) found that measures of anxiety showed a small positive correlation with aesthetic judgement. He suggested that this may not be indicative of a particularly high level of anxiety *per se*, but rather that individuals with a greater interest in aesthetic values may be more able and willing to recognise and report unpleasant emotions and anxiety themselves. Knapp and Wulff (1963) reported the results of a study on art preference which they describe as being suggestive of a relationship between abstract painting and general neuroticism, although significant values were not obtained. However, these findings do not provide a substantial basis for the prediction of an association of any nature between neuroticism and like or dislike of surreal art.

Extraversion is concerned with the preferred levels of quality and intensity for interpersonal interactions, and activity and stimulation. An early exploration by Burt (1939) divided subjects at the more extreme ends of the extraversion spectrum into four personality combinations, namely introvert/extravert and stable/unstable. The patterns of preference for painting styles were different for each of these types. The largest proportion of stable extraverts liked realistic pictures, unstable extraverts tended to prefer romantic art, stable introverts preferred classical art and unstable introverts liked impressionistic styles. The preferences of subjects who were less extreme in their introversion/extraversion showed no particular leanings towards any one type of painting. Eysenck (1941) suggested that the bipolar factor separating preferences for modern and traditional paintings was correlated with extraversion. However, one of the findings of Cardinet (1958) in research using 195 pairs of pictures in 22 categories, with 180 subjects, was that introverts preferred modern and more abstract paintings. Robertoux *et al.* (1971) found no association between introversion and tolerance of representational distortion in pictures. Past experimental evidence therefore provides contradictory indications of the nature of any association between extraversion and artistic preference.

9.7 PERSONALITY AND MONEY

Consumption nearly always involves the use of money. People have to accumulate, store and exchange money for goods. Are personality factors related to money usage? There is a surprising dearth of work in this field (Lim and Teo, 1997; Furnham and Argyle, 1998). Money is imbued with meaning, as is clear from the following quote by Wiseman (1974):

> One thinks of kleptomaniacs, or of the women who drain men of their resources, to whom money, which they are always striving to take away, symbolizes a whole series of introjected objects that have been withheld from them, or of depressive characters who from fear of starvation regard money as potential food. There are those men to whom money signifies their potency, who experience any loss of money as a castration, or who are inclined, when in danger, to sacrifice money in a sort of 'prophylactic self-castration'. There are, in addition, people who – according to their attitudes of the moment towards taking, giving, or withholding – accumulate or spend money, or alternate between accumulation and spending, quite impulsively, without regard for the real significance of money, and often to their detriment every man has, and the pricelessness of objects, and the price on the outlaw's head; there are forty pieces of silver and also the double indemnity of one's own life.
>
> Behind its apparent sameness lie the many meanings of money. Blood-money does not buy the same thing as bride-money, and a king's ransom is not the same kind of fortune as a lottery prize. The great exchangeability of money is deceptive; it enables us to buy the appearance of things, their physical form, as in the case of a 'bought woman', while what we thought we had bought eludes us.
>
> (Wiseman, 1974, pp.13–14)

There have been a few studies on personality, individual differences and money beliefs and behaviours. Luft (1957) found that a person's weekly income determines how he or she is perceived by peers. Rich men were regarded as relatively healthy, happy and well adjusted, while poor people were seen as maladjusted and unhappy. Rim (1982) looked at the relationship between personality and attitudes towards money, and observed that stable extraverts seemed to be more open, comfortable and carefree about their money than unstable introverts. However, he found that personality variables appeared to be only weak predictors of money-related attitudes and behaviour.

McClure (1984) gave 159 American shoppers a 22-item questionnaire about money, including items on spending habits, perceived control over finances, importance of money in one's life, preferences about monetary privacy, and conflict resulting from money. He found that extraverts tended to be more extravagant and less stingy than introverts. People with strong feelings of control over their money reported less general anxiety, and tended to be more extraverted. Neurotic introverts considered money to be more important in their lives, and were more private about it than stable introverts. Despite clear links to personality, the results showed that the attitudes measured in the questionnaire were unrelated to demographic differences in gender, education, occupation or religion.

Furnham (1984) found that older, less well-educated people believed their early childhood to be poorer than did young better-educated people, reflecting both the average increased standard of living and the class structure of society. Overall, he found few differences in the subjects' perception of money in the past, but a large number regarding their perception of money in the future. Older people were more worried about the future than younger people, possibly because they had greater financial responsibility – for families, children and mortgages. Richer people were more concerned about the future than poorer people. Conservative (right-wing) voters believed that the country's economic future was bright, while Labour (left-wing) voters and those with high levels of alienation and conservative social attitudes believed that it would get worse. Although these questions may seem vague they are not trivial, because presumably people act on their beliefs about future trends in terms of saving, spending and investing (Rubinstein, 1981). Thus if one believes that future economic trends mean that one might be substantially worse off, one might take steps to avoid this eventuality.

Hanley and Wilhelm (1992) investigated the relationship between self-esteem and attitudes towards money. As predicted, they found that compulsive spenders have relatively lower self-esteem than 'normal' consumers, and that compulsive spenders have beliefs about money which reflect its symbolic ability to enhance self-esteem. They note:

> Descriptively, the findings of this study show that there are significant differences between a sample of compulsive spenders and a sample of 'normal' consumers on five of the six money attitude and belief dimensions

under study. Compulsive spenders reported a greater likelihood than 'normal' consumers to be preoccupied with the importance of money as a solution to problems and to use money as a means of comparison. Additionally, compulsive spenders were more likely to report the need to spend money in a manner which was reflective of status and power. In contrast, the compulsive spenders were less likely than 'normal' consumers to take a traditional, more conservative approach to money. Compulsive spenders were more likely to report that they did not have enough money for their needs, especially in comparison to friends. Finally, compulsive spenders reported a greater tendency than did 'normal' consumers to feel a sense of conflict over the spending of money.

(Hanley and Wilhelm, 1992, pp.16–17)

Lynn (1994) looked at national differences in attitudes to money in 43 countries. There were statistically significant negative associations between the valuation of money and per capita income among most nation groups, and people from more affluent countries attached less value to money. Males attached more value to money than females. One possible explanation for this sex difference is that males generally tend to be more competitive. There were also strong correlations between the valuation of money and competitiveness across nations.

The results were not dissimilar to those reported from related American studies (Rubinstein, 1981; Yamauchi and Templer, 1982). Attitudes towards money are by no means unidimensional: factor analytical results yielded six clearly interpretable factors that bore many similarities to the factors found by Yamauchi and Templer (1982), such as power, retention and inadequacy, as well as the hypothetical factors derived from psychoanalytic theory (Fenichel, 1947). Whereas some of the factors were clearly linked to clinical traits of anxiety and obsessionality, others were more closely related to power and the way in which individuals obtain money. In addition, some factors more than others proved to be related to the demographic and belief variables. Obsession with money showed significant differences according to sex, education, income and all of the belief variables (i.e. alienation, Protestant work ethic and conservatism), whereas the inadequacy factors showed no significant differences on either set of variables. These differences would not have been predicted by psychoanalytic theory. It should also be noted that feelings of alienation did not discriminate very clearly, so casting doubt on a narrowly clinical approach to money beliefs and attitudes.

A great deal of research has attempted to investigate the emotional underpinning of money pathology. One emotion frequently linked with money is *guilt*. This has been associated with Puritan values of asceticism, denial and anhedonia (Furnham, 1990). Puritanism preaches the sinfulness of self-indulgence, waste and ostentatious consumption. Values such as conscientiousness, punctuality, thrift and sobriety caused people with these beliefs (or this socialisation) to be guilty not about the acquisition of money, but more about the spending of it. Puritanism is not antagonistic to the concept of money or receiving equitable rewards for hard work, but it opposes money gained too easily (e.g. by gambling or inheritance) or dishonestly or sinfully (and particularly frivolously) spent.

Guilt about money, or indeed about anything, can cause a sense of discomfort, dishonesty, unhappiness and even self-loathing. This guilt may be consciously felt and steps taken to reduce it. Goldberg and Lewis (1978) believe that guilt about money may result in psychosomatic complaints, which are transferred to feelings of depression. Psychoanalysts have documented cases of fear of affluence in individuals schooled in the Puritan ethic. The basis of this fear is apparently *loss of control.* Money controls the individual, it dictates how and where one lives, it can prescribe and proscribe who are one's friends and associates, and it can limit as much as liberate one's social activities. The Puritan ethic focuses on limits and the conservation of such things as time, money, resources and even emotions. If money were in superabundance there would seem to be little (and certainly less) reason to exercise any control over it. In this sense one could lose the need for control. Maintaining control – over physical factors and emotions – provides a person with the illusion of a sense of security.

Psychoanalysts believe that one reason why those who suddenly become rich may be unable to deal with their wealth is that they lack the self-discipline and, of course, the actual experience to handle it. 'Where controls have not been internalized and realistic self-discipline has not evolved, the individual is dependent upon external controls to provide a sense of security' (Goldberg and Lewis, 1978, p.75). For many individuals, the possession of large amounts of money seems to imply that they can use it irrespective of the consequences, and this uncontrolled behaviour creates anxiety. Paradoxically, if the money dries up or disappears, order and security are restored to life. Furthermore, if an individual has made sudden and dramatic changes to their life, getting rid of the money and all that it bought may mean a return to normality.

As well as being associated with guilt, money can represent *security.* Studies of the self-made, very rich in the USA have shown a much greater than chance incidence of these rich people having experienced early parental death, divorce or some other major deprivation (Cox and Cooper, 1990). Psychoanalysts believe that, in adulthood, they set out to amass so much money that they would never be stranded again. Having had to assume adult responsibilities at an early age, they may have felt the need to demonstrate both to themselves and to others their lack of need to depend on parents. The desire to amass wealth may therefore be nothing more than a quest for emotional rather than physical security.

For psychoanalysts, money greed may be related more to orality than to anality (Goldberg and Lewis, 1978). They point here to terms like 'bread' and 'dough' referring to money. The money-hungry person who seeks and devours money with little regard for social etiquette reacts to money as a starving person does to food. This behaviour, it is said, derives from a deprived infancy. Psychoanalytic writers have tried hard to categorise people in terms of the underlying dynamics of their money pathology, the most common and powerful of which are *security, power, love* and *freedom* (Goldberg and Lewis, 1978).

Forman (1987) argued that, of all the neuroses, the money neurosis is most widespread. Like all neurotic processes, it involves unresolved conflict associated with fear and anxiety that may relate directly to maladaptive, self-defeating, irrational behaviour. Money cannot buy love and affection, personal states of mind, such as inner peace, self-esteem or contentment, or particular social attributes, such as power, status or security. Forman believed that too many people believe a simple equation like 'money equals love' (or self-worth, or freedom, power or security). In his book, Forman (1987) describes the following five classic neurotic types.

1. The *miser* who hoards money, tends not to admit to being niggardly, has a terrible fear of losing funds, and tends to be distrustful, yet has trouble enjoying the benefits of money.
2. The *spendthrift* who tends to be compulsive and uncontrolled in his or her spending, particularly when depressed and feeling worthless and rejected. Spending is an instant but short-lived gratification that frequently leads to guilt.
3. The *tycoon* who is totally absorbed with money-making which is seen as the best way to gain power status and approval. They argue that the more money they have, the better control they have over their world and the happier they are likely to be.
4. The *bargain hunter* who compulsively hunts bargains even if they are not wanted because getting things for a lower price makes them feel superior. They feel angry and depressed if they have to pay the asking price or cannot bring the price down significantly.
5. The *gambler* who feels exhilarated and optimistic when taking chances. They tend to find it difficult to stop even when they are losing, because of the sense of power they achieve when winning.

Forman considers in some detail several of the more fascinating neuroses associated with everyday financial and economic affairs such as saving, paying insurance and taxes, making a will and using credit cards. He does not speculate directly on the relationship between those various money complexes, appearing to suggest that they are all related to the same basic pathology. He developed a forced-choice (ipsative) questionnaire and a way for individuals to self-diagnose, the idea being that if one agrees with the majority of items in any one section, one may have that pathology.

Furnham (1996) has undertaken some empirical evaluation of the Forman (1987) scale and typology. He argued that most psychological research in this area appears to have concentrated on a limited number of 'money complexes', and hence this multidimensional questionnaire has the advantage of examining different manifestations of the same disorder. It is possible that the five money types outlined by Forman (1987) are related to other established psychological variables. Thus one may expect *spendthrift* to be positively correlated, but all other scales to be negatively correlated, with the Protestant work ethic (Furnham, 1990). It is also likely that *miser* and *tycoon* are positively correlated with neuroticism. However, it is probable that individual scores on these five money-attitudes subscales are most closely correlated with socio-political beliefs and attitudes to work, both of which are partly concerned with the generation and distribution of wealth (Furnham, 1984, 1990).

The subscale of money pathology appeared to indicate that, while being a miser or a spendthrift seemed to be unrelated to the other subscales, they were moderately positively correlated with and all systematically related to the simple 20-item sanity scale (where a low score indicated 'insanity'). Indeed, it was this scale that was most clearly and strongly related to the various attitudinal scores. However, the totalled money pathology scale (including all five specific money pathology subscales, which totalled 50 items) was also correlated with many of the work- and economics-related beliefs and values scales. Thus despite the attempts of clinical, organisational and social psychologists to taxonomise different money-related attitudes, the psychometric properties of many of their devised questionnaires remain relatively weak.

However, it was the regressional analysis which demonstrated that the more people endorse the work ethic, the more they are indeed 'obsessed' by money. In fact, the second chapter of Weber's monograph is almost exclusively concerned with the amassing (but not the spending) of money.

These results are similar to those of Furnham (1984), who also found that political beliefs (in that case, voting patterns), the Protestant work ethic (PWE) and sex were statistically significant correlates of money attitudes. Using canonical correlations, he found that females who endorsed the work ethic tended to be more obsessed with money. Similarly, Lynn (1994) found that Protestant work ethic beliefs and attitudes to saving money were closely related. He also observed consistent sex differences in attitudes to money. Tang's (1992, 1993) research on money ethics also established the link between attitudes to money and the work ethic beliefs.

Furnham (1990), in his review of the work ethic, noted that both a historical view of the writing on the Protestant work ethic and what limited empirical research there has been suggest that PWE beliefs are associated with security, collecting, miserliness and saving, but also with autonomy and power. At the heart of the Protestant work ethic is an obsession with money as a sign of success (and grace), and hence a powerful psychological indicator of PWE beliefs.

Tang (1992, 1993, 1995) and colleagues (Tang and Gilbert, 1995; Tang et al., 1997) have done much empirical research on what Tang called the Money Ethic Scale (MES). He believes that attitudes to money have an *affective* component (good, evil), a *cognitive* component (how it relates to achievement, respect, freedom) and a *behavioural* component. He set out to develop and validate a clear, straightforward, multidimensional scale.

Tang and Gilbert (1995) found that intrinsic job satisfaction was related to the concept that money is symbolic of freedom and power, while extrinsic job satisfaction was related to the notion that money is not an evil. He found that his (mental health) workers with self-reported low organisational stress tended to believe that money was inherently good. Furthermore, those who claimed that they budgeted their money carefully tended to be older, with lower income, higher self-esteem and low organisational stress. As before, those who endorsed Protestant work ethic values tended to believe that money represented an achievement and was inherently good.

Using a shortened version of the scale, Tang (1995) found many correlates of the total score, which indicates people's general positive attitude towards money – it represents success, not evil, yet they budget carefully. He found that individuals who showed a very positive attitude to money expressed strong economic and political values but not religious values, and they tended to be older, with lower income. Thus individuals who value money tend to show greater dissatisfaction, no doubt because of the perceived inequity between pay reality and expectations. Tang (1995) argues that there are various rewards for productivity, including job redesign, goal-setting, contingent payment and participation in decision-making – for individuals who endorse the money ethic are those who are motivated by extrinsic rewards, and will be most interested in and satisfied by profit- or gain-sharing bonuses and other contingent payment methods of compensation.

Certainly the literature on money beliefs and behaviours does appear to indicate that they are related to personality (particularly clinical) traits. If indeed consumption is strongly related to money attitudes, it seems logical that personality traits will have an important role in our understanding of patterns of consumption.

9.8 CONCLUSION

The idea that personality is related to regular patterns of consumption, of possession acquisition and display, of aesthetic preference and of money attitudes has led to piecemeal research in the area for over 50 years. Overall the results have been disappointing, with personality appearing to account for a disappointingly small amount of variance. As has been noted many times, there are both theoretical and methodological reasons for this. The primary reason lies in the measurement of consumption – it is expensive, difficult and time-consuming to obtain reliable figures on individual patterns of purchasing and consumption over time. Collecting data on brand preference and purchasing, shop usage and actual consumption of products is not easy. It is this data which needs to be related to personality measures that are both reliable and valid, *and* which one expects for theoretical reasons to be related to consumption behaviour.

It should be acknowledged that many other variables are related to consumer behaviour. There are cultural, social and situational influences on consumer preference, and equally there are household, salesperson and advertising influences on this behaviour. Customers need money (or credit) and product availability, as well as the will to purchase goods. Personality traits may relate to many of these factors independently – sensitivity to advertising, preference for certain stores, susceptibility to influence by sales staff, etc.

Researchers in consumer behaviour have long been interested in consumer motivation, values and involvement. A better and more up-to-date understanding of the personality trait literature would significantly enhance their findings in this important area.

REFERENCES

Albanese, P. (1990) Personality consumer behaviour and marketing research. *Research in Consumer Behaviour* 4, 1–41.

Assael, H. (1987) *Consumer behaviour and marketing action*. Boston, MA: Kent.

Belk, R. (1991) The ineluctable mysteries of possessions. *Journal of Social Behaviour and Personality* 6, 17–53.

Bell, S., Holbrook, M. and Soloman, M. (1991) Combining aesthetic and social value to explain preferences for product styles with the incorporation of personality and ensemble effects. *Journal of Social Behaviour and Personality* 6, 243–74.

Black, D. (1996) Compulsive buying: a review. *Journal of Clinical Psychiatry* 57, 50–55.

Boone, L. (1970) The search for the consumer innovator. *Journal of Business* 43, 135–40.

Bridgeman, J. and Slade, P. (1996) Shoplifting and eating disorders. *European Disorders Review* 4, 133–43.

Brody, R. and Cunningham, S. (1968) Personality variables and the consumer decision process. *Journal of Marketing Research* 5, 50–57.

Browne, B. and Kaldenberg, D. (1997) Conceptualizing self-monitoring links to materialism and product involvement. *Journal of Consumer Marketing* 14, 31–42.

Bruce, G. and Wilt, R. (1970) Personality correlates of innovative behaviours. *Journal of Marketing Research* 7, 259–60.

Burroughs, W., Drews, D. and Hallman, W. (1991) Predicting personality from personal possessions. *Journal of Social Behaviour and Personality* 6, 147–63.

Burt, C. (1933) *How the mind works*. London: Allen & Unwin.

Burt, C. (1939) The factorial analysis of emotional traits. *Character and Personality* 7, 238–54, 285–90.

Cardinet, J. (1958) Préférences esthétiques et personnalité. *Année Psychologique* 58, 45–69.

Child, I.L. (1962) Personal preferences as an expression of aesthetic sensitivity. *Journal of Personality* 30, 496–512.

Child, I.L. (1965) Personality correlates of aesthetic judgement in college students. *Journal of Personality* 33, 476–511.

Claycamp, H. (1965) Characteristics of owners of thrift deposits in commercial and savings and loan associations. *Journal of Marketing Research* 2, 163–70.

Cohen, J. (1968) The role of personality in consumer behaviour. In Kassargian, H. and Robertson, T. (eds), *Perspectives in consumer behaviour*. Glenview, IL: Scott Foresman, 220–34.

Cohen, J. and Golden, E. (1972) Informational social influence and product evaluation. *Journal of Applied Psychology* 50, 54–9.

Cox, C. and Cooper, C. (1990) *High flyers*. Oxford: Basil Blackwell.

Dolich, I. (1969) Congruence relationships between self-images and product brands. *Journal of Marketing Research* 5, 50–63.

Engel, J., Blackwell, R. and Miniard, O. (1995) *Consumer behaviour*. Fort Worth, TX: Dryden Press.

Evans, F. (1959) Psychological and objective factors in the production of brand choice: Ford vs. Chevrolet. *Journal of Business* 32, 340–69.

Eysenck, H.J. (1940) The general factor in aesthetic judgements. *British Journal of Psychology* 31, 94–102.

Eysenck, H.J. (1941) 'Type'-factors in aesthetic judgements. *British Journal of Psychology* 31, 262–70.

Fenichel, O. (1947) The drive to amass wealth. In Fenichel, O. and Rapoport, O. (eds), *The collected papers of O. Fenichel*. New York: Norton.

Forman, N. (1987) *Mind over money*. Toronto: Doubleday.

Foxall, G. (1980) *Consumer behaviour: a practical guide*. London: Croom Helm.

Foxall, G. and Goldsmith, R. (1989) Personality and consumer research: another look. *Journal of the Market Research Society* 30, 111–25.

Fry, J. (1971) Personality variables and cigarette brand choice. *Journal of Marketing Research* 8, 298–304.

Furnham, A. (1984) Many sides of the coin: the psychology of money usage. *Personality and Individual Differences* 5, 95–100.

Furnham, A. (1990) *The Protestant work ethic*. London: Routledge.

Furnham, A. (1996) Attitudinal correlates and demographic predictors of monetary beliefs and behaviours. *Journal of Organizational Behaviour* 17, 375–89.

Furnham, A. and Argyle, M. (1998) *The psychology of money*. London: Routledge.

Furnham, A. and Avison, M. (1998) Personality and preference for surreal art. *Personality and Individual Differences* 23, 923–35.

Furnham, A.F. and Bunyan, M. (1988) Personality and art preferences. *European Journal of Personality* 2, 67–74.

Goldberg, H. and Lewis, R. (1978) *Money madness: the psychology of saving, spending, loving and hating money*. London: Springwood.

Grubb, E. and Hupp, G. (1968) Perception of self-generalized stereotypes and brand selection. *Journal of Marketing Research* 5, 58–63.

Gunter, B. and Furnham, A. (1992) *Consumer profiles: an introduction to psychographics*. London: Routledge.

Gutman, J. and Mills, M. (1982) Fashion life-style, self-concept, shopping orientation, and store patronage: an integrative analysis. *Journal of Retailing* 58, 64–86.

Haire, M. (1950) Projective techniques in marketing research. *Journal of Marketing* 14, 649–56.

Hanley, A. and Wilhelm, M. (1992) Compulsive buying: an exploration into self-esteem and money attitudes. *Journal of Economic Psychology* 13, 5–11.

Hawkins, D., Best, R. and Coney, K. (1996) *Consumer behaviour: implications for marketing strategy.* Boston, MA: Irwin.

Holbrook, M. (1993) Nostalgia and consumption preferences. *Journal of Consumer Research* 20, 245–56.

Holbrook, M. and Schindler, R. (1994) Age, sex, and attitude toward the past as predictors of consumers' aesthetic tastes for cultural products. *Journal of Marketing Research* 31, 417–22.

Jackson, D. (1967) *Manuals for the Personality Research Form.* London, Ontario: University of Western Ontario.

Juhasz, J. and Paxson, L. (1978) Personality and preference for painting style. *Perceptual and Motor Skills* 46, 347–9.

Kassarjian, H. (1971) Personality and consumer behaviour: a review. *Journal of Marketing Research* 8, 409–18.

Kassarjian, H. and Sheffet, M. (1991) Personality and consumer behaviour: an update. In Kassarjian, H. and Robertson, T. (eds), *Perspectives in consumer behaviour.* Englewood Cliffs, NJ: Prentice Hall, 281–303.

Kernan, J. (1971) The CAD instrument in behaviour diagnosis. Proceedings of the second ACR Conference, 307–12.

Klein, M. (1983) *Discover your real self.* London: Hutchinson.

Knapp, R. and Wulff, A. (1963) Preferences for abstract and representational art. *Journal of Social Psychology* 60, 255–62.

Kopenen, A. (1960) Personality characteristics of purchasers. *Journal of Advertising Research* 1, 6–12.

Kuehn, A. (1963) Demonstration of a relationship between psychological factors and brand choice. *Journal of Business* 36, 237–41.

Lastovicka, J. and Joachimsthaler, E. (1988) Improving the detection of personality–behaviour relationships in consumer research. *Journal of Consumer Research* 14, 583–7.

Lim, V. and Teo, T. (1997) Sex, money and financial hardship. *Journal of Economic Psychology* 18, 369–86.

Litle, P. and Zuckerman, M. (1986) Sensation-seeking and music preferences. *Personality and Individual Differences* 4, 575–8.

Luft, J. (1957) Monetary value and the perception of persons. *Journal of Social Psychology* 46, 245–51.

Lynn, R. (1994) *The secret of the miracle economy.* London: Social Affairs Unit.

McClure, R. (1984) The relationship between money attitudes and overall pathology. *Psychology* 21, 4–6.

Maital, M. (1982) *Minds, markets and money: the psychological foundations of economic behaviour.* New York: Basic Books.

Marcus, A. (1965) Obtaining group measures from personality test scores. *Psychological Reports* 17, 523–31.

Massy, W., Frank, R. and Lodahl, R. (1968) *Purchasing behaviour and personal attributes.* Philadelphia, PA: University of Pennsylvania Press.

Mooradian, T. and Oliver, J. (1996) Shopping motives and the five-factor model. *Psychological Reports* 78, 579–92.

Moore, D., Harris, W. and Chen, H. (1995) Affect intensity: an individual difference response to advertising appeals. *Journal of Consumer Research* 22, 154–64.

Netemeyer, R., Burton, S. and Lichtenstein, D. (1995) Trait aspects of vanity. *Journal of Consumer Research* 21, 612–26.

Noerager, J. (1979) An assessment of CAO. *Journal of Marketing Research* **16**, 53–9.

O'Guinn, T. and Faber, R. (1989) Compulsive buying: a phenomenological exploration. *Journal of Consumer Research* **16**, 147–57.

Peel, E.A. (1945) On identifying aesthetic types. *British Journal of Psychology* **35**, 61–9.

Plummer, J. (1985) How personality makes a difference. *Journal of Advertising Research* **24**, 27–30.

Raju, P. (1980) Optimum stimulation level: its relationship to personality demographics and exploratory behaviour. *Journal of Consumer Research* **7**, 272–82.

Richin, M. and Dawson, S. (1992) A consumer values orientation for materialism and its measurement: scale development and validation. *Journal of Consumer Research* **19**, 303–16.

Rim, Y. (1982) Personality and attitudes connected with money. Paper presented at the European Conference on Economic Psychology, Edinburgh, August 1982.

Robertoux, P., Carlier, M. and Chaguiboff, J. (1971) Preference for non-objective art: personal and psychological determiners. *British Journal of Psychology* **62**, 105–10.

Robertson, T. and Myers, J. (1969) Personality correlates of opinion leadership and innovative buying behaviour. *Journal of Marketing Research* **6**, 164–8.

Rubinstein, W. (1981) Survey report on money. *Psychology Today* **5**, 24–44.

Schiffman, L. and Kanuk, L. (1983) *Consumer behaviour.* Englewood Cliffs, NJ: Prentice-Hall.

Snyder, A. (1974) The self-monitoring of expressive behaviour. *Journal of Personality and Social Psychology* **30**, 526–75.

Snyder, M. (1987) *Public appearances, private realities: the psychology of self-monitoring.* New York: M.H. Freeman.

Sparks, D. and Tucker, W. (1971) A multivariate analysis of personality and product use. *Journal of Marketing Research* **8**, 67–70.

Sproles, E. and Sproles, G. (1990) Consumer decision-making styles as a function of individual learning styles. *Journal of Consumer Affairs* **24**, 134–7.

Steenkamp, J. and Baumgartner, H. (1992) The role of optimum stimulation level in exploratory consumer behaviour. *Journal of Consumer Research* **19**, 434–48.

Tang, T. (1992) The meaning of money revisited. *Journal of Organizational Behaviour* **13**, 197–202.

Tang, T. (1993) The meaning of money. *Journal of Organizational Behaviour* **14**, 93–9.

Tang, T. (1995) The development of a short money ethic scale. *Personality and Individual Differences* **19**, 809–16.

Tang, T. and Gilbert, P. (1995) Attitudes towards money as related to intrinsic and extrinsic job satisfaction, stress, and work-related attitudes. *Personality and Individual Differences* **19**, 327–32.

Tang, T., Furnham, A. and Davis, E. (1997) A cross-cultural comparison of the money ethic. Unpublished paper.

Tobacyck, J.J., Myers, H. and Bailey, L. (1981) Field-dependence, sensation-seeking and preference for paintings. *Journal of Personality Assessment* **45**, 270–77.

Tucker, W. and Painter, J. (1961) Personality and product use. *Journal of Applied Psychology* **45**, 325–9.

Vitz, P. and Johnson, D. (1965) Masculinity of smokers and the masculinity of cigarette images. *Journal of Applied Psychology* **49**, 155–9.

Webster, F. and Von Pechmann, F. (1970) A replication of the shopping-list study. *Journal of Marketing* **34**, 61–3.

Wells, W. and Beard, A. (1973) Personality and consumer behaviour. In Ward, S. and Robertson, T. (eds), *Consumer behaviour.* Englewood Cliffs, NJ: Prentice-Hall.

Westfall, R. (1962) Psychological factors in predicting brand choice. *Journal of Marketing* **26**, 1–17.

White, I. (1967) The perception of value in products. In Newman, J. (ed.), *On knowing the consumer.* New York: Wiley, 90–106.

Wilkie, W. (1990) *Consumer behaviour.* New York: Wiley.

Wilson, G.D., Ausman, J. and Matthews, T.R. (1973) Conservatism and art preferences. *Journal of Personality and Social Psychology* **25**, 286–9.

Wiseman. T. (1974) *The money motive.* London: Hodder & Stoughton.

Worthing, P., Venkatesan, M. and Smith, S. (1973) Personality and product use revisited. *Journal of Applied Psychology* **57**, 179–83.

Yamauchi, K. and Templer, D. (1982) The development of a money attitude scale. *Journal of Personality Assessment* **46**, 522–8.

Zaleski, Z. (1984) Sensation-seeking and preference for emotional visual stimuli. *Personality and Individual Differences* **5**, 609–11.

Zuckerman, M., Neary, R.S. and Brustman, B.A. (1970) Sensation-seeking scale correlates in experience (smoking, drugs, alcohol, 'hallucinations' and sex) and preference for complexity (designs) In *Proceedings of the 78th Annual Convention of the American Psychological Association.* Washington, DC: American Psychological Association, 317–18.

Zuckerman, M., Eysenck, S.B.G. and Eysenck, H.J. (1978) Sensation-seeking in England and America: cross-cultural, age and sex comparisons. *Journal of Consulting and Clinical Psychology* **46**, 139–49.

Zuckerman, M., Ulrich, R.S. and McLaughlin, J. (1993) Sensation-seeking and reactions to nature paintings. *Personality and Individual Differences* **15**, 563–76.

10

Conclusion

INTRODUCTION

This book has attempted a very different approach for a personality text. As noted in the introduction, all personality theorists attempt to describe and explain how personality relates to various aspects of social behaviour (e.g. health, work, leisure, consumption). It is possible to construct a grid with theorists represented by the rows and behaviours by the columns. Of course some writers have little interest in, or not much to say about, certain specific areas, so there are gaps in the grid. Equally, many accept that personality factors do not relate equally strongly to all aspects of social behaviour. Psychologists, for instance, do not write much about work behaviours. What most textbooks do is construct the chapters/sections of the book around the rows (theorists), whereas this book attempts to do so via the columns (social behaviours).

This final chapter is divided into three sections. The first section deals with some of the interesting but neglected areas that do not fit neatly into the other chapters of the book. Hence we have sections entitled 'personality and creativity', 'personality and handwriting' and 'personality and humour'. It is important to note that personality and individual differences may *not* be powerfully predictive of *all* forms of social behaviour. Thus we have reviewed a section on personality and graphology because, although many people believe that personality can be assessed from handwriting, all of the reliable available evidence suggests that it cannot. It is impossible to cover all areas of human behaviour in which personality differences have a direct impact, but some of the more interesting and currently researched areas will be considered.

The second section of this chapter considers some of the issues concerning the measurement of personality. Do people fake on personality tests? If so, what can we do about it? Are people accurate at predicting their own scores or those of others? Can people pick out their correct scores derived from personality tests? These issues are relevant for both measurement and an understanding of some of the processes underlying personality.

The third section considers briefly the circumstances under which personality test scores do and do not predict social behaviour.

10.2 PERSONALITY AND CREATIVITY

Can creativity be measured? Can it be taught? Is creativity closely linked to personality traits? Why are some people more creative than others? Are particularly creative people prone to madness? As Loehle points out: 'The path of creativity is strewn with the bones of those consumed by the vultures of mediocrity, accountability, and responsibility. One cannot schedule creative breakthroughs, budget for them, or prove them in advance to a review panel' (Loehle, 1990, p.129).

There is much disagreement and confusion in the literature with regard to the term 'creativity'. Several authors have come to the conclusion that 'creativity is almost infinite' (Torrance, 1974). A central feature of the definition is that creativity is the ability to produce work that is both novel and innovative. Essentially, creativity denotes a person's capacity to produce new or original ideas, insights, inventions or artistic products which are accepted by experts as being of aesthetic, scientific, social or technological value. Other peripheral features of the definition include the idea that creativity puts different, disparate ideas together, and that it has the power to stir the emotions (Lubart, 1994). Judgement about creativity inevitably involves social consensus, as there is no absolute, objective definition. There are subtle differences between a creative performance, the creative person and creative potential.

However, four major approaches to the study of creativity can be clearly identified:

1. the *creative process* approach, which focuses on the cognitive factors underlying creativity;
2. the *creative person* approach, which focuses on the personality correlates of creativity;
3. the *creative product* approach, which emphasises the importance of the creative products as a defining criterion in the study of creativity;
4. the *creative situation* approach, which focuses on the environmental, social and situational factors that might influence creative production (Brown, 1989; Stumpf, 1995).

Western definitions of creativity emphasise a product-oriented, originality-based phenomenon, whereas many Eastern views stress creativity as a way of expressing an inner truth, or in terms of self-growth.

Lubart (1994), in reviewing various ideas about the sources of creativity, has described five different approaches. The *mystical* conception sees creativity as divine intervention. The *psychoanalytic* approach sees creativity as arising from the tension between conscious reality and unconscious drives. The popular *cognitive* approach stresses the quality and organisation of a person's knowledge and thinking style. The *social psychological* approach focuses on the match between personality variables (independence of judgement, self-confidence, attraction to complexity, aesthetic orientation and risk-taking) as well as motivational and socio-cultural environmental factors thought to be linked to creativity. Finally, the *confluences* or *synthesis* approach attempts to explain how the (agreed) components of creativity (i.e. intelligence, knowledge, thinking style, personality, motivation and environment) interact to produce creative people and products.

The fact that creativity has been operationalised in so many ways is shown by the diversity of the existing methods for measuring it. Hocevar and Bachelor (1989) and Lubart (1994) presented a taxonomy of the available measures, which consisted of the following eight categories: divergent thinking tests; attitudes and interest inventories; personality inventories; biographical inventories; ratings by peers, teachers and supervisors; judgements of products; ratings of eminence; and self-reported creative activities.

Due to the different ways in which researchers have approached creativity, a major methodological problem has emerged, namely the 'process versus product criterion issue' (Brown, 1989). A disagreement has developed around the question of whether creativity should be viewed as a *cognitive ability* that is *normally distributed* in the general population, i.e. as a trait, or whether it should be defined in terms of *exceptional real-life creative production* which very few individuals manage to achieve.

The advocates of the trait approach have attempted to discover the essence of the creative process and to develop appropriate instruments for measuring it. Several concepts have been introduced as being 'at the heart' of the creative process. As Brown (1989) noted, since the early twentieth century creativity has been viewed as (1) an aspect of intelligence, (2) a largely unconscious process, (3) one of the stages of problem-solving and (4) an associative process (Guilford, 1956; Wallach and Kogan, 1965; Torrance, 1974). 'Divergence of thinking' (DT), a construct originally presented by Guilford (1956), was considered by supporters of the trait approach to be the basic thinking style which characterises creativity, consisting of abilities such as 'fluency', 'originality', 'flexibility' and 'elaboration'.

More recent approaches have been componential, attempting to understand creative thinking and production in terms of specific processes. Thus Feldhusen (1995) argued that there were three elements which were essential, and which operated interactively to determine creativity. These were meta-cognitive skills (guessing causes, redefining new use of familiar actions, and seeing the implications of some actions), a knowledge base, and personality (defined by their terms of motivation, attitudes, values and styles). With regard to traits, they isolated high energy levels (drive), independence, positive self-concept and sensitivity to details and patterns.

Those authors who support the notion that real-life achievement is the criterion for creativity believe that 'creativity has no meaning except in relation to the creative product' (Fox, 1963; cited in Brown, 1989). They criticise the trait approach on both methodological and theoretical grounds (Helson *et al.*, 1995). Commenting on the value of DT tests, Brown (1989) argued that:

1. the tests are so closely related to particular theoretical viewpoints that criterion and construct validity are interwoven;
2. any process that increases productivity in general will increase the scores on DT tests;
3. extraneous factors may determine performance on DT tests;
4. there is little evidence of criterion validity.

Along the same lines, Hocevar and Bachelor (1989), who criticised the measures used in the study of creativity, suggested that researchers should focus only on those studies that involve a measure of *real-life creativity*. Such measures may be of four kinds:

1. eminence based on overt production criteria, such as patent awards and number of publications;
2. eminence based on professional recognition criteria;
3. judgements of products;
4. social recognition criteria, such as judgements by teachers, peers and supervisors (Hocevar and Bachelor, 1989).

Woodman and Schoenfeldt (1989) have pointed out that studies of person-ality characteristics associated with creativity have waxed and waned in popularity over the years. Attempts have been made to delineate the core characteristics of the creative personality, yet despite the convergence of results, it has proved difficult to generalise the findings across various creative fields of endeavour. They do note a move from an interest in traits to an interest in cognitive styles or abilities. However, they present an interactionist model with five components:

• antecedent conditions such as birth order and early socialisation;
• personality variables which are divided into traits (locus of control, dogmatism, autonomy), cognitive styles (divergent thinking, perceptual openness) and person factors (values, intention to behave);
• situational values such as distal physical and cultural variables, as well as proximate influences such as role models, organisational rewards and punishments;
• creative behaviours, which can take many forms;
• consequences – which may of course involve the non-recognition of genuinely creative work, and vice versa.

Although these interactionist models seem intuitively appealing, they represent little more than a long list of variables without any description of the creative process itself. However, Eysenck's (1994) work is different. He suggests that there are three major variables that interactively relate to creativity as an achievement. These are cognitive variables (intelligence, knowledge, technical skills, special talents), environmental variables (politico-religious, cultural, socio-economic and educational factors) and personality variables (internal motivation, confidence, non-conformity and trait creativity). For Eysenck, it is the process of over-inclusive or allusive thinking that characterises both psychotic and creative thinking.

> What do we find? Creativity can be measured directly as a trait, but this only correlates moderately with creative achievement; it is necessary but not a sufficient ingredient. It interacts in a probably multiplicative fashion with other variables like intelligence, motivation, and personality. Creativity is indexed by certain cognitive styles (overinclusiveness, allusive thinking, looseness or 'slippage' of ideation), which increases fluency and originality. This type of cognitive style is closely related to psychoticism, and accounts for the many links between psychosis and creativity. Psychosis as such is of course likely to *prevent* creative achievement, in spite of being related to the trait of creativity; it constitutes a negative factor in the multiplicative relationship between the factors making for creative achievement.
>
> Psychoticism is linked directly with both trait creativity and achievement creativity, the link being overinclusiveness.
>
> (Eysenck, 1994, p.232)

Various studies have looked specifically at the relationship between personality and creativity using a variety of methods (Stavridou and Furnham, 1996). Gelade (1997) gave the five factor NEO Personality Inventory (NEO-PI) to a group of advertising and design creatives, and to a comparable group of professionals and managers in occupations that were not apparently creative. The results confirmed the hypotheses. Compared to the 'non-creatives', the 'commercial creatives' were more neurotic (particularly in terms of angry hostility, depression, self-consciousness, impulsivity and vulnerability), more extraverted (especially in terms of gregariousness and excitement-seeking), more open to experiences (particularly fantasy, aesthetics and feelings) and less conscientious (particularly in terms of overall competence, order, self-discipline and deliberation).

McCrae (1987) found that divergent thinking – one index of creativity – was consistently associated with self-reports and peer ratings of *openness to experience*, but not with extraversion, neuroticism, agreeableness or conscientiousness. However, he notes:

> Creative ability does not inevitably lead to recognized creativity, and a variety of personality traits may be involved in being conceived as creative. Conscientious individuals may complete their creative projects more often;

extraverts may exhibit them more readily; adjusted individuals may be less distracted from creative work by personal problems. . . . smart extraverts make intelligent conversation, smart introverts read difficult books; conscientious individuals use their intellectual gifts, lackadaisical individuals do not. Openness to experience and divergent thinking abilities may also interact as mutually necessary conditions for creativity, the former providing the inclination and the latter providing the aptitude for original thinking.

(McCrae, 1987, p.1264)

Using a battery of creativity tests, Aguilar-Alonso (1996) found as predicted that psychoticism and extraversion were significant predictors. High P scorers were more verbally creative and flexible than low P scorers. Moreover, extraverts were more original, fluent and flexible than introverts, but the neuroticism factor was uncorrelated.

Eysenck (1993) pointed out that the criterion conflict (trait vs. achievement creativity) is partly reinforced by the fact that there is a discrepancy between the shape of the distribution of creativity when measured by tests of divergent thinking, compared to when it is measured as unique real-life achievement. Creativity as a trait measured by DT tests shows a normal, Gaussian-type distribution. However, creativity as achievement shows a skewed (J-shaped) distribution which follows the Price law (Price, 1963). This means that most of the creative achievements in a field are made by just a few individuals. Eysenck (1993) pointed out the similarity of this distribution discrepancy to that between intelligence and income. Just as intelligence is a necessary but not sufficient causal condition for high income, in the same way trait creativity (fluency, originality, etc.) is a necessary but not sufficient condition for achievement creativity. Eysenck (1993) went further and suggested a model in which, apart from trait creativity, many other factors (cognitive, environmental and personality related) are acting *synergistically* (in a multiplicative way) to give rise to real-life creative achievement. This model is able to explain why DT tests do not correlate strongly with achievement criteria.

A similar model which also synthesises a variety of previous research in the field was suggested by Amabile (1983). She argued that creativity can best be conceptualised as a behaviour resulting from a particular constellation of personal characteristics, cognitive abilities and social environments. Within models such as the above-mentioned ones, trait creativity can be seen as one of the important cognitive aspects of creative behaviour and, as such, it is an interesting and promising construct in its own right that merits attention and study.

The study of the personality characteristics of creative people has been one of the main approaches to creativity (Brown, 1989). Personality has been regarded as a major driving force leading to creative performance, and the synthetic models of Amabile (1983) and Eysenck (1993), presented above, both consider personality factors to be important for creative achievement.

Eysenck (1993) suggested that personality can be seen as a link between trait and achievement creativity, a link which 'translates' creative abilities into real-life creative performance.

Mansfield and Busse (1981) have stressed the importance of various developmental variables which they claim are predictive of creativity. These include low emotionality of the parent–child relationship, parental autonomy-fostering, parental intellectual stimulation, and receiving an apprenticeship.

For over 30 years, studies have examined the relationship between creativity and psychopathology (Cattell and Drevdahl, 1955; MacKinnon, 1962; Dellas and Gaier, 1970; Goertzel et al., 1978; Jamisson, 1988). Most of these studies concluded that there are clear signs of psychopathology (especially psychoses) among famous creators, and they pointed to a link between creativity and psychopathology, a link that is sometimes considered to be so powerful that it can almost predict abnormal personality for all creative geniuses. Eysenck (1993) pointed out that much of the debate about whether or not creative geniuses are psychotic could easily be aborted by disregarding the false assumption that psychiatric abnormality is categorical rather than dimensional. According to Eysenck and Eysenck (1976), psychopathology can be conceptualised as an exaggeration/extension of underlying personality traits. Accordingly, psychosis lies at the extreme end of the distribution of 'psychoticism', a hypothetical dispositional personality trait which is conceived of as a continuum 'ranging from normal to psychotic'. Psychoticism has been described as consisting of several characteristics, one of which is creativity. Other characteristics include aggressiveness, impersonal and anti-social behaviour, coldness, egocentricity, impulsivity, unempathic behaviour and tough-mindedness. The assumption of Eysenck (1993), therefore, is that creative people possess the personality characteristics of psychoticism at a higher level than the mean normal individual and that, if adequate control is missing or if they experience stressful situations, then they may develop psychosis. Eysenck's (1993) position can be summarised as follows. Provided that (1) there is a link between psychosis and creativity and (2) psychoticism taps a unitary dimension underlying susceptibility to psychotic illness, then it is postulated that the important personality factor which acts synergistically with trait creativity (originality) and which may – under favourable environmental conditions – lead to real-life creative achievement, is psychoticism. In fact, numerous studies have found a correlation between psychoticism and trait creativity (Woody and Claridge, 1977; Rawlings, 1985), and also between psychoticism and achievement–creativity (Rushton, 1990).

What then is the common factor (or factors) underlying this relationship between psychoticism and the creative process? It could be argued that common *information-processing patterns* can be found in both creative people and psychotics. Close examination of the theories developed in order to explain the cognitive deficit in psychotics (Hemsley, 1991) and those relating to the cognitive aspects of creativity (Martindale, 1981) reveals many similarities.

Most of the theories relating to the cognitive deficit in schizophrenia seem to propose that there is a deficit in selective attention mechanisms, which results in schizophrenics being unable to inhibit irrelevant information from entering consciousness (Hemsley, 1991). Consequently, many unrelated ideas become interconnected, resulting in a 'widening of the associative horizons' (Eysenck, 1993) of schizophrenics. Evidence that schizophrenics, as well as normals who obtain high scores on psychoticism scales, are characterised by 'wide associative horizons', i.e. they produce more unusual associations between words and ideas compared to normals and low-psychoticism scorers, comes from a significant number of studies (Miller and Chapman, 1983).

Many studies have directly examined the hypothesis that a mechanism of reduced cognitive inhibition occurring during selective attention is responsible for the 'widening' of associative connections. Most of these studies have used a 'negative priming' (Tipper, 1985) paradigm to measure inhibition. Negative priming refers to the delay in responding to a current target object when this object has been a distracter to be inhibited on a previous display. In other words, if an ignored object on a prime display is the same as the object to be named on a subsequent probe display, naming latencies are impaired.

Bullen and Hemsley (1984), using a negative-priming word task and the Eysenck Personality Questionnaire (EPQ) as a measure of psychotic tendencies, found a significant negative correlation between psychoticism (P) and the magnitude of the inhibitory negative-priming effect. High-P scorers showed reduced cognitive inhibition compared to low-P scorers. No other correlations between the negative-priming task and any of the rest of the personality scales of the EPQ were obtained.

Beech et al. (1989) studied the effect of chlorpromazine (a drug routinely administered to reduce schizophrenic symptomatology) on negative priming. They found that, although negative priming was observed in both the drug and the placebo conditions, the effect was stronger in the drug condition. A drug which reduces the symptoms of schizophrenia was found to increase cognitive inhibition.

Theories developed to explain the creative process show many similarities to the theoretical views about schizophrenia. A number of authors have suggested that the creative process is an associative one. Mednick (1962) proposed that individuals who show low creativity have a small number of strong, stereotyped associative responses to a given stimulus, compared to highly creative individuals. Wallach (1970) suggested that what is important in creativity is the generating of associates, and that attention deployment is the process underlying this generation. Creative individuals are able to attend to many aspects of a given stimulus, and thus produce more and more varied associations. The similarity of the theories mentioned above to the notion of 'wide associative horizons' which characterise schizophrenics is more than clear. Martindale (1981) postulated that creative people have a high resting level of activation, and that they are oversensitive to stimuli. However, they also have a low level of inhibition, so that the more they are stimulated, the more their level of arousal drops, favouring creative performance. Again, the notions of reduced inhibition and mood fluctuation (arousal levels rising and falling) are common notions in the literature on schizophrenia.

A number of studies have reported results which support the above theories. MacKinnon (1962), in his study of architects, found that rated creativity correlated by 0.50 with a measure of unusualness of mental associations on a word association test. Similarly, Gough (1976) reported that the scores on two word association tests – a general one and a scientific word-list – correlated with rated creativity in a sample of engineering students and industrial reward scientists (cited in Eysenck, 1993). Andreasen and Powers (1975) administered the Goldstein-Sheerer Objective Sorting Test to a group of highly creative writers, and found them to be 'overconclusive'.

Finally, a small number of studies have contrasted the attentional and information-processing strategies of both schizophrenics (and high-P scorers) and creative individuals. Rawlings (1985) used the EPQ, two subscales of the Wallach-Kogan (1965) creativity test and a dichotic shadowing task (as a measure of cognitive inhibition) on a group of 30 undergraduate students. The dichotic shadowing task consisted of two conditions. In the 'focused attention' condition, subjects were instructed to shadow with one ear but also to try to remember as many words as possible from the secondary channel. Inhibition was measured in terms of the number of errors (omissions and intrusions). The author found that performance on the shadowing task was positively correlated with creativity scores and with psychoticism scores on the 'divided attention' condition. However, the pattern of results was reversed on the focused attention condition and, moreover, the correlation between psychoticism and creativity was not statistically significant.

It seems, therefore, that there is no doubt that certain personality traits are important for explaining and predicting creativity. This may account for as much as one-quarter to one-third of the variance in explaining the causes of creative work. As has been pointed out, possessing certain traits, such as openness to experience or tough-mindedness (psychoticism), is probably necessary but not sufficient. To ensure that a person fulfils his or her potential, other requisite cognitive and situational variables need to be present.

10.3 PERSONALITY AND HANDWRITING

Is graphology valid? Is an individual's personality manifest/apparent in their handwriting? Although the term 'graphology' goes back to 1871, when it was first used by the French cleric *Michon*, the belief that personality is somehow manifest in handwriting existed before this date. Furnham (1988) has noted that, since the beginning of this century, there has been increasing interest in graphology. Graphology books tell one both what factors to look at (e.g. size, slant, zone, pressure) and what traits (e.g. temperament, mental, social, work and moral) are 'revealed'. There are various schools of graphology, each with a slightly different history, approach and 'theory'. However, what appears to be most obviously missing from the area is not a method of analysis so much as a theory of how or why individual differences are manifested in handwriting. For instance, is one to assume that personality traits are the result of genetic biological differences that predispose all social behaviour, including handwriting, or is handwriting style, like other social behaviours, a product of complex primary, secondary and tertiary education? Thus there is no mechanistic or process explanation for what occurs.

Eysenck and Gudjonsson (1986) believe that there appear to be two different basic approaches to the assessment of both handwriting and personality (holistic vs. analytic). This gives four basic types of analysis.

Holistic analysis of handwriting This is basically impressionistic. The graphologist, using his or her experience and insight, offers a general description of the kind of personality he or she believes the handwriting discloses.

Analytic analysis of handwriting This uses measurement of the constituents of the handwriting, such as slant, pressure, etc. These specific, objective and tabulated measures are then converted into personality assessment on the basis of a formula or code.

Holistic analysis of personality This is also impressionistic, and may be done after an interview, when a trained psychologist offers a personality description on the basis of his or her questions, observations and intuitions.

Analytic analysis of personality This involves the application of psychometrically assessed, reliable and valid personality tests (questionnaires, physiological responses to a person, and the various grade-scores obtained).

As a result of this fourfold classification there are quite different approaches to the evaluation of the validity of graphological analysis in the prediction of personality. These are as follows. *Holistic matching* is the impressionistic interpretation of writing matched with an impressionistic account of personality. *Holistic correlation* is the impressionistic interpretation of writing correlated with a quantitative assessment of personality. *Analytic matching* involves the measurement of the constituents of the handwriting matched with an impressionistic account of personality. *Analytic correlation* is the measurement of the constituents of the handwriting correlated with a quantitative assessment of personality. Most of the studies have been of the last type, but few have found any effects.

Furnham (1988) listed the conclusions drawn from six studies conducted in the 1970s and 1980s:

1. 'It was concluded that the analyst could not accurately predict personality from handwriting.' This was based on a study by Vestewig, Santee, and Moss (1976) from Wright State University, who asked six handwriting experts to rate 48 specimens of handwriting on 15 personal variables.

2. 'No evidence was found for the validity of graphological signs.' This is from Lester, McLaughlin, and Nosal (1977), who used 16 graphological signs of extraversion to try to predict from handwriting samples the extraversion of 109 subjects whose personality test scores were known.

3. 'Thus the results did not support the claim that the three handwriting measures were valid indices of extraversion.' This is based on the study by Rosenthal and Lines (1978), who attempted to correlate three graphological indices with the extraversion scores of 58 students.

4. 'There is thus little support here for the validity of graphological analysis.' This was based on a recent study by Eysenck and Gudjonsson (1986), who employed a professional graphologist to analyze handwriting from 99 subjects and then fill out personality questionnaires as she thought would have been done by the respondents.

5. 'The graphologists did not perform significantly better than a chance model.' This was the conclusion of Ben-Shaktar and colleagues (1986) at the Hebrew University, who asked graphologists to judge the profession, out of eight possibilities, of 40 successful professionals.

6. 'Although the literature on the topic suffers from significant methodological negligence, the general trend of findings is to suggest that graphology is not a viable assessment method.' This conclusion comes from Klimoski and Rafael (1983), based at Ohio State University, after a careful review of the literature.

(Furnham, 1988, p.65)

Furnham and Gunter (1987) also found far fewer correlations than would be expected by chance between 13 different measures and Eysenck's EPQ. They believed that graphological evidence was *not* related to personality, and noted:

Even if graphological analyses were valid, the *theoretical* basis of the method appears weak, non-explicit, and nonparsimonious. Furthermore, it is unclear why it should be used if clearly valid and reliable measures exist to measure the same thing (i.e. personality) more cheaply, accurately, and efficiently. Perhaps one should be forced to conclude, rather uncharacteristically for researchers, that no further work needs to be done in this field.

(Furnham and Gunter, 1987, p.434)

A more recent study using Cattell's 16 PF simply concluded:

Whilst this does not purport to be a definitive assessment of handwriting analysis of self-report personality questionnaires, it does add to the body of information that points to the superiority of the questionnaire approach and once more calls the validity of handwriting analysis into question.

(Bushnell, 1996, p.17)

More recent studies have come to the same conclusion. Edwards and Armitage (1992) found that graphologists assigned 65 per cent of scripts to the correct categories (i.e. high-flyers vs. low-flyers), but that a control group of non-graphologists had a 59 per cent success rate. They claimed their results showed that graphologists failed to substantiate claims made on their behalf.

Tett and Palmer (1997) found a high level of inter-rater agreement when coders were trained to measure specific bad handwriting elements supposedly linked to personality traits. However, when correlating these measures with a test measuring 15 normal personality traits (the Jackson Personality Inventory), they found that only 5 per cent were significant in the expected direction, and 4 per cent in the opposite direction. As before, the researchers concluded that handwriting analysis is of limited value.

Ben-Shaktar et al. (1986) conducted a major and well-controlled study, and reached the following conclusions:

1. Although it would not be surprising if it were found that sloppy handwriting characterized sloppy writers, stylized calligraphy indicated some artistic flair, and bold, energetic people had bold, energetic handwriting, there is no reason to believe that traits such as honesty, insight, leadership, responsibility, warmth, and promiscuity find any kind of expression in graphological features. ... Some may have no somatic expression in graphological features. Some may have no somatic expression at all. Indeed, if a correspondence were to be empirically found between graphological features and such traits, it would be a major theoretical challenge to account for it.

2. There are not enough constraints in graphological analysis, and the very richness of handwriting can be its downfall. Unless the graphologist makes firm commitments to the nature of the correspondence between handwriting and personality, one can find *ad hoc* corroboration for any claim.

3. The a priori intuitions supporting graphology listed above operate on a much wider range of texts than those graphologists find acceptable. As graphologists practise their craft, it appears that from a graphological viewpoint, handwriting – rather than being a robust and stable form of expressive behaviour – is actually extremely sensitive to extraneous influences that have nothing to do with personality (e.g. whether the script is copied or not, or the paper is lined or not).

4. It is noteworthy that most graphologists decline to predict the sex of the writer from handwriting, although even lay people can diagnose a writer's sex from handwriting correctly about 70% of the time. They explain this by insisting that handwriting only reveals psychological, rather than biological, gender. Although common sense would agree that some women are masculine and some men are effeminate, it would be somewhat perverse to argue against the presumption that most women must be feminine and most men masculine. Could the graphologists simply be reluctant to predict so readily verifiable – or falsifiable – a variable?

(Ben-Shaktar *et al.*, 1986, p.652)

In another review, Neter and Ben-Shaktar (1989) asked 63 graphologists and 51 non-graphologists to rate 1223 scripts. They found that psychologists with no knowledge of graphology outperformed the graphologists on all dimensions, and they suggested that the limited validity of handwriting analysis is usually based on the script's content rather than on its style.

However, the careful and comprehensive reviews by Dean (1992) and Dean *et al.* (1992) go further in attempting to examine size effects in this literature, and in trying to explain why, if the empirical research literature is almost uniformly negative, it has not shaken graphologists' or lay people's faith in this type of analysis. Dean (1992) found over 60 reliability and 140 effect size study results for his analysis. The effect size is the mean correlation (weighted by number of scripts) between personality as predicted from the handwriting (by graphologists or others), and personality determined by tests or ratings. After looking at 1519 correlations, he concluded that effect sizes are too low to be useful, and that non-graphologists are generally as good at handwriting analysis as graphologists! He admits that there *is* an effect, but suggests that at least some of it is due to content, not actual writing, and that graphology is not valid or reliable enough to be useful. As a challenge he concludes: 'Should graphologists wish to challenge the above conclusions, all they need do is present a meta-analysis of properly controlled tests that demonstrates an adequate effect size. Nothing else will do' (Dean, 1992, p.301).

Finally, Dean *et al.* (1992) attempted to explain the puzzle for many scientists – why, if all the evidence suggests that graphology is barely related to any personality variable, do clients of graphologists attest to their accuracy? They list 26 reasons why clients are convinced that graphology works, *none* of which actually requires that it is true. Interestingly, this may account for some graphologists' unshakeable beliefs in their 'art'. For various (placebo-type) reasons clients believe that graphology works, which increases the graphologists' belief in their own skill. Hence each reinforces the other, despite the possibility that there remains no validity in graphological analysis.

Thus we have a situation where many people are convinced that hand-writing is linked to personality, yet all of the good evidence suggests this is not true. As Driver *et al.* (1996) have concluded:

> While a few articles have proposed that graphology is a valid and useful selection technique, the overwhelming results of well-controlled empirical studies have been that the technique has not demonstrated acceptable validity. A review of relevant literature regarding both theory and research indicates that, while the procedure may have an intuitive appeal, graphology should not be used in a selection context.
>
> (Driver *et al.*, 1996, p.78)

10.4 PERSONALITY AND HUMOUR

Why do some people self-evidently enjoy aggressive or sexual humour, while others prefer intellectual or black humour? Is personality related to humour creation (e.g. telling jokes, making puns) and/or just appreciation of making jokes? Do people who can make us laugh have quite different personality traits to those who do not or cannot? Are professional humorists clearly distinguishable as creators vs. performers of humour, and do both differ in personality terms from amateur humorists?

The ancient Greeks saw humour as being related to the humours – clearly, sanguine types were more humorous than melancholic types. Perhaps the first psychologists to work in this area were psychoanalysts, but since World War Two there has been a sporadic interest shown by trait theorists.

Researchers in this area have considered humour creativity to be unrelated to humour appreciation. The former is concerned with perceiving and describing people, objects or situations in an incongruous way (i.e. humorously). The latter is the enjoyment of these descriptions. Thus we have four possible types, namely individuals who are high/high (frequently making witty remarks/jokes and seeking out other people or situations where there is humour), low/low (serious people who do not enjoy telling or hearing humorous stories), high/low (people who enjoy telling jokes but show little appreciation when told them by others) and low/high (people who love to laugh and do so frequently, but are not much given to creating humour) (Ziv, 1984).

Freud wrote a number of papers on humour, and was clearly fascinated by its functions, as well as by the techniques/mechanics of making jokes. Jokes, like dreams, provide an insight into the unconscious. They are important defence mechanisms, and suppressing them can lead to serious consequences. Freud divided jokes into two classes, namely the innocent/trivial and the tendentious. The latter served two major purposes – aggression (satire) or sex.

Thus the purpose of the most interesting jokes is the expression of sexual or aggressive feelings which would otherwise be barred. Furthermore, the amount and timing of laughter correspond to the psychical energy saved by not having to repress. As Kline (1977) writes: 'In jokes veritas: thus like dreams and many forms of art Freud and his followers saw jokes as a socially accepted and socially shared mechanism of expressing what is normally forbidden.'

Kline (1977) has pointed out that Freudian theory is a fecund source of testable, but infrequently well tested, hypotheses.

1. Individuals finding aggressive jokes funniest will be those in whom aggression is normally repressed.
2. Individuals finding sexual jokes funniest will be those whose sexuality is normally repressed. In this instance we can be more specific.
   (a) Anal jokes will appeal most to those fixated at the anal level (this is partly supported, in any case, by the commonplace observation of primary school humour).
   (b) Oral jokes will appeal to those fixated at the oral level. (To quote Bridget Brophy: in air-cunnilingus you meet a better class of fellatio.)
   (c) Homosexual and transvestite jokes will appeal to those with the relevant tastes.
3. Those whose main defence mechanism is repression and who have a strong superego will be humourless (they will not laugh at jokes).
4. Psychopaths should not find jokes amusing, for they have no need to lift repression in this way.
5. Wits will be more neurotic than the normal population.

All these hypotheses, it will be noticed, refer to the best-known aspects of psychoanalytic theories of humour, namely the purpose of jokes. However, hypotheses can be derived from the theories of joke-work. Thus:

1. highly repressed individuals prefer jokes with complex joke-work to 'simple' jokes; and
2. joke deprivation should produce increased dreaming and/or direct expression of impulses, a hypothesis derived from both aspects of psychoanalytic theory.

(Kline, 1997, pp.10–11)

Other perspectives have been less fanciful and more empirically minded. The usual empirical method of examining the relationship between personality and humour first involves classifying humour by obtaining jokes, cartoons, recordings and videos, and rating these so that they can be grouped into different types of humour, such as satire, aggressive, sexual, etc. Preference for each type is then correlated with scores on personality questionnaires. In a series of increasingly sophisticated studies, Ruch (1992) has developed a

3 WD Humour Test, which measures what are starting to be recognised as the three fundamental unrelated dimensions of humour, namely incongruity resolution, nonsense and sexual humour. Whilst there have been many piecemeal studies of this sort, Leventhal and Sofer (1977) have noted that a large number of these studies were poor and not theoretically based. The three major problems appear to be:

1. the categorisation of humour – there has yet to be any consensus in this area;
2. choosing the most salient personality factors independent of other relevant demographic factors and the possibly confounding effect of mood;
3. too little theory-building and too much naive psychometric work.

Humour creates a response when it is synthesised within an emotional category.

Leventhal and Sofer (1977) state:

> We concluded that the traditional individual difference approach to humour has not been fruitful for both methodological and conceptual reasons, and instead suggested that humour research should apply personality models to the sociocultural, cognitive, and affective factors in humour. In reviewing these models, we stressed that each looks at the humour experience from a different perspective: the sociocultural model describes from an external perspective the factors dealt with by the cognitive and emotion models from an internal, mediating perspective.
>
> Second, the models suggest a sequential theory of the humour experience – the social situation establishing the conditions (initial perception and readiness) for the action of cognitive processes that construct incongruity units (perceptual interpretations) and then integrate these units at a second stage with an effective category. These factors taken together make up the humour experience.
>
> Finally, individual differences exist in each of these domains – in sociocultural background, in roles and role relationships, in cognitive factors for the understanding of rule structures, in intellectual temperament responsible for forming incongruity units, and in expressiveness and willingness to enjoy or sustain emotional experience. The study of individual differences in each of these areas will require the development of refined measuring devices and the use of these measures in an experimental setting where situational factors are varied. Only when we can predict which subjects will be affected by specific situational variables and not by others can we be sure that our individual difference measures are assessing a specific, underlying, conceptual factor. If the study of humour now seems overwhelmingly complex, we can take heart in the fact that our efforts will be long-term and hopefully bring us more than a few laughs and a good deal of enlightenment on the nature of emotional processes and their relationship to thought.
>
> (Leventhal and Sofer, 1977, p.346)

According to Leventhal and Sofer (1977), there are three main approaches to the psychology of humour. The *social* psychological approach concentrates on the social meaning of humour, the contexts or occasions for it, and the effects of humour on group facilitation. Social psychologists have always been interested in how humour can generate a sense of group solidarity/belongingness, provide a safety valve for dealing with group leisure, and help individuals cope with threatening, negative experiences. The *cognitive* psychologists are primarily interested in how and why people understand jokes. For instance, they have shown a curvilinear relationship between the difficulty of understanding a joke and its perceived funniness. Cognitive psychologists have long been interested in how people process information. Finally, the *emotional* theory suggests either that humour has arousal functions or that humour can be used by individuals to modify their arousal levels as well as to express affect.

Trait theorists have also investigated humour. Ziv (1984) has attempted to use Eysenckian theory to investigate the relationship between personality and humour. Stable extraverts obviously enjoy humour more than introverts for various reasons – it strengthens group cohesiveness, and it provides more options for social reinforcement. Ziv (1984) believes that there are sex, age and intelligence correlates of human appreciation of humour – females more than males, adolescents more than adults, and more rather than less intelligent people enjoy humour.

Although he provides no data in support of his categorisation, Ziv (1984) attempted to describe humour appreciation in the four different Eysenckian quadrants. Hence the *neurotic extravert* likes humour to express aggression (in an acceptable way) and be accepted by the group. Short jokes, practical jokes and skits/comedy are apparently favoured. The *stable extravert* supposedly quite enjoys jokes at their own expense, and approves of others who can laugh at themselves. The *neurotic introvert* enjoys satire, black humour and cartoons/written humour but is not, by definition, a very cheerful person. Finally, the *stable introvert* supposedly favours absurd or incongruous situations and the problem-solving process involved in decoding them.

Ziv (1984) has provided the following table (Table 10.1). For him, the creation of humour is much more closely related to creativity and divergent thinking styles. He notes the importance of family background and education – frequently a poor family struggling for subsistence in an atmosphere of parental conflict.

> The humour that develops in such a situation is both a defence mechanism and a means of coping with difficulties; it attaches and distorts reality, makes it funny, and therefore makes it tolerable. Of course, an unhappy childhood will not produce a humorist if talent is lacking.
>
> (Ziv, 1984, p.139)

Most successful humorists also had relatively poor school records and experience of school. According to Ziv (1984), most are insecure and use their humour as a way to gain acceptance and love. From his review of the literature, he believes that most professional humorists are highly intelligent (among the top 5 per cent) and score particularly well on creativity tests.

Ziv (1984) notes that many professional humorists are notably introverted – serious people who are not prone much to laughter. Writers are more introverted than performers, but even the latter tend to be unstable (neurotic), and characterised by anxiety, depression and low self-esteem. However, they find that their humour gives them power over others and an ability to compensate for their feelings of inferiority.

Ruch (1992), a leading researcher in the field, has spent the previous decade developing a reliable and valid measure of humour appreciation and generation. Having developed a robust and sensitive measure of humour appreciation and creation, Ruch et al. (1997) were able to examine the relationship between personality and humour. Köhler and Ruch (1998) gave a cross-section of German adults the Eysenck EPQ and the humour creation/appreciation tests. They found that overall sense of humour was strongly positively correlated with extraversion, less so with psychoticism (P), and negatively correlated with neuroticism. There were few correlations between personality and detailed humour appreciation, but a clear pattern for humour

Table 10.1 Personality and humour performances[a]

Humour category	Personality type			
	Emotional extravert	Stable extravert	Emotional introvert	Stable introvert
Functions				
Aggressive	xx	x	x	
Sexual	x	x		
Social (general)		x	x	x
Social (interpersonal)	x	xx		
Defence against anxiety			x	x
Self-disparaging		x	x	xx
Intellectual		x	x	xx
Techniques				
Written/cartoons				xx
Narrated or acted	x	xx		
Situations				
Numerous	xx	x		

[a] x denotes preference; xx denotes strong preference.
Source: Ziv, A. (1984) Personality and sense of humour. Springer Publishing Company, Inc., New York 10012. Used by permission.

creativity. Tough-minded people in particular and also extraverts tended to do better on tests of humour production.

These authors note that, compared to introverts, extraverts are more cheerful, less serious, able to produce more (but not necessarily funnier) punch-lines, and tend to appreciate jokes and cartoons. The latter tendency is consistent across studies, but is not always statistically significant. High-P (Psychoticism) scorers are clearly more creative and original in their humour, while low-P scorers enjoy jokes and cartoons which contain punch-lines with fully resolvable incongruities. Neurotics tend not to enjoy humour, and fail to appreciate the possibilities of using humour as an antidote to negative affect.

Ruch (1992) argued that the two dimensions of humour which he isolated lead to various testable hypotheses with regard to the relationship between personality and humour. Because of the incongruity-resolving dimension of humour, it may be linked to measures of stimulation preference because humour is often unpredictable, complex, surprising and perplexing. Thus he assumed that personality variables such as ambiguity tolerance, conservatism and sensation-seeking should provide the clearest conceptual link to an appreciation of the individual properties in humour. He reviewed the many studies which indeed related these three variables to humour appreciation, and his results showed that intolerance of ambiguity was a significant predictor of the funniness of sexual humour, based on the incongruity-resolution structure of jokes. Furthermore, sensation-seeking was a logical and consistent predictor, showing that the low sensation-seeker dislikes nonsense humour and regards it as aversive, but gives higher ratings of funniness to incongruity-resolution humour. Sensation-seeking is a trait defined by the need for varied, novel and complex situations, so it is not surprising that it is strongly positively correlated with particular types of humour appreciation.

Ruch notes:

> Because humour is related to many psychic phenomena, there is a need for a standardized humour test in several fields within psychology. One aim . . . is to draw the attention of personality research to this field again; decades ago, humour was an integrated field of inquiry for personality psychology. The picture that psychology draws of man will remain particularly incomplete, if such a genuine human ability as the appreciation of humour remains a missing element . . .
>
> The results demonstrate a close interlocking between appreciation of humour and personality. A potential use of the humour test as a means of the objective assessment of personality traits is discussed. The review of the studies also demonstrates several unresolved issues in the assessment of the appreciation of humour.

(Ruch, 1992, p.71–2)

Once again we find evidence that personality traits are modestly but reliably related to both humour production and humour appreciation.

10.5 LYING ON PERSONALITY QUESTIONNAIRES

Whether it is called lying, faking, dissimulation or showing a socially desirable response bias, the problem of people not telling the truth on personality questionnaires presents a fundamental difficulty for the researcher and the applied person trying to select individuals.

Perhaps the most common objection to the use of personality inventories is that because people can lie or 'fake good' on self-report measures, the latter must be invalid because they do not yield true scores, especially on the assessment of undesirable traits or behaviour patterns. The issue continues to attract research interest (Helmes and Holden, 1986; Christiansen *et al.*, 1994; Goffin and Woods, 1995; Zickar and Drasgow, 1996). One of three related objections is frequently made: people *deliberately sabotage* the results by making random responses; there is *motivation distortion* or faking to achieve a particular profile (positive or desirable); *sheer ignorance*, whereby the respondent, through lack of self-insight, cannot rather than will not accurately report on his or her attitude, beliefs or behaviours. Academic discussion of these issues has revolved around the controversy concerning whether the term 'faking' implies conscious or unconscious efforts to distort response patterns. For most lay people, the term 'fake' would imply a conscious effort at distortion, which would not necessarily be related to unconscious efforts at test distortion.

Classically there are four methods used to catch questionnaire liars. The first is the most simple, but it is quietly effective – tell people not to lie. That is, *present clear instructions about quick and honest responding*. Let the respondents know that lies are frequent, and hence that testers are quite good at detecting them when they occur. Although this does not prevent exaggeration, subterfuge or selective memory, it usually serves to reduce many lies and inhibit the majority. Goffin and Woods (1995) demonstrated clearly that the threat of faking detection reduced faking.

The second method is to use a *lie scale*. Consider the following questions: 'Do you always wash your hands before a meal?', 'Have you *ever* been late for an appointment?', 'Have you *ever* taken the credit for something someone else did?' If you answer YES, NO, NO, then you are probably a liar. There is some debate as to what the scales measure and which are the best available, but they are useful for research purposes.

The third method encourages people to lie. Questionnaires are typically given to three groups of people. One-third of the respondents are asked to 'fake good' (i.e. to lie by putting themselves in a positive light), one-third are asked to 'fake bad' (i.e. to lie by putting themselves in a negative light) and the remainder are asked to tell the truth. The aim is to obtain a *profile or template of a liar*. This method yields a template of the responses of the fake-good liar (and a template of the responses of the fake-bad liar is also occasionally useful), so that one can match up the responses of the respondent with the 'known' responses of liars.

The fourth method is the forced-choice or *ipsative method*. People will not usually admit to negative behaviour such as absenteeism-related hypochondriasis, pilfering or encouraging stock shrinkage, politicking and back-stabbing. A way of catching the ingratiator, the liar or the cleaner-than-clean employee is to give him or her a choice between two equally desirable or undesirable behaviours. However, the method does rely on a careful and judicious assessment of the equivalence of misdeeds. If those two indiscretions are equal, then ask people which they are *more likely* to do or have done. It is easy to generate such questions (e.g. 'Have you/are you more likely to (a) make a private call on company time/expenses, (b) take home company stationery?'). This method forces candidates to admit the undesirable side of their behaviour. Other more recent methods have looked at response latency or the time spent answering questions. The results suggest that when people lie they take longer to respond. Holden and Hobbs (1995) showed that time spent responding to individual questions could correctly discriminate (82 per cent correct) between individuals who were being honest and those who were requested to answer in such a way as to be hired for a job.

In his critical review of ways to prevent or reduce social desirability bias, Nederhof (1985) lists seven such methods. Three deal with other-deceptive, situational determinants, one deals with selection of interviewers, one with choice of respondents, and two with the data-collection situation.

1. *Forced-choice items* – respondents choose between two items that are equal in desirability, and hence their choice cannot be seen to be influenced by social desirability.
2. *Neutral questions* – only questions which are neutral with regards to social desirability are included.
3. *Randomized response technique* – this technique allows respondents to answer one or two randomly selected items, with the interviewer not knowing which item was answered.
4. *Self-administered questionnaires* – this reduces the salience of social cues by isolating the respondent.
5. *Bogus pipeline* – respondents are led to believe that the machine to which they are attached can detect whether or not they are speaking the truth.
6. *Selecting interviewers* – social desirability is reduced when respondents are similar to their interviewers, who must also be 'warm and person-oriented'.
7. *Proxy respondents* – instead of interviewing the respondent, someone who knows him or her well is questioned about the behaviour of the target person.

In conclusion, no one method excels completely and under all conditions in coping with social desirability bias. Most methods were shown to be at best reasonable palliatives. A combination of one or several prevention methods and one detection method seems the best choice available. It should be noted that the exact effectiveness with regard to both other-deception and self-deception of most of the prevention methods has yet to be determined empirically.

(Nederhof, 1985, p.276)

Various important conclusions appeared from the recent review of the literature (Furnham, 1986). The first was that no matter who the participants were (e.g. students, policemen, army recruits, employed people), they showed a similar pattern of faking (Burbeck and Furnham, 1984). Secondly, most studies have simply asked participants to fake good or bad, but some have asked them to fake according to other instructions (e.g. to fake a librarian or a mental patient), although the results have usually been predictable (Furnham and Henderson, 1983; Archer et al., 1987; Furnham and Craig, 1987; Furnham, 1990a). Thirdly, studies conducted in 'real life' as opposed to 'experimental' settings have yielded comparable results. Fourthly, testing occasions can be shown to be differentially dissimulation prone, and this proneness can be measured from the test results (Michaelis and Eysenck, 1971). This suggests that experimental work using *any* population group, and using fake good and bad instructions, would yield comparatively robust results and replicable faking templates. Finally, studies conducted on different questionnaires have shown that most, but not all, dimensions can be faked (Furnham, 1990a).

There has been a fair amount of research on the fakeability of self-report, personality measures used specifically in organisational settings (Furnham and Craig, 1987). Recent studies of faked response-set characteristics in applied settings have shown that it is relatively easy to fake some of the most widely used and respected measures (Archer et al., 1987). In a study of actual applicants to the British Metropolitan Police Force, Burbeck and Furnham (1984) found that applicants had identical profiles to those student subjects who had been asked to fake skilfully on the questionnaire. The desire to be accepted as police recruits had led them to fake a socially desirable response pattern, which in this instance meant scoring high on extraversion and low on neuroticism. This conclusion is unwarranted in the absence of independent evidence, and needs to be established. More recently, Furnham (1990b) set out to examine the fakeability of three questionnaires used for personality assessment in applied and occupational settings, namely the 16 PF, the Myers-Briggs Type Indicator and the Fundamental Interpersonal Relations Orientation – Behaviour (FIRO-B), which are extensively used in occupational selection and assessment in the UK. All of the tests proved to be extremely sensitive to faking, especially the 16 PF. Furnham (1990b) drew the following conclusions from the results:

First, in many instances the means and profiles of the two faking groups were not totally extreme, showing that extremity is not necessarily an indicator of faking; second, whereas some results may have been predicted or anticipated, others which may have yielded significant difference did not; third, not all findings were linear and often too much or too little of a quality or trait was considered equally good or bad; finally, faking is not easy and there is no clear agreement as to what constitutes a good or bad response.

(Furnham, 1990b, p.709)

The results of the Jungian Myers-Briggs questionnaire are shown in Table 10.2.

Some of the results showed a linear pattern (extraversion good–introversion bad), but some showed a curvilinear pattern in which extremes are bad. Moreover, nearly all (7 out of 8) of the fake good vs. control comparisons were significantly different, yet just over 50 per cent (5 out of 8) of the fake good vs. fake bad and fake bad vs. control comparisons (6 out of 8) were significantly different. The ideal fake good profile is ESTJ (practical realists, matter-of-fact, with a natural head for business; like to organise and run activities), while the ideal fake bad profile is ISTP (cool onlookers, quiet, reserved, observing and analysing life with detached curiosity and unexpected flashes of original humour). The control group, on the other hand, tended to be ENFP (warmly enthusiastic, high-spirited, ingenious and imaginative). According to the manual, occupations likely to be attractive to ESTJ include administrators, computer specialists, scientists, judges, doctors and teachers, while for ISTP they include health service workers, and private household and factory workers. People with an ENFP profile are likely to be engineers, scientists or professionals.

Table 10.2 Means and analysis of variance results for the Myers-Briggs Type Indicator (MBTI)

| Factor | Means | | | ANOVA | Post hoc comparisons | | |
	Fake good	Control	Fake bad	F level	FG C	FG FB	FB C
1. Extraversion	19.01	15.19	9.05	15.62***		*	*
2. Introversion	7.18	13.66	19.40	17.93***	*	*	*
3. Sensing	15.13	6.42	22.50	28.66***	*	*	*
4. Intuiting	12.54	18.00	10.80	10.60***	*		*
5. Thinking	16.13	7.19	21.10	17.62***	*		*
6. Feeling	8.59	13.38	10.40	4.10*	*		
7. Judging	16.90	9.28	8.85	8.89***	*		*
8. Perceiving	10.68	18.47	20.70	11.61***	*	*	

***$P < 0.001$; **$P < 0.01$; *$P < 0.05$.

Reprinted from *Personality and Individual Differences*, **11**, Furnham, A., The fakeability of the 16PF Myers-Briggs and Firo-B personality measures, Page No's. 711–16, Copyright (1990), with permission from Elsevier Science.

Nearly all of the faking studies have required subjects to 'fake good' in order to examine the socially desirable profile. However, this method may have relatively low ecological validity because faking good in one context may not be equivalent to faking good in another. For instance, if a personality test was to be given at an interview for a job as an actor, the fake good profile would presumably be quite different to that of the ideal candidate aiming to join the army as an officer-cadet. Few studies have required subjects to fake particular profiles. However, that by Velicar and Weiner (1975) is an exception, as their study required subjects to fake a salesman, a librarian and their ideal self. As predicted, they found large differences between the resultant profiles, suggesting that subjects can fake many types of ideal or good professional profiles.

Furnham (1990c) asked over 50 subjects to complete four personality measures used in personnel selection. Based on a latin-square design, they were asked to fill them in as if they were trying to present themselves as ideal candidates for the job of librarian, advertising executive or banker, while on one questionnaire they gave 'honest' true responses. For comparison, note the results from the Myers-Briggs Type Indicator (Table 10.3).

Advertisers were perceived as having the highest extraversion, feeling and judging scores, while librarians had the exact opposite scores. The fake banker profile had the highest thinking and lowest feeling scores. Overall, the thinking–feeling dimension showed the most dramatic differences.

More recent studies have examined the fakeability of the very popular Big Five measures. Topping and O'Gorman (1997) asked students either to respond honestly or to fake good when completing the NEO Big Five measures. They also asked judges who had known each student for at least 12 months to rate them on the 12 dimensions. As predicted, they found that the fake good group had higher scores on agreeableness, conscientiousness and extraversion, but lower neuroticism scores. They also found correlations of between 0.49 and 0.60 between the honest self-report and the other rated reports. However, the correlation between the fake good and the observers was as low as $r = 0.09$. They concluded that, consistent with popular beliefs, deliberate attempts to fake do seriously compromise the reliability of tests.

Furnham (1997) also examined the fakeability of the Costa and McCrae (1988) Big Five measure of personality. The results are shown in Table 10.4.

Post hoc analysis showed that all comparisons between fake good and fake bad groups as well as between controls and fake bad groups were statistically significant, with fake bad individuals scoring lower on each dimension except neuroticism, where the score was higher. The fake good vs. control comparisons showed that only three of the five differences reached the level of statistical significance. Control participants had higher neuroticism, lower agreeableness and lower conscientiousness scores than the fake good group. The dimensions which showed the greatest difference between the groups

Table 10.3 Means and analysis of variance for the four faking groups. Reprinted by permission of Transaction Publishers. "Faking personality questionnaires: fabricating different profiles for different purposes" by Furnham, A. in *Current Psychology: Research and Reviews* **9**, 46–55, 1990. Copyright © 1990 by Transaction Publishers; all rights reserved.

| | Means | | | | ANOVA | | Post hoc comparisons | | | | | |
| | Fake librarian | Fake advertiser | Fake banker | Control | | | | | | | | |
	FL	FA	FB	C	Levels F		FL FA	FL FB	FL C	FA FB	FA C	FB C
Myers-Briggs												
Extraversion	4.73	22.92	17.50	15.33	28.59***		*	*	*		*	
Introversion	23.93	4.84	10.50	12.93	26.37***		*	*	*		*	*
Sensing	28.33	3.23	20.83	8.73	41.58***		*		*			*
Intuiting	5.20	22.30	8.08	15.20	31.08***						*	*
Thinking	23.73	14.07	28.75	10.06	17.13***					*		*
Feeling	4.46	10.38	1.33	9.60	11.63***					*		*
Judging	1.79	27.69	22.41	14.46	79.12***		*		*	*	*	*
Perceiving	13.80	6.08	27.69	1.73	74.44***		*		*	*	*	*
KAI	101.93	79.15	116.16	58.40	30.17***		*		*			*

*** $P < 0.001$, ** $P < 0.01$, * $P < 0.05$.

Table 10.4 Means (and standard deviations) of the two faking and control groups

	Fake good (FG) (n=25)	Control (C) (n=20)	Fake bad (FB) (n=25)	F-level	Scheffe tests[a]		
					FG/C	FG/B	FB/C
Neuroticism	20.80 (8.97)	34.50 (9.63)	45.68 (13.25)	32.39***	*	*	*
Extraversion	47.52 (8.90)	43.20 (6.50)	22.44 (9.26)	62.00***		*	*
Openness	44.68 (6.32)	43.60 (4.09)	27.24 (6.80)	65.01***		*	*
Agreeableness	47.24 (5.76)	39.05 (5.90)	17.44 (4.98)	190.26***	*	*	*
Conscientiousness	54.00 (9.11)	39.15 (9.69)	17.20 (6.67)	118.15***	*	*	*

[a] The Scheffe tests compared the scores on fake good and control group scores (FG/C), fake good and fake bad groups (FG/FB) and fake bad and control groups (FB/C) which were significant at $P < 0.05$.
*$P < 0.05$, ***$P < 0.01$.
Source: Furnham, A. (1997) Knowing and faking one's five-factor personality score. *Journal of Personality Assessment* **69**, 229–43. Reproduced with permission.

were first conscientiousness and secondly agreeableness, suggesting that these are perhaps the most fakeable dimensions.

The characteristics of the fake-good profile which emerged from the three studies was of a non-neurotic, extraverted, conscientious person. Surprisingly, perhaps, neuroticism showed the least difference between the groups and conscientiousness the most. The standard deviation suggested a reasonable amount of variation within each group under each condition, certainly not indicating unanimity with regard to faking responses.

However, studies such as this cannot answer the following questions. Under what conditions do participants fake, or for what jobs and organisations? Clearly this is a very important question, but one that is difficult to answer in an experimental setting. Are there any individual differences, subgroups or cultural correlates of faking? Again, the answer is important and would depend primarily on different individuals or group concepts of ideal or optional characteristics for the situation, job or organisation. Does the degree of faking affect the reliability and validity of the scales? Before these important and interesting questions can be answered, it is first necessary to establish the degree and direction of faking in popularly used questionnaires.

Faking studies can reveal what a participant (in general) believes to be desirable or normal. Similarly, faking can show an employer what a prospective employee thinks are the most desirable traits for the job. In addition, they may provide a useful template of typical faked responses that could be used actually to detect people lying in the questionnaire. On the other hand, there is increasing evidence from studies on the consistency and stability of socially desirable responses to suggest that these may have trait-like qualities that relate to naivety. Furnham (1986) has argued that the reason why mental health measures are so susceptible to faking (and correlated with measures of social desirability) is that giving socially desirable responses could itself be an index of mental illness. Thus it is possible that if people fake on application questionnaires, then they are likely to be unreliable employees, either because they are mentally unstable or else because they are prone to ingratiation and dissimulation in order to achieve some end. On the other hand, it should be pointed out that participants who are able to fake 'good' in psychiatric settings are typically better adjusted. It is possible that some mild forms of 'faking good' are highly appropriate for job applicants, in that the total absence of efforts at distortion may have psychological correlates.

The fact that people fake on personality tests is important, but it is not damning for the validity of such tests. Furthermore, the study of how, when and why people fake provides interesting and useful data in its own right.

10.6 PREDICTING ONE'S OWN AND OTHERS' PERSONALITY SCORES

Can people predict their own personality scores? Is the ability to predict scores accurately a way of validating a test? Does a significant positive correlation between an estimate and a test-derived score mean that either or both are correct – the person being assessed or the psychologist who devised the test? What does it mean if individuals cannot predict their own score?

Various studies have looked at participants' ability to predict their own extraversion scores (Blaz, 1983). Semin *et al.* (1981) demonstrated a conceptual overlap between lay-produced and 'scientific' conceptions of extraversion–introversion, and hence it was expected – and shown – that people accurately predict their own scores. In one of the first studies in the area, Vingoe (1966) asked participants to estimate their extraversion score on a seven-point scale, which was compared with the Eysenck Personality Inventory (EPI) score. He found that introverts were more aware of their introversion than extraverts were of their extraversion. Harrison and McLaughlin (1969) found correlations of 0.72 and 0.56 between 243 participants' estimates of their own extraversion and neuroticism, respectively, compared with their actual scores resulting from the EPI. Similarly, Gray (1972) replicated this study on a sample of 131 nurses and found correlations of 0.48 for extraversion and 0.21 for neuroticism.

Furnham (1990a) looked at participants' ability to predict their scores on three quite diverse measures. A total of 56 participants completed three questionnaires (the Morningness–Eveningness Questionnaire, the FIRO-B and the Myers-Briggs Type Indicator), and then estimated the scores on each dimension (15 in total) for themselves and for another person whom they knew well. The results showed significant positive correlations on 10 of the 15 dimensions for the participants themselves. The dimensions which they were best at estimating were morningness–eveningness, extraversion and thinking on the Myers-Briggs Type Indicator, and wanted and expressed inclusion on the FIRO-B. Eight correlations reached the level of significance with regard to their ability to predict another known individual's scores, but were weaker for their own estimate–actual correlations. The variables that subjects claimed most familiarity with were, in rank order, extraversion–introversion, morningness–eveningness and thinking–feeling, which supports the idea that familiarity is related.

Another reason for the relatively low correlations between a person's actual and estimated scores may be due to their useful tendency to overestimate socially desirable characteristics (e.g. extraversion, thinking) and to underestimate socially undesirable characteristics (e.g. neuroticism, sensing).

However good people may be at estimating their extraversion and neuroticism, there is evidence that this ability does not generalise to all personality dimensions. For instance, Furnham and Henderson (1983) found that participants were unable to predict their scores on an assertiveness inventory or on a locus of control scale. Similarly, they could not correctly predict their Lie score from the Eysenck Personality Questionnaire (EPQ). Indeed, they were even worse at predicting some of these scores for another nominated person, occasionally obtaining significant negative correlations.

The question remains, therefore, as to which personality trait dimension scores people in general are able and unable to predict with any degree of accuracy, and whether some individuals are significantly better than others at predicting their own scores. Theoretically, it may be assumed that people are able to predict scores for dimensions which they understand, or when they have some frame or schema of reference for potential behaviours which they can use effectively. For example, if an individual was required to estimate his or her extraversion or psychoticism score accurately, he or she would have to be familiar with the concept, be clear about the situations or phenomena to which it applied, and be aware of how he or she compared with a fairly wide range of other people. Concepts such as extraversion and neuroticism and, to a lesser extent, conscientiousness, are part of everyday language, frequently discussed with respect to a variety of settings, and social comparisons are often made. Hence it may be postulated that they could be significantly predicted (Goldberg, 1992). Indeed, in a validity study, Costa and McCrae (1988) found the highest correlations between questionnaire-derived scores and adjective-based self-reports for conscientiousness, neuroticism and extraversion. On the other hand, 16PF dimensions such as Harria-Premsia or

Alaxia-Protension, whatever their 'jargon' terms, are less often discussed, and hence presumably less easy to predict (Furnham, 1989). Thus, to do this task well, a participant needs to access and use a detailed, user-friendly framework concerning personality traits. His or her inability to do so indicates either a non-existent, incorrect or poorly formed category, or an inability to use it comparatively. However, it could be argued that the obscurity of a factor title does not necessarily mean that the concept(s) represented by that factor are obscure and, likewise, that a poorly formed category cannot be described by a commonly used word.

An interesting and related question concerns whether accuracy of self-prediction is a question of main effects or of interaction. That is, it may be that certain individuals are highly sensitive to detecting personality traits (from related social behaviour) in others as a function of their own personality. Thus neurotics may be highly sensitive to the manifestations of neuroticism (or stability) in others. This explanation stresses individual differences rather than cultural factors, such as how well known a concept may be.

Furnham (1997) reported on three studies, each examining students' ability to predict their Big Five scores. The results are shown in Table 10.5.

Table 10.5 Correlations between estimated and 'actual' NEO-FFI test scores for self and other[a]

Studies	Estimated and 'actual' self			Estimated and 'actual' other			'Actual' self and 'actual' other			Estimated self and estimated other		
	1	2	3	1	2	3	1	2	3	1	2	3
Neuroticism	***	***	***	**	***			*		*	***	**
	0.63	0.56	0.34	0.33	0.47	0.00	0.04	0.27	0.15	0.27	0.43	0.30
Extraversion	***	***	***	***			***			*	***	
	0.58	0.59	0.40	0.36	0.19	0.02	0.33	−0.01	0.17	0.26	0.47	0.09
Openness		**	***		**			*	*	***	***	***
	0.20	0.41	0.40	0.01	0.29	0.09	0.00	−0.21	0.23	0.39	0.53	0.53
Agreeableness	***	**	**		**	***				***	**	***
	0.48	0.39	0.30	0.18	0.32	0.55	0.09	−0.05	0.00	0.57	0.28	0.55
Conscientiousness	***	***	***	***					**	***	***	***
	0.62	0.51	0.59	0.41	0.17	0.20	0.04	0.10	0.41	0.21	0.44	0.49

$*P < 0.05$, $**P < 0.01$, $***P < 0.001$.

[a] Study 1, Study 2, Study 3.

Source: Furnham, A. (1997) Knowing and faking one's five-factor personality score. *Journal of Personality Assessment* **69**, 229–43. Reproduced with permission.

The participants were clearly able to estimate their personality score fairly accurately. Overall, they were best at predicting conscientiousness (mean $r = 0.57$) followed by extraversion (mean $r = 0.52$) and neuroticism (mean $r = 0.51$). They were least good at predicting their openness-to-experience score (mean $r = 0.33$), where one of the studies showed a non-significant result.

The second section (estimated other and actual other scores) revealed less consistent findings across the three studies. In two out of three studies, the participants were able to predict the neuroticism, agreeableness and conscientiousness of their acquaintances (nominated other). In the third group only one of the five correlations was significant, which may be an indication of how well the participants knew each other.

The third section (actual self and actual other scores) shows 5 out of 15 significant correlations, four being positive and one being negative. As predicted, this section showed that, overall, participants were dissimilar to each other in their actual personality test-derived scores. The fourth section (estimated self and estimated other) looked much like the first in that most of the correlations were positive and significant. However, here the highest mean correlation between the two estimated scores across the three samples was for openness-to-experience and agreeableness, and the lowest for extraversion (mean $r = 0.27$). Thus although the participants believed (by estimation) that they were like their acquaintances (section 4), the data for the relationship between the actual scores (section 3) show that they were not.

This study has replicated findings from other studies (Vingoe, 1966; Gray, 1972; Funder, 1980; Blaz, 1983; Furnham and Henderson, 1983; Furnham, 1989), but using the Big Five personality measures. Those factors which have been shown to be part of everyday lay theories or conversation (e.g. extraversion and conscientiousness) show the highest correlations between actual and estimated scores. It seems that about 30 per cent of the variance could be accounted for in the case of conscientiousness, and it appeared that participants had more difficulty in grasping the concepts of openness to experience and agreeableness as they are used in the 'technical sense' by personality theorists. All of the five personality factor domains were, of course, obtained from natural language. Goldberg (1992) investigated trait terms, which represent an objective measure of usage within everyday lay language, and found that the domain of agreeableness had most, and that of openness to experience had least trait words in English.

However, the question remains as to why some dimensions can be predicted and others cannot. Furnham (1988) has argued that the more popular and well known the concept in lay usage, the more likely participants are to understand, fake or predict their own score. Provided, of course, that the meaning of the concept in lay usage is correct (i.e. similar to that used by the test constructor), it may be assumed that individuals can accurately predict their own scores. Participants certainly seemed to be relatively unfamiliar with the concept of openness to experience, but grasped it once it had been fully described. Yet because this had not been absorbed in their implicit personality theory, all of the correlations between actual and estimate scores were low (Furnham, 1988).

Another possible reason for the relatively low correlations between a person's actual and estimated scores may be their useful tendency to over-estimate socially desirable characteristics (extraversion and conscientiousness) and to underestimate socially undesirable characteristics (neuroticism). Some evidence for this view comes from the correlations between the socially desirable faked scores on all items and the self-actual and self-estimated scores (Furnham, 1990c). The fact that individuals appear to be less accurate (but not significantly so) at predicting others' personality scores is also apparent. People assume that they are like the individuals they know, who are frequently their acquaintances – hence the large number of significant positive correlations (13 out of 15) between self- and other-estimated scores – but because they are not like their acquaintances (33 per cent were significant, four positive and one negative), their estimates of their actual score are poor. The assumption that other individuals are like oneself restricts one's ability to predict accurately the behaviour of others, or at least their own scores on personality inventories. This phenomenon of 'assumed similarity' has been described by Cook (1979).

However, one flaw in these studies was the fact that they did not determine, match or control for the length and nature of the acquaintanceship. This clearly varied between nominating pairs, and could account for the unstable findings between replications. Nevertheless, these results are consistent with others in the area, some of which did control for the nature of the acquaintanceship (Costa and McCrae, 1988).

The major problem with these studies lies in obtaining an objective criterion against which to evaluate the judgements. Instead of arguing that individuals' own personality estimations do or do not accurately reflect the assessment of psychological instruments, it may be just as meaningful to argue precisely the opposite, concluding that it is the assessment devices of psychologists that do not seem to be able to judge very accurately individuals' actual personalities. Thus studies may be more accurately described as a comparison of two types of personality assessment – a formal test vs. an intuitive judgement. The task for the participants required them to predict their own scores, not their personality *per se*, and it is entirely reasonable that they should be able to predict scores after they have observed the types of questions the personality questionnaire used to measure the various dimensions of their personality. Moreover, formal personality scores are reasonable criteria of accuracy if the measure has good construct validity. Of course, if personality measures were invalid, they would not yield results clearly in accordance with empirically testable hypotheses derived from a hypothetical framework which is clearly not the same (Furnham, 1986).

The fact that individuals can predict some (but not all) of their (valid) personality (and those of others) is both interesting and important. It often reveals how much they understand about personality traits and how well they understand themselves and others?

10.7 ACCEPTING PERSONALITY TEST FEEDBACK

Can individuals correctly pick out their scored personality profile? Do people accept their (accurately scored) personality feedback? Can people be fooled into accepting bogus, nonsense feedback? Are some personality types more likely to accept some types of feedback than others.

The 'Barnum effect' refers to the phenomenon whereby individuals tend to accept bogus personality feedback as being true of themselves, whether it is universally valid of everyone, trivial or even untrue, because it is supposedly derived from personality assessment procedures such as questionnaires, or graphological or astrological analysis. Forer (1949) was the first to demonstrate what he called the 'fallacy of personal validation', which suggested that people frequently accept as correct generalised, vague and bogus descriptions of themselves which have a high base-rate occurrence in the general population. This later became known as the Barnum effect because of the two sayings of that person: 'there is a fool born every minute' and 'a little something for everybody'. The effect has been and can be easily demonstrated by showing that people accept as true feedback about themselves which was not, so they believed, obtained from some test or insight, but chosen because it is true (or believed to be true) for all people. That is, individuals can be fooled by astrologers and graphologists (and psychologists) because they do not recognise the high base-rate validity (i.e. general applicability) of most bogus feedback, instead believing it to be partially true of themselves.

Several studies which have considered the influence of personality factors on the Barnum effect have attempted to show that the acceptance of feedback is consistent with particular traits. In this sense, the literature has as much to do with self-verification (Swann, 1987), namely the notion that individuals are highly motivated to verify their self-conceptions even if those are negative (Forer, 1968). Many studies in this area are seriously handicapped by tautology, in that the independent variable (personality) and the dependent variable (feedback) are almost identical. Carrier (1963), using trait measures from the Edwards Personal Preference Schedule (EPPS), found that the suggestibility of students (i.e. the extent to which they accepted Barnum statements) was related to achievement, deference and introception among males, and to abasement, introception and endurance among females. However, Carrier pointed out that these relationships may be a result of the particular situation within which the test was carried out, and may not be generalised to other studies. In other words, the generalisability was threatened by possible experimental artefacts.

Mosher (1965) used the Marlowe-Crowne Social Desirability (M-CSD) scale to measure approval-seeking behaviour and vulnerable self-esteem, as it was thought to relate to gaining approval from the psychologist by accepting bogus feedback. His findings, which were completely self-obvious, revealed that subjects scoring high on the M-CSD were more likely to accept favourable fake personality interpretations, but significantly less likely to accept unfavourable ones. High scorers on the need-for-approval measures are those who endorse implausible but socially desirable characteristics. Snyder and Larson (1972) also found that individuals with a high need for social approval did not necessarily accept all of the feedback, and the high external locus of control correlated positively with acceptance. Later Orpen and Jamotte (1975) found that all three of the personality factors which they used played a relatively significant role in determining acceptance – that is, authoritarians, those with a high need for approval and those with an external locus of control tend to be more accepting of the (general, bogus personality) feedback than those who score low on authoritarianism, have a low need for approval and an internal locus of control. However, Fichten and Sunerton (1983) did not replicate this finding with locus of control, but did find that neuroticism correlated with both reading frequency and belief in horoscopes.

Another study by Snyder and Clair (1977) looked at the effects of insecurity on the acceptance of personality interpretations, both as a trait and as a situational manipulation. The major finding of this study was that the greater the insecurity of the participants, the greater was the acceptance of feedback. Ruzzene and Noller (1986) noted that individuals who exhibited high levels of desire for feedback did not discriminate between favourable (positive) and unfavourable (negative) accurate feedback, or between accurate and inaccurate favourable feedback. In other words, desire for feedback *per se* did not affect the acceptability of feedback.

Various studies have related extraversion and neuroticism to the acceptance of bogus feedback. Layne and Ally (1980) used the Eysenck Personality Inventory, and found that the more accurate the feedback, the more positively it was accepted. Neurotics endorsed neurotic (and accurate) feedback more than stable (inaccurate) feedback, and stable people endorsed stable (and accurate) feedback more than neurotic (inaccurate) feedback. This suggests that some personality variables were logically and predictably related to feedback acceptance. Yet Kelly *et al.* (1986) found no relationship between extraversion and neuroticism and ratings of uniqueness on the perceived accuracy of favourable and unfavourable Barnum profiles.

Furnham and Varian (1988) looked at the way in which introverts/ extraverts and neurotics/non-neurotics accepted general vs. specific positive and negative feedback. They found that extraverts, compared to introverts, showed a significantly greater acceptance of general positive and specific positive feedback. Compared to non-neurotics, neurotics showed a greater acceptance of general positive, specific positive and general negative feedback, but not specific negative feedback. Neurotic extraverts showed significantly more acceptance of general and specific negative feedback. The impulsiveness and low reflectiveness of extraverts accounts for their readiness to accept positive feedback, or the fact that being more sociable, which is a desirable trait, actually results in receiving more positive feedback in everyday life, which was confirmed in this study. Because both introverts and extraverts perceive extraversion as a more desirable or ideal trait than introversion, it is possible that extraverts accept positive feedback as being more accurate than negative feedback (but not vice versa) precisely because it is true.

Neurotics tended to accept feedback more than non-neurotics, particularly a high base rate or positive feedback. This confirms previous findings in this area (Layne, 1978; Layne and Ally, 1980; Fichten and Sunerton, 1983), although Kelly *et al.* (1986) found no significant effects. Subjects in the 'hysteric' quadrant of the EPQ most readily accepted general and specific negative feedback. Wilson (1981), in reviewing the work on suggestibility, noted that extravert neurotics were shown to be most suggestible to all types of outside influence. It is no doubt the high anxiety level of neurotics that leads them to accept high base-rate bogus information as being true. Thus it is possible that neurotics seek out feedback from professionals such as astrologers, graphologists or psychotherapists which may well be bogus, so confirming the suspicion of many cynics that it is often the worried, depressed and unsure who visit fortune-tellers and the like (Snyder and Shenkel, 1975).

Furnham (1989b) used the 16PF and looked at the relationship between the acceptance of general and specific positive and negative feedback. The results seem to suggest that factors associated with extraversion (*affectia, surgency* and *parmia*) are positively related to the acceptance of positive feedback, while factors associated with neuroticism (*low ego strength, guilty* and *high ergic tension*) are positively related to the acceptance of negative feedback. However, it is true that submission–dominance, obviously related to extraversion, was not related to the acceptance of positive feedback, thus throwing some doubt on the point.

Yet these results are in accordance with those of Layne and Ally (1980), Fichten and Sunerton (1983) and Furnham and Varian (1988). That is, work on the relationship between extraversion and neuroticism as it relates to diverse issues such as suggestibility, mental health and values substantiates these results. Even alternative approaches such as that of Gray (1981) can be interpreted within the paradigm. Gray (1981) has proposed that extraverts respond mainly to reward (positive feedback) and introverts to punishment (negative feedback), which accounts for the positive correlation between extraversion-related factors and positive feedback. Moreover, neuroticism seems to be particularly associated with negative social influences, such as the acceptance of irrational or maladaptive information about oneself (Wilson, 1981).

In a second study, Furnham (1989a) gave subjects 30 trait words as feedback (15 positive and 15 negative words) 2 weeks after completing the EPQ. Predictably, individuals accepted more positive than negative feedback. Extraverts tend to accept positive and reject negative feedback, the precise opposite being true of introverts. Those scoring higher on the neuroticism and psychoticism subscales tended to rate the negative feedback as more accurate than those who scored lower on these scales. The results of the study confirm previous work on extraversion, but suggest that neuroticism is correlated only with the acceptance of negative feedback.

However, without doubt the most interesting and potentially important findings are those relating to the largest correlation, namely that between neuroticism and the acceptance of negative feedback. Cognitive theories of depression suggest that the aetiology and maintenance of depression, anxiety and other neurotic states may in part be due to the information-processing strategies of particular individuals. The low self-esteem of neurotics may well be due to their propensity to accept as true negative (and bogus) feedback about themselves. On the other hand, it may be particularly adaptive to reject negative feedback, or at least to be discriminating about its accuracy (Swann, 1987). It may also be a manifestation of the neurotic paradox that neurotics seek out personality feedback from psychologists and astrologers, but that, particularly in the case of the latter, they can be reassured that it is nearly always positive.

Fletcher *et al.* (1996) found that subjects who completed the 16PF were able to identify their test-derived personality more accurately than would be expected by chance. However, they did find that education, sex and personality were related to the acceptance of feedback. Three personality factors accounted for 22 per cent of the variance in accuracy ratings – these were mental capacity, conscientiousness and imaginativeness. They note:

> To define which personality characteristics those giving feedback should be wary of would be difficult: on the other hand, some evidence suggests that individuals with less positive characteristics are less likely to seek test feedback anyway.
>
> (Fletcher *et al.*, 1996, p.155)

Again, research in this area seems to indicate quite clearly that personality traits are systematically linked to whether people accept true or bogus feedback about themselves.

10.8 WHEN PERSONALITY TRAITS PREDICT SOCIAL BEHAVIOUR

Critical reviews and meta-analyses of studies examining the behaviour correlates of personality traits in very diverse areas, ranging from consumption to education, and from health to work, have tended to make the same fundamental points. Personality traits are likely to be *significant predictors* of behaviour, accounting for between 5 and 50 per cent of the variance (and more typically 30 per cent) if, and only if, the following five factors are taken into account.

1. First, the (social) behaviour that is related to personality dimension needs to be *reliably*, *accurately* and *sensitively* measured. Whether it is behaviour in the classroom or in the clinic, the factory or the football pitch, it is important that *multiple (aggregated) measures* are used, ideally measured by different methods (multi-trait, multi-method). Too often, single-response or single-behavioural measures are used which are highly unreliable and therefore invalid. Most of the behaviours that applied researchers try to predict are indeed complex, e.g. absenteeism, addictive (drug-related) behaviour, or even leisure pursuits. It is often very difficult to obtain subtle and reliable measures of what people buy, how they vote, how hard they work, etc., but there is no excuse for not attempting to do this. To believe that personality is not (empirically) predictive of behaviour may simply be the result of the latter (the dependent variable) not being very reliably or validly measured. Measurement or observation, test and self-report all have widely known and subtle biases, and the best measures attempt to use more than one method on more than one occasion in order to minimise bias. It is important that data is *aggregated* – that is, multiple recordings are needed to ensure reliability. Finally, because of the systematic biases inherent in all forms of data collection (e.g. self-report, observation, test) it is ideally best to obtain measures from *multiple sources*. In short, it may be difficult to 'prove' that personality predicts behaviour, not because it is not the case, but because of the measure of the behaviour one is using to try to predict the problem.

2. Secondly, the personality trait(s) themselves need to be measured properly. There are literally thousands of personality tests, but they differ enormously, not only in the theory (if any) on which they are based, but also in their psychometric properties. It is clear that each concept measured needs to be reliably measured – there must be evidence of test, re-test, split half and internal reliability. This needs to be the case at whatever level the trait is measured (e.g. the superfactor level such as extraversion, or the primary factor level, such as impulsivity and sociability). The trait also needs to show sufficient evidence of validity (content, concurrent construct, predictive, convergent, divergent). Simply saying that a scale measures something reliably is not sufficient. For instance, many single traits are multifactional; others are almost identical, with quite differently named traits. Tests that are popularly used (by applied researchers) are often not the most satisfactory in terms of their psychometric properties. Over the past decade, psychometric research has progressed to a point where many sophisticated, validated measures are available from which the applied researcher can choose. Again, to use a personality test with poor or unproven psychometric properties to measure a trait, and then to argue on the basis of poor correlates that personality tests do not predict social behaviour, is unjustified. Too many studies have been based on outdated, commercially well-advertised but poorly constructed tests.

3. Thirdly, self-evidently but not always obviously, either to researchers or to reviewers, the trait must be logically and theoretically related to the behaviour. Not all traits are relevant to all behaviours (see Section 10.3). Some traits are clearly more salient in some areas of life than others. Thus extraversion is more relevant to work and leisure than to consumption, while conscientiousness is probably more relevant to education and health-related issues than to leisure pursuits. For too long researchers compared multiple-trait measures with multiple behavioural measures, observed that about 10 per cent of the (very numerous) correlations were significant (and rather small), but then concluded that personality factors appeared to be poor predictors of that type of behaviour. As researchers showed in the occupational sphere, if one examined only those correlations which one expected to be significant *for good theoretical reasons*, the pattern looked completely different. Although far fewer correlations (or their statistical equivalent) were expected to be significant, a much higher percentage were or tended to be larger. However, in order to make these predictions, it is necessary to have both a theoretically sound personality theory (and test) and a good understanding of the organisation and other constraints on organisational behaviour. The 'shot-gun' approach is bad science. Where researchers have attempted to understand a particular process related to traits (e.g. stimulation levels in extraversion), it is possible to derive and test sensible relationships to specific social behaviours.

4. Neither personality variables nor social behaviours in any sphere or setting are likely to be random. People select and choose situations – be they educational, religious, or related to work, leisure or environment, etc. – and, when possible, change them. Hence one finds a certain degree of natural homogeneity among people in self-selected groups. This restriction of range and reduced variability can have an important impact on the statistical relationships one expects to find unless it is 'corrected for'. Moreover, social behaviour in all settings is constrained. The sheer amount of money available inevitably affects consumption patterns; work colleagues, organisational structure and equipment can have a powerful effect on work output. If these behaviours were totally 'unconstrained', it is quite possible that there would be much greater variety, and it is likely they would be much more closely related to personality variables. Thus, for various reasons, the real and even powerful relationship between personality and social behaviour may not be apparent, even though both variables are well measured and theoretically related.

5. Many other factors as well as personality traits inevitably affect the relationship between personality and social behaviour. These include intelligence and other ability factors, demographic factors such as age, sex and class, and socio-cultural factors. Sometimes personality factors act as a moderator variable between, say, demographic variables and social behaviours. For instance, in Europe smoking is closely correlated with sex

and class. Working-class women are most likely to smoke. However, extraverts are more likely to take up smoking and to continue the habit. Thus demographic factors may influence the uptake of a habit, but personality factors influence its continuation. In this sense, personality factors may play an important but indirect role in the relationship between individual difference variables and all kinds of social behaviour.

Reviews of the role of personality factors in predicting behaviour have often found grounds for pessimism. Mischel (1968), in his critical book, set back personality research for 15 years because he argued that situational variables predict some behaviour more than personality traits. However, as we saw in Chapter 1, there has been a powerful resurgence of the trait approach with considerable optimism concerning the predictive validity of traits (Matthews and Deary, 1998). There is no doubt that systematic individual differences are logically and powerfully related to many aspects of social behaviour. The evidence for this is highly equivocal, and this is more often the result of poor research and theorising than of actual facts.

REFERENCES

Aguilar-Alonso, A. (1996) Personality and creativity. *Personality and Individual Differences* 21, 959–69.

Amabile, T. (1983) The social psychology of creativity: a componential conceptualization. *Journal of Personality and Social Psychology* 45, 357–67.

Andreasen, N. and Powers, P. (1975) Creativity and psychosis: an examination of conceptual style. *Archives of General Psychiatry* 32, 70–73.

Archer, R., Gordon, R. and Kirchner. F. (1987) MMPI response set characteristics among adolescents. *Journal of Personality Assessment* 51, 506–16.

Beech, A., Baylis, C., Smithson, P. and Claridge, G. (1989) Individual differences in schizotyping as reflected in measures of cognitive inhibition. *British Journal of Clinical Psychology* 28, 117–29.

Ben-Shaktar, G., Bar-Hillel, M., Bilin, F., Ben-Abba, E. and Flug, A. (1986) Can graphology predict occupational success? Two empirical studies and some methodological ruminations. *Journal of Applied Psychology* 71, 645–53.

Blaz, M. (1983) Perceived extraversion in a best friend. *Perceptual and Motor Skills* 53, 891–4.

Brown, R. (1989) Creativity: what are we to measure? In Glover, J., Ronning, R. and Reynolds, C. (eds), *Handbook of creativity*. Cambridge: Cambridge University Press.

Bullen, J. and Hemsley, D. (1984) Psychoticism and visual recognition threshold. *Personality and Individual Differences* 5, 633–48.

Burbeck, E. and Furnham, A. (1984) Personality and police selection. *Personality and Individual Differences* 5, 257–63.

Bushnell, I. (1996) A comparison of the validity of handwriting analysis with that of the Cattell 16PF. *International Journal of Selection and Assessment* 4, 12–17.

Carrier, N.A. (1963) Need correlates of 'gullibility'. *Journal of Abnormal Social Psychology* 66, 84–6.

Cattell, R. and Drevdahl, J. (1955) A comparison of the personality profile (16PF) of eminent researchers with that of eminent teachers and administrators, and of the general population. *British Journal of Psychology* 40, 248–61.

Christiansen, M., Goffin, R., Johnson, N. and Rothstein, N. (1994) Correcting for 16PF faking. *Personnel Psychology* 47, 847–60.

Cook, M. (1979) *Perceiving others.* London: Methuen.

Costa, P. and McCrae, R. (1988) *The NEO-PI/FFI manual supplement.* Odessa, FL: Psychological Assessment Resources.

Dean, G. (1992) The bottom line: effect size. In Beyerstein, B. and Beyerstein, D. (eds), *The write stuff: evaluations of graphology.* Buffalo, NY: Prometheus Books, 269–340.

Dean, G., Kelley, I., Sakofoke, D. and Furnham, A. (1992) Graphology and human judgement. In Beyerstein, B. and Beyerstein, D. (eds), *The write stuff: evaluations of graphology.* Buffalo, NY: Prometheus Books, 342–96.

Dellas, M. and Gaier, E. (1970) Identification of creativity: the individual. *Psychological Bulletin* 73, 55–73.

Driver, R., Buckley, M. and Frink, D. (1996) Should we write off graphology? *International Journal of Selection and Assessment* 6, 78–84.

Edwards, A. and Armitage, P. (1992) An experiment to test the discriminating ability of graphologists. *Personality and Individual Differences* 13, 69–74.

Eysenck, H. (1993) Creativity and personality: suggestions for a theory. *Psychological Inquiry* 4, 147–78.

Eysenck, H. (1994) *The measurement of creativity.* Unpublished paper.

Eysenck, H. and Eysenck, S. (1976) *Psychoticism as a dimension of personality.* London: Hodder & Stoughton.

Eysenck, H. and Gudjonsson, G. (1986) An empirical study of the validity of handwriting analysis. *Personality and Individual Differences* 7, 263–4.

Feldhusen, J. (1995) Creativity: a knowledge base, meta-cognitive skills and personality factors. *Journal of Creative Behaviour* 29, 255–68.

Fichten, C.S. and Sunerton, D. (1983) Popular horoscopes and the 'Barnum effect'. *Journal of Psychology* 114, 123–4.

Fletcher, C., Taylor, P. and Glanfield, K. (1996) Acceptance of personality questionnaire feedback. *Personality and Individual Differences* 20, 151–6.

Forer, B.R. (1949) The fallacy of personal validation: a classroom demonstration of gullibility. *Journal of Abnormal Social Psychology* 44, 118–23.

Forer, B.R. (1968) Personality validation and the person. *Psychological Reports* 23, 1214.

Funder, D. (1980) On seeing ourselves as others see us: self–other agreement and discrepancy in personality ratings. *Journal of Personality* 48, 473–93.

Furnham, A. (1986) Response bias, social desirability and dissimulation. *Personality and Individual Differences* 7, 385–400.

Furnham, A. (1988) Write and wrong: the validity of graphological analysis. *The Skeptical Inquirer,* 13, 64–9.

Furnham, A. (1989a) Personality and the acceptance of diagnostic feedback. *Personality and Individual Differences* 10, 1120–33.

Furnham, A. (1989b) Predicting one's own and others' 16PF scores. *Current Psychological Reviews and Research* 8, 30–37.

Furnham, A. (1990a) Can people accurately estimate their own personality test scores? *European Journal of Personality* 4, 319–27.

Furnham, A. (1990b) The fakeability of the 16PF Myers-Briggs and Firo-B personality measures. *Personality and Individual Differences* 11, 711–16.

Furnham, A. (1990c) Faking personality questionnaires: fabricating different profiles for different purposes. *Current Psychology: Research and Reviews* 9, 46–55.

Furnham, A. (1997) Knowing and faking one's five-factor personality score. *Journal of Personality Assessment* 69, 229–43.

Furnham, A. and Henderson, M. (1983) The mote in my brother's eye, and the beam in thine own: predicting one's own and others' personality test scores. *British Journal of Psychology,* 74, 381–9.

Furnham, A. and Craig, S. (1987) Fakeability and correlates of the Perception and Preference Inventory. *Personality and Individual Differences* 8, 459–70.

Furnham, A. and Gunter, B. (1987) Graphology and personality: another failure to validate graphological analysis. *Personality and Individual Differences* 8, 433–5.

Furnham, A. and Varian, C. (1988) Predicting and accepting personality test feedback. *Personality and Individual Differences* 9, 735–48.

Gelade, G. (1997) Creativity in conflict: the personality of the commercial creative. *Journal of Genetic Psychology* 158, 67–78.

Goertzel, M., Goertzel, V. and Goertzel, T. (1978) *Three hundred eminent personalities*. San Francisco, CA: Jossey-Bass.

Goffin, R. and Woods, D. (1995) Using personality testing for personnel selection: faking and test-taking instructions. *International Journal of Selection and Assessment* 3, 227–36.

Goldberg, L. (1992) The development of markers for the Big Five factor structure. *Psychological Assessment* 4, 26–42.

Gough, H. (1976) Studying creativity by means of the Word Association tasks. *Journal of Applied Psychology* 51, 348–53.

Gray, J. (1972) Self-rating and Eysenck Personality Inventory estimates of neuroticism and extraversion. *Psychological Reports* 30, 213–14.

Gray, J. (1981) A critique of Eysenck's Theory of Personality. In Eysenck, H. (ed.), *A model for personality*. Berlin: Springer-Verlag, 246–76.

Guildford, J. (1956) The structure of the intellect. *Psychological Bulletin* 53, 267–93.

Harrison, N.W. and McLaughlin, R.J. (1969) Self-rating validation of the Eysenck Personality Inventory. *British Journal of Social and Clinical Psychology* 8, 55–8.

Helmes, E. and Holden, R. (1986) Response styles and faking on the basic personality inventory. *Journal of Consulting and Clinical Psychology* 54, 853–9.

Helson, R., Roberts, B. and Agronick, G. (1995) Enduringness and change in creative personality and the prediction of occupational creativity. *Journal of Personality and Social Psychology* 69, 1173–83.

Hemsley, D. (1991) An experimental psychological model of schizophrenia. In Hafner, A., Gattaz, W. and Janzarik, F. (eds), *Search for the causes of schizophrenia*. Hiedelberg: Springer-Verlag.

Hocevar, D. and Bachelor, P. (1989) A taxonomy and critique of measurements used in the study of creativity. In Glover, J., Ronning, R. and Reynolds, C. (eds), *Handbook of creativity*. Cambridge: Cambridge University Press.

Holden, R. and Hobbs, N. (1995) Incremental validity of response latencies for detecting fakers on a personality test. *Journal of Research in Personality* 24, 362–72.

Jamisson, K. (1988) Manic-depressive illness and accomplishment. In Goodwin, F. and Jamisson, K. (eds), *Manic-depressive illness*. Oxford: Oxford University Press.

Kelly, I.W., Dickson, D.H. and Saklofske, D.H. (1986) Personality and the acceptance of Barnum statements under a condition of ambiguous relevance. *Percepual and Motor Skills* **63**, 795–800.

Kline, P. (1977) The psychoanalytic theory of humour and laughter. In Chapman, A. and Foot, H. (eds), *It's a funny thing, humour*. Oxford: Pergamon Press, 7–12.

Köhler, G. and Ruch, W. (1998) Source of variance in current sense of humour inventories: how much substance, how much method variance? *Humour* (in press).

Layne, C. (1978) Relationship between the 'Barnum effect' and Personality Response Inventory responses. *Journal of Clinical Psychology* **34**, 94–7.

Layne, C. and Ally, G. (1980) How and why people accept personality feedback. *Journal of Personality Assessment* **44**, 541–6.

Leventhal, H. and Sofer, M. (1977) Individual differences, personality and humour appreciation. In Chapman, A. and Foot, H. (eds), *It's a funny thing, humour*. Oxford: Pergamon Press.

Loehle, C. (1990) A guide to increased creativity in research – inspiration or perspiration. *BioScience* **40**, 123–9.

Lubart, T. (1994) Creativity. In Sternberg, R. (ed.), *Handbook of perception and cognition*. New York: Academic Press, 289–332.

McCrae, R. (1987) Creativity, divergent thinking, and openness to experience. *Journal of Personality and Social Psychology* **52**, 1258–65.

MacKinnon, D. (1962) The personality correlates of creativity: a study of American architects. In Vernon, P. (ed.), *Creativity*. Harmondsworth: Penguin.

Mansfield, R. and Busse, T. (1981) *The psychology of creativity and discovery*. Chicago, IL: Nelson-Hall.

Martindale, C. (1981) *Cognition and consciousness*. Homewood, IL: Dorsey.

Matthews, G. and Deary, I. (1998) *Personality traits*. Cambridge: Cambridge University Press.

Mednick, S. (1962) The association basis of the creative process. *Psychological Review* **69**, 220–32.

Michaelis, W. and Eysenck, H. (1971) The determination of personality inventory factor patterns and intercorrelations by changes in real life motivation. *Journal of Genetic Psychology* **118**, 223–34.

Mischel, W. (1968) *Personality and assessment*. New York: John Wiley.

Miller, E. and Chapman, L. (1983) Continued word associations in hypothetically psychosis-prone college students. *Journal of Abnormal Psychology* **92**, 468–78.

Mosher, D.L. (1965) Approval motive and acceptance of 'fake' personality test interpretations which differ in favourability. *Psychological Reports* **17**, 395–402.

Nederhof, A. (1985) Methods of coping with social desirability bias. *European Journal of Social Psychology* **15**, 263–80.

Neter, E. and Ben-Shaktar, G. (1989) The predictive validity of graphological inferences: a meta-analytic approach. *Personality and Individual Differences* **10**, 737–45.

Orpen, R. and Jamotte, A. (1975) The acceptance of generalized personality interpretations. *Journal of Social Psychology* **96**, 147–8.

Price, D. (1963) *Little science, big science*. New York: Columbia University Press.

Rawlings, D. (1985) Psychoticism, creativity and dichotic shadowing. *Personality and Individual Differences* 6, 737–42.

Ruch, W. (1992) Assessment of appreciation of humour. In Spielberg, C. and Butcher, J. (eds), *Advances in personality assessment*. Hillsdale, NJ: Lawrence Erlbaum Associates, 27–75.

Ruch, W., Köhler, G. and van Thriel, C. (1997) To be in good or bad humour. *Personality and Individual Differences* 22, 477–91.

Rushton, J. (1990) Creativity, intelligence and psychoticism. *Personality and Individual Differences* 11, 1291–8.

Ruzzene, M. and Noller, P. (1986) Feedback, motivation and reactions to personality interpretations that differ in favourability and accuracy. *Journal of Personality and Social Psychology* 51, 1293–9.

Semin, G., Rosch, E. and Chassein, J. (1981) A comparison of the common-sense and scientific conceptions of extraversion–introversion. *European Journal of Social Psychology* 11, 77–86.

Snyder, C.R. and Larson, G.R. (1972) A further look at student acceptance of general personality interpretations. *Journal of Consulting Clinical Psychology* 38, 384–8.

Snyder, C. and Shenkel, R. (1975) Astrologers, handwriting analyses, and sometimes psychologists' use of the P.T. Barnum effect. *Psychology Today* **March**, 52–4.

Snyder, C.R. and Clair, M.S. (1977) Does insecurity breed acceptance? Effects of trait and situational insecurity on acceptance of positive and negative diagnostic feedback. *Journal of Consulting Clinical Psychology* 45, 843–50.

Stavridou, A. and Furnham, A. (1996) The relationship between psychoticism, trait creativity and the attentional mechanism of cognitive inhibition. *Personality and Individual Differences* 21, 143–53.

Stumpf, H. (1995) Scientific creativity: a short overview. *Educational Psychology Review* 1, 225–41.

Swann, W. (1987) Identity negotiation: where two roads meet. *Journal of Personality and Social Psychology* 53, 1038–51.

Tett, R. and Palmer, C. (1997) The validity of handwriting elements in relation to self-report personality trait measures. *Personality and Individual Differences* 22, 11–18.

Tipper, P. (1985) The negative primary effect: inhibitory priming by ignored objects. *Quarterly Journal of Experimental Psychology* 37, 571–90.

Topping, G. and O'Gorman, J. (1997) Effects of faking set on validity of the NEO-FFI. *Personality and Individual Differences* 23, 117–24.

Torrance, E. (1974) *Torrance tests of creativity thinking: norms, technical manual.* Lexington: Ginn.

Velicar, W. and Weiner, B. (1975) Effects of sophistication and faking sets on the Eysenck Personality Inventory. *Psychological Reports* 37, 71–3.

Vingoe, F. (1966) Validity of the Eysenck Extraversion Scale as determined by self-ratings in normals. *British Journal of Social and Clinical Psychology* 5, 89–91.

Wallach, M. (1970) Creativity. In Mussen, P. (ed.), *Carmichael's manual of child psychology.* New York: Wiley.

Wallach, M. and Kogan, N. (1965) *Modes of thinking in young children.* New York: Holt, Rhinehart & Winston.

Wilson, G. (1981) Personality and social behaviour. In Eysenck, H.J. (ed.), *A model for personality.* Heidelberg: Springer-Verlag.

Woodman, R. and Schoenfeldt, L. (1989) Individual differences in creativity. In Glover, J., Ronning, R. and Reynolds, C. (eds), *Handbook of creativity*. New York: Plenum Press.

Woody, E. and Claridge, G. (1977) Psychoticism and thinking. *British Journal of Social and Clinical Psychology* 16, 241–8.

Zickar, M. and Drasgow, F. (1996) Detecting faking on a personality instrument using appropriateness measurement. *Applied Psychological Measurement* 20, 71–88.

Ziv, A. (1984) *Personality and sense of humour*. New York: Springer-Verlag.

Glossary

Accommodator: Someone who likes to *do* rather than just think about things.

Active generalisation: The recurrence of particular learned behaviour in a different situation from which the learning originally took place.

Agape: A selfless all-giving love.

Allocentric: Thinking about self in terms of family or work group.

Anomie: A sense of being alienated or apart from the rest of society.

Arousal theory: A theory that describes individual differences in personality in terms of physiological processes.

Ascending reticular activation system (ARAS): Situated at the base of the brain and involved in a wide range of psychological processes, such as motivation, emotion and conditioning.

Assimilator: Someone who functions at the abstract level producing models of how things work.

Attachment style: An individual's emotional orientation towards other people.

Attributional style: See explanatory style.

Authoritarianism: A personality trait said to be indicative of prejudice and intolerance towards minority groups. Right-wing authoritarianism was devised by Altemeyer and comprises authoritarian submission, authoritarian aggression and conventionalism.

Barnum Effect: The acceptance of positive, bland, bogus feedback about oneself as true.

Behaviour genetics: The study of the genetic determinants of all forms of observable behaviour.

Behaviourism: A theoretical tradition, sometimes called *black box* psychology, which emphasises the importance of the objective study of (observable) actual behaviour (response).

Big Five: The fundamental *higher-order* personality factors, namely extraversion, neuroticism, openness-to-experience, agreeableness, conscientiousness.

Biopsychosocial model: The view that one's health status is co-determined by psychological, physical and sociological factors.

Borderline personality disorder: Characterised by dramatic mood swings, unstable interpersonal relationships and an unstable sense of identity.

Bortner scale: A personality inventory used to assess the Type A behaviour pattern.

California Personality Inventory: An 18-scale personality test designed to measure the personality of *normal* people.

California Psychological Inventory (CPI): A standardised measure of personality among normal adult populations.

Cattell's 16PF: A standardised measure of sixteen personality factors developed by Raymond Cattell.

Child Behaviour Checklist: An inventory designed to measure behavioural problems and manifestations in children aged 4–16 years.

Clinical psychology: That branch of psychology concerned with the cause and cure of *abnormal* behaviour.

Cluster analysis: A statistical analysis that looks at the underlying clusters of items rated in a test (and plotted with dendograms).

Cognition: A term covering all of the following: conceiving, judging, perceiving, reasoning, remembering.

Cognitive closure: The act of drawing to a conclusion; resolving inconsistencies.

Cognitive psychology: That branch of psychology concerned with cognition (see above).

Cognitive style: See learning style.

Compliant-Aggressive-Detached (CAD) test: Psychological test that measures these three reactions.

Conservatism: A constellation of attitudes held by people who find change threatening and who want to preserve the existing order. Such attitudes are generally pro-religion, anti-hedonistic, pro law and order, and racist.

Constructionism: The notion that personality (indeed, all social reality) is not objective, but constructed by us in the process of describing and explaining what we experience.

Converger: Someone with practical skills who is good at problem solving.

Divergence of thinking: The opposite of convergence; seeking many alternatives.

Diverger: Someone with good imaginative capabilities who can generate new ideas.

Dogmatism: A system of beliefs about reality. Such beliefs are generally described as being *closed* as opposed to being *open*.

Economic psychology: That branch of psychology concerned with studying individual and group economic beliefs and behaviours (spending, saving, gambling, etc.)

Edwards Personal Preference Schedule (EPPS): A test that measures 15 needs (i.e. achievement, affiliation, dominance) and is used widely in vocational psychology.

EEG (electroencephalograph): An instrument that records electrical activity in the brain.

EPI (Eysenck Personality Inventory): A standardised measure of personality that predates the EPQ-R (Revised Eysenck Personality Questionnaire).

EPQ: Eysenck Personality Questionnaire (see EPI).

Eros: A passionate love characterised by a shorter and more intense relationship.

Experimental psychology: That approach to psychology which deploys the use of experimental methods to test hypotheses.

Explanatory style: A particular way of thinking that individuals use to make sense of events around them.

Extraversion: Opposite of introversion, indicating a sociable, outgoing, under-aroused indivual.

F (Fascist) scale: A somewhat outdated measure of authoritarianism.

Factor analysis: A statistical test based on correlations that seeks to look at the factors (dimensions) underlying a large number of observations.

FIRO-B: A test (Fundamental Interpersonal Relations Orientation-Behaviour) based on psychoanalytic ideas that measures three dimensions of personality.

Five-Factor Model (FFM): A model suggesting that personality can be described in terms of five major domains.

Forman Scale: A measure of money pathology.

Framingham Type A Scale: A measure of the Type A Behaviour Pattern.

Gordon Personality Profile: A multiple scale test that attempts a full profile of normal personality functioning.

Graphology: The quasi-scientific analysis of handwriting.

High School Personality Questionnaire: A personality inventory devised by Raymond Cattell for use among high school students (see also Cattell's 16PF).

Id: A Freudian term referring to unconscious forces and energies. One part (along with ego and superego) of the Freudian tripartite system.

Ideal partner hypothesis: The theory that we are attracted to individuals because they possess certain traits that we value.

Introversion: Opposite of extraversion, indicating inwardly looking, physiologically over-aroused individual not prone to seeking out company.

Jackson Personality Research Form: A personality test that measures 22 variables based on the theory of Murray (1930).

Jenkins Activity Survey: A measure of the Type A Behaviour Pattern.

Just world principle: The belief that the world is a just place and that people get what they deserve.

Learning style: The strategy that one adopts to master new and complex material. This strategy is believed to reflect the interplay between intelligence and personality.

Learning Styles Questionnaire: A test that measures four different styles in learning preferences (Activist, Reflector, Theorist, Pragmatist).

Leisure ethic: Opposite of the work ethic; a belief that it is morally correct to seek out and enjoy leisure activities.

Lie scale: A measure of *faking good* or dissimulation included in some measures of personality such as the EPQ.

Locus of control: The tendency to explain events as being under one's control (internal locus of control) or as being due to uncontrollable environmental influences (external locus of control).

Ludus: A game-playing love entailing deception and manipulation.

Major affective disorder: Characterised by a depressed mood, loss of appetite, reduced levels of energy and sleep disturbance.

Mania: A possessive and dependent love.

Marlowe-Crowne Social Desirability Scale (M-C50): A short test frequently used to detect lying, faking and dissimulation.

Maslow's hierarchy of needs: The theory that needs are arranged hierarchically from physiological needs (the most basic) through to self-actualisation needs.

MBTI (Myers-Briggs Type Indicator): Very popular test based on Jungian theory that is used to classify individuals into one of 16 types.

Meta-analysis: A statistical technique used to look at the overall results (trends) in a series of studies on the same topic.

Money Ethic Scale (MES): A short questionnaire looking at ethical attitudes and beliefs relating to money.

Monozygotic twins: Identical twins (of same sex) unlike fraternal (dizygotic) twins.

Morningness-Eveningness Questionnaire: A questionnaire measuring individual differences in chrono-biology (time of day preferences).

Negative priming: This refers to the delay in responding to a current target object when this object has been a detractor to be inhibited on a previous display.

Neo Freudian: The New Freudians, who accept psychoanalytic conceptions of unconscious conflict, but differ from Freud in particular ways; Adler, Jung and others, who adapted aspects of Freud's theory.

Neurosis: A term used to describe a broad range of personality problems such as high levels of anxiety, lack of self-esteem and mood swings.

Neuroticism: Minor nervous disorder, characterised by such things as anxiety, phobia, depression, hypochondriasis.

Occupational psychology: That branch of psychology dedicated to the understanding of behaviour in the work place.

Operant conditioning: A form of learning in which a reinforcer, such as food, is given only if the person/animal performs the appropriate instrumental response, such as pressing a lever.

Optimal dissimilarity hypothesis: We are attracted to people who are only slightly different from ourselves.

Optimal outbreeding hypothesis: This is based on the finding that some animals have shown a preference to breed with those who are somewhat different.

Passive generalisation: The natural generalisation of responses over time, conditions and situations (without effort or reward).

Personality: An enduring set of internal characteristics, partly inherited, partly learnt, that endure over time and result in stable, predictable behaviour patterns.

Personality test: Usually a self-report questionnaire designed to measure specific personality traits.

Personality theory: A theory that attempts to explain (as well as describe) the processes and mechanisms that lead to individual differences in personality traits.

Phrenology: Also called craniology: a method that supposedly measures mental characteristics and capacities by observation of the prominence of areas on the external surface of the skull.

Pragma: Similar to computer-matching love and requires a committed and compatible partner.

Principal components analysis: A statistical technique used to reduce a large number of related items (or scales) to descriptive factors, components or domains.

Protestant work ethic: A set of beliefs and practices that foster independence, mastery, success and, ultimately, wealth.

Psychoanalysis: A theory of personality and a method of therapy formulated by Sigmund Freud.

Psychological Screening Inventory: A short diagnostic tool to determine the seriousness of pathology.

Psychometrics: Mathematical and measurement aspects of psychological research often associated with ability and personality testing.

Psychopathic deviate scale: A subscale of the MMPI which measures disregard for social and moral norms.

Psychoticism: The third major personality domain in H. Eysenck's model of personality. The others are extraversion and neuroticism. Persons scoring high on psychoticism tend to be hostile, cold, aggressive, and have poor interpersonal relations.

Reaction formulation: A psychoanalytic term: a defence mechanism where a forbidden *impulse* is turned into its opposite (hate becomes love).

Repulsion hypothesis: The theory that we are repulsed by dissimilar people.

Right-wing authoritarianism: See authoritarianism.

Schizophrenia: A serious psychotic mental disorder characterised by marked disturbances of thought, withdrawal, inappropriate or flat emotional response, delusions and hallucinations.

Self-actualisation: The highest need in Maslow's theory. Self-actualised individuals have reached their highest potential (see Maslow's hierarchy of needs).

Self-concept theory: Theories that stress the importance of self-concept as a determinant of social behaviour.

Self-monitoring: The sensitive and consistent monitoring (and adaptation) of the images of self, projected in everyday social interaction.

Self-theorists: One of a number of *third-force* theorists who argue that the concept of self (self-esteem, self-image) is at the centre of personality differences.

Sensation-seeking inventory: An inventory that measures the extent to which individuals are thrill seekers.

Similarity hypothesis: The theory that we are attracted to people who are similar to ourselves.

Social dominance orientation: The belief in group inequality and that some groups are better than others. This construct is a good predictor of prejudice and intolerance.

Sport psychology: That branch of psychology dedicated to understanding preference for and success at all sports.

Storge: Natural affection; the merging of friendship and love.

Substance use disorder: Disorder involving continued use of substances such as marijuana.

Tender-mindedness: H. Eysenck's third personality dimension (psychoticism) is also sometimes referred to as tender-mindedness vs. tough-mindedness (see psychoticism).

Trait theory: The idea that people differ with regard to a limited number of fundamental underlying attributes (traits) that partially determine consistent and stable social behaviour.

Type A Behaviour Pattern (TABP): This behavioural pattern is characterised by a sense of urgency, competitiveness, hostility and impatience.

Type B: Sometimes used to describe individuals who are not Type A.

Type theory: The idea that people can be classified into unique and distinguished types.

Vickers scale: A personality inventory often used to assess the Type A Behaviour.

Wallach-Kogan Creativity Test: One of the better tests of creativity, based on rating the liking of pictures.

Index